BETWEEN THE WATERS

Newton H. Winchell's birch-bark canoe, shown here on the campus of the University of Minnesota c. 1910. It was used to map the geological formations of Minnesota and completed the last officially recorded excursion along the Northwest Trail in 1878. Photo from Winchell's *Aborigines of Minnesota*

BETWEEN THE WATERS

TRACING THE NORTHWEST TRAIL
FROM LAKE SUPERIOR TO THE MISSISSIPPI

LARRY LUUKKONEN

Dovetailed Press LLC
Duluth, Minnesota

First Edition

Soft Bound
ISBN 13 - 978-0-9765890-3-7
ISBN 10 - 0-9765890-3-6

Hard Bound
ISBN 13 - 978-0-9765890-4-4
ISBN 10 - 0-9765890-4-4

Library of Congress Control Number: 2007925580

Printed and bound in the United States of America by Bang Printing, Brainerd, MN

Book layout and design by Marlene Wisuri

Publisher's Cataloging-in-Publication
(Provided by Quality Books, Inc.)

Luukkonen, Larry.
    Between the waters : tracing the old Northwest Trail
 from Lake Superior to the Mississippi / Larry Luukkonen.
    p. cm.
    Includes bibliographical references and index.
    LCCN 2007925580
    Soft Bound
    ISBN-13: 9780976589037
    ISBN-10: 0976589036

    Hard Bound
    ISBN- 13: 9780976589044
    ISBN- 10: 0976589044

    1. Minnesota--History--To 1858. 2. Trails--Minnesota
 --History. 3. Minnesota--Description and travel.
    I. Title.

    F606.L88 2007   977.6

                        QBI07-600107

Cover Images:
Front cover - photograph of the St. Louis River by Allen Anway.
Back cover - detail from the 1806 map by Sergeant Antoine Nau.

Dovetailed Press LLC
5263 North Shore Drive
Duluth, MN 55804
www.dovetailedpress.com

Dovetailed Press LLC

Dedication

To my parents, Arnold and Vivian Luukkonen

Acknowledgments

I would like to thank all those who in some way helped in the preparation of this book. I am grateful to my friends and colleagues for their encouragement and patience. I am especially indebted to Allen Anway, Rod Boehlke, Steve Cummings, Biz Robbins, Roberta Malwitz, and Marlene Wisuri for their assistance in selecting materials and for their helpful comments. Last but not least, I appreciate the many readers of my serial articles in the *Aitkin Independent Age* who have expressed their enjoyment each time a new story appears. I hope you all enjoy this literary journey along the Northwest Trail as much as I have enjoyed writing it.

"For he lives twice who can at once employ
The present well and e'en the past enjoy."

CONTENTS

Part I ⊸ The Route West

Part II ⊸ The People of the Trail

Preface

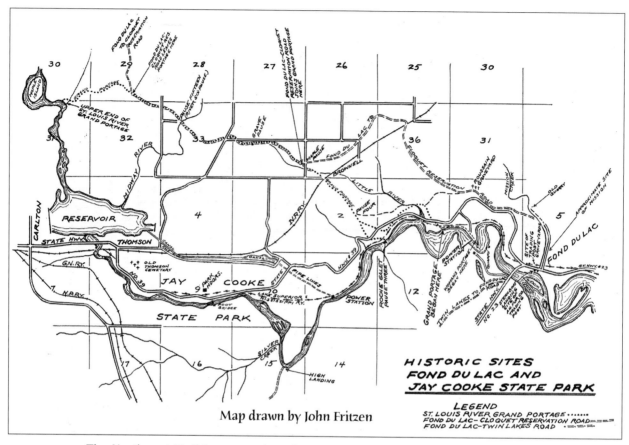

Map drawn by John Fritzen

HISTORIC SITES FOND DU LAC AND JAY COOKE STATE PARK

LEGEND
ST. LOUIS RIVER GRAND PORTAGE ·······
FOND DU LAC – CLOQUET RESERVATION ROAD ════
FOND DU LAC – TWIN LAKES ROAD ·═·═·═·

The Northwest Trail is now anchored on either end by Minnesota state parks—Jay Cooke State Park on the St. Louis River and Savanna State Park at Sandy Lake.

On a summer day in 1878, Minnesota State Geologist Newton H. Winchell's voyageurs, Paul Morrison and John Lightbody, guided their birch-bark canoe carefully down the St. Louis River toward the eastern terminus of the Prairie Portage. They passed the East Savanna River, but declined the chance to follow that stream to the Savanna Portage in favor of the longer but less demanding route by way of Prairie Lake and River. Winchell and his voyageurs had spent several months exploring the geological features along the waterways of northern Minnesota, and now they pointed the bow of their craft toward home. They apparently gave little thought to the significance of their voyage, but their journey down the St. Louis River and transit of the Prairie Portage were the last officially recorded excursions along that historic waterway.

Winchell and his men were by no means the only persons who used part of the ancient network of rivers and portages referred to as the "Northwest Trail," but their passage over a portion of it in 1878 marked the end of an era, when waterways were the dominant means of travel.

What was the "Northwest Trail?" Very simply, it was a land and water route that connected Lake Superior and the Great Lakes with the Mississippi River at

The famous
Swinging Bridge
over the St. Louis
River at Jay Cooke
State Park.
Photo by Allen Anway

Sandy Lake. During its heyday (c. 1650-1850), the Northwest Trail was widely known as a major travel and trade artery. It served many purposes including an avenue by which early explorers and missionaries entered what is now Minnesota, a favorite pathway for traders, and a migration route for indigenous people. Also, part of its course was briefly considered a means of defining the international boundary separating the United States from Canada.

Until now the story of the route between the waters and its various uses has been largely overshadowed by Minnesota's legendary Boundary Waters. While certainly a significant waterway, particularly in terms of the history of the western Canadian fur trade, the Boundary Waters were geographically and historically on the periphery of Minnesota. However, the exploration and development of northern Minnesota was inextricably connected with places and events along the Northwest Trail.

The story of the Northwest Trail is one of portages and rivers that provided a route west from the Great Lakes through the interior of Minnesota. Beginning at the western end of Lake Superior, the route continued up the St. Louis River and around a series of difficult rapids and formidable waterfalls to the height of land separating the Great Lakes watershed from the Mississippi River watershed. Once across the drainage divide, it ultimately led to Sandy Lake and the Mississippi River.

Sandy Lake was a hub of travel on the Mississippi headwaters with trails and canoe routes radiating outward in all directions like the spokes of a wheel. In winter, when the frozen ground rendered large sections of the surrounding territory passable, dog sleds traveling over frozen trails or "winter roads" provided direct communication with isolated villages at locations such as Leech Lake and Mille Lacs. Actually, winter sledding was faster than canoeing. Winter or summer travelers could always follow the river from Sandy Lake and either journey down the Mississippi or proceed upstream toward Cass Lake, up the Turtle River, across the height of land and down the Mud River to Lower Red Lake. By following the Red Lake River to the Red River of the North, traders bound for western Canada could then easily travel downstream to Lake Winnipeg to access the Saskatchewan River, flowing from the Rocky Mountains. This route was an alternative to using the series of lakes and streams along the present border between the United States and Canada.

For a time, early explorers believed somewhere in the web of winter trails and summer waterways west of Lake Superior lay the passage to the "South Sea" (Pacific Ocean). Certainly the verbal accounts of the streams were similar to the descriptions of rivers thought to be the key to the famous Northwest Passage, the all-water route across North America to the Orient. As early as 1534, Jacques Cartier thought he had indeed found the Northwest Passage when he saw the St. Lawrence River.

At first glance, it is easy to see why the entrance to the St. Lawrence River looked like the fabled route to the Indies. After Cartier's journey, it was prominently marked on navigation charts as the *Fleuve Saint-Laurent*, because of the tremendous volume of water discharged at its entrance. Subsequent references to places farther west like *Le Sault de la Chine* (The Rapids of China) and *La Mer de l'Ouest* (The Sea of the West) show that many truly believed the St. Lawrence, and the great chain of inland seas it drained must indeed be the elusive shortcut to the wealth of China and the East Indies.

At the western end of the chain of lakes was Lake Superior, named by the French, because it was the uppermost or first of the *Grand Lacs*. Superior was the focus of a number of rivers flowing from the north, south, and west. Three of the waterways–the Pigeon River, the Kaministiquia River, and the St. Louis River–originated west of Lake Superior. Two of these streams, the Pigeon and the Kaministiquia, have been extensively studied because of their connection with Canadian exploration and the fur trade. In contrast, the St. Louis River has received less attention, though it was an important alternate way to the Northwest.

The story of the Northwest Trail deserves telling not only to show its role in the early history of Minnesota, but also to place the stories of the other trade routes in perspective. Crossing the bar at the entrance to the St. Louis River marked the beginning of a notable journey over a series of portages and streams that collectively comprised the Northwest Trail. Descriptions of this route, taken from the letters and journals of explorers, travelers, traders, and government officials, include references to innumerable interesting places, colorful personalities, and a host of curious place-names.

The focus of this book is regional in its scope stretching from Lake Superior to the Mississippi River. The sources that describe the history of the route comprise four major categories. Part I concerns the route itself and its component parts as well as efforts to map it. Part II discusses the people who used the trail and contributed to its history. Part III deals with the trading posts and the various traders who resided at Fond du Lac and Sandy Lake. Finally, Part IV covers the changing frontier as reflected in the descriptions of the people and developments that occurred along the trail after 1850.

Regardless of their destination, all those who passed over the North West Trail shared a common experience. Like the early traveler threading his way among the myriad lakes and streams, the reader can trace the story of this ancient and historic pathway. Hopefully, somewhere along the way he or she can also relive the adventures of those who first followed the twisting courses of the rivers or the faintly visible portages between the waters.

Scenic overlook on the Continental Divide in Savanna Portage State Park.
Minnesota Department of Natural Resources

With its rushing water and jagged rock formations,
the St. Louis River was a formidable route to travel.
Photo by Allen Anway

Part I ⚬⟲⟳⚬ *The Route West*

Chapter 1 ✂ The River at the End of the Lake

Any attempt to describe exploration and trade in northern Minnesota from 1650 to 1850 must inevitably mention certain key routes that made those undertakings possible. One prominent route was the Northwest Trail. Named by a voyageur, the trail was comprised of a network of waterways, portages, and an alternative winter road, which connected Lake Superior to the Mississippi River. Anchoring each end of the trail were the villages and later trading establishments of Fond du Lac and Sandy Lake. Between those sites was the largest single physical feature of the Northwest Trail—the St. Louis River. The river formed more than two thirds of the total length of this important travel route.[1]

To appreciate the importance of the Northwest Trail as a major travel and trade artery, it is necessary to know the documentary resources which describe the trail and the activities which took place on it. Also important are the natural features of the route and the place-names encountered along the way as they provide the setting for events. The natural features and distinctive place-names also made the route unique. Place-names were especially important because they signified reference points, which were later included on maps or in written descriptions of the country.

Lake Superior's North Shore Streams

Of course the story of the Northwest Trail and its chief natural feature, the St. Louis River, is much older than the fur trade. It is certainly older than the exploits of the first European explorers in search of the fabled Northwest Passage or even the advent of the first human inhabitants in the region. It is a tale that began with the geological processes that created the rugged terrain, which in turn influenced the contours of the streams draining the land west of Lake Superior. Such natural forces played an important part in determining which waterways would ultimately be most useful for travel, trade, or exploration.

Geologists have described various forces that shaped the waterways of northern Minnesota. The source of the St. Louis River was once actually the original source of the Mississippi River, the St. Louis being but a separate insignificant tributary to Lake Superior. The ancient Mississippi headwaters began in Seven Beaver Lake, where the St. Louis originates today. The river flowed southwest following the course of the East and West Savanna rivers and eventually joined the present Mississippi west of Sandy Lake.[2]

A major change to the drainage system of northeastern Minnesota occurred sometime in the past, when the St. Louis River fed by glacial meltwater cut through an ancient natural barrier known as the Duluth Escarpment, which separated it from the headwaters of the Mississippi. The result of this sudden change had a profound impact on both streams. The former headwaters of the Mississippi were redirected sharply to the east near the present town of Floodwood, Minnesota. This main stream became the headwaters of the St. Louis, which discharged its flow into Lake Superior. Even though the volume of water eventually decreased following the glacial period, the now much enlarged St. Louis River remained a major tributary of the great lake.[3]

In contrast, the Mississippi, which approaches to within a few miles of the St. Louis River at Sandy Lake, became dependent on a new source of water provided by lakes and wetlands to the northwest originating near present-day Lake Itasca. The network of lakes and streams created by the change in the course of the ancient Mississippi and the growth of the St. Louis River furnished the original inhabitants of the region with a convenient but rugged connection between water routes, which ultimately became the Northwest Trail.

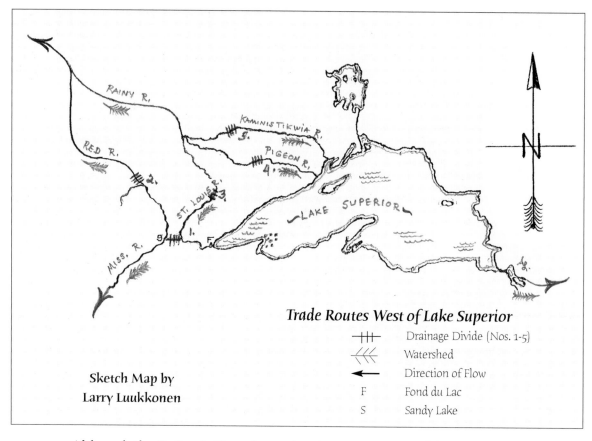

Trade Routes West of Lake Superior

┼┼┼	Drainage Divide (Nos. 1-5)
⟨⟨⟨	Watershed
←	Direction of Flow
F	Fond du Lac
S	Sandy Lake

**Sketch Map by
Larry Luukkonen**

Although the St. Louis River formed an important part of the eastern portion of the Northwest Trail, it was only one of three rivers offering a passage westward from Lake Superior. Though many streams dot Lake Superior's shore, only the Kaministiquia, Pigeon and St. Louis rivers became prominent as trade routes to the west. These rivers share certain common characteristics which determined their use as a route of travel and commerce. These characteristics are also reflected in various place-names which are still commonly used along each stream.[4]

The common natural features of the rivers were described by geologist Newton Horace Winchell. The first is the sudden and steep descent of all the rivers as they approach Lake Superior. All the western streams are marked by waterfalls within two to ten miles of their entry into the lake. Because of the precipitous fall in elevation, most of the streams along Superior's famous North Shore are simply not navigable. Parts of the Kaministiquia, Pigeon, and St. Louis rivers, however, are navigable farther west by canoe, albeit with some major obstacles. Then as now, anyone attempting to canoe the streams had to portage around formidable barriers.[5]

For example, the famous Dalles of the St. Louis, which, prior to the construction of a series of hydroelectric dams at the beginning of the twentieth century, included at least three significant waterfalls. "Dalles" is a French word meaning a rapid in a narrow gorge having a flat rocky bottom. During a trip through the region in 1820, Henry Rowe Schoolcraft described the narrow gorge and the sharp drop in elevation. He estimated the river fell two hundred and twenty feet along the Grand Portage.[6]

A North Shore stream as photographed by Allen Anway.

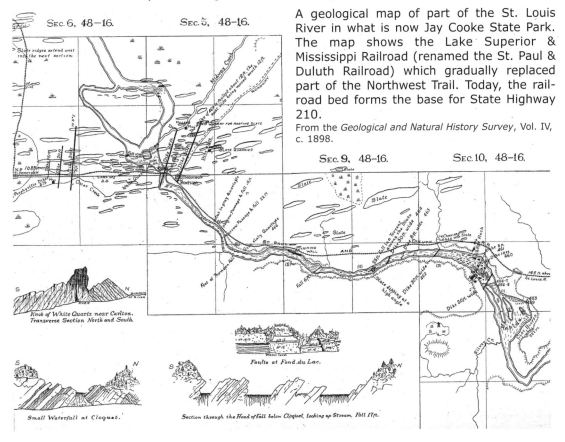

A geological map of part of the St. Louis River in what is now Jay Cooke State Park. The map shows the Lake Superior & Mississippi Railroad (renamed the St. Paul & Duluth Railroad) which gradually replaced part of the Northwest Trail. Today, the railroad bed forms the base for State Highway 210.
From the *Geological and Natural History Survey*, Vol. IV, c. 1898.

John Disturnell, writing in the *St. Paul Press*, July 26th, 1870, described the Dalles of the St. Louis as "a scene of attractions rarely equaled and never excelled. There Nature is seen in her original, pristine wildness." Today, regardless of the dams, when the St. Louis River is in full flood, it is still a force to be respected and its wild churning waters provide a breathtaking spectacle. Of all the places along the St. Louis River, the Dalles were the most scenic and the most treacherous. They were known to the Ojibway as the *Kitchi Kakabikang* or "The Great Falls."[7]

The Dalles of the St. Louis River.

Photo by Allen Anway

Another common characteristic of the St. Louis River, which is shared by other rivers along Superior's shores, is the seasonal fluctuation of stream flow. Flooding caused danger in some sections of the rivers and rendered others simply impassable. The North West Company's Geographer David Thompson recounted a ride he experienced down the St. Louis River in May of 1798. Along the way, his men noticed marks on the trees indicating the depth of the river in full flood was from six to eight feet above the level at the time of his visit. Fortunately, his voyageurs were highly experienced and knew each of the portages around the worst sections, including the Dalles of the St. Louis.[8]

Conditions change with the seasons, and by midsummer the St. Louis displays many sections of shoal water. Sometimes it was necessary to make a series of short portages around shallow spots. There were also instances where the passengers and cargo were unloaded while the voyageurs hurriedly built small dams called "sluices" in the shallow stream to obtain sufficient water to float a canoe. Once completed, the canoe was carefully

Shoal water on the St. Louis River.
Photo by Allen Anway

guided through the shallows before re-embarking. The voyageurs referred to the process of lightening the load to float the canoe as a *décharge.*[9]

The seasonal fluctuation in water level on the St. Louis influenced travel as well as the amount of trade goods brought into the interior. The extremes in water level also shortened or lengthened travel routes. Portages such as the Savanna could vary in length because of high water. In some cases, it was simply easier to move certain kinds of goods in wintertime, when stretches of normally swampy ground, once frozen and snow covered, provided easy passage for dog sleds.

A dog sled of the type often used as pictured in Thomas L. McKenney's *Sketches of a Tour to the Lakes*, 1827.

Another similarity among the rivers occurs following winter runoff and spring rainstorms. Sandbars form at the entrance to each stream along the shores of Lake Superior only to have parts washed away by sudden torrents. Perhaps the most notable baymouth bar in the world is the permanent sandbar, which extends across the mouth of the St. Louis River.[10] Pierced in two locations for ship canals, the resulting component parts are known today as "Minnesota Point" and "Wisconsin Point." The St. Louis River's massive baymouth bar was known to the Ojibway as *Shagawamik* or "a long narrow point." A similar name, *Jagawamikong* or *Shagawaumikong,* was given by them to the sandbar near Ashland, Wisconsin, from which the name Chequamegon Bay is derived.[11]

Although geographer Joseph Nicollet's 1842 map showed the depth at the mouth to the St. Louis River as "8 feet on the bar," that depth was not constant. Reverend

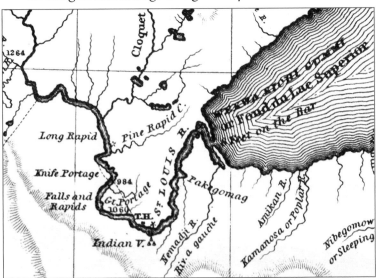

A detail from Joseph Nicollet's map showing the mouth of the St. Louis River.

Alfred Brunson, a Methodist missionary, traveled the same route as Nicollet and observed how seasonal fluctuations in water level and silt deposits altered passage over the bar. The enormous volume of water flowing into Lake Superior nearly upset Brunson's canoe. He recorded how the flow swept the silt from the entrance of the St. Louis and created a channel so deep he could not reach bottom with a thirty foot weighted line. The same buildup of sediment occurs today, and it is necessary to periodically employ dredges to keep the ship channels open.[12]

The possibility of traveling from one watershed to another by short portages marks yet another characteristic of the St. Louis River. In an era when waterways were the only practical means of penetrating the wilderness, all three river systems were connected to a web of smaller streams that gave extraordinary access to the country through which they flowed.[13]

Each of the three major rivers was connected to at least one adjoining watershed. For example, the Kaministiquia River afforded access from the Great Lakes by a series of portages through Lac des Mille Lacs, Pickerel, and Sturgeon lakes to the Maligne River and Lac la Croix, forming a link with streams flowing into Hudson Bay. Similarly, the Pigeon River route connected the Great Lakes with Hudson Bay. The St. Louis River was connected by portages with the Great Lakes, Mississippi River, and Hudson Bay watersheds. It was the interconnection of three watersheds that made the St. Louis River a central feature on the Northwest Trail and accounts for the use of that route by numerous travelers.

Heavy winter snows and abundant summer rains were critical elements for making the St. Louis River a dependable water route. In fact, each of the three watersheds that originate in Minnesota depends on the annual precipitation, which, to a large extent, is stored in the state's wetlands. A glance at any map of Minnesota's waterways quickly affirms that water flows out of the state but none flows in. The sustained flow in the St. Louis River depends on the large concentration of wetlands adjacent to the river that release their water slowly over the course of the summer.[14]

The amount of water in the St. Louis River also influenced the shape and size of watercraft. Canoes used on the shallow northern waters were modified to include a flat bottom and broad beam which drew less water. The basic design of the light birch-bark canoes built by local craftsmen remained virtually unchanged. Even the dimensions of the canoes were given in the old French measurements including fathoms or *brasses* (64 inches) for length, *pieds* (12.79 inches) for width, and *pouces* (1.125 inches) for depth.[15]

The overall length of the canoes used in the fur trade varied from two to six fathoms, The typical freight canoe was the four and a half fathom (twenty-four foot) *canot du maître*, also known as the *maître canot*, great canoe, North canoe, *rabeska*, or *nadoué chiman*. In practice, most of the canoes used on the Northwest Trail were in all probability "light canoes" or *canots léger* about three fathoms (sixteen feet) long. To the French, the light canoe was known as a *canot*, *canau* (pl. *canaux*), *encorse de bouleau*, or *petite embarcation*. Where large canoes were employed on the St. Louis, records indicate they were frequently damaged because of the rocky river bottom.[16]

The St. Louis River, while similar in many ways to other North Shore streams, also has some unique attributes. As travelers journey from east to west along the river, there is a gradual but perceptible change from the rugged topography of the Laurentian Highlands, with its boreal forest cover, to a rolling countryside and vegetation typical of the Great Lakes area.

The changing features were recorded by explorer and geographer David Thompson during his 1798 voyage along the Northwest Trail. On a single page of his notebook are references to his rough track survey notes, celestial observations, comments about the rivers, wildlife, topography, trees, and the people he met along the way. For example, he described his travel down the East Savanna and St. Louis rivers:

> We entered a Brook of seven feet wide, three feet deep, by two miles an hour, and descended it for twelve miles, but its windings will extend it to twenty miles, in which distance it receives one brook from the southward, and two from the northward, which increased it to ten yards wide, seven feet deep by 1 3/4 miles an hour. We now entered the river St. Louis, a bold stream of about one hundred yards in width by eight feet in depth, the current three miles an hour.[17]

Included in his narrative are references to trees like the hemlock found along the Grand Portage of the St. Louis and to the "Plaine Tree," a Canadian term for the red or swamp maple (*Acer rubrum*), growing along the river.[18]

The Northwest Trail also differed from the other northern routes in the number and frequency of portages. For example, there were three major portages on the St. Louis River, compared to ten times that number from the Grand Portage of the Pigeon River to Lac La Croix. In addition, the portages found along the Northwest Trail are as a rule longer and more difficult than their northern counterparts. The Pigeon River-Lac La Croix route includes twenty-nine portages having a total distance of fifteen miles. In contrast, the three major portages (Grand, Knife, and Savanna) which make up the Northwest Trail cover the same distance. Of course all routes were adversely affected by low water which lengthened the distance at each carrying place.[19]

Another trademark of the St. Louis River is its dark brown "coffee-colored" water. The color of the St. Louis differs markedly from some of the North Shore streams. The dark-colored water contains tannic acid, which is present in the decayed vegetation found in the vast swamplands bordering part of the course of the river. These extensive swamps provide the source of water for many of the tributaries of the St. Louis, hence the concentration of color. While most freshwater streams exhibit some dark stain in the water, the color of the St. Louis River has been the subject of commentary throughout its recorded history. Author Walter O'Meara remarked how the brown frothing rapids reminded him of a river of root beer.[20]

Finally, an interesting similarity shared by each of the three major rivers does not concern natural features at all. At issue was the true location of the boundary between Canada and the United States. The boundary was supposed to follow the established canoe route west of Lake Superior; however, there was confusion over which route to follow because of vague wording in the peace treaty, concluded at Paris in 1783, that ended the American Revolutionary War. The boundary issue remained unresolved.

Part of the dilemma facing those trying to establish the boundary was the need to determine which river system constituted the customary route of travel. Geographer David Thompson favored the St. Louis River as the easiest route and believed its fine estuary was the "Long Lake" referred to in the peace treaty. Thompson was supported by explorer Alexander Mackenzie who saw the Northwest Trail as the quickest route to the Mississippi. MacKenzie remarked:

> "...the St. Louis passes within a short distance of a branch of the Mississippi [at Savanna Portage], where it becomes navigable for canoes. This will appear more evident from consulting the map [Thompson's]; and if the navigation of the Mississippi is considered as of any consequence by this country from that part of the globe, such is the nearest way to get at it."[21]

One of the provisions of the Treaty of Ghent ending the War of 1812, called for a special boundary commission to examine the St. Louis, Pigeon, and Kaministiquia rivers and establish a border between Canada and the United States. The British proposed the St. Louis River as the boundary and Thompson actually surveyed it in 1825, however, the United States countered with a claim that the Kaministiquia River was the proper boundary. Both sides' extreme claims regarding the boundary were never recognized. The only thing that developed from the survey of 1825 was a better understanding of the topography of northern Minnesota and the course of the St. Louis River. The boundary issue remained unresolved until the signing of the Webster-Ashburton Treaty on August 9th, 1842.[22]

Language and Geography

Travelers who used the various described routes west from Lake Superior would likely have noticed some of the common characteristics of the North Shore streams. Each stream, however, held many of its own secrets. Travelers canoeing along the St. Louis River encountered a variety of portages, rapids, and other unique features including villages and trading posts. All of those features had descriptive names. Over time, individuals recorded information about the names of certain landmarks, and in some cases, included facts concerning the origin or meaning of the names—but this was not an easy task.

One difficulty confronting both early travelers along the Northwest Trail and scholars concerned with recording the place-names was the different spelling used for the same word. In addition, the lack of written native languages and the different dialects spoken by various branches or bands within the same tribe further hampered efforts to correctly record names. These difficulties of mispronunciation of place-names and the frequent use of phonetic spelling caused a search for the true origin or meaning of a name.[23]

A very good example of the importance associated with a system of orthography, or style of spelling, appears in the various renditions of the tribal name Ojibway. Ojibwa, Outchibouec, Otjibwe, Ojibue, Chippewa, and Chippeway are but a few examples. Recently, yet another version, Ojibwe, has been added to the list. For the sake of continuity, the author has elected to use the spelling "Ojibway," which has been used for almost two centuries. It was the preferred spelling according to William Whipple Warren, the noted historian of the tribe. Warren was acknowledged by everyone who knew him to be exceptionally fluent in the language, and he favored Ojibway as "embodying the truest pronunciation." Trader Henry Mower Rice described Warren's linguistic ability with a ringing endorsement. "He was one of the most eloquent and fluent speakers I ever heard. The Indians said he understood their language better than themselves."[24]

To further compound the problem of determining place-names, persons sometimes completely ignored the original name of a landmark and simply used a new name. For example, it was not unusual for a place-name of long-standing to be replaced by the name of a new resident or of a prominent person. An example of this can be seen in the names given to Lake Superior during the seventeenth century. Aspiring authors, explorers, and some map makers routinely changed names with the intention of flattering someone to curry favor or to impress their readers.

Newton Winchell, in his *Geological and Natural History of Minnesota, Geology of Minnesota*, Vol. I of the Final Report, published in 1884, included a chart showing several different names which were used during the French regime in Canada to describe Lake Superior. For example, Samuel de Champlain referred to Lake Superior as the *Grand Lac* on his *Carte de la Nouvelle France* or "Map of New France," published in 1632.[25]

In 1666, Father Claude Allouez suggested renaming Lake Superior *Lac Tracy* to honor Alexander Prouville, Marquis de Tracy, who was sent to New France in the capacity of Lieutenant General for French America with orders to subdue the Iroquois. The *Jesuit Relations* for 1670 and 1671 contain a detailed chart of Lake Superior, labeled *Lac Tracy ou Supérieur* (Lake Tracy or Superior). Although the name *Lac Tracy* appeared on a few maps, it never achieved common acceptance.[26]

In 1680, Father Louis Hennepin referred to Lake Superior as *Lac Condé*, in deference to Louis II de Bourbon, Prince of Condé; but like the other names, it too, never gained widespread popularity. Travelers simply referred to the big lake as *Lac Supérieur*.[27]

The French-Canadian voyageurs understood the Indian names for geographical features and in most cases translated the local name into French. In so doing, they frequently managed to preserve the essential meaning. However, difficulties often arose concerning the pronunciation and consequent misspelling of the original Indian names at the hands of illiterate voyageurs. Father Frederic Baraga commented about this problem in his *Dictionary of the Otchipwe Language*:

> It should be kept in mind that all these names, which at the present time, designate towns, rivers, lakes, etc., have been thus disfigured by voyageurs, who pronounced them according to the best of their knowledge, without giving a thought they were destroying words and rendering them incomprehensible, in spite of the reclamations of Indianologists who were anxious to preserve the true pronunciation; but usage has prevailed and is still the case in our day.[28]

As the French explored and traded ever farther westward along the Great Lakes, their language became the language of the fur trade. At times various words spoken by different tribes were incorporated into the vocabulary of the trader, and in some cases either a French word or spelling was given to aboriginal terms. The Ojibway word *makak* (a birch-bark tub) is a typical example. Several different spellings exist, including the French version *makaque* and the English version mocock.[29]

The fur trade spawned a cross-cultural exchange not only of goods but also of language. Interesting examples of this exchange survive today in the form of the names used to describe various bands of the Chippewa tribe. In Minnesota, the *Bois Forte*, *Fond du Lac*, and *Mille Lacs* bands use French names. The same is true for Wisconsin bands which use *Lac du Flambeau*, *Lac Courte Oreilles*, and *Lac Vieux Desert*.[30] The acceptance of the French language as the language of the fur trade and its continued use by various tribes can be seen in Minnesota. It is also apparent in other parts of the United States. Some examples from other locations are the names *Gros Ventre*, *Nez Percé*, and *Iroquois*.

Many interesting old place-names, such as Grand Portage and Knife Falls, remain in common use today. These names, although long since anglicized, are constant reminders of the former presence of the French and are especially significant to anyone who wishes to retrace the route of the Northwest Trail. We have already noted a succession of names used to describe Lake Superior. In fact, the very name of the greatest of the Great Lakes, Superior, was derived from the French *supérieur*, meaning "upper" or "higher" in reference to its elevation or relationship with the other lakes. The French term was similar to a translation of the Ojibway name *Kitchigami*, meaning "great water" or "great lake." Lake Superior was also referred to by Father Baraga as *Otchipwe-Kitchigami* or "Great Lake of the Ojibway." Additional changes from Ojibway names to French are also found along the Northwest Trail.[31]

Mileposts in the Wilderness

To travel on the Northwest Trail is to experience a variety of historic place-names. The indigenous people gave distinctive names to various physical features which were faithfully preserved in many early travel accounts. The names they chose were easy to remember because they so aptly captured the very essence of the places described. In fact, travelers measured their progress along the Northwest Trail and other similar routes by these landmarks as if they were mileposts in the wilderness. For example, the mouth of the St. Louis River is often referred to as "the entrance" or "the entry." This early place-name is frequently mentioned by travelers. The entry forms a narrow opening in a long crescent shaped sandbar which separates the deep waters of Lake Superior from the large shallow lake known today as Superior Bay.

After passing through the entry, Allouez Bay appears to the far left. It was named for the Jesuit missionary Father Claude Allouez, who first mapped the shores of Lake Superior. Close by the entry on the bay side is a small river known to the early French and English traders as *La rivière á Gauche*, or "The Left-Hand River," because it was on the left-hand side of anyone entering Superior Bay from Lake Superior. The French name was taken from the Ojibway *Nemadji*, meaning essentially the same thing, "The Left-Hand River." In more recent times, the name of the river was changed back to the original Ojibway version of *Nemadji*.

The Nemadji or "The Left Hand River"
Photo by Allen Anway

Most travelers bound for the interior turned right and headed in a north-westerly direction for about three miles before turning left and passing through a narrow opening between Connor's Point on the south and Rice's Point on the north which was formerly known as *Wubishingweka* or a "narrow point covered with little pines." Both points of land were renamed for early residents in the area.

Paddling through the narrows separating the two points, the traveler enters another sheltered lake known as St. Louis Bay. The river flows through the middle of St. Louis Bay, which is characterized by many indentations, until the stream gradually narrows and begins a serpentine course. Upstream, the route ahead passes between two mountains, and the prospect of a leisurely passage toward the southwest seems assured. Any thoughts of an uneventful passage, however, are quickly dispelled upon arrival at the head of navigation at a place appropriately named *Fond du Lac*, or "the end of the lake."

The name Fond du Lac is an example of a term having several meanings. Initially it meant the far or western end of Lake Superior. It also referred to the head of navigation on the St. Louis River. In addition, it was used to denote the area drained by the St. Louis River, an administrative division or "department" of a fur trading company, a village of indigenous people, and a small settlement located approximately twenty river miles upstream from the mouth of the St. Louis River.

Truly the site of the village of Fond du Lac was "the end of the lake" for it represented the point at which practical navigation ended. Joseph Nicollet's 1842 map is marked near the mouth of the St. Louis River, "*Wekwa Kitchi Gummi* or Fond du Lac Superior." His version of Fond du Lac retained its French meaning as the "end" or "bottom of Lake Superior." Father Frederic Baraga referred to the Ojibway name for the area near the actual village of Fond du Lac as *Waiekwâkitchigami,* or "It is the end [of the] big water." Another Ojibway name used to describe the river at the foot of the first rapids was *Nagadjiwanag* or "the place where the water [of the lake] stops."[32]

During the French regime in Canada, the St. Louis River, the greatest single tributary to Lake Superior, was commonly known as, *La rivière du fond du Lac Supérieur* or "The River at the End of Lake Superior." Eighteenth century French maps used this highly descriptive name instead of "St. Louis," when referring to the river. A few used both names. In fact, who first applied the name "St. Louis" to the river and when is unclear. After the acquisition of New France by Great Britain in 1763, many English map makers simply continued to refer to the St. Louis as the "River at the End of the Lake" or the "Fond du Lac River." The name St. Louis did not become standard on maps until the very end of the eighteenth century.[33]

Today, we usually credit the name of the river to Louis IX (St. Louis), the crusading King of France, but during the eighteenth century, references to St. Louis were also commonly made in connection with the Order of St. Louis. Created by Louis XIV in 1693, the Royal and Military Order of St. Louis was an order of merit symbolized by a knight's cross. Membership in the order was bestowed upon worthy officers by the king. A number of officers serving in New France, including the famous explorer Pierre Gaultier de Varennes, Sieur de la Vérendrye, were recipients of the Order of St. Louis. Whether the name of the river was directly intended to honor King Louis IX, or made in reference to the prestigious military order of merit named after him, poses an interesting question. The story behind the naming of the St. Louis River, like many early terms used in connection with geographic locations, includes a variety of possible explanations.[34]

During the eighteenth century, the Montreal based North West Company referred to the region west of Lake Superior as the "Fond du Lac Department" or "the Fond du Lac." It was one of the many trading areas of the company and covered a territory that included everything west from Lake Superior extending as far as the Red River of the North, south to the Snake River, and north as far as the present border with Canada. The name given to the area continued in popular use long after the North West Company ceased operations in the region. Of course Fond du Lac was merely one name. There were other names of equal interest.

Early traders commonly referred to regions similar to the *Fond du Lac* that were known for their natural resources or other distinct attributes such as the abundant wild rice found in the *Folle Avoine* (Fool's Oats or False Oats) country near the headwaters of the St. Croix River, or the many lakes typical of the *Mille Lacs* or "Thousand Lakes" country. Unfortunately, present usage has largely forsaken the old French names such as *Fond du Lac*, *Folle Avoine*, and *Mille Lacs* when they pertain to a geographic region.[35]

Farther west along the Northwest Trail, additional place-names are encountered chiefly in connection with the rapids and portages of the St. Louis. About two miles beyond the site of the village of Fond du Lac lies the lower end or "foot" of the first portage known as a *Portage des Femme* or "Portage of the Woman." This short carrying place was realy the first part of the *Grand Portage* or "Great Carrying Place" of the the St. Louis. Approximately two miles above the Grand Portage lies *Le Portage des Couteaux* (Portage of the Knives), so named from the sharp upturned slate lining the trail. Between the head of the Grand Portage and the Portage of the Knives were two additional short portages both known as *Portage des Femme*.

Above the portages, additional obstacles were encountered such as the Pine Rapids, the Grand Rapids of the St. Louis, the Long Rapids, and the *Cloutier* or *Cloquet Rapids*.[36] Beyond these landmarks are still more rapids and streams which either flow into or are a feature of the St. Louis, such as three streams which retain their French identity. They are the *Prairie*, *Savanne* (Savanna), and *Embarras* (Floodwood) rivers.

There are also many lakes in the area with exotic names such as *Ga-mitawangagamag sagaigan* meaning "Place-of-the-bare-sand-lake." The French called it *Lac du Sables* or *Lac des Sables* meaning literally, "Lake of the Sands" or Sandy Lake. Although sometimes erroneously referred to as "Big" Sandy Lake, there is no historical basis for the use of the word "big" in reference to the lake. Like so many other place-names it has been tampered with by persons who lack even a rudimentary knowledge of the actual history of the lake or the meaning of the name.[37]

Southeast of Sandy Lake is *Kitchi-manominikani sagaigan* or "Great Wild Oats (Rice) Lake." Known to the French voyageurs as *Grand Lac du Folle Avoine* or "Great Lake of the False (or Fool's) Oats," it is referred to today as Lake "Minnewawa," which is a made-up name, or nonsense term, first created by a real-estate promoter in 1913. The true name of this historically significant lake has been replaced by a fabrication consisting of a Dakota word *minne* and a Cree word *wawa* supposedly signifying "water of the wild goose." The perpetrator of this interesting fraud was evidently not only ignorant of the two languages he borrowed from but also unaware of the eternal enmity which existed between the two tribes that would have effectively precluded the concoction of such a term in the first place. Sadly, "Minnewawa" is but one more example of a new term applied to an historic body of water that in truth lacks both meaningful substance or authenticity.[38]

Chapter 1 - The River at the End of the Lake
Notes

1.   Laurence Oliphant, *Minnesota and the Far West* (Edinburgh, 1855), p. 187. Oliphant's voyageur guide Le Fêve referred to the water and land route between Lake Superior and the Mississippi River as "the Northwest Trail."

2.   Richard W. Ojakangas and Charles L. Matsch, *Minnesota's Geology* (Minneapolis, 1982), pp. 161-167.

3.   Ibid. p. 111, Figure 7-19 (b). Two maps on page 111, explain the geological process of "stream piracy" by the St. Louis River; see also Charles R. Van Hise and Charles K. Leith, *The Geology of the Lake Superior Region*, United States Geological Survey Monographs, vol. 52 (Washington D.C., 1911), p. 113; Van Hise and Leith's work was referred to in an article by Professor Irving Harlow Hart, "The Geologic Origin of the Savanna and Prairie Portages," *Minnesota History*, vol. 13, no. 4 (December, 1932), pp. 403-407. Hart, an archivist at the State Teachers College in Cedar Falls, Iowa, performed much pioneering research on the early history of the Savanna Portage, Sandy Lake, and the Mississippi River.

4.   Eric W. Morse, *Fur Trade Canoe Routes of Canada! Then and Now* (Ottawa, 1969) , pp. 27-32. Although Morse is primarily concerned with Canadian waterways, the general characteristics of trade routes are discussed.

5.   Newton H. Winchell assisted by Warren Upham, *The Geological and Natural History Survey of Minnesota, 1872-1882, The Geology of Minnesota*, vol. 1, of the Final Report (Minneapolis, 1884), p. 135.

6.   Mentor L. Williams (ed.), *Schoolcraft's Narrative Journal of Travels* (East Lansing, 1992), p. 142, includes Schoolcraft's description of the St. Louis River and the Grand Portage.

7.   John Disturnell, *The Great Lakes, or Inland Seas of America* (Philadelphia, 1871), pp. 145-148; Joseph A. Gilfillan, "Minnesota Geographical Names Derived From the Chippewa Language," *The Geological and Natural History Survey of Minnesota*, Fifteenth Annual Report for the Year 1886 (1887), p. 458. The entire glossary was reprinted in *The Minnesota Archaeologist*, vol. 35, no. 4 (1976), pp. 25-51.

8.   David Thompson, Diary No. 9, May 8th, 1798. Copies of Thompson's manuscript diaries are in the collections of the Minnesota Historical Society. His travels on the Northwest Trail are described in Diary No. 9 and in his published narrative begun in the 1840s. Several versions of his work include: J. B. Tyrrell (ed.), *David Thompson's Narrative of His Explorations in Western America, 1784-1812* (Toronto, 1916); Richard Glover (ed.), *David Thompson's Narrative, 1784-1812* (Toronto, 1962); and Victor G. Hopwood (ed.), *David Thompson: Travels in Western North America, 1784-1812* (Toronto, 1971). Thompson's manuscript diary contains information not found in the published editions and is well worth consulting.

9.   Morse, *Canoe Routes*, pp. 5-14; and Grace Lee Nute, *The Voyageur* (1931; reprint ed., St. Paul, 1955), pp. 35-74. Both works include the various methods of moving canoes and cargo on rivers including the décharge.

10.   Ojakangas-Marsch, *Minnesota's Geology*, pp. 169-170. The authors include an explanation of the forming of the "baymouth bar" at the entrance to the St. Louis River. For an Ojibway account of the creation of the sandbar at the mouth of the St. Louis River, see William Whipple Warren, *History of the Ojibway People* (1885; reprint ed., St. Paul, 1984), p. 81.

11.   Gilfillan, "Minnesota Geographic Names," p. 457; see also, Chrysostum Verwyst, "A Glossary of Chippewa Indian Names of Rivers, Lakes, and Villages," *Acta et Dicta*, vol. 4, no. 2 (July, 1916), p. 257. Chequamegon is an English version of the French *Chagoumigon*, which in turn is a corruption of the Ojibway term *Jagawamikong* or *Shagawaumikong*, meaning "a long sandy point."

12   Alfred Brunson, *A Western Pioneer*, 2 vols. (New York, 1872), vol. 1, p. 178, contains a vivid description of the conditions confronting canoeists at the mouth of the St. Louis River.

13.   Williams (ed.), *Schoolcraft's Narrative Journal*, pp. 441-443, and 446-447, for James Doty's comments on the streams connecting Lake Superior with the Mississippi.

14. Glover, *Thompson's Narrative*, p. 210.

15. Edwin Tappen Adney and Howard I. Chapelle, *The Bark Canoes and Skin Boats of North America* (Washington, D.C., 1964), pp. 8, and 135-153.

16. There are several early references to the use of "light canoes" on the St. Louis River. A British military memorandum c. 1777, found in "Papers From Canadian Archives, 1767-1814," *Collections of the State Historical Society of Wisconsin*, vol.,12 (Madison, 1892), p. 43, mentions the use of light canoes west of Lake Superior; reference to a light canoe is also found in Glover, *Thompson's Narrative*, p. 207; and Williams (ed.), *Schoolcraft's Narrative Journal*, p. 143. Schoolcraft mentions exchanging two large canoes for four smaller ones above the Grand Portage of the St. Louis in 1820.

17. Glover, *Thompson's Narrative*, p. 210.

18. *Collections of the State Historical Society of Wisconsin*, vol. 16, (Madison, 1902) p.197, n.

19. The six portages along the route from Lake Superior to the Mississippi River were: (1) the Woman's Portage (located at the foot of the Grand Portage of the St. Louis River), (2) the Grand Portage of the St. Louis (beginning at Roche Galet), (3) two Woman's Portages (one on either bank at the head of the Grand Portage of the St. Louis), (4) the Knife Portage, (5) the Pine Island Portage, and (6) either the Prairie Portage or the Savanna Portage to the adjoining Mississippi watershed. For those traveling farther up the St. Louis toward Lake Vermilion, the portage between the headwaters of the St. Louis and Pike rivers connected the St. Louis-Great Lakes watershed with that of Hudson Bay.

20. Williams (ed.), *Schoolcraft's Narrative Journal*, p. 481. Trowbridge mentioned the dark river water in his journal entry for Sunday, July 9th, 1820; Charles Lanman, *A Canoe Voyage up the Mississippi River and Around Lake Superior* (New York, 1847). p. 21, stated, "The water is perfectly clear, but of a rich snuff color, owing probably to the swamps out of which it runs;" Walter O'Meara, *We Made it Through the Winter* (St. Paul, 1974), p. 100.

21. *Alexander MacKenzie, Voyages From Montreal on the River St. Laurence Through the Continent of North America to the Frozen and Pacific Oceans in the Years 1789 and 1793 with a Preliminary Account of the Rise, Progress, and Present State of the Fur Trade*, in Master Works of Canadian Authors (1801; reprint ed., Toronto, 1927), p. 64.

22. For a detailed study of the Minnesota-Canadian boundary see: William E. Lass, *Minnesota's Boundary With Canada: Its Evolution Since 1783* (St. Paul, 1980); and Francis M. Carroll, *A Good and Wise Measure: The Search for the Canadian-American Boundary, 1783-1842* (Toronto, 2001).

23. Gilfillan, "Minnesota Geographical Names," p. 451; For a good introduction to Ojibway place-names in Minnesota see Alan R. Woolworth, "Indian Place Names of the Minnesota Region," *The Minnesota Archaeologist*, vol. 35, no. 4 (December, 1976), pp. 3-12. Other sources of Ojibway names pertaining to the area of the Northwest Trail can be found in Mary W. Berthel, "Place Names of the Mille Lacs Region," *Minnesota History*, vol. 21, no. 4 (December, 1940), pp. 345-352; Alan H. Hartley, "The Expansion of Ojibway and French Place-Names into the Lake Superior Region in the Seventeenth Century," *Names*, vol. 28 (March, 1980), pp. 43-68; Karen Daniels Petersen (ed.), "Ojibway and Dakota Place Names in Minnesota," *The Minnesota Archaeologist*, vol. 25, no. 1(1963) pp. 5-40; *Warren Upham, Minnesota Geographic Names: Their Origin and Historic Significance* (1920; reprint ed., St. Paul, 1969), and Verwyst, "Glossary," pp. 253-274.

24. Warren, *History of the Ojibway*, p. 37.

25. Winchell and Upham, *Geological and Natural History Survey, 1872-1882, The Geology of Minnesota*, vol. 1 of the Final Report (Minneapolis, 1884), plate 1, "Historical Chart Showing the Geographical Names and Their Dates Prior to Nicollet's Map of 1841." The authors date Nicollet's map to 1841 and others date it to 1843. The map itself bears the date 1842, and a scale-down version was printed to accompany a report released in 1843.

26. *Collections of the State Historical Society of Wisconsin*, vol. 16, (Madison, 1902), p. 31. Father Claude Allouez proposed renaming Lake Superior *Lac Tracy* for Alexander de Prouville, Marquis de Tracy and Governor-General of New France. Allouez declared the lake "...will henceforth bear Monsieur de Tracy's name, in recognition of indebtedness to him on the part of the people of

those regions." That indebtedness was due to the temporary relief afforded New France and the Great Lakes tribes from the sporadic attacks of the Iroquois. The Marquis was specifically sent to the colony with a contingent of seasoned troops of the Carignan-Salières Regiment with orders to crush the Iroquois.

27.   John Gilmary Shea, *Discovery and Exploration of the Mississippi River Valley* (New York, 1853), p. 113. This early translation of Father Louis Hennepin's work identifies *Lac Buade* (Mille Lacs), or the "Lake of the "Issati," and *Lac Condé* (Superior), but says nothing about the Northwest Trail.

28   Frederic Baraga, *A Dictionary of the Otchipwe Language*, In 2 parts (1878; reprint ed., Minneapolis, 1973), part 1, p. 297.

29.   Ibid., part 2, p. 207.

30.   The various Minnesota bands of Ojibway having French names include the *Bois Forte* (Strong Wood), *Fond du Lac* (End of the Lake), and *Mille Lac* (A Thousand Lakes). The Wisconsin bands include the *Lac du Flambeau* (Lake of the Torch), *Lac Courte Oreilles*, (Lake of the Short Ears), and *Lac Vieux Desert*, which Schoolcraft translated as "Lake of the Old Wintering Grounds." For a commentary on Schoolcraft's mastery of French, see Philip P. Mason (ed.), *Schoolcraft's Expedition to Lake Itasca* (East Lansing, 1993), p. 68.

31.   Gilfillan, "Geographical Names," p. 457.

32.   Ibid., p. 458. For a brief history of the village site see Sister Bernard Coleman, *Where the Water Stops: Fond du Lac Reservation* (Duluth, 1967).

33.   Ellworth T. Carlstedt, "A History of the Fond du Lac Trading Posts With Some Mention of the Fond du Lac Department," unpublished manuscript, University of Minnesota, December 9th, 1933, pp. 3-5. Carlstedt listed the various names given to the river from 1703 to 1921. The earliest mention of the name St. Louis is on a map he identified as "Charlevoix-Bellin" (1744). The river is marked "River St. Louis or of Fond du Lac."

34.   Warren Upham, in *Magazine of History*, vol. 4, no. 4 (October, 1906), p. 196, believed the name of the St. Louis River commemorated the investiture of Pierre Gaultier de Varennes, Sieur de la Vérendrye with the Cross of the Order of St. Louis; Louise Phelps Kellogg, *The French Régime in Wisconsin and the Northwest* (Madison, 1925), p. 296, stated the Order of St. Louis was the highest ambition of every Canadian army officer. Given the prestige accorded the recipient, the story of Sieur La Vérendrye naming the river after he received the coveted knight's cross sounds plausible. Coleman, *Where The Water Stops*, p. 3, states the St. Louis River was named by Sieur La Vérendrye in honor of Louis, King of France, but she does not indicate which Louis. Unfortunately, Sieur La Vérendrye was awarded the Cross of St. Louis in 1749, five years after the name St. Louis first appeared on a map. Furthermore, he died in December of 1749, before he could return to the Lake Superior country. If the story of his naming the St. Louis River is true, he most likely named it before he received the award. The question is when?

35.   *Collections of the State Historical Society of Wisconsin*, vol. 16 (Madison, 1902), p. 114, includes a copy of a letter written in 1684 by Daniel Greysolon, Sieur Du Lhut, wherein he refers to the *Folle Avoines*. The French traders referred to the Menominee Indians as the *Folle Avoines*. Menominee is merely an English version of the French word *Malouminé* or "False Oats Men."

36.   Gilfillan, "Minnesota Geographical Names," p. 456. The Ojibway name of the Cloquet River is *Ga-bitotigweiag-zibii* or "The-river-that-runs-parallel-or-double-with Lake Superior." All of the rapids situated along the St. Louis River were named for natural features except the Cloutier or Cloquet Rapids. This obstacle was apparently named for a voyageur who broke his canoe in the rapids. The unfortunate man's name, or a variation of it, was later applied to the river; See, Williams (ed.), *Schoolcraft's Narrative Journal*, p. 66, for Schoolcraft's comments on the voyageurs propensity to name every landmark along a stream; Larry Luukkonen, *Cloquet: The Story Behind the Name* (Cloquet, Minnesota, 2000).

37.   Ibid., p. 458, The Ojibway name, *Ga-mitawonggagumag-sagaigun*, refers to the character of the soil in which the lake is situated, hence the name "The-place-of-bare-sand-lake," or Sandy Lake.

38.   Ibid., The correct Ojibway name for this lake is *Kitchi-manominikani-sagaiigun* or "The-great-place-of-false-oats [great wild rice]-lake." The voyageurs called it *Grand Lac du Folle Avoine*.

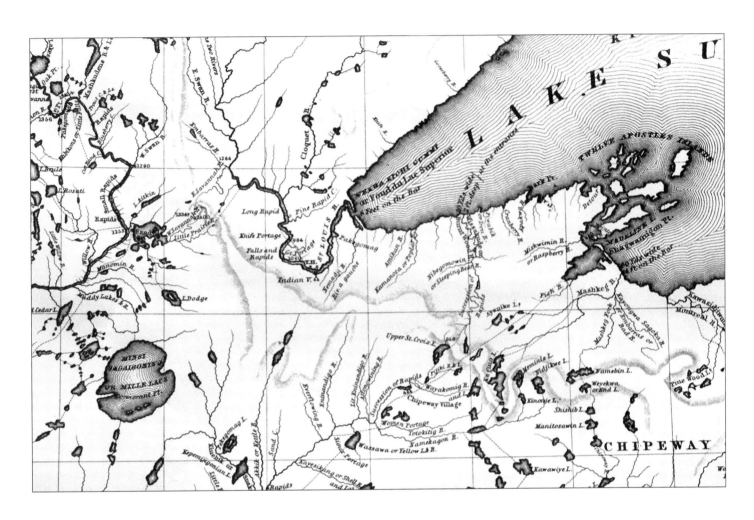

A section of Joseph Nicollet's map, printed in 1843, showing the territory between Lake Superior and the Mississippi River. The map is a scale-down copy of one produced in 1842 for the Bureau of the Corps of Topographical Engineers. U.S. Army Corps of Engineers

The St. Louis River.
Photo by Allen Anway

Voyageur portaging with his pack.
Sketch after Frederic Remington, from the collection of the Carlton County Historical Society

Chapter 2 ✎ River Routes and Winter Roads

It is with good reason that early travelers liberally sprinkled the countryside along the Northwest Trail with interesting and colorful place-names. Although distinctive landmarks abound to help one find the way, such places are better remembered when associated with a name. If the name concerns a prominent or readily identifiable feature, so much the better. Some of the most interesting place-names are found along the various portages and waterways that crisscrossed the country west of Lake Superior.

Portages were significant stops during any journey along the Northwest Trail; and many early travelers' journals contain vivid descriptions of them. In fact, the word "portage" is a French word meaning "carrying place," and is most often associated with canoe travel. Like so many other interesting terms, we have adopted the word portage into the English language without its original pronunciation. To "portage" means one has to get out of the canoe and carry it to a distant location. The process can be quite unforgettable if one retraces some of the carrying places found on the Northwest Trail.

Portages and Posés on the St. Louis River

There were several notable portages along the route from Lake Superior to the Mississippi, and their unforgettable qualities were mentioned by a host of travelers. Starting at the head of navigation on Lake Superior it was necessary to cross these portages: the Grand Portage of the St. Louis, which was approximately seven miles long and contained nineteen *posés* or rest points; and the Knife Portage, one and a half miles long with three *posés*. In addition, two portages crossed the height of land at different points. These were the Prairie and Savanna portages. The length of the Savanna Portage varied with the amount of water available. Generally described as being six miles in length, the number of rest points on the Savanna Portage varied from twelve to thirteen depending upon which of several paths were used. The Prairie Portage was about five miles long with eleven rest points.[1]

In his book, *Fur Trade Canoe Routes of Canada*, author Eric Morse lists three desirable qualities of a portage: directness, gradient, and footing. Each of the portages on the Northwest Trail had at least two of these essential attributes.[2] Beginning with the Grand Portage of the St. Louis, the chief challenge was gradient. Here the river falls over five hundred and seventy feet in the relatively short distance from Knife Falls to St. Louis Bay, and the traveler was forced to carry all of his baggage and canoe over a long and steep portage. Gradient also dictated the best type of craft to use on inland waters.

The high waves encountered on Lake Superior required the fur traders to travel by either a twenty-eight foot North canoe, a *bateau*, or a six-oared

Mackinaw boat. Once past the river's mouth, however, such large craft were unsuitable for interior navigation on shallow, fast moving streams. Instead, the voyageurs unloaded them at the "foot," or lower end of the Grand Portage. Smaller canoes, more adapted for use in the river, were kept at the upper end, or "head," of the portage by the fur companies.[3]

After unloading the cargo, the large North canoes, *bateaux*, or Mackinaw boats were either returned to the fur post or hauled up on the river bank and carefully stored for the return trip. The birch-bark canoes were particularly susceptible to damage from excessive drying and were carefully placed upside down and completely covered with bushes to protect their pitched seams from direct exposure to sunlight. The same procedure was followed for the smaller canoes used on the upper reaches of the river. Once the boats were unloaded and properly stored, the procession over the portage began.[4]

The procedure followed at the Grand Portage of the St. Louis is worth noting because it was repeated at other portages in the same way. Passengers disembarked and usually carried their own personal baggage. Cargo, consisting of bales of furs or trade goods, was carried by the boatsmen or *voyageurs*. The bales or *pièces*, weighing on average seventy-five pounds apiece, were then unloaded and carried to the first rest point or *posé*. The Ojibway referred to a *posé* as *opuggid-diwanan* or "the place of putting down the pack."[5]

When everything had been brought up to the first rest point, the procedure was then repeated to reach the second rest point and so on until the portage was completed. Various reasons have been given for this method of portaging ranging from prevention of pilferage to allowing the men carrying the bundles of goods an opportunity to rest from their burdens. Apparently, the men preferred to carry heavy loads for short distances and rest on the return trip rather than make one long exhausting trip across the full length of the portage.

The length of a portage was measured by the number of *posés*. The distance between *posés* varied in length from about a third to a half a mile. The number of *posés* was indicative of the difficulty encountered in crossing a portage rather than in terms of a measurable distance. The higher the number, the more difficult the portage.[6]

The crossing of the Grand Portage of the St. Louis involved a series of steps. Beginning at the head of navigation, a typical canoe party proceeded approximately two miles upstream against the current at which point they discharged passengers and some cargo at a place called the *Portage des Femme*, or "Portage of the Woman." Here the travelers found a path leading to the foot of a steep bank from which, after ascending carefully by means of hand holds scooped in the hill side, they observed an imposing view of the countryside. The hill was estimated as being two hundred feet above the river by Lieutenant James Allen, who crossed the Grand Portage in 1832. He calculated the gradient at the beginning of the Woman's Portage to be about forty-five degrees.

The travelers rested after climbing the steep hill. Meanwhile, the voyageurs escorting the lightened canoes proceeded farther upstream into the rapids, each pushing against the current with a *pique de fond*, or "setting pole," until they arrived at the true beginning of the Grand Portage known as *Roche Galet*, or "Shingle Rock." The portage was located near the mouth of a tributary known as the Little River. Once there, the voyageurs unloaded the balance of the cargo and began the pattern of moving the packs from one rest point to the next. From *Roche Galet*, the voyageurs, having met the passengers previously discharged at the Woman's Portage, proceeded overland. Frequently, however, passengers did not wait at *Roche Galet* but instead struck out across the portage, each carrying his own baggage, independent of the voyageurs laboring behind them who were weighed down under heavy bales.[7]

This scene showing men poling their canoes up the rapids at Sault Sainte Marie was repeated many times along the Northwest Trail. Once the voyageurs reached the drainage divide they ceremoniously "threw away" their setting poles. Library of Congress

Trade goods and furs were usually packed in bales covered with sheeting or canvas and secured by twine. These packages were carried by means of a tumpline strapped across the forehead and secured to the base of the pack. Plenty of stories abound as to the number of *pièces* and other merchandise carried by experienced voyageurs. It is said that George Bonga carried as many as three bales at a time, each one weighing approximately seventy-five pounds. Bonga was a large man and equal to the task.[8]

The Grand Portage of the St. Louis was described by most who passed over it as being approximately seven miles long with nineteen *posés* interspersed according to the terrain. In 1825, geographer David Thompson and his son Samuel, measured the length of the Grand Portage of the St. Louis while working for the International Boundary Commission, established under the Treaty of Ghent (1815). Their survey showed the portage as being eleven thousand nine hundred fifteen yards long.[9]

Many of the rest points along the trail had highly descriptive names such as: *Roche Galet, passe a l'Ours,* Maple *posé*, River Six *posé* (also referred to as the Six Pause River or Midway River), and The Grave. While crossing the portage on Friday, July 7th, 1820, James Doty, a member of Governor Lewis Cass' Northwestern Expedition, remarked about the last-named *posé*. The name originated with a Frenchman named Machone whose wife was buried there. A lone wooden cross stood at the head of her grave to mark the spot. The other names of the remaining rest points have been forgotten over time. The original United States land survey of the area in 1868, clearly shows the original voyageurs' portage, but no rest points are delineated.[10]

The 1868 government survey notes not only include a description of the Grand Portage of the St. Louis, but also describe the "Grand Portage Wagon Road" built over a portion of the original trail. The wagon road was known locally by a number of names including the "Military Road," or the "Government Road." It was reportedly built in 1857 with government funds, hence the name. The wagon road was constructed after the Ojibway abandoned their original village on *Nikig* (Otter) Island in the St. Louis River opposite the old American Fur Company post at Fond du Lac. The new village was located upstream on the bluff overlooking the future site of the city of Cloquet, Minnesota. Their encampment was within the boundaries of the newly created Fond du Lac Indian Reservation, established by treaty in 1854. As noted, the wagon road followed portions of the original Grand Portage of the St. Louis and was built to facilitate the movement of necessary supplies by ox cart from the head of navigation to a point on the St. Louis River opposite the new village site. It reportedly remained in use until 1907.[11]

Henry Schoolcraft described his experiences crossing the Grand Portage of the St. Louis. Schoolcraft, who filled the positions of geologist and mineralogist on the Northwestern Expedition of 1820, later published his account of the journey. His description of the portage began at the newly established (1817) American Fur Company post at the village of Fond du Lac on July 6th, 1820:

> We left the establishment at ten o'clock in the morning. The river is ascended two miles further, to the foot of the Grand Portage. Here the goods are all landed and the carrying commences... The first part of this portage is excessively rough, and the fatigue was rendered almost insupportable by the heat of the day, the thermometer standing at 82° at noon. With the assistance of the Indians...we proceeded however, with all our baggage, five pauses, and encamped at twilight.[12]

The next day, in spite of rain that made the red clay of the steep muddy trail exceptionally slippery, the party continued across the portage the distance of ten *posés*. The following day, July 8th, Schoolcraft and his companions resumed their journey over the remaining four posés and reached the head of the portage in time to dry their damp baggage, repair their canoes, and prepare for the journey the following day. Schoolcraft remarked further:

> The fall of the St. Louis River, between the extremes of this portage is very great, being one continued chain of rapids and falls... It is here that the river forces a passage through a chain of mountains...and renders the traveling excessively toilsome.[13]

James D. Doty, another member of the Northwestern Expedition, made the following comments upon completing the transit of the Grand Portage:

> Saturday, July 8, 1820. By 4 o'clock we had everything across the portage, for all which we were blessing our stars... This is considered a difficult portage and it is reckoned fortunate to pass it in 3 days. We had 20 Indians to assist us—a long talk was held with them this afternoon and

many valuable presents made, with which they appeared highly pleased.[14]

While the gradient of the Grand Portage of the St. Louis, particularly at its foot near the village of Fond du Lac, was quite steep and treacherous, there were other disagreeable aspects to portaging.

Regardless of the physical features of the Grand Portage, the region was well-known for its voracious mosquitoes, which descended in clouds covering the sweltering passengers as well as the voyageurs laboring with paddle or setting pole. Even in the shade of the overhanging trees which lined the route of the portage, there was barely a breeze sufficient to disturb the stifling humidity of a midsummer's day or drive away the swarms of ever-present insects. Nothing but tightly woven cloth or netting was effective against these creatures who probed every garment for an unguarded spot so they might satisfy their craving for a blood meal. To those Indians and voyageurs who habitually went *au natural*, or nearly so, to save their few precious articles of clothing, there was no relief from the stinging hordes. Even if they had anointed any exposed flesh with bear oil, it would have washed off as they climbed in and out of the water.[15]

Above all the hustle and bustle of portaging could be heard the continuous roar of water rushing over rock ledges. The ancient geological formations found in the St. Louis River tilt upward at impossible angles, forming immense barriers over which the brown foaming flood pours unrelentingly. Although the balance of the route along the Grand Portage of the St. Louis was located some distance away from the river, travelers could catch a glimpse of the rapids shrouded in mist near the end of the portage. A few travelers made side trips from the portage for a closer look at the spectacular scenery found near the waterfalls, especially when the river was swollen with spring runoff. Then as now, the thundering torrents of water served to hold the observer spellbound with their power. Today, the sight of the roaring flood rushing wildly over jagged rock formations still impresses persons viewing the prospect for the first time, and moves the more thoughtful traveler to record the scene in diary, letter, or with camera.

The St. Louis River in flood. Photo by Allen Anway

After reaching the head of the Grand Portage at Maple Island, the traveler had the option of continuing by water or using a second "Woman's Portage." It should be noted here that any short portage which required the partial unloading of passengers and baggage was referred to as a "Woman's Portage," since by custom the women in the party had to carry the baggage from one point to the next, leaving the men free to manage the canoes. Above Maple Island, the traveler actually found two Woman's Portages, one on either side of the river.[16]

The voyageurs struggled with bringing the partially loaded canoes through the rapids, around the western side of Maple Island, and up a three foot *chute d'eau*, or "cascade," in the river. From the head of the Grand Portage of the St. Louis the route extended upstream to the next carrying place known to the Ojibway as *Mokomaninigaming*. French voyageurs and traders such as Jean Baptiste Perrault called it *Le Portage des Couteaux*. Doctor Douglass Houghton referred to the portage as the *Portage aux Couteau*. Most travelers simply referred to it as "Knife Portage."[17]

The river channel above the head of the Grand Portage and for the next few miles is exceedingly rocky, interspersed with shallows, rapids, and deep pools. The voyageurs poling their canoes upstream had to frequently disembark and carefully guide their fragile craft over the sharp upturned rock formations. This was a difficult task given the dark water which obscured some obstacles hidden beneath the surface. While a man was negotiating a seemingly shallow stretch of the river, it was not uncommon for him to suddenly step off a rock ledge and find himself over his head. Such sudden surprises undoubtedly prompted many a *sacré* from the voyageurs.[18]

Le Portage des Couteaux was situated on the west bank of the river about two miles above Maple Island. To the voyageur toiling upstream against a powerful current, the sight of a unique rock formation standing in the middle of the river was a familiar landmark. Known locally as "Fortress Island" for its resemblance to a ruined castle, the imposing rock formation is located at the foot of the three mile long Knife Rapids and about two hundred feet north of the foot of the Knife Portage. It was familiar to all who used the Northwest Trail, but to the voyageur it spelled the beginning of a short but painful carrying place. Normally, the current of the Knife Rapids was too strong, and the traveler had little choice but to cross the rugged portage.

The old and the new.
A view of pristine Fortress Island against a backdrop of modern industrial development.
Photo by Larry Luukkonen

Fortress Island, a landmark in the St. Louis River.
Carlton County Historical Society

The chief feature of Knife Portage was poor footing. Here the path overland was paved with sharp upturned slate rock. Henry Schoolcraft, who first crossed the Knife Portage on Sunday, July 9th, 1820, likened the slate to:

...the leaves of a book standing edgewise. The effect of this arrangement of the strata, upon the mockasins [sic] and feet of the voyageurs, who cross this portage has led to its name–the portage of the knives. At the lower end of it, this slate forms a lone standing pile, or pyramid, in the centre of the river, of eighty or ninety feet in height, and supporting in its crevices a few stunted cedars and pines.[19]

When traveling by canoe, both voyageurs and travelers routinely traded their heavy leather boots or shoes for Indian moccasins. This was done not only because the footwear was easy to obtain but also because moccasins reduced the chance of damaging the inside of the frail birch-bark craft. Leather moccasins, however, became soft after repeated soaking in the river brought about by the need to get in and out of the canoe to guide it over rocks and rapids. By the time the weary voyageur or traveler reached Knife Falls, his moccasins were very likely extremely soft and pliable. When subjected to travel over the harsh surface of the portage, the wet leather was easily cut by the upturned slate.

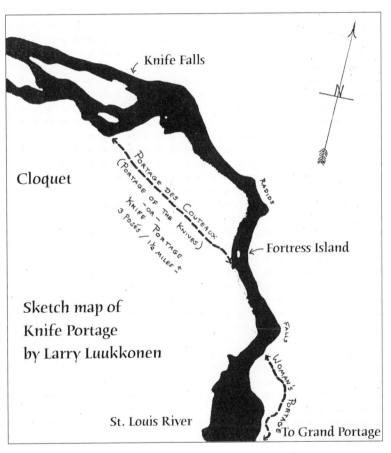

Sketch map of
Knife Portage
by Larry Luukkonen

Various estimates exist regarding the length of the Knife Portage; some calculated it as being two miles long, while others insisted it was only a mile to a mile and a half. David Thompson's map of the river listed the Knife Portage as being two thousand twenty-nine yards long. James Doty, a member of the Cass Expedition, commented on the Knife Portage in his journal entry for Sunday, July 9th, 1820:

It is called the knife portage because of its being entire ledges of stone lying on an angle of 90°. They are sharp and pierce the feet at almost every step. It was three pauses and is about 1 mile long. I walked it in less than half an hour...[20]

Doty went on to record that at the head of the portage he viewed Knife Falls, which he estimated had a perpendicular drop of about twelve feet. He thought the falls offered one of the finest views he had seen thus far on the trip.

On reaching the head or western point of the Knife Portage, the traveler encountered a series of converging overland trails. These trails connected with other points on the river and also with an Indian village and sugar camp to the west at Perch Lake as well as points farther inland. Above the Knife Portage, the St. Louis River turned gently to the north below a bluff overlooking the river. Several islands dot the surface of the St. Louis, but no obstacle other than a few shallow spots confronted the voyageurs in this section of the river.

Chief Naganub of Fond du Lac, c. 1880.
Photo by William McLeish, Minnesota Historical Society

Sketch map of the St. Louis River from the head of the Grand Portage near Maple Island to the Paw-paw-sco-me-me-tig islands drawn by Reverend Edmund Ely based on a description given to him by Chief Naganub in 1862.
Carlton County Historical Society

Above the head of the Knife Portage, the river is navigable for a little more than a mile before encountering shallow rapids near two islands known collectively as *Paw-paw-sco-me-me-tig* or *Papashkominitigong*, which was translated as "a treeless island," "Bald Island," or "Bald River Island," by missionaries. The

Canadian voyageurs called it simply "Plain Island" for the "Plaine Tree" or red maple found growing there as previously noted. The island consists of two parts separated by a small channel, and is clearly shown on a map dating from 1862. The map was based on a sketch drawn for Reverend Edmund Franklin Ely by Fond du Lac Chief Naganub (also spelled Nahgahub). Naganub's map depicts the section of the St. Louis River from the head of the Grand Portage as far as the *Paw-paw-sco-me-me-tig* islands.[21]

Farther upstream are a series of four rapids known in order as the Pine Island Rapids, the Grand Rapids of the St. Louis, followed by the Long Rapids, and the Cloutier or Cloquet Rapids. At the foot of the series of rapids, the voyageurs had to resort once again to the use of setting poles as they slowly pushed their canoes upstream against the current. When traveling upstream through rapids, ordinary canoe paddles were useless. If travelers wished to avoid poling a canoe upstream, they used Pine Island Portage. It began below the Pine Island Rapids on the west side of the river, and terminated above the Long Rapids.[22]

Above the Grand Rapids of the St. Louis was a place the Ojibway called *Che-ba-gah-me-goons* or "little grave." Fur trader William Alexander Aitkin lost a young child there, and for many years travelers remarked about the small grave enclosed with cedar pickets overlooking the rapids.[23]

Proceeding upstream from the Long Rapids, the voyageurs encountered the next obstacle—the Cloquet or Cloutier Rapids. Beginning some distance below the mouth of the Cloquet River, the rapids constituted a serious obstacle in periods of high water, when submerged rocks in the river bed posed a threat to the unwary voyageurs. Long a favorite fishing spot of the Ojibway, the Cloutier or Cloquet Rapids reportedly received its name from a voyageur who broke his canoe on the rocks at that location. The rapids share their name with the nearby river and the city of Cloquet, located several miles downstream at Knife Falls.[24]

Above the rapids, the Cloquet River, originally known as the Rapid River, enters the St. Louis from the northeast. The Cloquet River is characterized by a series of rough rapids just above its junction with the St. Louis River.

Beyond the Cloquet River, the course of the St. Louis turns to the west. Continuing upstream, the river is characterized by a fairly smooth stretch of water broken here and there by small rapids. About a mile west of the confluence of the Cloquet River at a location known to the Ojibway as *Ashkibwakaning* or "swamp potato place," a brook enters from the south. The brook, which originates far to the south at Perch Lake, is known variously as Stoney Brook or Wild Rice River. Beyond this point, the St. Louis River continues in a westerly direction until it intersects the Prairie Portage, the first of two portages which connect it with the Mississippi.

Crossing the Divide

The Prairie Portage started rather inauspiciously at the mouth of a small stream which flows into the St. Louis near the center of Section 27, Township 51

North, Range 20 West, in St. Louis County. The portage followed the stream toward its source in a generally southwesterly direction. The fur trader Jean Baptiste Perrault followed the Prairie Portage in the fall of 1784, and left a good description of its course. The portage passed a small lake near the height of land, located a short distance north of Prairie Lake, and continued about a half mile south until it struck the north shore of Prairie Lake. Prairie Lake, also called by the Ojibway *Mashkode-onigami-sagaigan* (Prairie Portage Lake), is the source of the *Mashkode sibi*, or Prairie River, which flows along a westerly course into Sandy Lake and eventually the Mississippi River.[25]

Scene along the Prairie River. Sandy Lake is just around the bend.
Photo by Larry Luukkonen

Embarking on Prairie Lake, travelers paddled south toward a small island. Once near the island, they turned west toward a point which slightly obscures the beginning of the Prairie River. The Prairie River, also known as the Prairie Portage River, derived its name from the grass found along the banks near its origin. *Prairie* is a French term for "meadow."

There is only a modest change in elevation along the entire length of the Prairie River as it flows westward from Prairie Lake, hence its meandering course. Only one rapid of note interrupted the voyage on the Prairie River, and Jean Baptiste Perrault described it as the scene of a canoe mishap where a boat and its contents belonging to trader Alexander Kay was lost in 1784. This rapid was normally avoided by making a short portage called appropriately the Pine Portage after the abundant pine growing in the vicinity at that time.[26]

Although there are a number of references in early accounts to the Prairie Portage, after the 1790s, few travelers mentioned it. The primary reason for the decline in use began when a series of storms littered portions of the route with fallen trees and debris, which rendered it all but impassible for canoes. Known to some as the "Indian route" or the "winter route," part of the Prairie Portage continued to be used in a limited way in summer by local inhabitants and as a winter route for dog sleds.[27]

In contrast to the Prairie Portage, the Savanna Portage has been described by many writers. Most travelers continued their voyage up the St. Louis River a short distance to the present-day town of Floodwood, Minnesota, site of the junction of three rivers. Here, one could either continue upstream and eventually portage into Lake Vermilion, or take the Savanna River to the southwest, or canoe northwest up the *Embarras* River. *Embarras* is a French word meaning "an obstruction," in reference to what were described by travelers as "rafts" of timber and debris annually washed downstream. The Ojibway called the river *Angwassago-sibi*, or the "Driftwood River." The name was later changed to the Floodwood

River.[28] Based on early references in journals and reports, most fur traders continued along the Northwest Trail and followed the Savanna River toward the Savanna Portage and Sandy Lake.

Leaving the broad St. Louis behind, intrepid voyageurs began to encounter floating debris as the Savanna became ever more meandering. As they progressed toward the river's source, the low banks were covered with stands of tall grass and scattered trees, hence the river's name meaning "grassland."

Shortly before arriving at the eastern end of the Savanna Portage, the river is intersected by a small brook with a barely perceptible current flowing from the northwest. A short distance up this brook travelers encountered the first *posé* of the Savanna Portage. During times of high water, the voyageurs would push their canoes from this first rest point as far up the stream as possible, leaving the passengers to walk along a flimsy network of trail corduroy until they reached dry land somewhere near the third *posé*. The footing was so bad that gentlemen were carried across the portage rather than wallow in the mire.

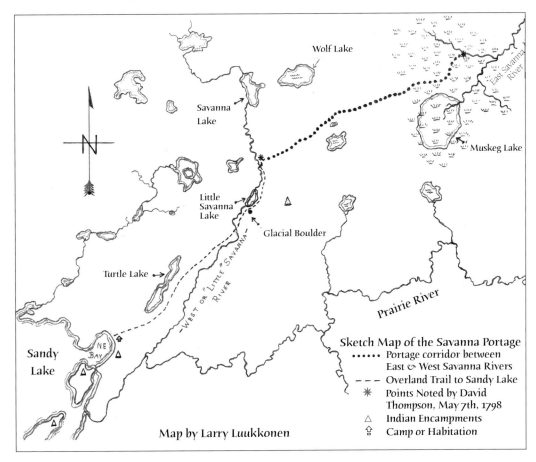

Wolf Lake

East Savanna River

Savanna Lake

Muskeg Lake

Little Savanna Lake

Glacial Boulder

West or "Little" Savanna River

Turtle Lake

Prairie River

Sketch Map of the Savanna Portage
• • • • • Portage corridor between East & West Savanna Rivers
– – – Overland Trail to Sandy Lake
✳ Points Noted by David Thompson, May 7th, 1798
△ Indian Encampments
⌂ Camp or Habitation

Sandy Lake

NE BAY

Map by Larry Luukkonen

Of all the places on the Northwest Trail, the portage between the Savanna and Little Savanna rivers was perhaps the most memorable part of the journey for those who crossed the height of land. The Savanna Portage was a key spot along the famous route from Lake Superior, and all river traffic inward or outward had to pass over its rough course.

An indication of the relative difficulty of the various portages along the Northwest Trail can be determined by comparing the distance covered on a given portage with the number of *posés*. Based on these figures, the two most physically demanding portages were the Grand Portage of the St. Louis, covering an estimated length of seven miles with nineteen *posés*; and, the Savanna Portage, with an estimated distance of six miles and thirteen *posés*. To those who had to travel over the Savanna, it offered by far the most challenging conditions for portaging that could be imagined. Doctor Joseph Norwood, who crossed the Savanna Portage in the summer of 1848, described it as, "The worst carrying place in the Northwest."[29]

The Savanna Portage connected the Savanna River, a tributary of the St. Louis, with the Little Savanna River, which in turn flowed into the Prairie River, Sandy Lake, and ultimately, the Mississippi River. The Little Savanna River derived its name from Little Savanna Lake, in accordance with the Indian custom of naming streams for the lakes they flow through. Known today as the East and West Savanna rivers, these streams were thus designated by Henry Schoolcraft in 1820. Ironically, Schoolcraft, who eventually became a renowned American ethnologist for his study of the Ojibway, seems to have had a peculiar penchant for changing place-names given to various features by the very people he later found to be quite fascinating. The naming of the East Savanna and West Savanna rivers are just two examples of his early handiwork.[30]

Each of the portages along the Northwest Trail linking Lake Superior to the Mississippi has its unique attributes. The Savanna Portage, like the Prairie Portage, is significant, for here is found the height of land which separates the watersheds. In the case of the Savanna Portage, the height of land is a large trackless swamp from which both the Savanna and Little Savanna rivers receive their water.

Photo of the Little or West Savanna River below the Savanna Portage. Note the lush grassy meadow or savanna from which both the stream and portage derive their names.

Photo by Larry Luukkonen

When considering the length of the Savanna Portage, one should bear in mind that the route consisted of several components. At least two trails connected the Savanna and Little Savanna rivers, each approximately six miles long. An overland trail extended another six miles from the western end of the portage as far as Northeast Bay on Sandy Lake. The overland trail was used during periods of drought when river travel was impractical because of low water. Frequently described as being simply six or six and a half miles long with twelve or thirteen *posés*, the Savanna Portage's true length depended on the amount of water available in the rivers to float a canoe. Nowhere along the old Northwest Trail was abundant water more crucial than where the western end of the Savanna Portage intersected the Little Savanna River. Low water in the Little Savanna effectively doubled the length of the portage from the commonly cited six mile course to twelve miles.

Thus far no historical account of the Savanna Portage has mentioned the system of trails or the overland extension of the portage to Northeast Bay, although many early travelers refer to the overland trail in their journals. To anyone canoeing the Little or West Savanna River today, the need to lighten a canoe in order to navigate the stream during periods of low water is obvious; yet, the connection between the conditions in the Little Savanna River and the descriptions of travelers using the overland trail has not been made by any writers to date.

Some of the first documented references to the overland extension of the Savanna Portage were made by Captain David Bates Douglass and Henry Schoolcraft. Both men were part of the Northwestern Expedition undertaken by Governor Lewis Cass in the summer of 1820. As the expedition worked its way up the St. Louis River, it was plagued by low water. Cass sent Schoolcraft and thirteen other men from the expedition, along with two Indian guides, overland from Knife Falls with instructions to obtain help at the American Fur Company's post at Sandy Lake and meet him at the Savanna Portage.

After arriving at Sandy Lake, Schoolcraft procured the necessary help and started for the portage. In recounting his experiences, Schoolcraft left the following interesting description of his efforts including mention of the overland trail:

> This morning we embarked, accompanied by one of the clerks [John H. Fairbanks] of the company's establishment, and sixteen Indians of the Sandy Lake band, to meet the expedition on the Savanna Portage, and assist in carrying the baggage across. On going a league we landed in a bay on the northeast shore of the lake, and proceeded along an old trail, leading to the west end of the portage, where we arrived about twelve o'clock...[31]

Meanwhile, Cass and the main party in seven canoes continued their slow journey up the St. Louis and Savanna rivers until they encountered the portage. After much difficulty in making the crossing, the party finally rendezvoused with Schoolcraft.

Captain Douglass not only recorded the rigors of crossing the portage but also left an interesting account of the overland trail:

> Embarked our canoes at an early hour for the descent of the river. There is here a good route by land which I took as being much the shortest on account of the windings of the river. At about two miles down, the path crosses the river to the west side at a place the canoes have to be lightened to pass a shallow rapid of about 300 yards in length. Another mile and another of these occurs about a half mile in length. Below this the path, by going somewhat westerly, comes to the head of a bay of Sandy Lake—at which Mr. Fairbanks had left the canoes of his party, and thence paddling an hour brought me to the fort.[32]

Douglass' account matches specific geographic features that are still visible today. Other early accounts also mention the overland trail to Sandy Lake, but are less descriptive. Nevertheless, the fact early travel accounts highlight the frequent need to use the overland trail extension along the Little Savanna River is significant. Reverend Edmund Ely remarked during a crossing of the portage in 1833 about a "winter road" twelve miles long. In 1849, Reverend John H. Pitezel and a party of missionaries arrived at the east end of the Savanna Portage. He stated in his journal, "We now had some twelve miles of land portage, and about four across Sandy Lake." Lastly, the English traveler Laurence Oliphant remarked on arriving at the east end of the portage:

> We had a portage of sixteen miles before us for the following day, and, according to the account of the Indian from whom we had just parted, there was scarcely any water in the Little Savanna where we hoped to launch our canoes.

He went on to say, "This portage is always necessary; but at other times of the year when there is more water, the distance is considerably reduced."[33]

One year after Oliphant's crossing, a correspondent for the *Missouri Republican* en route to St. Paul from the newly established city of Superior, Wisconsin, observed:

> This portage is generally sixteen miles long, but the late equinoctial storm (to which we were exposed for three days) had made the creeks navigable, and reduced it to seven miles.[34]

In this last case, sudden storms produced high water, which allowed the use of the Little or West Savanna River all the way to Sandy Lake. Interestingly enough, the correspondent gave the same optimum distance for the crossing as Lawrence Oliphant.

That the track of the portage changed is without a doubt if, one considers similar developments along the Grand Portage of the St. Louis. For example, there is a definite similarity to improvements made over time to the Grand Portage of the St. Louis mentioned earlier and the overland extension of the Savanna Portage.

Modern accounts purporting to tell the history of the Savanna Portage state the portage passed out of use with the coming of the railroad. This is simply not correct. The building of the Northern Pacific Railroad through the region in 1870 only opened up the area near the right-of-way. Persons wishing to travel from any point along the railroad into the interior still had to resort to the network of waterways, portages, or overland trails which crisscrossed the countryside.[35]

Also, while heavy usage of the Savanna Portage tapered off after the dissolution of the American Fur Company (1847), local use continued uninterrupted. To imply that the entire portage was completely abandoned is not true, considering there is both written and physical evidence to the contrary. For example, an Ojibway sugar camp located on an eighty acre allotment belonging to the Grasshopper family was connected to an alternate trail or portage between the East and West Savanna rivers. The alternate trail terminated on a hill overlooking Little Savanna Lake.[36]

Government survey notes describe other trails intersecting both the Savanna and Prairie rivers, which in turn connected with Indian villages or seasonal camps to the east. Furthermore, visual evidence of the existence of the Savanna Portage was recorded by the government surveyors who crossed it as they ran their lines. Clearly, these trails could be easily identified and were still used by the Ojibway and a few early settlers in the region or they would have long since been obliterated.[37]

It is significant to note that the Sandy Lake area has always held an attraction for indigenous people because of its abundant groves of birch and sugar maple, wild rice beds, and renowned fisheries. The Ojibway, who lived at Ga-mitawan-gagamag (Sandy Lake) were only the latest in a series of inhabitants to know the area and its resources. They used the trails and portages and continued to dwell on or near Sandy Lake as others had done before them.

By the dawn of the twentieth century, settlers on the east side of Sandy Lake also found the old trail extremely convenient as a means of access to their newly established homesteads. In fact, interviews with early residents in the area indicate that when it became necessary to improve access to their homes, a tote road suitable for automobiles was built over a considerable portion of the old trail leading from the west end of the portage to Northeast Bay on Sandy Lake, thereby connecting part of the Savanna Portage with Sandy Lake.

At the same time that portions of the old trail were being converted to roads, other sections of the portage became "lost" for various reasons. One issue that continues to excite interest is the exact location of the east and west ends of the portage. Efforts to locate the Savanna Portage since 1926 have assumed there were two points connected by a single trail, but early accounts suggest there were at least three routes. Moreover, recent attempts to uncover the trail are further confounded by what appear to be discrepancies in the descriptions of eyewitnesses.

Laurence Oliphant crossed the Savanna Portage in 1854, and described two distinct paths. His voyageurs took a different route to the Little Savanna River than the one he followed with his companions. Later, he remarked sighting his voyageurs with the canoe from a height of land overlooking Little Savanna Lake.[38]

The assumption that there was a single discernible trail runs contrary to both eyewitness accounts as well as the demonstrable experience on other portages, noted earlier. We have already seen how the Grand Portage of the St. Louis was enhanced by incorporating several different trails, including the Grand Portage Wagon Road, to improve travel. Part of the problem with relocating important segments of the Savanna Portage may also be the type of sources consulted and the use of evidence not subject to verification.

A good example of the pitfalls awaiting those who do not consider evidence closely can clearly be seen in the description of the western end of the Savanna Portage. Some of the most valuable early references to the Northwest Trail and its component parts are contained in the rough track survey notes made by North West Company Geographer David Thompson, who traveled the extent of the trail in the spring of 1798.

Thompson's notes contain a wealth of information, but they have been largely overlooked in the published accounts of the Savanna Portage. Instead, it appears whenever authors have consulted his writings, they have relied on the published versions of his notes, which omit some vital information. One reason the field notes are not used more often may be because of Thompson's handwriting, which is hard to read. Another may be the endless records of observations and other information that are not only difficult to decipher but also meaningless to one not familiar with the methods of gathering information for map making.

Yet, in spite of their shortcomings, David Thompson's original notes clearly spell out the location of the western terminus of the Savanna Portage. Buried amid a long list of compass bearings and estimated travel distances is a description of the approach to the western end of the portage that has eluded writers for decades:

> ...for the last 100 yards we have the main brook [Little Savanna River] on the left and go up a very small arm of about 3 feet wide. It is 1 1/2 to 2 feet deep of a moderate current. It comes from the swamps and a little lake on the left of the portage.[39]

Thompson not only recorded the features of the west end, but described the Savanna Portage in his notebook and observed the latitude and longitude of the eastern terminus while waiting for his voyageurs to catch up. A comparison of the distances between given points determined by Thompson's observations with the distances between these same locations on modern maps show that at times he was off by as much as a mile. On the other hand, Thompson's longitude for the Sandy Lake post, taken with the instruments of his day, is remarkably close to the same point on modern maps, which is amazing considering he had to work alone under less than ideal conditions.

Thompson's account of the Savanna Portage is only one of many. Doctor Alexander Wolcott, who accompanied Governor Lewis Cass in 1820, described in great detail the approach to the east end of the portage and other features along the way:

> The length of the Savannah [sic] portage is six miles, and is passed in thirteen pauses. The first three pauses are shockingly bad. It is not only a bed of mire, but the difficulty of passing it is greatly increased by fallen trees, limbs and sharp knots of the Pitch pine, in some places on the surface, in others imbedded one or two feet below.[40]

Wolcott noted the various features he passed as he made his way to the west end of the portage. His description not only contains a noteworthy explanation as to why the Savanna Portage was such a difficult route, but also provides the reader with details as to the type of vegetation found there:

> Old voyageurs say, that this part [the first three posés of the east end] of the portage was formerly covered with a heavy bog, or a kind of peat, upon which the walking was very good, but that during a dry season, it accidentally caught fire and burnt over the surface of the earth so as to lower its level two or three feet when it became miry, and subject to inundation from the Savannah river. The country, after passing the third pause, changes in a short distance, from a marsh to a region of sand hills covered mostly with white and yellow pine, intermixed with aspen.[41]

Other travelers described different types of vegetation along the portage supporting the contention that there was more than one route west. Doctor Douglass Houghton, who passed over the Savanna Portage in 1832, noted the following scene after arriving at the east end of the trail:

> The voyageurs soon after commenced carrying the goods one pause on the portage. This pause is extremely muddy and they frequently sank with loads nearly to the hip in mud and water. At the end of this pause the portage passed two pauses through a tamarack swamp of the worst kind. The mud so deep that the voyageurs sank nearly to their waists. Having passed over this a short distance farther brought us to dry land timbered chiefly with elm and basswood where we encamped for the night our voyageurs being almost completely worn out.[42]

The various descriptions of the portage ought to encourage a careful reading of the early travel accounts. These records not only reveal hidden secrets of the trail, but also explain why certain modes of transportation we are accustomed to associate with the fur trade and the region were in fact more widely used than previously imagined.

The difficulties encountered along the Savanna Portage, especially on the east end, were sufficient reason for some travelers to take easier routes across country. The use of a second trail to cross the Savanna was just one option. Some travelers resorted to traveling at different times of the year when conditions offered fewer delays. The physical barriers encountered along the Savanna and other places on the Northwest Trail encouraged the use of winter travel whenever possible and on a scale hardly imagined by previous writers. Most readers are perhaps accustomed to thinking of traders and trappers on snowshoes, or as the French called them *raquettes*, trekking through the forest trailing a toboggan, but there were other means of transportation as well.

Overland to Sandy Lake by Dog Sled and Horse Train

When one thinks of those who ventured into the wilderness west of Lake Superior, one usually associates their journey with canoe routes and portages on the St. Louis, Savanna, or Prairie rivers. Perhaps this connection is because so many travelers made their trips in the spring of the year. However, other early narratives contain references to year-round use. In fact, records show that a "winter road" or trail made up one of the major routes connecting the Great Lakes with the Mississippi River.[43]

Travelers using the Northwest Trail had a choice of three ways to reach the Mississippi River at Sandy Lake. The first two were by way of the Savanna Portage and the Prairie Portage, routes previously discussed. The third route was by way of an overland trail or winter road. The notion of routinely traveling a winter road spanning the distance from Sandy Lake to Fond du Lac and even points beyond is something quite different from the usual winter fur gathering trip, or *une dérouine*, undertaken by dog sled. Such short trips are mentioned frequently in the journals of northern travelers and were made by traders who had advanced goods to trappers on credit. The trips were intended to resupply the trapper and collect the furs already gathered to keep them out of the hands of rival traders. The latter had no scruples about buying a trapper's catch for a little more than he could expect to make from his trader.

So instead of an image of sweating voyageurs laboriously toiling upstream with setting poles and paddles or carefully running rapids, one is confronted with a different picture—that of processions of dog sleds wending their way along frozen trails through a gleaming white forest. Why was it necessary to have a winter route in country that is blessed with so many fine rivers and lakes? Perhaps the best answer can be found in the experiences of a fur trader named John Hay in the summer of 1794. The difficulties Hay experienced underscored the need for an alternate route.

John Hay was one of a number of fur traders, known collectively to their contemporaries as the "South Traders," whose way to the rich fur areas of the Northwest followed the south shore of Lake Superior to the mouth of the St. Louis River and along the Northwest Trail to Sandy Lake. Some of these traders left the main route at Sandy Lake and spent the season at trading areas such as along the Crow Wing River or locations in the lake country of central Minnesota. Others pursued a course up the Mississippi to Upper Red Cedar Lake (Cass Lake), then turned up the Turtle River, portaged over the height of land separating the Mississippi from the Red River watershed, and then continued on to their trading grounds along the Red River of the North or adjacent streams. The difficulties they experienced are exemplified in Hay's account and the need for an alternate way of gaining access to the interior is clearly apparent.[44]

Hay's exploits negotiating the rivers and portages along the Northwest Trail were recorded in a narrative entitled "Description of the Route from Makina [sic] to the Interior parts of the Northwest by the south side of Lake Superior." Hay departed from Mackinac Island on June 7th, 1794, bound for Fond du Lac, but owing to bad weather, did not arrive at the "End of the Lake" until July 20th.

Already late in the summer, Hay's party found the water level of the St. Louis River very low and the normally formidable rushing rapids tamed. Portions of the river were exceedingly hard to negotiate because of a lack of sufficient water and the jagged rocks. By the time he reached the foot of the Knife Portage, near the present city of Cloquet, there was barely enough water to float his canoes:

> This river in the Spring is very high and even in the Summer when you have a Couple days Rains gives sufficient water–the time I was in it, there was only 7 & 8 In [inches] Water.[45]

Further upstream at a place Hay called the "Bald Island" (Paw-paw-sco-me-me-tig), there was hardly any water at all. His men toiled up the river until they reached the small stream signaling the beginning of the Prairie Portage. Marching overland about five miles, Hay reached Prairie Lake and set out once again by canoe. Taking a bearing on the little island in the middle of the lake, Hay set his course for the entrance of the Prairie River.

The Prairie River proved to be so shallow and meandering that Hay's men were forced to make little dams in order to have sufficient water to float the canoes. Eventually, they were forced to wade down the stream carrying all their belongings and trade goods on their backs. In all, it took them seven days to get to Sandy Lake. Normally, it was a journey that one could reasonably expect to make in three or four days:

> We found the water so low obliged to make dams–Made near 19 leagues in this Manner by Sluices in Seven Day time which brought [us] to Lac des Sables or Sand Lake.–this makes altogether 50 Leagues from Sayer's fort [Fort St. Louis located near the entry of the St. Louis River], and which took 26 days March....[46]

John Hay's story is one of the few describing the Prairie River trade route and its recognizable features. It is also an account of how a regular trading party managed to make a crossing under less than ideal conditions. Because of obstructions, the route was considered impassible but those obstructions did not spell the end of the Prairie River route.

John Hay's experiences on the St. Louis River and on the Prairie Portage were the result of seasonal variations in waterfall. The use of the rivers, as noted earlier, was strictly dependent on the amount of water available to float a canoe. In spite of the use of special broad beamed canoes, traffic on northern rivers in mid and late summer was fraught with difficulty lest the fragile birch-bark craft be pierced by a sharp rock in the shoal water.

Given the challenges facing canoe parties trying to navigate the St. Louis and other rivers, it was no wonder the traders opted for winter transportation. Paul Beaulieu, a noted government interpreter and one familiar with the fur trade and trade routes, remarked that some goods, "...were stowed at Fond du Lac Depot to be transported by Dog traines during winter to Sandy Lake."[47]

From depots such as Fond du Lac, sleds with trade goods were sent west by way of the winter trail to other posts, and furs sent east to La Pointe. Accounts of a brisk winter trade and the experiences of those who used the winter trail shed new light on the methods of travel and the techniques for moving goods in the wilderness.

Typical winter scene on the overland trail from Fond du Lac to Sandy Lake. Photo by Allen Anway

The route of a typical trader traveling by dog sled from Fond du Lac to Sandy Lake followed portions of the Grand Portage of the St. Louis. If conditions were right and the rapids in the St. Louis River safely frozen over, the dog sled crossed the river at Maple Island near the head of the portage and continued to Fond du Lac. Known locally as the "Three Foot Rapids" after their height, these rapids proved to be a serious obstacle to dog or horse-drawn sleds.

Once across the river, the trail forked. One branch led in a fairly direct path northwest toward the head of the Knife Falls. The second branch headed almost due west. Skirting the south shore of Long Lake, now known as Big Lake, the winter trail continued southwesterly beyond the lake and wound around the south end of Perch Lake in Carlton County. Passing an Indian village and burial ground, the trail gradually led northwest. It followed a height of land until it reached Prairie Lake in southern St. Louis County. The trail continued around the south end of Prairie Lake, striking the Prairie River below a rapids that also marked the end of the Pine Portage. From this point, the trail followed the frozen river bed to Sandy Lake.[48]

Many winter trails used frozen lakes, rivers, and swamps because of the flat surface and ease of travel. One had to be constantly alert, however, for obstructions and other impediments to travel–especially near rapids, where constantly flowing water meant thin ice. In spite of potential danger, winter "expresses," or light dog sleds, sped back and forth along frozen trails carrying correspondence and local news between far-flung trading posts. Heavier sleds drawn either by dogs or horses traveled more slowly with their loads of merchandise and furs.[49]

The favorite means of conveyance in winter was the dog sled. Judging from the comments of eyewitnesses, large numbers of such sleds, known as *carioles*, operated in the wilderness. The *cariole* was constructed of ash or oak boards turned up at the front like a toboggan. It was provided with a backrest and the sides were enclosed with hide.[50]

Another type of early sled was formed by two runners supported with many cross pieces lashed with rawhide at regular intervals. No nails were used in the construction of heavy sleds. Instead, every component in the sled was lashed with rawhide and fastened in such a way that it would flex or twist under the weight of the load when crossing rough terrain. Nails would pull out if subjected to the rough treatment accorded a horse-drawn sled. These sleds were strong enough to be drawn by a horse and stand up to the punishment provided by rocks and other hazards on the trail.

The sleds, whether dog-drawn or pulled by horses, were referred to as a "train" or "traine," after the French word *traîneau* meaning "sled" or *traîneau de glace* meaning an "ice sled." The latter term undoubtedly referred to the ice ruts found on the winter roads or the use of sleds on frozen lakes and rivers. The terms "dog trains" or "horse trains" also referred to a procession of sleds.[51]

Other types of winter conveyances included cutters, or light sleighs, pulled by horses. Trader William Alexander Aitkin had a horse drawn cutter at his Sandy Lake post. Reverend Edmund Ely mentioned Aitkin's sleigh in his journal entry for December 25th, 1833:

> Today, being Christmas, Mr. Aitkin gave an entertainment to Messrs. Abbott & Scott [competitors]. this morning went to Mr. Abbot's & sung with the children–returned with Mr. Aitkin who came across the Lake in his Horse & Cutter.[52]

A few days later, on January 8th, 1834, Ely recorded the departure of a procession of sleds bound for Fond du Lac. "Today Mr. A. started off–Horse trains for Fondulac & is to follow in the Morning with a dog train."[53]

From descriptions such as Ely's, it is clear the depots at Fond du Lac, Sandy Lake, and Leech Lake, were situated at year-round commercial crossroads. Not only were these posts handy for summer canoe traffic, but also useful in winter.

For example, trails radiated outward like spokes in a wheel from Aitkin's post at the junction of the Sandy Lake and Mississippi rivers. One is clearly shown on an 1832 map following a string of lakes and portages to Leech Lake. Another trail led south following the course of the Sandy Lake River, and then across country to Mille Lacs. The most heavily traveled trail, however, led east from Sandy Lake to Fond du Lac.[54]

It was not always easy traveling in the winter. Conditions on the trail varied with the weather and terrain. Ely commented about his experiences while en route from Sandy Lake to Leech Lake in March of 1834:

> This morning left Sandy Lake, on my way to Leech Lake, accompanied by one man & a dog train to Carry my Baggage. There are also in company, a son of Mr. Du Fault of Red Lake with 2 men & a man of Mr. Davenport's of Leech Lake–in all 6–and 3 trains–drawn by 8 dogs. Do not know the distance we have traveled–probably about 10 Leagues [30 miles]. The traveling has been very bad today–especially across the Grand Moshkig [muskeg], where the snow was nearly all washed away &–quite wet–was very hard for the dogs, as it was bare ground most of the way.[55]

The winter road that connected Fond du Lac with Sandy Lake also intersected a route that extended east. With this overland link, it was possible to go by dog sled from Sandy Lake all the way to the village of La Pointe on Madeline Island. Undoubtedly a major reason for establishing a winter route was the difficulty encountered in navigating from La Pointe to Fond du Lac in summer–especially passing the entry with its constantly shifting sandbar or the spring ice floes, which, if driven by a fickle wind, could effectively seal the entry for weeks at a time until finally blown away.[56]

During the era of the American Fur Company's operation in western Lake Superior (1817-1847), the use of overland winter travel for the movement of trade goods and cargo was by all indications highly developed.[57] The idea of using sleds for long hauls, however, was not foolproof. At times weather conditions could interrupt traffic, particularly if the sleds used a route that crossed Lake Superior. Reverend Ely noted in his diary on February 17th, 1834, that Mr. "Aitkins" left this morning with a horse train for Fond du Lac and La Pointe. Nine days later he wrote:

> About noon, Mr. Aitkins arrived alone, from fondulac. He had, with great difficulty proceeded on his way to Le Pt. [La Pointe] as far as Burnt River [Bois Brûlé or Brule River], where beyond whh [which], the lake was not frozen. It was therefore impossible to proceed with a Horse. He sent out two men by Land, & himself & Mr. Cotte, who accompanied him, returned to F. [fond du Lac].[58]

Fast sleds, or "expresses," routinely made the trip from La Pointe to Sandy Lake relaying messages, hauling mail, or company personnel. Reverend Ely's journal entry for March 1st, 1834, noted the arrival of one of these sleds and his disappointment at not hearing more from old friends:

> McDonald arrived near sunset, from Le Pointe—bringing an express from Sault Ste. Maries. I received a letter from my beloved friend Mrs. Mary S. Wright of rome N. Y. & also from sister Delia Cook, Le Pointe. Was much disappointed in not receiving more letters or papers. Cannot think that most of my beloved friends in the states have forgotten me.[59]

There were other references to the trail from La Pointe to Sandy Lake, but the exact location of parts of the trail is difficult to determine. Like most winter trails, portions of it disappeared in spring along with the melting snow. Only the general route would have been carefully noted by the sled drivers who used it every season. Like portions of the Savanna and Prairie portages, some parts of the winter road located on dry land survived only to be duly noted in the government land survey notes in the 1860s and 1870s. Subsequent settlement activity has undoubtedly obliterated much of the route, making relocation of the complete trail today highly problematical.

Thus far we have examined the physical features of the Northwest Trail, which gave rise to place-names that in turn served as guideposts along the portages and winter roads used by the early traveler. The next phase in the history of the route involved the gathering of geographic information and efforts to map the route.

Little Savanna Lake as seen from the Savanna Portage. The West or Little Savanna River is hidden in the reeds on the extreme right of the picture.
Photo by Larry Luukkonen

Chapter 2 - River Routes and Winter Roads
Notes

1. For details concerning the Grand Portage of the St. Louis, see Lieutenant James Allen, *Journal of an "Expedition into the Indian country," to the source of the Mississippi, made under the authority of the War Department in 1832*, in U.S. House *Executive Documents*, no. 323, 23rd Congress 1st Session, 1833-1834, p. 328; Philip P. Mason (ed.), *Schoolcraft's Expedition to Lake Itasca* (East Lansing, 1993), pp. 193-194. Allen recorded the length of the Grand Portage as nine miles with nineteen *posés*. Others credit the portage as being seven miles long; John Fritzen, "Portages and Old Trails In and Adjacent to Jay Cook State Park," unpublished manuscript, Carlton County Historical Society, Cloquet, Minnesota, c. 1935.

    Descriptions of the Knife Portage are found in Mentor L. Williams (ed.), *Schoolcraft's Narrative Journal of Travels* (East Lansing, 1992), pp. 143, 426, and 480-481.

    For the Savanna Portage see Williams (ed.), *Schoolcraft's Narrative Journal*, pp. 143-151; Sydney W. Jackman, John F. Freeman eds., assisted by Donald S. Rickard and James L. Carter, *American Voyageur: The Journal of David Bates Douglass* (Marquette, 1969), pp. 76-78; Mason, *Lake Itasca*, pp. 12, 195, 246-247, and 321-323; Nancy L. Woolworth, with research by Alan R. Woolworth, "Savanna Portage Southwest," unpublished manuscript, Savanna Portage State Park, 1969, offers a useful compendium of travelers' accounts of the Savanna Portage and Newton H. Winchell's description (1878) of the Prairie Portage, pp. 65-66.

    For the Prairie Portage see John Hay, "Journal in the N.W. by S. side of L. Superior," in James MacKay, "Extracts from Capt. MacKay's Journal–and Others," *Publications of the State Historical Society of Wisconsin, Proceedings of the Society at its Sixty-third Annual Meeting, October 21, 1915* (Madison, 1916), p. 205. Hay's account includes the following description of the Prairie Portage: "This Carryg [carrying] place has 11 Rests and abt [about] 5 miles."

2. Eric C. Morse, *Fur Trade Canoe Routes of Canada! Then and Now* (Ottawa, 1969), p. 32.

3. Edwin Tappen Adney and Charles I. Chapelle, *The Bark Canoes and Skin Boats of North America* (Washington, D.C., 1964), pp. 135-153; Grace Lee Nute, *The Voyageur* (1931; reprint ed., St. Paul, 1955), pp. 23-32, describe the basic types of craft used in western Lake Superior. Four types of canoes frequently mentioned in connection with the fur trade include: the *canot du maître*, or the large Montreal canoe used on the Great Lakes; the *canot du nord*, or "North" canoe used on inland waters; a variant of both types called a *canot bâtard*, or "bastard" canoe; and the *canot léger*, or "light canoe" used on shallow streams such as the St. Louis River. Practically speaking, there was no difference between these various types except length, width, and depth. Furthermore, there was no exact pattern and each canoe only roughly approximated an ideal type; John Nelson Davidson, "Missions On Chequamegon Bay," in *Collections of the State Historical Society of Wisconsin*, vol. 12 (Madison, 1892), pp. 442-443, mentions the canoes used in the fur trade varied in length from ten to thirty feet. The larger canoes carried two to three tons of lading. In addition to canoes, bateaux, forty feet long and ten to twelve feet wide, were used in lake commerce. These craft carried five tons of lading and were usually propelled by six oarsmen; Tim Cochran and Hawk Tolson, *A Good Boat Speaks for Itself* (Minneapolis, 2002), pp. 69-80, describe a third type of craft, the Mackinaw boat. Note the phonetic spelling of "Mackinaw" used in relation to the type of boat instead of the normal French spelling of *Mackinac*, which is a shortened version of *Michilimackinac*.

4. Alexander Henry, *Travels & Adventures in Canada and the Indian Territories Between the Years 1760 and 1776*, ed. by James Bain (1809; reprint ed., Boston, 1901), p. 264, describes the measures used to protect the fragile birch-bark canoes, while wintering at Beaver Lake north of the Hudson's Bay Company's Cumberland House. The canoes were buried in moist sand to keep the bark from splitting. Other travelers submerged their canoes in rivers or lakes, sometimes with disastrous results as in the case of Nicholas Perrot, quoted in Emma Helen Blair (ed. and trans.), *The Indian Tribes of the Upper Mississippi Valley and Region of the Great Lakes, as described by Nicholas Perrot,...,Bacqueville de la Potherie,...,Morrell Marston,..., and Thomas Forsyth,...*, 2 vols.... (Cleveland, 1911-1912), vol. 1, p. 245. Perrot remarked: "At that time [1686] I was in the

country of the Scioux [sic], where the ice had broken up all our canoes, and I was compelled to spend the summer there...."

5.   Grace Lee Nute, *The Voyageur*, pp. 45-48; Several different spellings exist for the Ojibway expression "putting down the pack." The one used here is taken from historian Elliott Coues (ed.), *The Expeditions of Zebulon Montgomery Pike*, 3 vols. in 2 (1895; reprint ed., Minneapolis, 1965), vol. 1, p. 136, n. 48.

6.   Williams (ed.), *Schoolcraft's Narrative Journal*, pp. 142, and 425.

7.   Mason (ed.), *Lake Itasca*, pp. 192-194.

8.   Kenneth W. Porter, "Relations Between Negroes and Indians Within the Present Limits of the United States," *Journal of Negro History*, vol. 17(July, 1932), pp. 361-363.

9.   David Thompson's 1826 map of the St. Louis River was filed by order of the Board of Commissioners under Article 6.C.7 of the Treaty of Ghent. See U.S. House *Executive Document* No. 451, 25th Congress, 2nd Session, July 3rd, 1838.

10.   See Williams (ed.), *Schoolcraft's Narrative Journal*, pp. 425, 446 and 480, for James Doty's and Charles Christopher Trowbridge's observations along the Grand Portage of the St. Louis.

11.   Details concerning the Grand Portage Wagon Road constructed over portions of the old Grand Portage can be found in John Fritzen, "Portages;" pp. 4, 15-19, and 27-28; N. H. Winchell, *The Geological and Natural History Survey of Minnesota, 1896-1898, The Geology of Minnesota*, vol. 4 of the Final Report (St. Paul, 1899), Plate 87, contains a map showing the route of the Fond du Lac to Cloquet (or Grand Portage) Wagon Road.

12.   Williams (ed.), *Schoolcraft's Narrative Journal*, p. 141.

13.   Ibid., p.142.

14.   Ibid., p. 426.

15.   Mason (ed.), *Lake Itasca*, pp. 320-323.

16.   Fritzen, "*Portages*," pp. 12-13. Schoolcraft later encamped at another "Woman's Portage" on the St. Croix River. For a comparison see Mason, *Lake Itasca*, p. 88.

17.   The Knife Portage is mentioned by Schoolcraft and James Doty in Williams (ed.), *Schoolcraft's Narrative Journal*, pp. 143 and 426. For the Schoolcraft Expedition in 1832, see Mason (ed.), *Lake Itasca*, p. 12. For Lt. Allen's description, see pp. 194-195 (see also n. 1 above for Allen's complete official report); For Doctor Houghton's description see p. 245; The Ojibway name for Knife Portage is listed in Chrysostum Verwyst, "A Glossary of Chippewa Indian names of Rivers, Lakes, and Villages," *Acta et Dicta*, vol. 4, no. 2 (July, 1916), p. 258. When compiling his glossary, Verwyst followed the system of orthography developed by Bishop Frederic Baraga.

18.   See Williams (ed.), *Narrative Journal*, p. 481, for Charles Christopher Trowbridge's description of the problems encountered by the voyageurs in the dark waters of the St. Louis River.

19.   Ibid., p. 143.

20.   Ibid., p. 426.

21.   See Verwyst, "Glossary," p. 258, for the various translations and meaning of the island's name including "Bald" or "Bare Island." The terms suggest the island was once cleared (for a garden?).

22.   Douglass (ed.), *American Voyageur*, p. 75.

23.   John H. Pitezel, *Lights and Shades of Missionary Life* (Cincinnati, 1861), pp. 285-286.

24.   Larry Luukkonen, *Cloquet: The Story Behind the Name* (Cloquet, Minnesota, 2000).

25.   Another contemporary account of the Prairie Portage can be found in John Hay's "Journal in the N.W.," p. 205.

26.   For an account of Alexander Kay's experience on the Prairie River, see Jean Baptiste Perrault, "Narrative of the Travels and Adventures of a Merchant Voyageur...May, 1783 (to 1820)," *Historical Collections and Researches Made by the Michigan Pioneer and Historical Society*, vol. 37 (1909-1910), p. 525; Louis-P. Cormier, *Jean-Baptiste Perrault marchand voyageur parti de Montreal le 28e de mai, 1783* (Montreal, 1978), p. 44, offers a more recent account.

27.   Douglass (ed.), *American Voyageur*, p. 76.

28.   Verwyst, "Glossary," p. 260.

29.   See Dr. Joseph Norwood's account in David Dale Owen, *Report of a Geological Survey of Wisconsin, Iowa, and Minnesota; and Incidentally of a Portion of Nebraska* (Philadelphia, 1852), pp. 300-301.

30. Williams (ed.), *Schoolcraft's Narrative Journal*, p. 151.

31. Ibid., 149.

32. Douglass (ed.), *American Voyageur*, pp. 78-79.

33. Laurence Oliphant, *Minnesota and the Far West* (Edinburgh, 1855), pp. 184-188.

34. "A Voyage from Lake Superior to St. Paul in a Bark Canoe," *Superior Chronicle*, vol. 1, nos. 25-26 (Tuesday, December 11th, 1855), n.p.

35. J. William Trygg, "Composite Maps of United States Land Surveyor's Original Plats and Field Notes," Sheets 13 and 14, Minnesota Series (Ely, Minnesota, 1966). The lack of roads or trails on early maps shows rather convincingly that waterways and existing trails retained their importance as a means of access to the hinterland well into the twentieth century and long after the building of the railroad network. The waterways continued to serve the local population and some routes were recorded on the first survey maps. Trygg's useful index to the original government plats and survey notes shows early portages, winter roads, and other cultural features along the Northwest Trail.

36. The various allotments were assigned numbers. For example, the Grasshopper family allotment is recorded in Savanna Portage State Park as Outside Fond du Lac 422.

37. Part of the Savanna Portage is shown in Sections 2 and 3 of the original United States Survey of Balsam Township made in 1874, as filed in the Minnesota Secretary of State's Office, St. Paul. A copy of the survey, together with the field notes, is on file at the Aitkin County Land Department, Aitkin, Minnesota.

38. Oliphant, *Minnesota*, p. 187-188; and Interview with Herbert William Larson, Saturday, September 4th, 1982. Laurence Oliphant used an alternative trail when portaging from the East Savanna River to the West Savanna in the summer of 1854. Mr. Larson described a similar trail and identified the location of the overland trail that connected the west end of the Savanna Portage with Northeast Bay on Sandy Lake.

39. David Thompson, Diary No. 9, May 7th, 1798. A copy of the original can be found in the collections of the Minnesota Historical Society.

40. Williams (ed.), *Schoolcraft's Narrative Journal*, p. 151.

41. Ibid.

42. Mason (ed.), *Lake Itasca*, p. 246.

43. Edmund Franklin Ely's Journals (Numbers 1 to 3) contain numerous references to the arrival and departure of dog and horse-drawn sleds at Sandy Lake. In fact, Ely made a tour by dog sled from Sandy Lake to Leech Lake, then to Fond du Lac in the winter of 1833-1834. The original journals are in the collections of the Northeast Minnesota Historical Center, University of Minnesota, Duluth (hereafter cited as NEMHC). Typescript copies of the journals are in the collections of the Minnesota Historical Society.

44. Harry W. Duckworth, "The Last Coureurs de Bois," *The Beaver*, outfit 314 no. 2, (Spring, 1984), pp. 4-12. The "South Traders" and their sphere of operation are aptly described by Duckworth. Early research by historians such as John Napier Bell and Grace Lee Nute, called attention to the influx of traders by way of the Northwest Trail, but surprisingly little has been written about them or the routes they followed in pursuit of the fur trade.

45. John Hay, "Journal in the NW," p. 204.

46. Ibid., p. 205.

47. Paul Beaulieu, unpublished manuscript included in Henry M. Rice Papers, Minnesota Historical Society, St. Paul, nd. A handwritten note at the top of the first page identifies the manuscript as Beaulieu's with the date 1880 [?]. The manuscript consists of fourteen typewritten pages marked "Transferred from Beaulieu Papers Jan. 16th, 1950."

48. See J. William Trygg "Composite Maps," Sheet 14, for details on the overland trail from Fond du Lac to Sandy Lake. Ironically, the most famous transit of this trail took place in the summer of 1820, not during the winter. The occasion was the cross-country trek by certain members of Governor Cass' Northwestern Expedition. The overland travel of part of the expedition was due to low water in the St. Louis River. For an account of the progress of this group see Williams (ed.), *Schoolcraft's Narrative Journal*, pp. 143-148, 426-429, and 481-483.

49. Nute, The Voyageur, p. 92.

50. For descriptions of the carioles or dog sleds employed in the fur trade see Nute, pp. 94; Eri H. Day, "Sketches of the Northwest," *Historical Collections and Researches Made by the Michigan Pioneer and Historical Society*, vol. 14 (Lansing, 1889), pp. 240-241; "The Diary of Archibald N. McLeod," in Charles M. Gates (ed.), *Five Fur Traders of the Northwest* (St. Paul, 1965), pp. 152 n. 38, and 154, and 228; Philip H. Godsell, *Arctic Trader: An Account of Twenty Years With the Hudson's Bay Company* (New York, 1934), pp. 49 and 145, includes photographs of the cariole still in use in remote areas of Canada in the early twentieth century.

51. Similar sleds to those described in the previous note, called traineau and drawn either by dogs or horses, are mentioned in "The Diary of Hugh Faries," in Charles M. Gates (ed.), *Five Fur Traders of the Northwest* (St. Paul, 1965), pp. 219 n. 29, 220, 226, and 228.

52. Edmund Franklin Ely, Diary No. 3, Wednesday, December 25th, 1833, p. 6. NEMHC.

53. Ibid., Diary No. 3, Wednesday, January 8th, 1834, p. 10. NEMHC.

54. Lt. Allen, "Journal," (see chap. 2, n. 1 above).

55. Ely, Diary No. 3, Tuesday, March 4th, 1834, p. 22. NEMHC.

56. Hamilton Nelson Ross, *La Pointe: Village Outpost* (St. Paul, 1960), p. 115.

57. Ibid., pp. 138-139. Portions of an overland trail from the site of Superior, Wisconsin, to the town of Bayfield, are shown on a map drawn by Ross.

58. Ely, Diary No. 3, Monday, February 17th, 1834, p. 19. NEMHC.

59. Ibid., Diary No. 3, Saturday, March, 1st, 1834, p.22. NEMHC.

Spring breakup on the St. Louis River.
Photo by Allen Anway

Jesuit map of Lake Superior attributed to Father Claude Allouez and Father Superior
Claude Dablon. The map appeared in the *Jesuit Relations* for 1670-1671.
Minneaota Historical Society.

Chapter 3 ❧ Mapping the Old Northwest Trail

The story of the Northwest Trail is indeed a very ancient one. Unlike the famous border-lakes canoe route so aptly described in Grace Lee Nute's *Voyageur's Highway*, surprisingly little attention has been given to the route which led northwest up the valley of the St. Louis River. Aside from a few stories of specific portages and trading posts, no really comprehensive study has been done of the Northwest Trail between the Great Lakes and the Mississippi. Certainly no one has described the first geographic information about this important route. What we do know about this wilderness route is largely based on travelers' tales and clues provided on period maps.

At first, the existence of the St. Louis River, with its unique physical features and intriguing place-names, was unknown to anyone outside of the local aboriginal inhabitants. In time, however, word of rivers that led to unknown lands began to reach the French settlements clustered along the St. Lawrence River. The exploration and mapping of the Great Lakes region during the seventeenth century were generally undertaken for one or more of the following reasons. Some exploration was based on a desire to extend the benefits of the Christian faith. Other exploration focused on the search for the Northwest Passage. Still, other exploration involved participation in the fur trade by traders who operated either with or without official permission. The line separating exploration, evangelism, and the fur trade was often blurred. Most voyages of discovery were little more than thinly disguised trading adventures.[1]

Allouez and Du Lhut

At first, vague stories of wild rivers, great lakes and salt water seas to the west inspired the curiosity of the new inhabitants on the St. Lawrence. The French, beginning with figures such as Samuel de Champlain, were motivated to investigate the tales and verify their truth for themselves. Maps published following each exploration reflected many new details about the wilderness.[2] In the process, knowledge of Lake Superior and the St. Louis River as possible routes to the west attracted the attention of French traders and missionaries. In fact, as early as 1623, Etienne Brulé may have reached the west end of Lake Superior. In 1642, Father Hierosme (Jerome) Lalement, a Jesuit missionary, referred to Lake Superior and a large river flowing into it from the west. He, in turn, received his information from two missionaries, Charles Raymbault and Isaac Jogues, who were familiar with the area near Sault Sainte Marie. Father Pierre René Ménard was actually the first missionary to venture into the Lake Superior region in 1660. Unfortunately, he was either abandoned or became separated from his guides and perished in the wilderness.[3]

The famous trading partners Pierre d'Esprit Radisson and Medard Chouart, Sieur de Groseilliers, may have seen the western end of Lake Superior and the St. Louis River during their voyage to the interior in 1659-1660. They claimed to have crossed from the south side of the lake near Fond du Lac to the north side to meet a band of Cree hunters. The appearance of the name *Rivière des Groseilliers* (Gooseberry River) on seventeenth century French maps of Lake Superior may tempt one to presume Radisson and Groseilliers discovered the stream, but aside from the name given to this feature, there is insufficient documentation to support any claim Radisson and Groseilliers actually explored the shores of Lake Superior or the water routes to the western country.[4]

A number of French traders headed by Antoine Trottier also went "up to Lake Superior" in 1660. How far they traveled along the shores of the lake or if they reached the Gooseberry River is not known. The Ojibway referred to the stream as the *Jabomini Sibi*, but there is no evidence of their presence near the river at the time of Radisson and Groseillier's supposed visit.[5]

There were, however, two men associated with the exploration of Lake Superior and the territory to the west who contributed a great deal to the knowledge of the area. They were Father Claude Allouez, a Jesuit missionary, and Captain Daniel Greysolon, Sieur Du Lhut. Both were part of a larger effort underway during the later half of the seventeenth century to gather useful information about the western country and map the bounds of New France.

Following the voyages of Radisson and Groseilliers in 1659-1660, the French focused on the Northwest as the logical area to find a passage to the South Sea (Pacific Ocean). Unfortunately, Radisson and Groseillier's description of the area they explored west of Lake Superior was vague. A systematic gathering of geographic information was needed to precisely record the extent of their discoveries. The necessary expertise in gathering such information was provided by the Jesuits, who lead the way in western exploration and mapping. It was one of their order, Father Claude Allouez, who first accurately charted the entire shoreline of Lake Superior. Father Allouez came to Canada in 1658 and began his mission work in 1665. In that year, he started exploring and mapping the coast of Lake Superior in a birch-bark canoe with two Indian guides.

During his first year of exploration, Allouez only traveled as far as a place he called *Pointe du Saint Esprit*, near the present-day town of Ashland, Wisconsin. Here he encountered remnants of a band of Christian *Tionontate* (Tobacco Hurons), who previously dwelt west of the Hurons at Nottawasaga Bay and were allied with them. They fled west to escape the Iroquois assault on the Indian settlements known as Huronia in 1649. Allouez established a mission at Pointe du Saint Esprit to minister to the needs of the refugees before resuming his exploration of the lake the following year.[6]

Meaningful details regarding the size of Lake Superior and the entrance to the St. Louis River either remained undiscovered or unreported until 1666. In that year, Father Allouez, traveling west along the south shore of Lake Superior, stopped briefly at the mouth of the St. Louis River before continuing his trip around the lake. Allouez traced the outline of the lake–including the way to Lake Nipigon–carefully noting important features.[7]

The information pertaining to the configuration of Lake Superior gathered by Allouez was later incorporated into a map that includes an extremely accurate rendition of the shoreline and islands of the lake. Published in the *Jesuit Relations* of 1670-1671, the strikingly modern view provided by the Lake Superior map was probably the result of a collaborative effort by Father Allouez and Father Superior Claude Dablon. There were, however, few place-names or reference points marked on the map.[8]

Studying the Jesuit map of Lake Superior discloses that Allouez was aware of the existence of two rivers leading toward the west: the Kaministiquia and the St. Louis. In the case of the latter stream, Allouez shows the mouth of the St. Louis River, which he called the *Fond du Lac Supérieur*, and includes a margin note, *R. pour aller au Nadouessi a 60 lieues vers le couchant*. Translated, the note informs the reader this is the "river that goes to the *Nadouessi* (Sioux or Dakota), sixty leagues to the west"[9]

The margin notes of Father Allouez indicate he knew vaguely where the St. Louis River originated, but the map does not trace the river to its source, show the Dakota villages, or include sufficient information beyond the shoreline of the lake to show that Allouez could have traveled inland any distance. Father Allouez gave some interesting information about the people dwelling to the west:

> There are people dwelling to the west of this place [Ashland, Wisconsin] toward the great river named Messipi. They are forty or fifty l e a g u e s from this place. Providence has furnished them a kind of marsh rye, which they go and harvest toward the end of summer. They gave me some when I was at the head of Lake Tracy [Superior], where I saw them.

He added a warning, "Yet they are warlike, and have conducted hostilities against all their neighbors, by whom they are held in extreme fear."[10]

After Father Allouez visited the entrance of the St. Louis River, other explorers ranged over the country near Lake Superior. In 1676, Governor-General Frontenac reportedly sent his engineer Hugues Randin to Sault Sainte Marie on Lake Superior to mediate a dispute and invite the people of the area to trade with the French.[11]

However, the Jesuits and the governor were not the only people interested in gathering geographic information and exploring the interior of New France. Members of other religious orders, such as the Récollets and Sulpicians, vied with the Jesuits for a share of the missionary work in the west and any wealth to be gained from the fur trade. In fact, political intrigue among competing groups sometimes hindered individuals seeking to further exploration.[12]

Antoine de la Mothe-Cadillac pointed out to Frontenac that the Jesuits not only owned considerable property in New France, but also enjoyed disproportionate influence in the colony. Frontenac evidently sought to counteract some of the Jesuit presence in frontier missionary work by having the Sulpicians of Montreal work with the Iroquois as a means of offsetting English influence among that tribe. In the same manner, the Récollet Order of the Franciscans was encouraged to undertake new western missionary efforts. The most famous member of that order to operate in the west was Father Louis Hennepin. Frontenac's use of trusted military officers, such as Daniel Greysolon, is merely another manifestation of the political rivalry that existed in New France.[13]

Also arrayed in opposition to the Jesuits were the *coureurs de bois*, the outlaw or unlicensed traders who ranged the western wilderness of New France. Unfortunately, because of the very nature of their operations, the extent of geographic knowledge possessed by the coureurs des bois remains largely a mystery. Whether they used the Northwest Trail to gain access to the country west of Lake Superior is largely a matter of conjecture.[14] There was one man, however, who did explore the unknown land west and north of the great lake and left a record of his travels to complement the fine map produced from the work of Father Allouez.

Daniel Greysolon, Sieur du Lhut was usually referred to by his title, but it was spelled in a variety of ways (e.g., Du Luc, Du Lud, Du Lude, Du Lut, Du Lhu, Du Lhut, and Du Luth). Although he signed his will "Dulhut," spelling conventions of the time were not always followed. The spelling of Du Lhut's title used here is consistent with that of other names of the period such as, Le Sueur, La Hontan, and La Vérendrye. Although the young French nobleman from Saint-Germain-Laval enjoyed the prestige of a title, there was no estate or income to go with it.

An artist's impression of Daniel Greysolon, Sieur Du Lhut, which appeared in Harper's *New Monthly Magazine*, September, 1893.

The lack of a personal fortune or an income-producing estate undoubtedly provided a powerful motivation to succeed.[15]

Du Lhut was a member of the *petite noblesse* (lessor nobility) and began his career in the army which was customary for a member of his social class. In 1657, he was commissioned an ensign for a company of troops based in Lyons. Later he served as a Gendarme of the Royal Guard, a unit made up exclusively of the sons of noblemen.

It is reported that Du Lhut first arrived in New France in 1672, at the head of a detachment of marines. He was related to a wealthy colonial merchant, Jacques Patron, and apparently sought his fortune in the new colony. He settled in Montreal with his brother Claude, but shortly thereafter returned to France to participate in a war with the Dutch. He rejoined the Gendarmes of the Royal Guard and also served as a squire for the Marquis de

Lassay. Du Lhut distinguished himself during campaigns in Franche-Comté and at the battle of Seneffe.[16]

Following his successful military career in Europe, Du Lhut returned to New France and, armed with a commission from Governor Frontenac, sought to make peace among the western tribes and explore the unknown country west of Lake Superior. In September of 1678, Du Lhut left the colony with a small party, which included seven Frenchmen and three Indian slaves, to explore the south shore of Lake Superior as far as the St. Louis River. The first year he spent the winter on Lake Huron before proceeding to Lake Superior, where he had a series of momentous meetings with local tribes.[17]

About the same time Du Lhut set out for Lake Superior, three French *coureurs des bois* named Dupuy, Lamonde, and Pierre Moreau, otherwise known as La Taupine, also journeyed to the western end of Lake Superior. Apparently, their voyage was successful, for Moreau returned in 1679 with nine hundred beaver skins obtained through unlicensed trade with the Indians near the mouth of the St. Louis River.[18]

Thinking La Taupine's companions were in league with Du Lhut, the *Intendant* (chief administrative officer for the colony), Jacques Duchesnau, was prejudiced against Du Lhut and denounced him in a report of November 10th, 1679, to the Minister of Marine. Later, La Salle, upon hearing of the incident, felt Du Lhut had violated his own exclusive right to trade in the west and denounced him in a report prepared at Fort Frontenac on August 22nd, 1682. Duchesnau's successor, Jacques De Meules, also sent an unfavorable report to France which eventually resulted in Du Lhut receiving a reprimand from the King in July, 1684.[19]

Meanwhile, Du Lhut, wholly unaware of the intrigues in the east, arrived at the Fond du Lac, and traveled into the interior most likely by way of the Northwest Trail. If Du Lhut reached the Mississippi River at Sandy Lake, his was the first recorded crossing of the Northwest Trail. It appears Du Lhut used this route to visit the Nadouesioux (Dakota) villages, clustered along the western shore of a large lake in north central Minnesota, where on July 2nd, 1679, he planted the King's arms. The lake was later renamed *Lac Buade* in honor of the family name of the Governor of New France, Louis de Buade, Comte de Frontenac. At each village, he in turn repeated the ceremony of claiming the land for Louis XIV and invited the residents to send delegates to a grand council at Fond du Lac.[20]

After his visit to the Dakota, Du Lhut returned to the west end of Lake Superior. On September 15th, 1679, he convened a great council of tribes near the mouth of the St. Louis River to insure a lasting peace and promote trade in the region. The peace agreement, which resulted from this meeting, existed relatively intact from 1679 until 1736. As a result of the peace negotiations, the Dakota allowed the Ojibway of Lake Superior the privilege of hunting and trapping on Dakota land south and west of Fond du Lac in exchange for providing French trade goods.[21]

Following the grand council at Fond du Lac, Du Lhut began the second part of his expedition to contact the northwestern tribes and convince them to trade with New France. Du Lhut traveled along the north shore of the great lake looking for a water route west that might intersect the customary trade routes used by the Cree and Monsoni to bring their furs to Hudson Bay. He built a fort and spent the winter of 1679-1680 at the Kaministiquia River.[22]

In the spring of 1680, Du Lhut decided to pay the Dakota another visit. It was during his travels that Du Lhut heard about a small group of Frenchmen traveling with the Dakota. The Frenchmen had been sent by Du Lhut's rival La Salle to locate the source of the Mississippi River, but were taken prisoner by a band of Dakota. With his exploration to the north and west interrupted by the episode with the Dakota and La Salle's scouting expedition, Du Lhut decided to have no further dealings with the bands west of Fond du Lac and instead returned to the French post at Michilimackinac.[23]

In 1683, Du Lhut returned to Lake Superior by way of the south shore with fifteen canoes loaded with supplies as well as a three year commission to win over the Cree and Monsoni. He was instructed to encourage those Indians to trade with the French rather than bring their furs to the English posts on Hudson Bay. Instead of following the Northwest Trail, he continued along the shore of Lake Superior to the Nipigon River and followed that stream to Lake Nipigon where he established Fort La Tourette named for his younger brother, Claude Greysolon, Sieur de la Tourette. In 1685, Du Lhut also built a second fort three miles upstream from the mouth of the Kaministiquia River. These forts successfully interdicted the flow of furs to Hudson Bay and by 1686, reportedly cost the Hudson's Bay Company a loss in excess of twenty-five thousand pounds.[24]

Unfortunately, Du Lhut's goals of building a successful western fur trade network and exploring the waterways leading to the northwest were periodically interrupted. The hostility of the Dakota and the need to rescue La Salle's scouting party were but the first setbacks. Du Lhut was also denounced by enemies including La Salle who considered him his chief rival in western exploration. In 1684, Du Lhut was temporarily placed in command of Michilimackinac and meted out justice to the murderers of two French traders at Sault Sainte Marie. Following that assignment, his services were repeatedly needed to defend the colony, thus preventing further exploration. During the last twenty-five years of his life, he suffered from gout and by 1702 he was incapacitated. He died in 1710.[25]

Taken collectively, the explorations of Father Allouez and Du Lhut provided hitherto unknown information about Lake Superior and the existence of the Northwest Trail. That body of knowledge, however, was not extensive and did not reach very far beyond the shores of Lake Superior.

French Map Makers

An examination of French maps produced from 1670 to 1755 shows a slow increase in the amount of information provided, including the location and relationship of lakes and rivers. Although the courses of major river systems, such as the Mississippi and St. Louis were often distorted, it is apparent that cartographers were trying to depict important elements of the various trade routes.

By the mid-eighteenth century, certain features of the Northwest Trail began to appear on maps of the West. For example, a map drawn by Nicolas Bellin in 1755 shows the headwaters of the St. Louis River connected by a short portage to Red Lake. Although the cartographer overlooked a number of intervening waterways, he tried to give the impression that a traveler could reach Red Lake, and ultimately Lake Winnipeg, by following the St. Louis River from Lake Superior.[26]

One curious feature depicted on Bellin's map, as well as other early maps, are lakes with outlets that flow in two directions at once. In Bellin's case, Red Lake is shown sitting astride the drainage divide, and the map shows the Mississippi River flowing out of one end and the Red River of the North flowing out of the other. Apparently what the map maker was trying to show was not so much the exact origin or course of the two rivers, but their relationship with respect to the geography of the surrounding country as it was then known, including the important connection provided by the Northwest Trail.

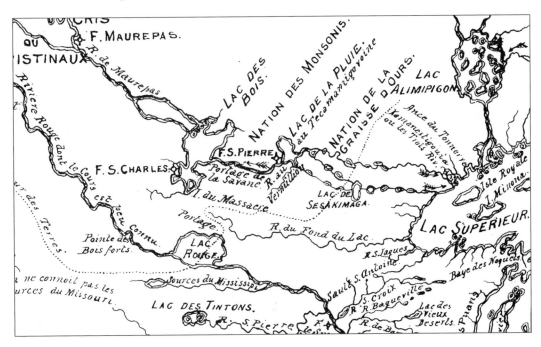

Nicolas Bellin's 1755 map of the Lake Superior area shows the extent of geographic knowledge toward the end of the French regime in Canada. Winchell, *Aborigines of Minnesota*

Invariably, early French maps show great distortion in the relationship of one watershed to another. Most streams west of Lake Superior are shown originating too far to the north or west. That particular pattern of distortion was caused in part by the lack of an accurate determination of latitude and longitude. Also, some knowledge of what actually existed in large areas of the Northwest was often based on second or third hand reports from Indian hunters or traders. The cartographer often could neither check the validity of the descriptions he received nor obtain additional information.[27]

In the case of Bellin's map, the lack of precise bearings from which a cartographer could construct an accurate map is reflected in the courses of the rivers and the distances between various points on the western edge. In addition, little was known of the country away from the rivers and lakes. It is no mere understatement that Bellin marked a large blank spot on his map northwest of Lake Superior the *Grand Entendue de Pays entierement Inconnue*, which, literally translated, tells the reader the "great extent of the country is entirely unknown." Detailed mapping, especially of the country along the Northwest Trail, would have to wait until the last decade of the eighteenth century.

While the distortion, which appeared on the edge of maps depicting areas to the west of the Great Lakes, was caused by the lack of navigational instruments and people with the necessary knowledge of how to use them, there were also other causes for error. Certainly fixing a position in the wilderness with few familiar landmarks for a bearing was a daunting task, but map makers of the period also tended to copy information published on previous maps, thus perpetuating discrepancies or outright errors.

A good example of an outstanding error repeated on early maps of Lake Superior is the large island shown on some French maps next to Isle Royale. Allouez showed one island on his map, but he called it Isle Minong. Subsequent cartographers—evidently hearing of an island called Isle Royale and and not knowing which was correct—dutifully reproduced both calling the second island Isle Minong or Isle Phelippeaux (or Philippeaux).[28]

Most explorers did not map their routes and unreliable descriptions can be found in their records. For example, although Du Lhut's travels took him into the interior, it is not always certain exactly which rivers he used since he did not mention their names or observe for latitude and longitude to determine either his position. Also, he did not mention known locations such as natural landmarks or Indian villages. Du Lhut's writings, while of great interest in determining his range of operations, lack sufficient detail for fixing some necessary locations with any certainty. Those travelers who made references to some known landmarks, often described them in either a French translation of an Indian name or simply used a phonetic spelling of what they thought the name sounded like.

Map makers wishing to depict the area west of Lake Superior continued to be hampered after Du Lhut's explorations because there were too few people traveling in the region with proper equipment or sufficient knowledge of how to fix a position in the wilderness. It is also quite possible some travelers or traders simply did not bother to report new information to the colonial authorities, even though the French government maintained the office of a royal hydrographer at Quebec. Traders who continued to operate in the western Great Lakes without a royal license were not about to tell anyone where they had been or how to get there.

The man responsible for keeping the maps of New France current in Du Lhut's time was Jean-Baptiste-Louis Franquelin. As a professional cartographer, Franquelin drafted eight maps of the Great Lakes area in the 1680s. His work influenced many subsequent cartographers such as Claude and Guillaume Del'Isle, whose *Carte du Canada*, printed in 1703, was the first map of New France with a reasonably accurate longitudinal grid. Franquelin's skill was sufficient to earn him an appointment as the official cartographer for the La Salle expedition (1684); and, in 1686, Franquelin was appointed *Hydrographe du Roy* at Quebec. Du Lhut and his cousin Henri de Tonti (or Tonty) provided Franquelin with useful information about the West based on their travels. As a result, in 1688, Franquelin produced a remarkably detailed map which included the St. Louis River, but his map still exhibited some of the distortions that plagued previous charts. There were, however, certain factors over which even the King's hydrographer had no control.[29]

The gathering of information for maps, including those depicting the Northwest Trail, was undoubtedly influenced when the trade west of Lake Superior became a monopoly. In 1696, orders were issued by King Louis XIV, abolishing all *congés* (licenses) and concentrating the fur trade at certain established posts complete with garrisons to enforce his orders. The royal orders were the latest in a series of measures undertaken to regulate the western trade. Although practically limited in their effectiveness, these acts were a response to the glut of furs on the European markets and the resultant depression in prices for furs. The royal edicts also had an unintended consequence. By limiting the number of legitimate traders, the orders also limited a dependable source of geographic information.[30]

Following the edicts closing the frontier, the major emphasis of French trade for the next seventeen years (1696 to 1713) was centered on Hudson Bay. The strategic James Bay posts, established by the Hudson's Bay Company after 1670, had been captured by Pierre de Troyes' expedition in 1686, thus insuring a bountiful trade for the French. Add to the closing of the western country and the change in emphasis in trading areas, a gradual increase in the intermittent warfare waged chiefly between the Dakota and Ojibway, plus a limited French presence, and the end result was that very little new information about the country north and west of Lake Superior appeared on period maps.[31]

Political events in Europe, however, had a direct impact on exploration and map making. After the Treaty of Utrecht in 1713, the amount of useful geographic information about the west contained on French maps changed noticeably. The treaty, which ended the last of the continental wars of Louis XIV, contained a provision which restored the James Bay trading posts to the Hudson's Bay Company. These new circumstances prompted the French to once more attempt to interdict the flow of furs coming to the English posts on Hudson Bay by opening trade routes and establishing strategically located trading posts to the northwest of Lake Superior. Geographic information gleaned from these western trading ventures ultimately appeared on new maps.

By the 1720s, it was apparent further extension of geographic knowledge and trade required not only opening new routes to the Northwest but also bypassing the increasingly belligerent Dakota. The increased level of intertribal conflict made exploration and trade on routes to the Northwest, including the Northwest Trail, a precarious undertaking. Clearly another route was needed—one that led far to the northwest, skirting the territory of the Dakota. Further exploration of the country by way of the Northwest Trail would have to wait.[32]

In the 1730s and 1740s, the chief representatives of French expansion in the west were Pierre Gaultier de Varennes, Sieur de la Vérendrye and his sons. According to historian Grace Lee Nute, Sieur de la Vérendrye (more commonly, La Vérendrye) was already a person of some importance in New France. A member of the third generation of a prominent Three Rivers family, he was the son of the governor of Three Rivers, and the grandson of Pierre Boucher, who published the first history of New France in 1664.[33]

Beginning in 1727, La Vérendrye visited Lake Nipigon to assess the available western routes. There he obtained a copy of a map of the rivers flowing into Lake Superior. The map, drawn by Assiniboine chief Ochagach, showed three water routes to the west, previously mentioned: the St. Louis, Pigeon, and Kaministiquia.

Among the interesting features of Ochagach's map are the interconnected river routes, which include the Northwest Trail. Although the French were certainly aware of the three water routes, they chose to follow the chain of lakes along Minnesota's present boundary. That particular route appeared to hold the greatest promise for the development of French trade in the Northwest without interference from the Dakota.[34]

In 1731, the elder La Vérendrye obtained permission from colonial authorities to explore the country west of Lake Winnipeg in the trading area called *la Mer de l'Ouest*, or literally "the Sea of the West." The trading area took its name from the mythical Sea of the West, which was supposedly in turn connected by the "Straits of Anian" to the South Sea (Pacific Ocean). Throughout the 1730s and 1740s, La Vérendrye and his sons explored the west as far as the foothills of the Rocky Mountains. Although the La Vérendrye family established a series of interior trading posts stretching west from Lake Superior, they failed to find an all water route to the South Sea. The elder La Vérendrye died in 1749, and the posts he and his sons had so laboriously carved out of the wilderness were instead leased to Jacques le Gardeur, Sieur de St. Pierre.[35]

Meanwhile, efforts to accurately describe the territory extending west from Fond du Lac in the 1730s and 1740s momentarily lapsed because of sporadic hostility between the Dakota and Ojibway. By the 1750s, La Vérendrye's youngest son returned to the area and traded at Sandy Lake and along the Mississippi River. Although he and others left a trail of documents supporting his presence in the country west of Lake Superior, he did not map the routes he traversed. The next opportunity to compile an accurate map of the Northwest Trail and surrounding country came in the last decade of the eighteenth century.

The capitulation of Montreal in 1760, and the departure of the last French garrison from Michilimackinac signaled the end of the era of French dominion in the Great Lakes. French merchants and traders from Montreal, however, continued to follow familiar trade routes west of Lake Superior in the years following the fall of New France. They were joined by enterprising Scots and Yankees who saw a profit to be made in the trade. Chief among these new traders was Alexander Henry the Elder; who, in conjunction with veteran trader Jean Baptiste Cadotte, were among the first to leave a record of their efforts to send men and goods to trade in the Fond du Lac area.[36]

Scarcely a decade had passed since the hostilities of the French and Indian War and Pontiac's Conspiracy when a new conflict erupted which threatened to disrupt trade by way of the Great Lakes. The protracted hostilities during the American Revolutionary War (1775 to 1783) prompted the Montreal traders to band together for mutual protection, eventually giving rise to the formation of the North West Company.

By the end of the Revolutionary War, the Montreal traders concentrated greater effort on tapping the fur resources west of Lake Superior, which had been visited by independent traders since the early years of the French regime in Canada. Who owned the territory west of Lake Superior was not only poorly defined on period maps but also obscured by the vague language of the peace treaty ending the war. Later negotiations, culminating in the Jay Treaty of 1794, allowed nationals from both the United States and Canada to trade in the disputed territory west of Lake Superior; but American traders had no significant presence in the area.

A Nor' Wester Leads the Way

In the late 1790s, the powerful North West Company of Montreal established a series of trading posts at major crossroads in Minnesota. Toward the close of the decade the company sent its geographer, a Welshman named David Thompson, to chart the northernmost source of the Mississippi River and to fix the location of its posts. Posts located within the area of the Northwest Territory claimed by both Great Britain and the newly independent United States were included. In the process of fulfilling his mapping assignment, Thompson created the first truly accurate chart of the vast expanse from Lake Superior to the Pacific Ocean, including the territory encompassing the Northwest Trail.

David Thompson was uniquely qualified for his task. He had studied navigation, or "practical astronomy" as it was known in the eighteenth century, and obtained the best navigational instruments and information then available. Thompson had worked for the Hudson's Bay Company as a geographer, but left that organization in 1797 to become the North West Company's Geographer. His first assignments included mapping the Northwest Trail.[37]

Thompson began his journey at the North West Company's Souris River post on February 26th, 1798. Traveling east by dog sled over the frozen country on what seemed like an impossible mission given the time of the year, he followed the Assiniboine River downstream. Arriving at the forks of the Assiniboine and Red rivers (present Winnipeg, Manitoba), he turned south along the familiar route of western traders bound for Lake Superior. He proceeded up the Red River of the North to the mouth of the Red Lake River stopping at several trading posts along the way to rest and obtain additional provisions.

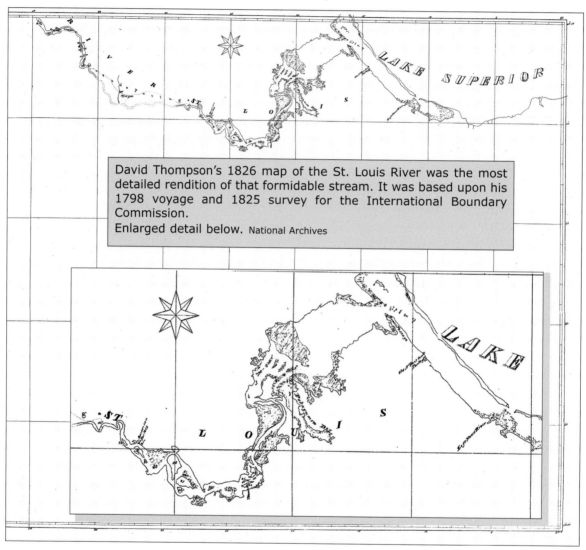

David Thompson's 1826 map of the St. Louis River was the most detailed rendition of that formidable stream. It was based upon his 1798 voyage and 1825 survey for the International Boundary Commission.
Enlarged detail below. National Archives

Thompson worked his way up the Red Lake River, until ice finally forced him to turn back to Jean Baptiste Cadotte's post, near present-day Red Lake Falls, Minnesota. Here he waited until April 9th, 1798, for the ice to break up. He traveled as far as Red Lake, where he found the lake was still frozen over. Thompson obtained a sled and hauled his canoe over the ice to the mouth of Mud River, located in the southeast corner of Lower Red Lake. Mud River, though an insignificant appearing body of water, nonetheless was an important link in the trade route Thompson was charting. Several trading posts were reportedly located on the shore of Red Lake near the mouth of Mud River.[38]

David Thompson proceeded up Mud River to a small lake at its source and from there to Turtle Lake. Twenty-five years after Thompson's visit, the Italian explorer Giacomo Constantino Beltrami declared a small lake he named "Lake Julia" to be the northern source of the Mississippi River, because, like Thompson's source, it appeared to have outlets which flowed into both Red Lake and the Mississippi River. Thompson's party completed its portage across the height of land to Turtle Lake, which Thompson declared to be the northernmost source of the Mississippi.[39]

From Turtle Lake, Thompson canoed down "Turtle Brook," as he called it, to Upper Red Cedar (Cass) Lake. Finding this lake also frozen over, he decided to stay at a trading post located at the mouth of Turtle River. The resident trader at Red Cedar Lake was absent. In his place, Thompson found John Sayer who was in charge of all the North West Company's posts in the Fond du Lac Department. From Sayer, Thompson learned a great deal about the country through which he had to pass. Most importantly, Sayer informed him not to proceed downstream beyond the mouth of the Sandy Lake River because of recent hostilities between the Dakota and Ojibway.[40]

David Thompson's trip along the trade route from the Red River to Lake Superior is significant for two major accomplishments. First, Thompson produced a remarkably accurate map showing Canada and a portion of the United States west of Lake Superior to the Pacific. Secondly, Thompson's seventy-seven notebooks were filled with rough track survey notes including compass bearings, latitude and longitude observations, and remarks about the flora and fauna of the country. After leaving Upper Red Cedar Lake he made the following observation about the meandering Mississippi River:

> Seeing a Pole before us at less than five hundred yards the four hands in the canoe paddled smartly for thirty five minutes before a current of 2 1/2 miles an hour to arrive at it, in which time we estimated we had passed over about three miles of the windings of the River. Meeting an Indian in his canoe ascending the river, he smoked with us, and on my remarking to him the crookedness of the River, he shook his head and said Snake make this River. I thought otherwise, for these windings break the current and make it navigable. I have always admired the formations of the Rivers, as directed by the finger of God for the most benevolent purpose.[41]

Thompson's course continued south on the meandering Mississippi. His journal entry for May 5th, 1798, recorded the violence prevalent in the country. "Met a Chippeway Man and Woman. She was paddling her husband, He was slightly stabbed in both shoulder blades with a knife." Later, while at Sandy Lake, Thompson elaborated on the story :

> On the 6th May we continued our route: in the course of the day we met an Indian and his Wife. The man had a large fresh scar across his nose,

and when smoking with us, asked if he was still not handsome; on arriving at Sand Lake we learned that the evening before, while drinking, another Indian had quarreled with him, and in a fit of jealousy had bit off his nose and thrown it away, but in the morning finding his nose was missing, he searched for, and found it, the part that remained was still bleeding, on which he stuck the part bitten off, without anything to keep it; it adhered, and taking a looking glass, exclaimed, "as yet I am not ugly." I was afterwards informed, the cure became complete, and only the scar remained.[42]

The historian Francis Parkman related that biting off the nose of an antagonist was "...a singular mode of revenge, much in vogue upon similar occasions among Indians of the upper lakes."

Far more sinister than this tale of a drunken frolic was the report Thompson received while at Red Lake Falls of the ambush and destruction of a Chippewa buffalo hunting party on February 19th, 1797. The group, numbering forty-six souls, was set upon by an estimated three hundred Dakota about one and a half day's march south of Sandy Lake. According to Thompson, buffalo could be found within a moderate two day walk in that area.[43]

Just before he left the Mississippi River at Sandy Lake, Thompson revealed the following prediction, which does not appear in his original journal entry for the date, but in a later published account of his explorations:

To the intelligent part of mankind, the sources of all the great rivers have always been subjects of curiosity; witness the expeditions undertaken; the sums of money expended, and the sufferings endured to discover the sources of the Nile, the research of ages. Whatever the Nile has been in ancient times in Arts and Arms, the noble valley of the Mississippi bids fair to be, and excluding its pompous, useless, Pyramids and other works; it's anglo saxon population will far exceed the Egyptians in all the arts of civilized life, and in pure religion. Although these are the predictions of a solitary traveler unknown to the world they will surely be verified (1798).[44]

On the afternoon of Sunday, May 6th, 1798, Thompson arrived at the mouth of the Sandy Lake River. He paused there long enough to measure both the width and depth of the Mississippi River and also took several observations to fix the precise point where the great river joined the Sandy Lake River at latitude 46.49.11 north longitude 93.49.7 west. Proceeding up the Sandy Lake River, Thompson noted the twisting course of the stream which he estimated carried him approximately two miles to gain the distance of half a mile. On entering Sandy Lake, Thompson took a compass bearing of south 14 degrees east for his course in the lake to the North West Company's trading post. He estimated the post to be about one and a half miles from the entrance to the river; however, the actual distance was greater.[45]

Arriving at the post at 6 p.m., Thompson secured provisions for his men and interviewed Charles Bousquet, the factor in charge of the Sandy Lake post. Later, since the evening was clear, he observed for latitude and longitude fixing the post at latitude 46.46.30 north longitude 93.44.17 west, variation 6 degrees east. During his travels, David Thompson recorded the latitude and longitude of not only the company's trading posts, but also the junctions of rivers and other important landmarks. Using these fixed points, together with his rough-track survey notes giving bearings and estimated distances traveled, he determined his position and obtained an accurate depiction of the country on his map.[46]

Although Thompson's records indicate he normally took observations of lunar distances, or "Lunars," to determine longitude, his journal entry for May 6th indicates he used his four foot achromatic telescope to take astronomical observations to time the eclipse of Jupiter's satellites to determine longitude. This painstaking method demanded precision, but also gave a more accurate position if done carefully. Thompson took many observations since he knew there were bound to be errors because of the primitive conditions he was operating under. By averaging the results of his observations, Thompson arrived at a fairly accurate position.[47]

Thompson's notes also contain interesting observations regarding the people he found at Sandy Lake. He observed that they appeared poor and ill-clad since most of the animals they depended upon were almost wholly destroyed by over hunting. The local residents subsisted on wild rice and sugar. He noted "we did not see a single duck in their canoes, ammunition being too scarce..."[48]

Thompson described the season's catch in various furs during his visit, most of which were obtained from the forests between the Mississippi and Lake Superior:

> He [Bousquet] showed me his winter hunt, in value fifty beaver skins. The Minks and Martens were inferior, the Lynxes appeared good, but the fur not so long as in the north. But the Fishers were uncommonly large, the color a rich glossy black brown, and the fur fine: the Beavers were mostly fall and spring skins, and as each were good in color and fur, but not a single Fox or Wolf. These animals are almost unknown, there being nothing for them to live on.[49]

On May 7th, Thompson departed Sandy Lake and ascended the "Savannah Brook" leading toward the Savanna Portage. He gave the first really accurate description of the western terminus of the portage as noted earlier. Upon arriving at the western end, he quickly passed over the portage to the east end, where he observed his position– latitude 46.50.3 north longitude 92.28.42 west variation 6 degrees east. He described the eastern end of the portage as terminating in a great swamp which extended as far north and south as he could see.

Thompson embarked on the East Savanna River. After following the winding river for an estimated twenty miles, he remarked, "We now entered the River St. Louis, a bold stream of about one hundred yards in width..."

At this point, he described an important observation respecting the rivers of northern Minnesota:

> Hitherto the width, depth and rate of current of the Brooks and Rivers are those of high water from the melting of snow. But as all of them, even the Red river, depend on the Snow and Rains for their supply of water; in the months of August, September and October they are all shoal.[50]

Thompson's canoe ride down the St. Louis was turbulent and at one point waves broke over the sides almost swamping the canoe. The St. Louis has many rapids, and there was always the potential of a sudden mishap. His notes indicate he noticed various natural features encountered along the way. Thompson described the Knife Portage as being one thousand five hundred seventy-six yards long. In 1825, he measured it again and found it to be two thousand twenty-nine yards in length.

After a voyage of four miles farther, consisting of almost all rapids, he arrived at the "Long Carrying Place," or the Grand Portage. He observed the flora, fauna, and physical features found along the river. Thompson estimated the fall of the St. Louis River to be four hundred seventeen feet, eleven inches from the mouth of the East Savanna to Lake Superior.[51]

David Thompson's description of the Northwest Trail concluded with his arrival at Fort St. Louis. This journey and many others produced a wealth of geographic information that he eventually incorporated into a gigantic map, which he completed for the North West Company in 1812. The map, which hung in the Great Hall at Fort William for many years not only described the exact location of all seventy-eight of the company's posts, but also filled in the blank spaces previously left on French maps of an earlier period. While his map represents an impressive accomplishment, David Thompson's work provided much useful information about the Mississippi headwaters and the St. Louis River for later explorers. His detailed notes give a remarkable picture of what he had found along the old Northwest Trail.[52]

In 1825, twenty-seven years after David Thompson's first springtime trip along the Northwest Trail, he and his son Samuel surveyed the St. Louis River for the British contingent of the Boundary Commission, created by the Treaty of Ghent. Given the vague descriptions of the border west of Lake Superior, David Thompson believed the St. Louis River route best represented the logical boundary between the United States and Canada. Among other things, the St. Louis estuary matched the description of the "long lake" mentioned in the treaty. In a series of letters to the British government, he tried to make a case for the northern border of Minnesota beginning at the mouth of the St. Louis River.

Thompson envisioned the border extending up the St. Louis and by a short portage to Lake Vermilion and thence along the old trade route from Grand Portage to Rainy Lake and eventually Lake of the Woods. Remarkably, even though Thompson was perhaps the best qualified man to discuss the geography west of Lake Superior, the government ignored him. In a letter on the subject, written in 1840, Thompson summarized the importance of the route:

> ...but the continuation of the Boundary, in nearly the same direction, through Lake Superior, leads to the fine estuary of the River St. Louis, and answers the description of the Long Lake [1783] the great thoroughfare of the fur trade, both to the interior, the Lake of the Woods, and to the rich countries of the Mississippi, and its branches; and to the Red River, and its streams; from whence the greater part of the fur trade then came.[53]

David Thompson's view that the logical border between the United States and Canada should follow the course of the St. Louis River was only briefly considered. A counter claim by the United States proposed that the provisions of the treaty ending the Revolutionary War established the boundary along the Kaministiquia River. Both claims concerning the St. Louis and the Kaministiquia rivers as the customary trade routes were ultimately rejected in favor of a compromise finally establishing the border in its present location extending west from Grand Portage. Concern over the border question and the activities of North West Company traders in territory claimed by the United States ultimately brought an official visit to the affected area.

Lieutenant Pike's Reconnaissance

In 1805, Lieutenant Zebulon Montgomery Pike was ordered by General James Wilkinson to conduct a reconnaissance of the Mississippi from St. Louis, Missouri, to its headwaters. As Pike's expedition proceeded north, it became apparent the trip would extend into the winter. He established a base camp at the mouth of the Swan River near the modern town of Little Falls, Minnesota, before proceeding further upstream. Pike experienced great difficulty in ascending the river once winter arrived. He also complained about the readings obtained from his navigational instruments, which suggests they were probably not of the highest quality for the type of work he was expected to perform.[54]

After undergoing great fatigue in ascending the frozen Mississippi on foot, his expedition halted for twelve days (January 8th to January 20th, 1806) at Sandy Lake while his men recuperated from the harsh conditions experienced on their winter journey up the great river. While there, Pike surveyed the lake and included detailed information in his journal about the Northwest Trail, which connected the North West Company's interior posts with Lake Superior.[55]

A manuscript map based on Pike's notes was prepared to accompany his journal of the Mississippi expedition shortly after he returned to St. Louis. The manuscript map, drawn under Pike's supervision by Sergeant Antoine Nau, is of particular interest since it includes a description of the Northwest Trail from Sandy Lake to Lake Superior, the exact location of company trading posts, the course of the Mississippi River, and, the Leech Lake River, commonly believed to be the major tributary of that stream.

The Nau map is highly significant, since it gives the exact location of the Sandy Lake post. The map also includes a curious rendition of the connection between Sandy Lake and the St. Louis River; however, it omits the Prairie portage. The description of the all-water route can be explained by several factors. First, what is shown as a water route on the map may have actually been intended to depict a winter road connecting the overland trail leading from Northeast Bay to the western end of the regular six mile portage. Secondly, the water route shown on the manuscript map appears to closely follow a small stream, which flows into Northeast Bay on Sandy Lake, and may have been used as a shortcut from the West Savanna River.[56]

Although Pike complained of the difficulty he was experiencing with his instruments in fixing locations of the posts and other details recorded in the Nau map, the manuscript map accurately gave the location of the Sandy Lake post with other prominent features. In spite of the care taken to obtain accurate measurements of latitude and longitude, it should be remembered that David Thompson's determination of various locations was also subject to error, as evidenced by his frequent observations and his practice of averaging the results derived from multiple bearings.

Certain locations on Nau's map were later distorted when a new and much reduced version of his original map was engraved by Francis Shallus to accompany the published version of Pike's journal of the Mississippi expedition printed by Nicholas King. The publication of Pike's notes and map was done at the request of Secretary of War, Henry Dearborn, for distribution to members of Congress in 1806. The new reduced version of the manuscript map was also included in a second account of Pike's expeditions on the Mississippi (1805-1806) and in the southwest (1806-1807) published in 1810. [57]

The Shallus map, although technically well-executed, resulted among other things in an incorrect location for the site of the North West Company's Sandy Lake trading post. The new map placed the location of the Sandy Lake post on the western shore and not on the tip of the peninsula on the southwest side of the lake as shown in the manuscript map. The error in the placement of the North West Company post resulted in subsequent descriptions of the post as being on a point in Northwest Bay.

In spite of the attempts to refine the manuscript map, that document and Pike's journal provide the first real detailed information about the country at the headwaters of the Mississippi and of the route separating the Great Lakes from that great river. Interestingly, Pike had no prior knowledge of the work of David Thompson until he visited the headquarters of the Fond du Lac Department of the North West Company at Leech Lake. His conversations with Chief Factor Hugh McGillis were particularly valuable since McGillis had been with Thompson in 1797 and undoubtedly knew of the scope of his work. It is also certain that later geographers knew of both the difficulties Pike experienced with his instruments in fixing the location of important features and of the geographical contributions of Thompson. An example can be found in a footnote on the Shallus map engraved for Nicholas King's edition of Pike's journal which indicates it was, "Reduced and corrected by the Astronomical Observations of Mr. Thompson at its source and of Captn. M. [Meriwether] Lewis where it receives the waters of the Missouri."[58]

Each succeeding explorer who traced the Northwest Trail borrowed to some degree from the knowledge first obtained by Thompson and Pike. Some, such as Lieutenant James Allen and Joseph N. Nicollet, improved on the information first set down by adding information not recorded by Thompson and Pike. Both Allen and Nicollet included trails as well as waterways on their respective maps. Nicollet's famous map, first published in 1842, included not only elevations at major junctions such as at the confluence of the East Savanna and St. Louis rivers, but also soundings at the entrance to rivers on Lake Superior and names for lakes previously unreported.[59]

Each successive mapping of the old Northwest Trail exposed new information. For example, James Allen, who commanded the military escort for Indian Agent Henry Schoolcraft's 1832 expedition to the headwaters of the Mississippi River, sketched and labeled the usual route used by the traders traveling from Lake Superior to the Red River of the North and beyond. He also included a description of the overland trail used by the traders and Indians traveling from Sandy Lake to Leech Lake. It was Joseph Nicollet, however, who completed the work first recorded by Thompson, Pike, and Allen when he traveled through northern Minnesota in the summers of 1836 and 1837.

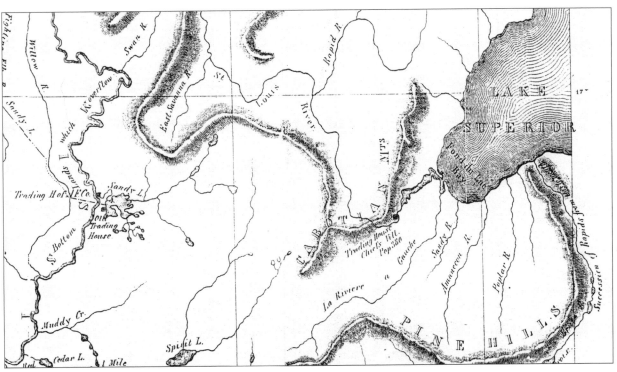

Lieutenant James Allen's map is based on his observations during the Schoolcraft Expedition of 1832. Allen's map, which accompanied his official report to Congress, is noticeably lacking in detail from Lake Superior to Sandy Lake. According to his journal, he was having a dreadful time managing his inexperienced crew and coping with the difficulties encountered along the St. Louis River. Compare with Nicollet's map at the end of Chapter 1. American State Papers, Military Affairs

Nicollet Maps the Route West

Joseph N. Nicollet's entry in the list of explorers and geographers who depicted the Northwest Trail occurred thirty years after Pike's famous Mississippi expedition. Nicollet, a French mathematician and geographer, spent several years on the American frontier and gathered information that he later published in both the form of a report and a magnificent map. The results of Nicollet's work, including his mapping activity in the country west of Lake Superior, were recorded in his journal.[60]

In 1836, Nicollet undertaking an expedition to explore the Mississippi River as far as its true source, followed in the footsteps of United States Indian Agent, Henry Schoolcraft, who had been guided to the supposed source at remote Elk Lake in 1832. The lake's name, which Schoolcraft changed to "Itasca," was formed from parts of two Latin words, *verum* or *veritas* meaning "true" or "truth" and *caput* meaning "head." Nicollet devoted several days to exploring the country surrounding Elk Lake, or Lake Itasca, conducted a detailed scientific examination of the headwaters of the Mississippi River and discovered the actual source. Following his work in the Lake Itasca area, Nicollet returned downstream where he encountered a valuable source of geographical information in the person of the chief trader for the American Fur Company, William Alexander Aitkin.

Nicollet spent an enjoyable evening at Aitkin's trading post, located at the confluence of the Mississippi and Sandy Lake rivers. Here, Nicollet had a long discussion regarding the geography of the region including the waterways. It was a region over which Aitkin held sway and of which he was very well-informed. Although the first meeting with Aitkin was of relatively short duration, the chief trader would eventually play a major role in Nicollet's plan to accurately map the region.[61]

The next opportunity Nicollet had to have a lengthy conversation with Aitkin regarding the geography of Minnesota came in the summer of 1837. Nicollet and Aitkin met at Fort Snelling, overlooking the junction of the Mississippi and St. Peter's (Minnesota) rivers, to witness the signing of the first treaty ceding Ojibway claims to certain lands in what was then Wisconsin Territory. Aitkin had submitted a successful traders' claim in the treaty for twenty-eight thousand dollars, and was on his way home via a roundabout route up the St. Croix River and then along the south shore of Lake Superior to Fond du Lac and ultimately Sandy Lake.

Nicollet joined Aitkin's party of traders and voyageurs bound for the American Fur Company's depot at La Pointe. To Nicollet, the trip afforded the chance of gathering important information about a region that was unknown to geographers. The St. Croix had not been mapped and the prospect of doing so apparently delighted Nicollet.[62]

Nicollet's famous 1842 map and his official report of 1843, which was intended to accompany the map, show details of the Northwest Trail never before included on a map of the region. In addition, his journal of the trips in 1836 and 1837 has been translated and published. It provides useful background for studying his travels through the countryside. The journal follows the day by day progress of Nicollet and his companions up the St. Croix River, across the height of land, down the Bois Brûlé River to Lake Superior, and as far as La Pointe on Madeline Island. Although Nicollet's journal ends there, his unpublished notes and maps tell the rest of the story. Leaving La Pointe after a short stay, Nicollet continued to record much valuable information about the countryside, sketched maps, and listed astronomical observations and calculations.

Nicollet's notes and sketch maps provide information about the St. Louis River, an important waterway whose description is missing from his published narrative. His detailed observations about the Northwest Trail from Fond du Lac to Sandy Lake include the rapids, portages, tributaries and other information not previously recorded. It also proved to be a very demanding trip for the rather frail geographer.

After negotiating the strenuous Grand Portage, the Knife Portage, and the abundant rapids found along the St. Louis River, the party carried their baggage across the swampy Savanna Portage before the current in the West Savanna River finally brought them to Aitkin's post at the outlet to Sandy Lake. The ordeal on the rivers and portages undoubttedly sapped Nicollet's strength for, according to his notes, he remained at Aitkin's residence in the trading post from August 20th until August 25th, recuperating before resuming his voyage down the Mississippi to Fort Snelling.[63]

Joseph Nicolas Nicollet, 1836.
Minnesota Historical Society

During his stay, Nicollet undoubtedly had intense conversations with Aitkin about the geography of northern Minnesota. As a case in point, a sketch map in his papers shows a detailed map of the Cloquet or Cloutier River, a principal tributary of the St. Louis, flowing into the latter stream from the northeast. Given his timetable on the St. Louis, it was impossible for Nicollet to have detoured to explore the Cloquet River as far as its source. Nicollet's detailed notes imply that he obtained the necessary information about the Cloquet River and other features directly from Aitkin. It is interesting to note here that Nicollet was the first of many travelers to use the name Cloquet to describe the major tributary of the St. Louis River.

As a source for information about the Cloquet River and other geographic features, William Aitkin was unparalleled. He had traveled all over northern Minnesota for twenty years and, as chief trader for the American Fur Company, proved to be an invaluable source of information to Joseph Nicollet. Nicollet's gratitude for Aitkin's assistance can be seen in subsequent correspondence which contain favorable references by Nicollet about William Aitkin.[64]

The story of the successive efforts by Nicollet and others to map the country between Lake Superior and the Mississippi River helps us better understand the experiences of early travelers who used the old Northwest Trail.

Chapter 3 - Mapping the Old Northwest Trail
Notes

1.   Three motives for exploration in New France included the search for the Northwest Passage, the location of copper mines on Lake Superior, and the fur trade. All are discussed in Helen E. Knuth, "Economic and Historical Background of Northeastern Minnesota Lands: Chippewa Indians of Lake Superior," in *Chippewa Indians III* (New York, 1974), pp. 188-189; The profit motive in exploration is discussed in John Bartlet Brebner, *The Explorers of North America: 1492-1806* (3rd printing, Cleveland, 1968), p. 290.

2.   Newton H. Winchell, *The Aborigines of Minnesota* (St. Paul, 1911), pp. 25-62, offers a brief summary of various maps produced depicting Minnesota from 1597 to 1763.

3.   For Brulé's explorations see Consul Wilshire Butterfield, *Brulé's Discoveries and Explorations* (Cleveland, 1898), pp. 107-109; Father Lalement's travels are summarized in Harold Hickerson, "Ethnohistory of the Chippewa of Lake Superior," *Chippewa Indians II* (New York, 1974), pp. 17-18; Reuben Gold Thwaites (ed.) *The Jesuit Relations and Allied Documents*, 74 vols.(Cleveland, 1896-1901), vol. 23, p. 225; See Emma Helen Blair, *The Indian Tribes of the Upper Mississippi Valley and Region of the Great Lakes*, 2 vols.(Cleveland, 1911), vol. 1, pp. 171-173; and Louise Phelps Kellogg, *Early Narratives of the Northwest*, 1634-1699 (New York, 1917), p. 25, for information on Father Ménard's travels in the country south of Lake Superior. Etienne Brulé may have preceded the Jesuit missionaries Jogues, Raymbault, Lalement, and Ménard to Lake Superior. His 1623 voyage reportedly followed the south shore of Lake Superior to the Brulé River (also known as the *Bois Brûlé* or Burnt Wood River), supposedly named for him, and possibly as far west as the St. Louis River. Brulé arrived in Canada in 1608 and was known to have mastered several Indian languages and served as an interpreter. His long tenure with the Indians came to a tragic end in 1632, when he was allegedly eaten by the Huron.

4.   Grace Lee Nute, *Caesars of the Wilderness* (New York, 1943); Warren Upham, "Groseilliers and Radisson, The First White Men in Minnesota, 1655-56, and 1659-60, and Their discovery of the Upper Mississippi River," *The Collections of the Minnesota Historical Society*, vol. 10 (1905), pp. 449-594; Nute's research examined the explorations of Pierre d'esprit Radisson and Medard Chouart, Sieur de Groseilliers. Upham credits these two intrepid explorers with the discovery of the "Upper Mississippi River." For the naming of the Gooseberry River see Chrysostum Verwyst, "A Glossary of Chippewa Names of Rivers, Lakes, and Villages," *Acta et Dicta*, vol. 4, no. 2 (July, 1916), p. 260. The Ojibway name for the Gooseberry River listed in Verwyst's Glossary poses an intriguing question. If Radisson and Groseilliers did not name the stream, who did? There is no report of an Ojibway settlement near the Gooseberry River at the time of their voyage.

5.   Louise Phelps Kellogg, *The French Régime in Wisconsin and the Northwest* (Madison, 1925), p. 115.

6.   For the explorations of Allouez, see *Collections of the State Historical Society of Wisconsin*, vol. 16 (Madison, 1902), pp. 32, 60, and 77; John Gilmary Shea, *Discovery and Exploration of the Mississippi Valley* (New York, 1853), pp. 67-69, and 86.

7.   Thwaites (ed.), *Jesuit Relations*, vol. 55, p. 94. The 1670-1671 map of Lake Superior may actually date to 1672.

8.   Kellogg, *French Régime*, pp. 154, and 158-159; *Collections of the State Historical Society of Wisconsin*, vol. 16 (Madison, 1902), pp. 62, 395-396; Knuth, *Chippewa Indians III*, p. 8; Thwaites (ed.), *Jesuit Relations*, vol. 54, pp. 135-139; Conrad E. Heidenreich, "Mapping the Great Lakes, The Period of Exploration, 1603-1700," in *Cartographica*, vol. 17, no. 2 (Autumn, 1980), p. 44; Kellogg states that Allouez probably had Jacques Marquette's help in preparing the chart. She also mentions Father Claude Dablon's appointment as Superior of the Northwest Missions and his interest in maps. According to Knuth, Dablon was interested in the discovery of the Northwest Passage to facilitate trade with Japan. Her position is reinforced by the *Jesuit Relations* and by Heidenreich's research. Dablon was an experienced map maker and could have assisted Allouez in the preparation of the Lake Superior map. In addition to his familiarity with the country, Dablon was in a favorable position to gain access to information for the mapping of New France. The Royal School of Hydrography at Quebec was staffed by the Jesuits.

9.   Thwaites (ed.), *Jesuit Relations*, vol. 15, p. 94.

10.   Ibid., p. 169; Justin Winsor, *Narrative and Critical History of America*, 8 vols. (Boston, 1889), vol. 4, p. 216, n. 4.

11.   Hickerson, *Chippewa Indians II*, p. 20. In 1671, Louis Armand de Lon d' Arce, Baron de La Hontan et Herleche paid an official visit to the Sault to claim the area for France.   He later wrote a book describing his travels. See Reuben Gold Thwaites (ed.), *New Voyages to North America*, 2 vols. (Chicago, 1905). Baron La Hontan's favorable reception by the Indians was noticed by Governor Frontenac (known to the Indians as *Ononthio* or Great Mountain) who was anxious to court the tribes living near Sault Sainte Marie and learn more about the country at the western end of Lake Superior. In 1676, Frontenac sent his engineer Hugues Randin to Sault Sainte Marie. Randin reportedly drew a map of Lake Superior and adjoining region based on a chart attributed to Louis Joliet.

12.   Brebner, *The Explorers*, pp. 139-140, n.1.

13.   Ibid., p. 151; Francis Parkman, *A Half-Century of Conflict* (3rd printing, New York, 1966), pp. 31, and 34-35. According to Parkman, La Mothe-Cadillac had "small love of priests and an aversion to Jesuits." In fact, he was quite candid about the inordinate influence of clerics in a memorial addressed to the Compte de Maurepas, c. 1699.

14.   Brebner, *The Explorers*, p.153. Some information must have come from the *coureurs des bois* given the appearance of new geographic features; such as the Fond du Lac or St. Louis River, which was included on maps of the western Lake Superior area.

15.   Lawrence J. Sommer (ed.), *Daniel Greysolon, Sieur DuLhut: A Tercentenary Tribute* (Duluth, 1979), pp. 5-74; and Milan Kovacovic, "Daniel Greysolon, Sieur DuLuth: An Introduction," quoted in Ryck Lydecker and Lawrence J. Sommer (eds.) *Duluth, Sketches of the Past: A Bicentennial Collection* (Duluth, 1976), pp. 19-25; For two early accounts of Du Lhut see William McLennan, "A Gentleman of the Royal Guard, Daniel de Gresollon [sic], Sieur Du L'hut," *Harper's New Monthly Magazine*, vol. 87, n. 520 (September, 1893), pp. 609-626, and Francis J. Schaefer, "Duluth, the Explorer of Northern and Central Minnesota," *Acta et Dicta*, vol. 3, no. 1 (July, 1911), pp. 22-40. Du Lhut has generally received sympathetic treatment from historians.

16.   It is questionable if Du Lhut could have accompanied a detachment of marines to Canada in 1672 as suggested in Sommer (p. 6) and Schaefer (p.23), since none were sent until November of 1683. Canada was under the administration of the *Ministère de la Marine* (Ministry of the Marine) and the troops raised for the defense of the colony included local militia and the *Compagnies franches de la Marine* or "free companies" as distinct from the royal marines which served on French warships. See Réne Chartrand, *The French Soldier in Colonial America*, Museum Restoration Service, Historical Arms Series, no. 18. (Bloomfield, Ontario, 1984), pp. 9-10.

17.   Kellogg, *French Régime*, p. 209, gives the names of Du Lhut's companions as the brothers Pepin (for whom Lake Pepin was named), Sieur de Maistre, Paul la Vigne, Sieur Bellegarde, and Sieur de la Rue.

18.   The little-known activities of the *coureurs des bois* are described in Edward D. Neal, "The Development of Trade on Lake Superior and its Tributaries During the French Regime," *Macalester College Contributions*, vol. 1, no. 77 (1890), pp. 103-104; see also Benjamin Sulte, "Les coureurs de bois au lac Supérieur, 1660," *Proceedings and Transactions of the Royal Society of Canada*, 3rd series, vol. 5 (1911), section 1, pp. 249-266; and W. B. Munro, "The Coureurs des Bois," *Proceedings of the Massachusetts Historical Society*, vol. 57 (1923-1924), pp. 192-205.

19.   *Collections of the State Historical Society of Wisconsin*, vol. 16 (Madison, 1902), pp. 107-109. La Salle's letter of 1682, as well as other charges against Du Lhut, should be taken with a grain of salt.

20.   William Watts Folwell, *A History of Minnesota*, 4 vols. (1921; reprint ed., St. Paul, 1956), vol. 1, pp. 22-23; John Fritzen, *The History of Fond du Lac and Jay Cooke State Park* (Duluth, 1978), p. 2. There is some disagreement regarding the exact route Du Lhut took from Fond du Lac to Mille Lacs. The most logical course would have been by canoe up the St. Louis River, or by way of the overland trail connecting Fond du Lac with the Mississippi at Sandy Lake. These were well-known routes.

21. See Kellogg, *Early Narratives*, pp. 329-334, for "Memoir of Duluth on the Sioux Country, 1678-1682" including the details of the Grand Council held at Fond du Lac.

22. Sommer, *Daniel Greysolon*, pp. 11-13.

23. Kellogg, *Early Narratives*, pp. 326 and 332-333; Kellogg, *French Régime*, p. 213. The rescue of La Salle's men, not only delayed Du Lhut's exploration, but also convinced him that any thought of using the Northwest Trail through Dakota country was out of the question. Du Lhut believed the Dakota were perfidious and says so rather indignantly in his "Memoir" cited above. Interestingly, La Salle never mentioned Du Lhut's actions in rescuing his men from the Dakota, only his dismay at the latter's encroachment on his trade monopoly.

24. Schaefer, "Duluth," pp. 35-36.

25. Kellogg, *French Régime*, pp. 225-226; Brebner, *Explorers*, pp. 293, 295, 297, and 313; *Collections of the State Historical Society of Wisconsin*, vol. 16 (Madison, 1902), p. 121. Du Lhut's ambitions are discussed in Kellogg and Brebner. Du Lhut has been described as having great influence over the Indians he encountered, but it appears he may simply have been following local custom whenever possible. Perhaps the most critical situation calling for serious attention to protocol was during the trial and execution of two Ojibway murderers at Sault Sainte Marie. Most accounts relate the two were shot by firing squad, but Du Lhut himself states in a letter of April 12th, 1684, "I put myself at the head of 42 Frenchmen, and, in sight of more than 400 men, and 200 steps from their fort, I had their heads broken." Death by a blow from what the French called a *casse-tête* or "head breaker" (war club) was the customary Ojibway method of execution.

26. See Winchell, *Aborigines*, p. 47, for part of Bellin's map showing northeastern Minnesota;

27. Heidenreich, "Great Lakes," pp. 53-57.

28. Verwyst, "Glossary," p. 254; L. J. Burpee (ed.), "Some Letters of David Thompson," *Canadian Historical Review*, vol. 4, no. 2 (June, 1923), pp. 114-115. See Verwyst for a definition of Minong. Isle Minong was later renamed Isle Phelypeaux (or Phillipeaux) after Louis Phelypeaux, Comte de Pontchartrain, Minister of Marine under King Louis XIV. The Ministry of Marine, organized in 1669, included within its jurisdiction not only the navy, but also France's overseas colonies. Lake Pontchartrain (Louisiana), Fort Pontchartrain on the site of present-day Detroit, and an island next to Isle Royale in Lake Superior were named for Louis Phelypeaux. Unfortunately, Isle Phelypeaux (or Isle Minong if you wish) existed only in the imagination of a cartographer. An interesting explanation for the origin of "Isle Phillipeaux" can be found in Burpee's account.

29. Kellogg, *French Régime*, p. 237. Jean-Baptiste-Louis Franquelin's contribution to geographical knowledge was the consolidation of the available geographic information from explorers such as Du Lhut and Henri Tonti.

30. On the subject of trade regulations, see Harold A. Innis, *The Fur Trade in Canada: An Introduction to Canadian Economic History* (New Haven, 1962), p. 66, n. 93. A royal ordinance (*Ordonnance du Roi au sujet des Vagabonds et Coureurs des Bois*), promulgated June 5th, 1673, was enacted to control the supply of furs by limiting trade. In spite of restrictive measures, the *coureurs des bois* continued to trade in the West and information concerning the various trade routes including the Northwest Trail continued to find its way to map makers such as Franquelin.

31. Innis, *Fur Trade*, p. 67. The various schemes to control the fur trade, and the activities of the coureurs des bois on western waters, took a new direction with the enactment of the *Déclaration du Roi* on May 21st, 1696, which abolished all licenses. Henceforth all trade in the interior was restricted to certain established posts. See "Memoir of Bougainville," *Collections of the State Historical Society of Wisconsin*, vol. 18 (Madison, 1908), pp. 167-195, for a list of the western posts and their locations in 1757 by Louis Antoine de Bougainville. Each post had a "dependancy" or assigned territory to trade in. Eventually, questions arose concerning the boundaries of the various dependancies which revealed the limited extent of geographic knowledge of the region west of Lake Superior.

32. In 1720, Father Pierre François Xavier de Charlevoix, a Jesuit historian, was ostensibly sent by the royal government to inspect the various missions in the Great Lakes. His real objective, however, was to explore possible routes to the western sea and report directly to the Duc d'Orleans, regent for the future King Louis XV. His three volume *Histoire de la Nouvelle France, a Journal d'un voyage fait par ordre du roi* (Paris, 1744) is based on his travels and experiences from 1720-1723.

33.   Grace Lee Nute, *Rainy River Country* (St. Paul, 1950), pp. 4-12; Lawrence J. Burpee (ed.), *Journals and Letters of Pierre Gaultier de Varennes de la Vérendrye and his Sons* (Toronto, 1927); Martin Kavanagh, *La Vérendrye, His Life and Times* (Brandon, Manitoba, 1967).

34.   Burpee, *La Vérendrye*, p. 53; Part of Ochagach's map is reproduced in Burpee. The sketch is entitled *Carte tracée par le Sauvage Ochagach,* or "Chart traced by the wild man Ochagach," and is inset at the top of a larger map entitled *Carte Physique des Terreins les plus élevés de la Partie Occidentale du Canada,* or literally a "Chart of the Physical Terrain [physical geography] and the many elevations in the Western Part of Canada," drawn by Philippe Buache and published by *l'Académie des Sciences*, September 4th,1754. Interestingly enough, no mention is made of La Vérendrye in the accompanying text, but Ochagach's map depicts the *Riv.* [river] *ou Fond du L.* [Lake] *Supérieur* entering a chain of lakes east of *Lac Tecamamiouen*, which indicates the French knew about the headwaters of the St. Louis River. Curiously, although the map is dated 1754, it still included the name *Tecamamiouen*, a French version of a *Monsoni* word which had been replaced by the French name *Lac la Pluie* or "Rainy Lake."

35.   Nute, *Rainy River*, pp. 11-12.

36.   *Collections of the State Historical Society of Wisconsin*, vol. 18 (Madison, 1908), p. 277; Alexander Henry, *Travels & Adventures In Canada and the Indian Territories Between the Years 1760 and 1776 By Alexander Henry Fur Trader,* James Bain (ed.), (1809; reprint ed., Boston, 1901).

37.   J. B. Tyrrell (ed.), *David Thompson's Narrative of His Explorations in Western America, 1784-1812* (Toronto, 1916); Richard Glover (ed.), *David Thompson's Narrative, 1784-1812* (Toronto, 1962); and, Victor E. Hopwood, *David Thompson's Travels in Western North America, 1784-1812* (Toronto, 1971). See also David Thompson, Diary No. 9, for details not covered in the various published accounts. A copy of portions of his diary is available at the Minnesota Historical Society.

38.   Grace Lee Nute, "Posts in the Minnesota Fur-Trading Area," *Minnesota History*, vol. 11, no. 4 (September, 1928), pp. 353-385.

39.   Hopwood, *Thompson's Travels*, pp. 185-186. In 1823, Giacomo Constantino Beltrami declared nearby Lake Julia the northernmost source of the Mississippi. Both he and Thompson had found the height of land separating the waters flowing south into the Mississippi from those flowing north into Hudson Bay. Beltrami was also aware of the western source of the Mississippi near Elk Lake (Lake Itasca), a fact which did not endear him to Henry Schoolcraft, the "discoverer" of the source of the Mississippi.

40.   Glover, *David Thompson's Narrative*, p. 205.

41.   Ibid., p. 206.

42.   Tyrrell, *David Thompson*, pp. 278-279; Glover, *David Thompson's Narrative*, pp. 206-207; Francis Parkman, *The Conspiracy of Pontiac* (10th ed., New York, 1966), p. 208. The encounter with the wounded man was recorded in David Thompson Diary No. 9 for May 6th, 1798, but the episode involving the brawl and nose biting was not included. Both Tyrrell and Glover mention it in their published versions, but Hopwood ignores it entirely.

43.   David Thompson, Diary No. 9 , May 7th, 1798. Copy in the Minnesota Historical Society collections; Tyrrell, *David Thompson*, pp. 263-264. The account of the ambush of the hunting party appears in Thompson's narrative while he rested at Cadotte's post.

44.   This paragraph was added by Thompson later and is included in all three printed versions of his travels cited here. In each case, the date 1798 appears at the end of the statement.

45.   Tyrrell, *David Thompson*, p. 281; Glover, *David Thompson's Narrative*, p. 208.

46.   For a description of Thompson's surveying methods see David Smyth, "David Thompson's Surveying Instruments and Methods In The Northwest, 1790-1812." *Cartographica*, vol. 18, no. 4 (1981), pp. 1-17.

47.   Ibid., p. 14. Thompson usually recorded "Lunars" or lunar distances to establish his location. Instead, he used his achromatic telescope to make the complex observation of the eclipse of Jupiter's moons. This tedious but more accurate procedure fascinated the Sandy Lake residents. To the Indians and voyageurs of the Northwest, Thompson was known as "Man-who-looks-at-the stars, *Koo-koo-sint,* or "the Star Man." To his first biographer, John B. Tyrrell, Thompson was "...the greatest practical land geographer who ever lived."

48. Glover, *David Thompson's Narrative*, p. 208.

49. Ibid., p. 209.

50. Ibid., p. 210.

51. David Thompson, Diary No. 9, May 7th-May 10th, 1798. Thompson's journal entries indicate it took three days to travel from Sandy Lake to Fort St. Louis.

52. Thompson made a revealing comment when he arrived at Fort St. Louis. "On Lake Superior a volume could be written; I have been twice around it, and six times over a great part, each survey correcting the preceding." Hopwood, *Thompson's Travels*, p. 189.

53. L. J. Burpee, *David Thompson*, p. 122.

54. Donald Jackson (ed.), *The Journals of Zebulon Montgomery Pike*, 2 vols. (Norman, 1966), vol. 1, pp. 280-281. Pike's letter to General Wilkinson dated Bellefontaine, July 2nd, 1806, describes the poor quality of his instruments.

55. Ibid., vol. 1, pp. 80-81. On January 14th and 15th, 1806, Pike took observations and toured the north side of Sandy Lake. On January 16th, he mapped, or as he described it, "Laid down Lake De Sable" in his notebook.

56. Ibid., vol. 1, pp. 457-458, Map 1. Antoine Nau's map consists of four sheets, each measuring thirty-nine inches by thirty-two inches.

57. Ibid., vol. 1, p. 459, Map 2.

58. Ibid., vol. 1, p. 452.

59. Joseph Nicollet's map was originally published in 1842, with a scale-down version printed in 1843 to accompany his official report. The Nicollet map was reprinted in 1965 from the original copper plate by the Minnesota Historical Society.

60. Martha Coleman Bray (ed.), André Fertey (trans.)*The Journals of Joseph N. Nicollet: A Scientist on the Mississippi Headwaters With Notes on Indian Life* (St. Paul, 1970). See Bray for the published portion of Nicollet's journal and documents relating to his work on the Mississippi River and his travels up the St. Croix River to La Pointe on Lake Superior.

61. Ibid., p. 135.

62. Ibid., p. 26.

63. For Nicollet's maps and observations from La Pointe to Sandy Lake see Joseph N. Nicollet Papers, c. 1834-1843, Minnesota Historical Society, Microfilm M-30 (6 rolls). roll 1[formerly roll 4], frame 45; roll 3, frames 20, 25, 35, and 560. Nicollet's notes and observations indicate he spent five days at Sandy Lake.

64. For Nicollet's sketch of the Cloquet River see Minnesota Historical Society, Microfilm M-30, roll 1, frame 45; For Nicollet's opinion of Aitkin see Nicollet to Sibley, November 27th, 1837, Sibley Papers, Minnesota Historical Society, St. Paul.

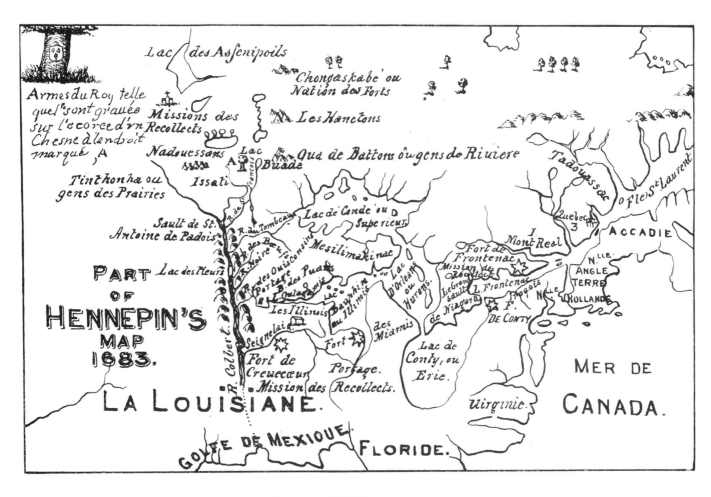

Part of Hennepin's map of 1683. Winchell, *Aborigines of Minnesota*

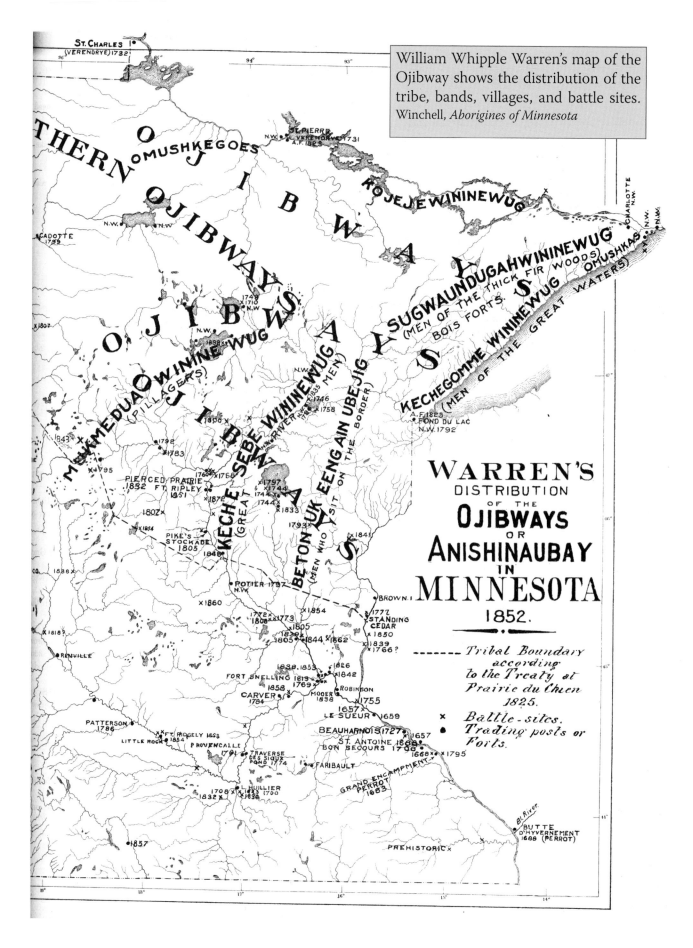

William Whipple Warren's map of the Ojibway shows the distribution of the tribe, bands, villages, and battle sites.
Winchell, *Aborigines of Minnesota*

WARREN'S
DISTRIBUTION
OF THE
OJIBWAYS
OR
ANISHINAUBAY
IN
MINNESOTA
1852.

------- *Tribal Boundary according to the Treaty at Prairie du Chien 1825.*

× *Battle-sites.*

● *Trading posts or Forts.*

Part II ⟶ The People of the Trail

Chapter 4 ✄ Westward Movement of the Ojibway

The people who used the Northwest Trail represented many groups including the Dakota and Ojibway tribes, European explorers, fur traders, government officials, missionaries, lumbermen, gold prospectors, iron miners, and an advance guard of settlers. Each has a tale to tell concerning their unique experiences on this historic route. The stories of the tribesmen, explorers, traders, and government officials, however, embody the earliest descriptions of the trail. One should also remember that the indigenous people, used it for the longest period of time and did not record their experiences.

Physical evidence identifies some of the prehistoric groups who may have used the trail, but it is only within relatively recent time that those early travelers can be identified. Most of the written documentation regarding the people who used the Northwest Trail and their origin only dates to the last half of the seventeenth century.

The Way West

Long before the Northwest Trail ever achieved fame as a fur trade route to the west, it was used by some people as a migration route, and by others as a war road. A number of major cultural groups existed in what is now Minnesota prior to the historical period (c.1650) and those groups undoubtedly followed the Northwest Trail. Of all the peoples, the Ojibway or Chippewa not only used the route, but also left oral accounts of their presence, which were later recorded. In the same way conflict brought about by the Ojibway migration is reflected in the origin of the tribal name.[1]

There are various explanations of the meaning of the name Ojibway. The Ojibway historian Warren states the name means "to roast till puckered up" after the tribal custom of wrapping captives in sheets of birch-bark and burning them alive. The torturing and ritual burning of captives was also attributed to neighboring tribes such as the Dakota. To the Ojibway, the Dakota were the *Naud-o-wa-se-wug*, or "our enemies." The term *Nâdowe* was also used synonymously with the French word *Iroquois*. Father Allouez referred to the Dakota as the "Iroquois of this country." The term *Naud-o-wa-se-wug* also accounts for the French name for the Dakota spelled variously *Nadouessiou* or *Nadouësioux*, from which the shortened version *Sioux* is derived. To the Ojibway, the Dakota were the *A-boin-ug*, or "the roasters," since they too were accustomed to burning captives alive. That the Ojibway took advantage of the highly combustible nature of birch-bark may represent their own peculiar variation on what was apparently a pervasive custom.[2] Stories such as these raise further questions as to the origin of the Ojibway.

Accounts of the origin of the Ojibway were passed down from generation to generation. In the nineteenth century many of these stories were systematically recorded by scholars intent on preserving the culture of what they believed to be a vanishing race. One notable example of those who were concerned, lest the story of these people be lost, was Henry Schoolcraft.

Schoolcraft's extensive writings represent a valuable compendium of knowledge about the Ojibway. His work benefitted from the talents of his brilliant wife, Jane Johnston Schoolcraft, whose ties by blood to the Lake Superior Chippewa certainly must have opened doors otherwise closed to the curious.[3]

Henry Rowe Schoolcraft
Minnesota Historical Society

Sketch of Jane Johnston
Schoolcraft
From J.V. Brower, *The Mississippi River and Its Source,* 1893

In addition to Schoolcraft, William Whipple Warren, who was himself part Ojibway, also collected many of the traditional accounts and wove them into his interesting *History of the Ojibway People.* Warren blended the traditional accounts of the Ojibway with the historic record of his day to set forth an account of the Ojibway migration from the Atlantic seaboard to the interior of Minnesota.

The Ojibway were—to use Warren's words—the "principal branches of the Algic [Algonquin] stock," and originated near the mouth of the St. Lawrence River. Warren includes in his story of the migration of the Ojibway, an allegory which explains how the tribe was led by a *Megis* (a type of sea shell used in wampum) through a succession of places beginning at the mouth of the St. Lawrence, to Lake Huron, to the outlet of Lake Superior at a place the French later called *Sault Sainte Marie*, to La Pointe, and, finally, to Minnesota via the north and south shores of Lake Superior.[4]

The westward migration of the Ojibway increasingly removed them from the scene of earlier conflicts to the shores of Lake Superior. Along the way, Warren related how they were attacked by the Five Nations of the Iroquois Confederation from their seat of power in the present state of

William Whipple Warren,
Ojibway historian, interpreter,
and legislator
Photo by Pepper, Minnesota Historical
Society

New York. The Iroquois, possessing the deadly firearms of the Dutch and English with whom they traded, waged a war of extermination against the Ojibway and others who either threatened their position as middlemen in the Great Lakes fur trade or who dared to trade directly with the French.

The clash between the Ojibway and the Iroquois occurred near early French settlements situated along the St. Lawrence Valley, where the Ojibway had come to trade. The Ojibway and the French eventually formed an alliance, since the Iroquois were opposed to either group developing direct trade with the western tribes.[5]

Unlike many of the other tribes opposed to the Iroquois, the Ojibway lived in semi-permanent settlements. Because of their seasonal movements, the Ojibway were comparatively less subject to an assault. Those who did live in permanent settlements, such as the fortified Huron villages known collectively as "Huronia," were eventually subjected to a massive Iroquois assault in 1649. The attack resulted in the destruction of the villages and the dispersion of the Hurons and others toward Lake Superior.

As the Ojibway moved west, they increasingly took on the role of middlemen in the fur trade between the western tribes and the French, thereby inviting the wrath of the Iroquois. Simultaneously, the Ojibway drew the Iroquois farther west into unfamiliar ground. As the supply of prime furs available to the Iroquois steadily declined, they were prompted to launch progressively deeper probes into the country west of Lake Ontario. Meanwhile, the Ojibway's growing commercial ties with the French meant they too had access to the murderous trade muskets, knives, and hatchets which they obtained in exchange for prime western furs. Finally, with the aid of French weapons, the Ojibway struck their enemies. In 1653, the Ojibway annihilated an Iroquois war party camped on a peninsula in Lake Superior west of Sault Sainte Marie (present-day Iroquois Point). In the later part of the seventeenth century the Ojibway increased their attacks on the Iroquois driving them from the land north of Lake Ontario.[6]

In spite of their heavy involvement with the fur trade, the Ojibway retained their unique cultural features to a far greater degree than any other Indian tribe. Scholars have credited this retention of a tribal identity to the flexible social system of the Ojibway, which was well suited to hunting and gathering. Their adaptability can readily be seen in the various social units employed at different times of the year.

Small social units, comprising the nuclear family, were characteristic of the band during the winter hunting season. Each family moved to a designated spot on the tribal hunting grounds. Although the seasonal dispersal by tribal members for hunting reduced pressure on the supply of available game throughout the hunting lands, it also meant the small Ojibway hunting parties were more vulnerable to either an attack by their enemies or starvation, an ever-present threat.

In early spring, several of the Ojibway family units would combine for the spring hunt, which generally occupied three or four weeks before the annual sugar gathering. Sugar making was followed by a general movement of the entire band to a favorite area lake for the summer fishing and berry picking. Here the band practiced a rudimentary type of agriculture to supplement the fruits of nature's bounty. In late summer the Ojibway harvested wild oats or rice, which was a staple of their diet, before dispersing once again to their winter hunting grounds.

Ojibway harvesting wild rice.
Photo by W.W. Latta, from the collection of Tom Amble

In addition to the simple yet adaptable social units, the political organization of the tribe also helped to retain tribal identity. There were clan and band chiefs, but no overall political leader for the whole tribe. Instead, tribal unity was based on a common language, kinship, and membership in clans.[7]

Another factor which enabled the Ojibway to adapt to the fur trade was that the Ojibway were more proficient fur hunters than many other tribes. They were encouraged by their traders to move into areas where other tribes had supposedly depleted the fur resource. For example, the Ojibway entered the Cree lands northwest of Lake Superior to glean furs the Cree did not take during their hunts. Interestingly enough, it has been established that the Cree actually obtained the bulk of their furs from barter and not trapping; hence their land yielded more furs to experienced Ojibway trappers than one would normally expect. The intensive trapping on the part of the Ojibway did not precipitate conflict with the Cree, since both tribes were highly specialized and did not effectively compete for the same resource in the same way.[8]

Lastly, the Ojibway tribal unity survived because they tended to live in remote forested areas on land not ordinarily suitable for agriculture. Even in more recent time, the Ojibway lands were not easily accessible, thus less liable to encroachment. Inaccessibility, coupled with the short growing season which limited the choice of crops, and the thin soil, all combined to discourage prospective farmers.[9]

The Ojibway summer settlement at a location known to the French as *Sault de Sainte Marie,* or the "Rapids of St. Mary," represented their largest historical assemblage, and from there they eventually spread toward the west. Sault Sainte Marie offered the Ojibway security and a food supply. The name given to the tribe by the French, that of *Saulteaux* or *Saulteurs,* meant "people of the *Sault,*" or "people of the rapids." The Dakota called the Ojibway *Ra-ra-to-oans* also meaning "people of the rapids." These of course were the more polite names the tribes gave to each other.

To the Ojibway at the Sault de Sainte Marie, the wealth of food, especially fresh fish available from the rapids of the St. Mary's River, meant the location was an ideal summer village site. The attributes at the Sault, however, did not prevent some members of the tribe from seeking further fortune to the west. One group, comprised of the Reindeer, Lynx, and Pike clans, moved northwest from the Sault de Sainte Marie along the shore of Lake Superior as far as the Pigeon River. They encountered other

Ojibway at Sault Sainte Marie.
Library of Congress, c. 1905

tribes as they pushed westward including a group known as the *Kinistinog*. The French called them the *Gens de Terre* or the "Men of the Land." We know them today as the Cree.

A larger group of the Ojibway moved west from the Sault along the south shore. They met and sometimes clashed with the local inhabitants. The people they encountered along the way, chiefly the *Outagami* (also known as the *Renard* or Fox Indians) and the Dakota, alternately traded and fought with the Ojibway. Eventually the Ojibway established a major village at *Jagawomikong* (Chequamegon Bay).[10]

Keeping their commercial and political ties with the French, the Ojibway strengthened their position as middlemen of the western fur trade by the time they reached Chequamegon Bay. They became part of a group known to the French as the "Upper Nation," or the "Far Indians," based on their remote geographic location.[11]

As noted earlier, of all the western tribes, the Ojibway proved to be the most adaptable culturally to the requirements of the fur trade as it evolved on the Great Lakes. That adaptability was tested when the Ojibway were compelled to move west in order to remain in the vanguard of the fur trade. The economic motivation provided by the fur trade and the continual need to obtain food helps explain their constant move westward.

At first the Ojibway waged war chiefly with the Iroquois Confederation. As further migration brought the tribe to the shores of Lake Superior, the focus of their sporadic warfare was directed toward the Dakota and Fox tribes. If Chequamegon Bay represented the westernmost Ojibway settlement along the southern beaches of Lake Superior, it did not remain so for long. Father Allouez related that the inhabitants of the village at Chequamegon were forced to retreat to Sault Sainte Marie in the 1660s. Dakota raids from the St. Croix and St. Louis rivers were intended to halt further Ojibway migration westward. The character of the Dakota raids was at first desultory, but soon changed into a determined campaign.[12]

By the time of the visit of Intendant Jean Talon's emissary, Simon François Daumant, Sieur de St. Lusson, to Sault Sainte Marie on June 14th, 1671, the Ojibway counted that location as their permanent home. They eventually returned to Chequamegon Bay after Du Lhut secured a peace between the Dakota and Assiniboine at the grand council, held near the mouth of the St. Louis River in the fall of 1679. The peace agreement he negotiated was fragile, but it lasted after Du Lhut left the country. From about 1680 to 1736, the Ojibway and Dakota maintained a mutually beneficial trading relationship in the region which included the Northwest Trail.[13]

Sometime after Du Lhut's visit, the Ojibway not only returned to the shores of Chequamegon Bay, but also continued to move slowly westward. William Warren credits Wa-me-gis-ug-o, a member of the Marten clan, with being the first to settle permanently near the mouth of the St. Louis River, most likely on Big (modern Clough) Island or Spirit Island, a short distance upstream from the mouth of the St. Louis. The Ojibway settled on islands in the St. Louis River for protection if any hostile war parties discovered them. Here, in the shelter of the islands and surrounded on all sides by water, the Ojibway had the advantage of not only seeing the approach of any potential enemies, but also having access to critical resources including an excellent fishery.[14]

The paucity of information regarding the people who settled about the entrance to the St. Louis River, suggests that the northern shore of the lake was nearly uninhabited. Du Lhut's account of his journey along the northern shore of Lake Superior does not mention any habitations of note, nor did Father Allouez mark any village sites west or north of *Mission du St. Esprit* on his map. Maps of the 1670s and 1680s show mostly Dakota names for physical features located west of Fond du Lac. A contemporary map drawn by Father Marquette also contained a warning in the margin about the Dakota living west of the mouth of the St. Louis River. It read, "They [the Dakota] comprise 15 villages and are very belligerent and the terror of their enemies."[15]

The first Ojibway village was a strategically significant site since it dominated the eastern end of the Northwest Trail. In the era of waterborne commerce, whoever controlled the narrow places along the waterways and connecting land routes controlled the entire region. The Ojibway village occupied a narrow place in the river, and it effectively blocked the route as either an avenue of commerce or as a war road for the Dakota. Up to 1736, the Dakota and Ojibway had an understanding which allowed the Ojibway to hunt game on Dakota hunting grounds west of Lake Superior in return for conveying the furs harvested by the Dakota to the French.[16]

In 1736, the mutually beneficial trading and hunting relationship between the Dakota and the Ojibway ended. Several causes for the end of the agreement include the expansion of French trade to the northwest, Ojibway trade with the Cree and Assiniboine who were at war with the Dakota, and the resentment by the Dakota of the trading advantages possessed by the Ojibway. The Ojibway response to the sudden enmity displayed by the Dakota was to seek further expansion to the west and an accommodation with the Cree and Assiniboine tribes. Although Warren mentions Dakota efforts to dislodge the Ojibway from their village in the St. Louis estuary with war parties, they were not effective. The next logical move in the Ojibway migration pattern was west to Sandy Lake.

The Contest for Sandy Lake

Among the traditional accounts of the Ojibway regarding the move to Sandy Lake is a story about the chance discovery of a Dakota village on Northeast Bay of Sandy Lake by a man and woman from Fond du Lac. The man's presence was detected by the Dakota who overtook and killed him as he fled back toward his village. The woman, being warned by her fleeing husband, escaped to her village and told what had happened. Her testimony may have triggered a retaliatory raid. Whatever explanation existed for the outbreak of intertribal warfare, what happened next shows that by the 1730s, Ojibway expansion followed the fur trade. By then, the Ojibway's movements were inextricably tied to growing French development along the chain of lakes to the north and on the Mississippi far to the south.[17]

An earlier discussion of French efforts to map the region west of Lake Superior mentioned a renewed interest after 1713 in opening routes to the northwest to interdict the trade in furs flowing toward the English posts on Hudson Bay. The French plan opened not only the way to the Hudson Bay trade, but also the route to the west, thus bypassing the Dakota, who dominated trade with many western tribes. While new plans were underway in the Northwest, far to the south the French established Fort Beauharnois and the mission of Saint Michael the Archangel in the heart of Dakota territory in 1727.

Located on the Mississippi near the present town of Frontenac, Minnesota, Fort Beauharnois was intended to be both a trading post and a mission for the Dakota. It was a significant post because it allowed the French to trade with the Dakota and monitor their activities south of the established routes along both the Northwest Trail and the border lakes, but the French plan proved unsuccessful and the fort was later abandoned in 1737.[18]

The most ambitious project undertaken by the French, however, lay to the north. During the 1730s, a chain of trading posts was established by Pierre Gaultier de Varennes, Sieur de la Vérendrye, his three sons, and his nephew Christophe DuFrost, Sieur de la Jémeraye. The posts extended west from Grand Portage along the lakes forming Minnesota's present boundary with Canada and eventually stretched as far west as the headwaters of the Saskatchewan River, known to the French as *La Fleuve de l'Ouest*, or "the River of the West."[19]

The trading area where La Vérendrye and his sons operated was known as La Mer de l'Ouest, since it was believed that a route existed from the headwaters of the Saskatchewan to the "Western Sea" and the "South Sea," or Pacific Ocean, as mentioned earlier in Chapter 2. The main French objective was to interdict trade between the Hudson's Bay Company and the western tribes. La Vérendrye was successful at opening trade routes and establishing a string of trading posts in the west, however, the loss of his eldest son and twenty companions compromised that success.

The Dakota were aware of the progress of the French in the northwest and resented the effort to bypass them and trade directly with tribes farther west. The practical result of French operations in the northwest meant the eventual destruction of the Dakota trade monopoly with the western tribes. Some tribes, such as the Cree and Assiniboine, were sworn enemies of the Dakota and welcomed the French trade goods and weapons. The extension of the Lake Superior Ojibway into the Dakota's northern hunting grounds, the attacks against Dakota villages as related by Warren, and the trading alliances the French concluded with the Ojibway band residing near Grand Portage, strained relations with the Dakota.

After suffering a series of reverses, the Dakota finally showed their displeasure with the French. In June of 1736, a party of nineteen French voyageurs, a Jesuit priest, Father Jean-Pierre Aulneau de la Touche, and La Vérendrye's eldest son, Jean-Baptiste Gaultier, were surprised by a war party and murdered on what is now known as Massacre Island in Lake of the Woods, not far from the French base at Fort St. Charles. The headless bodies of the unfortunates were brought to Fort St. Charles by their comrades and buried inside the fort walls.[20]

The attack at Lake of the Woods convinced the French of the need to redouble peace efforts on the frontier if trade and exploration were to continue. As long as the tribes continued to clash, trading parties could expect to be attacked without warning, disrupting contact with the far western posts. La Vérendrye's Indian allies urged him to strike back at the Dakota, but he realized his plan to expand into La Mer de l'Ouest was in jeopardy as long as the Dakota remained hostile.

While the official French policy of keeping peace on the frontier prevented La Vérendrye from attacking the Dakota, the Ojibway had no such reservations. Efforts to bring the warring parties together resulted in temporary lulls in fighting, but a true and lasting peace was never attained. The murder of the twenty-one Frenchmen at Massacre Island was merely one episode in a larger war being waged in northern Minnesota between the Dakota and Ojibway. The future of the fur trade in much of Minnesota and the Northwest rested on the outcome of that conflict. One key to dominating the trade lay in the control of the west end of the Northwest Trail at Sandy Lake.[21]

The traditional story of the Ojibway occupation of Sandy Lake as told by William Warren recounts a series of attacks at Sandy Lake and Mille Lac by the Ojibway, beginning about 1736, that eventually drove the Dakota out of their northern Minnesota villages. Warren's account is supplemented by a local story, previously mentioned, about the discovery of the Dakota village on the shores of Northeast Bay at Sandy Lake and the fate of the man who found it. The story offers an interesting insight to Warren's more detailed account of the occupation of the Dakota village at Sandy Lake. The main question remains, what was the key element in the decision of the Ojibway to go to war? Warren cites an important figure in the story of the Ojibway occupation of Sandy Lake—noted war chief Bi-aus-wah II.

Bi-aus-wah II had waged his first war against the Fox tribe who had killed his father, Bi-aus-wah I. He had witnessed the event when he was still a child, and he apparently brooded for years over the tragedy. Eventually, Bi-aus-wah II decided to summon members of the different tribal clans around Lake Superior to join him in a campaign against the Dakota. The decision to wage a war against them came when Bi-aus-wah II was middle-aged and after he had established himself at Fond du Lac. Warren states Bi-aus-wah's motive was revenge—whether for the death of his father, for the man killed after discovering the Dakota camp at Sandy Lake, or the murder of an Ojibway family is not clear. According to Warren, Bi-aus-wah II summoned men from as far away as Sault Sainte Marie, Grand Portage, and La Pointe to join his war party. Warren states the force was so large that if it passed in a single file, neither the head nor the tail of the column would be visible. Such a large war party was consistent with the recurring theme in Warren's narrative, namely the Ojibway war of conquest.[22]

From a strategic standpoint, however, Bi-aus-wah II must have realized that control of Sandy Lake and the western end of the Northwest Trail would give the Ojibway a major crossroads in the interior of Minnesota for further trade and expansion. Although Ojibway occupation of Fond du Lac and Sandy Lake strengthened the position of Bi-aus-wah's tribe, it also had unintended consequences in the form of opening the way for French traders. Thus it seems, the war waged against the Dakota in Minnesota was calculated to secure an abundant food supply and to improve the fortunes of the Ojibway in the fur trade and less about conquest for its own sake.[23]

Several aspects of the traditional story of the climactic attack on the Dakota village in the 1730s at Sandy Lake raise some questions. Warren states the force that set out from Fond du Lac was large, well-led, unexpected, and well-armed compared to its adversary. He also emphasizes that the Ojibway counted among their armament numerous muskets and a large store of powder and ball, whereas the Dakota had few firearms and relied heavily on the bow and barbed arrow. Their armament indicates that perhaps the Ojibway had some assistance from the French. Officially however, the French policy was to maintain peace among the western tribes.[24]

The size of the Ojibway force in Warren's description raises the issue of logistics. The effort involved with arming and sustaining so large a group in the field for a prolonged amount of time represented an enormous challenge even for European armies of the period, let alone aboriginal forces unfamiliar with such massive forays. Furthermore, when indigenous people waged war, they would normally fight in small war parties and forage off the land. It is known that Warren wrote for a nineteenth century audience and used terms they could relate to, but the scale of the operation at Sandy Lake is certainly not typical of aboriginal warfare. The record is not clear how the invading host was managed, only that it existed.[25]

Records show there were several village sites on Sandy Lake. Warren indicates that during the Dakota occupation, a large village was located on the east side of the lake on the tip of a point opposite the mouth of the Prairie River. The village may have consisted of earthen lodges, for the Dakota were known to have used such shelters.

A map showing the sites of villages, trading posts, and various battles entitled "Warren's Distribution of the Ojibway or *Anishinaubay* in Minnesota in 1852," was reproduced in Newton H. Winchell's *Aborigines of Minnesota*. The sites of battles fought at Sandy Lake along with the dates 1746 and 1758 are prominently marked on the map.[26]

If the Dakota were expelled from Sandy Lake by the first battle c. 1737, then the other two battle dates given on Warren's map might represent attempts by the Dakota to retake their village. The year 1746 is cited by Warren as the date of a retaliatory raid on Sandy Lake. The second date on Warren's map (1758) might represent a skirmish near a site known locally as "Battle Island." There are two distinct versions of that particular encounter.[27]

Historians say very little about the details of the first battle of Sandy Lake in the 1730s. The Dakota undoubtedly were astonished at the size of the force arrayed against them and the defense of the village collapsed. In Warren's traditional account of the battle, the Ojibway's overwhelming numbers insured victory and, to use an expression of the time, "put out the fires of the Dakota." Confronted by a large enemy force, the Dakota wisely abandoned the village. With their victory, the Ojibway gained control of the Northwest Trail and the door to the interior was open. Interestingly enough, the Ojibway did not immediately occupy the lake. Instead, some years later people from Bi-aus-wah's village moved into the area, first settling on the islands in Sandy Lake for protection, as they had done at Fond du Lac. Later they established a village on present-day Ponderosa Point opposite the mouth of the Prairie River.[28]

Once secure at Sandy Lake, the Ojibway extended their campaign outward occupying or attacking nearby village sites. Dakota villages at Leech, Winnipeg (Lake Winnibigoshish), Upper Red Cedar (Cass Lake), Red Lake, Gull Lake, Crow Wing, and Mille Lacs were occupied by the Ojibway.

The Ojibway found the old haunts of the Dakota favorable for the establishment of their own villages. The area around Sandy Lake was especially suitable for the maintenance of a fairly large population because of the abundant maple groves for the production of sugar, lush wild rice beds, and a plentiful supply of fish—especially tullibee. Birch trees were also present in large numbers for the construction of durable articles such as canoes and wigwams. A two day journey down the Mississippi River by birch-bark canoe brought hunting parties to the edge of the buffalo range near the present town of Little Falls, Minnesota. There are references to buffalo hunts originating at Sandy Lake. These hunts however, occurred on the "contested ground," an area claimed and vigorously defended by both the Dakota and Ojibway tribes.[29]

Warren mentioned two attempts by the Dakota to regain their old village site at Sandy Lake. He dated the first retaliatory raid about 1746. A large party of Dakota set out from their last stronghold at Leech Lake in a three pronged assault on various Ojibway villages, including one at Sandy Lake. The group sent against Sandy Lake supposedly drifted down the Mississippi River and accidentally met an Ojibway party destined to attack the Dakota village at Leech Lake. The battle began with a clash of scouts from both sides and quickly turned into a general melee. After a fierce contest, both sides retired from the battlefield. A notable aspect of the fight was the discovery after the battle of a dead Dakota brave with both feet partly amputated. The strange sight inspired the name of the lake near the Mississippi River, where the battle occurred: *Keesh-ke-sid-aboin sagaigun*, often translated "Lake of the cut-foot Dakota," or "Cut foot Sioux Lake." This short but bloody fight was not the last time a war party was sent against Sandy Lake. [30]

Warren related a second story about the attack on the Sandy Lake Ojibway. He told how a Dakota war party approached from Leech Lake by way of the Mississippi River with the intent of attacking the village at Sandy Lake. This time the Dakota succeeded in capturing some local women who were picking berries some distance upstream from the lake. The delay caused by the capture of the women allowed the village residents sufficient time to prepare a credible defense. The Dakota were driven off, but the story did not end there.

The same Dakota war party was later attacked by a contingent of the Sandy Lake Ojibway at the junction of the Crow Wing and the Mississippi rivers. At the first shot, the Ojibway prisoners overturned the canoes and swam to safety. The Dakota quickly regrouped and fought the Ojibway until both parties broke off the engagement the next day.[31] To what extent the Ojibway appreciated their new-found control of the Northwest Trail is difficult to assess; but while they remained on the islands in Sandy Lake, they were virtually unassailable. The following accounts tell the story of an effort by the Dakota to dislodge them.

The Story of Battle Island

Warren's map of the Ojibway in Minnesota includes the site of a battle near Sandy Lake in 1758, which may account for a story concerning an island in the lake referred to as Battle Island. Two versions of the story exist regarding an assault by a Dakota war party on an Ojibway village, located near Battle Island. Warren's history indicates the Ojibway first lived on the islands in the lake as a means of defense against retaliatory Dakota raids, so that aspect, plus the time period of the two stories, appear consistent with the date on the map. Other details, however, are inconsistent.[32]

The story of Battle Island is worth reviewing since it is a classic example of how two oral accounts may vary about the same historical incident. The Battle Island story is based on two different local sources. Both accounts of the battle were written by authors who conducted extensive research on the early history of Sandy Lake.

The first person to write about the story of Battle Island was Professor Irving H. Hart, an archivist at Iowa State Teachers College. Hart was an experienced researcher who devoted thirty-two years of his life to collecting information on historic sites and events in the region. Several articles based on his study of Sandy Lake were published by the Minnesota Historical Society.

The second author to describe the events near Battle Island was a professional writer, Clifford Greer. Greer was hired to research and write the history of the Sandy Lake area as part of a Works Progress Administration assignment in 1940-1941.

1881 Map of the Mississippi and Sandy Lake by Captain Charles J. Allen, Sheet 7 of 15. The map shows Long Point, present-day Ponderosa Point and Indian Point. The figure 1211 represents the elevation of the lake. There is no "Battle Island" or "Moose Gut Island" shown on the map and apparently none existed prior to the completion of the Sandy Lake Dam in 1895. U.S. Army Corps of Engineers

In the course of his work, Greer amassed a considerable amount of material including documents, secondary source materials, and a number of interviews. Clifford Greer's work was later published in 1967 under the title *Twelve Poses West*.[32]

Both Hart and Greer based their respective accounts of the battle on stories recited by local Indian women. Hart used a first person interview with Mrs. George Curtis, also known as Beengwa, who lived in the Sandy Lake area all of her life and related the story as it was originally told to her. Hart's interview with Beengwa was later published in *Minnesota History* in 1928.[33]

Greer's story was based on a secondhand account attributed to an Indian woman of the Rice Lake band. Neither Greer nor Hart included details of the actual interviews. In Hart's case, only his published version of the story survives. As for Greer, his source was secondhand to begin with and he had no convenient way of checking the authenticity of the traditional story.[34]

In Hart's version, a battle took place in 1768, when a hostile Dakota war party was discovered in the vicinity of Sandy Lake. Hart does not explain how he dated the incident to 1768, which is ten years after the date listed on Warren's map for the Dakota raid originating at Leech Lake. According to Hart, two Ojibway men were "fire hunting" deer south of Sandy Lake. Somehow they sensed that the Dakota were watching them. Pretending not to be aware of their foes, they suddenly made a dash for safety. After narrowly escaping their enemies, who fired on them as they fled, the two hunters hurried back to their village on Sandy Lake in time to warn of an impending attack. Why the Dakota blundered by attacking the two men prematurely when they could have waited and surprised the entire village is not clear.

Greer's version of the story has no date. It begins with a lone scout discovering signs of a Dakota war party south of Sandy Lake. He quickly hurried to inform his village. In both versions, the people of the village apparently have some time to prepare their defense. Hart's version has the attackers arriving near the village close behind their discoverers. Greer, on the other hand, mentions that a war council was called after hearing of the approach of the Dakota. The council determined that the attack would not come until after dark, so noncombatants (old men, women and children) were evacuated from the village to the safety of a small nearby island known as Battle Island.

Aerial photo of Sandy Lake. Compare this photograph showing "Battle Island" and "Moose Gut Island" with the 1881 map. U.S. Department of Agriculture photo, 1939

The two accounts differ markedly when it comes to describing the exact location of the Ojibway encampment on Sandy Lake. Hart contended the village was located on present-day Moose Gut Island opposite Long Point, which stretches from the southwest a considerable distance into Sandy Lake. Furthermore, he did not mention an evacuation of the noncombatants. Greer's source placed the village on a peninsula, now known as Indian Point, which projects into the lake from a northerly direction. Greer also gave information on the preparations for defense and evacuation.

The climax of Greer's account comes during a night attack. Confident that momentarily they would surprise a sleeping encampment, the Dakota used the cover of darkness to wade out into the shallows separating the mainland from the peninsula where the Ojibway village was located. Their stealthy movements caused barely a ripple on the dark water of the lake. Their caution in such exposed circumstances was well-founded, lest they be discovered.[35]

The grotesquely painted warriors advanced. Suddenly, midway across the open water, the darkness that enveloped them was shattered by explosions and bright flashes of gun powder as jets of brilliant orange flame stabbed out at the shadowy figures. The Sandy Lake Ojibway, after holding their fire until their enemies had waded into deep water, delivered a crushing volley of musketry at close range killing all but two of the attackers. In such wilderness encounters there were only the living and the dead. The Ojibway, lying in ambush, rushed forward to finish with knife or hatchet the survivors of their first volley of lead shot. In what seems like a remarkable act of self-restraint, Greer mentions the capture of two survivors. After having their ears symbolically amputated so they would heed a warning, the survivors were told to return home and tell their people that the inhabitants of Sandy Lake "wished to be left alone."

Greer's narrative differs from the predictable end of those captured in battle. The usual fate of captives was first to be subjected to humiliating and excruciating torture before being "knocked in the head" by a hatchet—the favorite method of execution. Lastly, the hapless victim's body was dismembered and the parts scattered to show the utter contempt the victor had for his foe. In former times, Warren relates, the unfortunate captive would be wrapped tightly in sheets of birch-bark and burned alive.[36]

It is interesting to note that over time prisoners, formerly enslaved or killed by their captors, were spared and exchanged, or held for ransom. The pattern of taking prisoners for exchange or ransom became increasingly common in the East. In the Great Lakes region, however, the old ways of "ask no quarter, give no quarter" persisted.

Professor Hart's account of the fight is quite different from Greer's, for he has the battle occurring between modern Moose Gut Island and Ponderosa Point. Unfortunately, Moose Gut Island did not exist before the construction of the Sandy Lake Dam in 1895. Hart notes no ambush or Dakota attempt to cross to "the island." Furthermore, Battle Island is only mentioned at the end of the story.[37]

Concerning how the combatants fought, Hart's source has both sides standing in the water shooting at each other. That the participants suffered themselves to be so exposed to hostile fire differed from normal Indian tactics. Perhaps the great distance separating Moose Gut Island from Ponderosa Point and, the relative inaccuracy of projectiles fired at long range from the smoothbore trade muskets used by combatants on both sides account for the display of bravado. It is also possible the attackers used a time-honored technique of jumping and dodging from side to side to disturb the aim of their enemies. In any event, Hart's version of the fight ends with the general retirement of the attackers after suffering many casualties. He neglects to mention either the number of casualties resulting from the battle or the number of captives.

The story of the battle, as told by Greer and Hart, raises as many questions as it answers. The one-sided nature of the fight, the disparity in the number of hunters who first encounter the enemy, the location of the village, the different names given to the island, the unknown number of combatants, and the descriptions of how the two sides fought, are all significant for evaluating the authenticity of the stories.

The tactics used by both sides do not conform to the usual type of ritual warfare practiced by the various tribes. For example, fighting from an exposed position was decidedly unpopular, for the Indian never liked to risk casualties. Even when a war party greatly outnumbered a foe, the slightest hint that something might go wrong or that the enemy had the potential to inflict great casualties would be enough to cancel a raid or even a lone ambush.[38]

The objective of war to the Indian was to prove oneself on the battlefield. That done, one was free to leave at any time—a factor which caused military officers of the era to severely question the effectiveness of Indian auxiliaries in war. Sometimes the desire to revenge a fancied insult or obtain someone else's head in retaliation for the murder of a relative would tempt a lone warrior to take extreme chances, but that was the exception. The Indian was no fool and he rarely took unnecessary risks, even in the heat of battle.

These stories of the victory of the Sandy Lake Ojibway over their adversaries might be rooted in oral tradition, but no one thus far has shown physical evidence of a major battle fought on Moose Gut Island, Ponderosa Point, or on Indian Point. In fact, none of the places-names mentioned in the stories existed before the twentieth century. If people have found items relating to the battle, they certainly have not shared the information. Authentic objects from the battle site could shed some light on the matter. Also, it is possible the conflicts were really not major battles at all.[39]

So an aura of mystery hangs over the story of Battle Island. Perhaps in the future more information either in the form of archaeological evidence or documents will be uncovered. Meanwhile, if there ever was a battle on Moose Gut Island, Indian Point, or some other location it was a very small affair—a skirmish at best, involving relatively few participants. In fact, the relatively small scale of Indian warfare in general explains not only what probably happened at Sandy Lake but also why it took so long for the Ojibway to finally gain control of the region and the Northwest Trail from the Dakota.[40]

If anything, the examples of traditional accounts cited by William Warren and others indicate the Dakota apparently did not quickly forget their old villages in northern Minnesota. They mounted several retaliatory raids against the Ojibway, possibly with the design of regaining their former territory. The traditional stories that have been handed down tell us the inhabitants of Sandy Lake and other occupied villages were subjected to a series of raids, but the result was always the same. The Ojibway prevailed, most likely because of their superior numbers, concentrated population, and armament.[41]

The Ojibway occupation of Sandy Lake after the 1730s insured for a time their position as middlemen in the fur trade west of Lake Superior. Ironically, although the Ojibway were victorious in their struggle with the Dakota, they eventually reached their territorial limit as roughly defined by the vast prairie country west of the Red River Valley and the parkland farther to the northwest. The continued position of the Ojibway as middlemen in the fur trade also reached its limit. The Northwest Trail was open and the way was now clear for French traders to risk visiting the villages in northern Minnesota relatively free from the fear of attack by the Dakota.[42]

Of course the tribal struggles, which were brought on in part by competition for trade, never really ceased. Hostilities flared up repeatedly throughout the rest of the eighteenth century and on into the nineteenth century and only ended with the expulsion of many Dakota following what has been referred to as the "Sioux Outbreak" in 1862.

An Unseen Visitor

The Ojibway paid a price for being the middlemen in the Great Lakes fur trade. Along with the amazing variety of trade goods acquired through contact with other groups was also the myriad of problems associated with that contact, especially health concerns caused by communicable diseases. At times, the Northwest Trail was the route by which pestilence entered the country. Ever since the initial contact between indigenous people and Europeans, health problems began to appear in both camps. Neither group had total natural immunity for certain diseases; and, when conditions were right, periodic outbreaks of disease decimated whole areas. The worst problems appear to have resulted from the spread of smallpox, although other common communicable diseases such as measles were equally lethal but less publicized.[43]

The first century of contact between indigenous people and Europeans in the Great Lakes region was characterized by numerous epidemics. Sometimes these outbreaks were the result of contact in war. For example, a large number of Ojibway from Lake Superior, possibly as far west as La Pointe, volunteered to assist the French under General Montcalm in their campaigns following the outbreak of the French and Indian War (1755-1763).[44]

The historian Francis Parkman showed that although the Ojibway were successful in many of their battles against the British forces, such as occurred at Fort William Henry in 1757, their victory was won at great cost because of the presence of smallpox. Following the surrender of the fort, some of the survivors of the siege were attacked by the Ojibway and other Indian auxiliaries. The unfortunate survivors suffered the wrath of the victors, and apparently those who were too sick or unable to leave their beds were swiftly killed with the tomahawk. In the process, the assailants unwittingly infected themselves with a particularly virulent strain of smallpox.[45] The contingent of Ojibway from Lake Superior, like other Indian allies of the French, contracted smallpox which they carried back to their villages and subsequently spread over the country.

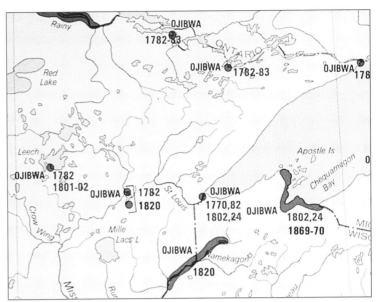

Epidemics along the Northwest Trail with locations and dates. No mention is made of the epidemics that struck Sandy Lake in 1850. Helen Tanner, *Atlas of Great Lakes Indian History*, courtesy of Newberry Library

There is no evidence the smallpox encountered at Fort William Henry extended as far west as the villages along the Northwest Trail, but an interesting traditional account of the origin of the name "Pillager" by the Ojibway historian Warren contains elements oddly similar to a plan proposed by Major-General Jeffrey Amherst for spreading smallpox among the Northwestern tribes opposed to the British during Pontiac's Conspiracy in 1763. General Amherst actually asked Colonel Henry Bouquet, "Could it not be contrived to send the Small-Pox among those disaffected tribes of Indians? We must on this occasion use every stratagem in our power to reduce them."[46] News of his scheme apparently circulated long afterward.

Warren defines the tribal name "Pillager" as being derived from the Ojibway *Muk-im-dua-win-in-e-wug*, or "Men who take by force," and therein lies the connection between the name and a plot to decimate the band because of hostile acts committed by them against a trader traveling on the Mississippi River.[47]

The traditional story related by Warren begins with the wholesale robbery of a sick trader from the lower reaches of the Mississippi by the Pillager band that occurred at Leech Lake in 1781. The trader later died from an unknown cause; and the band, in repentance for their boldness, sent a delegation to Mackinac Island with a large store of beaver skins to apparently "cover the dead." It appears from the story that the Pillagers were either following the custom of covering the grave of one wrongfully deceased with presents, or at the very least, paying belatedly for the articles they had taken from the trader. The British authorities at Mackinac Island received the Ojibway emissaries and the payment of beaver. Pardon was granted and presents given to the Pillagers on condition they not be opened until the delegation returned to their own country.[48]

Supposedly upon arriving at the Fond du Lac village, the delegation broke open the packages containing the presents and distributed them. Shortly thereafter, smallpox spread throughout the band, and it was said by some that the disease was sent to punish the Ojibway for what they had done. As the Pillagers traveled west along the Northwest Trail, they reportedly spread the disease to the inhabitants at Sandy Lake and other places along their march with disastrous results. On the surface the story sounds plausible, but there is another version.

William Warren claimed the story of the tainted trade goods was false. Instead, the chief of the Pillager band related to him another version which was apparently closer to the truth. The second story indicates the smallpox was actually brought into the country by Ojibway warriors and a contingent of Cree and Assiniboine, who formed a war party against the Gros Ventres. The war party contracted smallpox after attacking a village of their enemies on the Missouri River. Shortly thereafter, one by one, the attackers fell ill and died. They sought safety in dispersal. In an attempt to flee from the ravages of the smallpox, however, the warriors only hastened the spread of the disease.[49]

The second version of the story seems more truthful than the first. There is no mention of the commandant at Fort Mackinac, Lieutenant-Governor Patrick Sinclair, going to the trouble of infecting a band of Ojibway for action against a trader who apparently came up the Mississippi River from St. Louis, an area then controlled by the Spanish and Americans. Furthermore, the Ojibway were in league with the British against the Americans during the Revolutionary War, and it is highly unlikely the British would do anything to alienate their allies. In fact, a British led expedition against St. Louis in 1780, although unsuccessful, included a significant contingent of Ojibway. It is possible the Ojibway could have contracted the disease as a result of the 1780 expedition, but official reports did not mention the presence of smallpox at that time.

More recent research has disclosed the smallpox epidemic along the Northwest Trail was part of a larger pandemic that originated in Mexico in 1779 and swept north along the river systems as far as Alaska.[50] Thus, if a trader from the lower reaches of the Mississippi journeyed upstream, he could have very well been ill with the smallpox and infected the Pillager band without any help from infected trade goods from Mackinac.

From 1781 to 1783, the smallpox pandemic ravaged the frontier and disrupted the fur trade. Traders visiting Sandy Lake in 1781, remarked that everyone there was dead. Warren states there were only seven wigwams of survivors at Sandy Lake out of the once large native population that formerly resided there.[51]

Although disfigured for life by hideous pockmarks, those who somehow survived the smallpox were lucky. It is reported more men than women succumbed to smallpox because the women were supposedly better able to withstand the high fever caused by the contagion. The men, however, could not bear the high temperature and sought relief by immersing themselves in icy streams only to subject their already weakened constitutions to further shock and exposure, which proved fatal.[52]

An earlier unexplained outbreak of smallpox occurred at the Ojibway village of Fond du Lac in 1770, but the contagion was isolated there. There was no mention of smallpox being deliberately introduced into the local population then or any reason for such action. Contact through trade was sufficient to spread disease and it happened often along the Northwest Trail and elsewhere. After the smallpox pandemic of 1781, the disease reappeared in 1802 and 1824. In 1820, another common disease, measles, struck the village at Sandy Lake. Outbreaks of measles, dysentery, and scarlet fever also occurred at Sandy Lake during treaty payment in 1850.[53]

In 1832, local Ojibway at Fond du Lac and Sandy Lake were among many vaccinated against smallpox by Doctor Douglass Houghton as part of the itinerary of the expedition to the Mississippi headwaters led by United States Indian Agent Henry Schoolcraft. The vaccination program reduced the likelihood of fatalities from smallpox for those who received the shots, but there were other equally destructive diseases such as Asian cholera that menaced the frontier.[54]

While hostilities over hunting and trading were rekindled occasionally between the Dakota and Ojibway, the casualties from such skirmishes paled in relation to the fatalities caused by communicable diseases. Ironically, it seems that during periods of relative calm between the belligerents, these unseen dangers wrought the most destruction. Thus the Northwest Trail became not only a conduit for exploration, trade, and migration, but also the path for the scourge of the frontier. Diseases such as smallpox, like an enemy in ambush along a forest path, appeared quickly and without warning attacked their victims.

View of the pioneer cemetery located on the hill behind William Aitkin's trading post at Sandy Lake. The hill itself was a traditional burial ground. Photo by Larry Luukkonen

Chapter 4 - Westward Movement of the Ojibway
Notes

1.   George Irving Quimby, *Indian Life in the Upper Great Lakes, 11,000 B.C. to A.D. 1800* (Chicago, 1960), discusses the cultural eras prior to the historical period; Helen Hornbeck Tanner (ed.), *Atlas of Great Lakes Indian History* (Norman, 1987). Tanner's work is particularly useful in tracing the movement of the Ojibway in North America.

2.   William Whipple Warren, *History of the Ojibway People* (1885; reprint ed., St. Paul, 1984), pp. 106-107. Warren stated that the practice of torturing by fire was learned from the Fox Indians. Historian Francis Parkman relates similar accounts of the practice in *The Conspiracy of Pontiac* (10th ed.; New York, 1966), pp. 47-48. Other definitions of the tribal name exist ranging from the shape of moccasins to how meat was roasted on a spit.

3.   Philip P. Masson (ed.), *Schoolcraft's Expedition to Lake Itasca* (East Lansing, 1993), p. xv. Some of Schoolcraft's published works include: *Algic Researches, Historical and Statistical Information Respecting the History, Condition, and Prospects of the Indian Tribes of the United States, and Personal Memories of a Residence of Thirty Years with the Indian Tribes on the American Frontier.* In addition to its scholarly value, Schoolcraft's work provided the material for Henry Wadsworth Longfellow's *Hiawatha*.

4.   Warren, *History of the Ojibway*, pp. 76-81.

5.   Ibid., p. 124; The French policy of maintaining peace among the western Indian tribes is summarized in Francis Parkman, *A Half-Century of Conflict* (3rd printing, New York, 1966), pp. 194-195; Emma Helen Blair, *The Indian Tribes of the Upper Mississippi*, 2 vols. (Cleveland, 1911), vol. 1, pp. 231-234. The continuous conflict with the Iroquois at one point prompted Sieur Du Lhut to ask a fellow French officer, Nicolas Perrot, to encourage the western tribes to join with the French in an all-out war against the Iroquois.

6.   Louise Phelps Kellogg, *The French Régime in Wisconsin and the Northwest* (Madison, 1925), p. 103; and Warren, *History of the Ojibway*, p. 124, indicate the Iroquois never again made incursions into the Lake Superior region following their disastrous defeat at Iroquois Point in 1653. In fact, Tanner, *Atlas*, p. 4, states the Ojibway expanded eastward in the late seventeenth and early eighteenth centuries, and westward in the eighteenth and early nineteenth centuries. Alliances among tribes also changed. For example, a contingent of Iroquois joined with the Hurons and Ojibway in relieving the siege of Fort Ponchartrain (Fort Detroit) by the *Outagami* (also known as *O-dug-amee, Renard* or Fox) and *Mascoutin* Indians in 1712, during the *Outagami* (Fox) War as noted in the *Collections of the State Historical Society of Wisconsin*, vol. 16 (Madison, 1902), p. 284.

7.   See Quimby, *Indian Life*, pp. 122-127, for a description of Ojibway life including a list of clans (p. 126). The Ojibway social system continued in the area southwest of Hudson Bay as indicated in Arthur J. Ray, *Indians in the Fur trade: Their Role as Hunters, Trappers and Middlemen in the Lands Southwest of Hudson Bay, 1660-1870* (Toronto, 1974), p. 175. See Blair, *Indian Tribes*, vol. 2, pp. 259-260, for a discussion of the clan totems. She states the word "totem." is a corruption of *nind-otem* or *kitotem* meaning "my own family."

8.   Ibid., p. 104.

9.   Quimby, *Indian Life*, p. 126.

10.   Warren, *History of the Ojibway*, pp. 90-91 (see also chap. 1, n. 11 above.)

11.   For the identity of the "Far Indians" or "Upper Nation" see Parkman, *Half-Century*, p. 27; Harold Hickerson, "Ethnohistory of the Chippewa of Lake Superior," in *Chippewa Indians III* (New York, 1974), p. 18. The French used other generic terms such as *Sauvages*, for "men found in a wild state" or "wild men." The term was used in a general and not in a pejorative sense. Another generic term was "Ottawa," which was used synonymously with "trader" and applied to virtually all of the indigenous people in the Northwest.

12.   The trade with the Dakota is discussed in Blair, *Indian Tribes*, vol. 1 p. 277.

13.   Ibid., vol. 1, pp. 276-277, cites Claude Charles Le Roy, Bacqueville de la Potherie, who wrote a work about French Indian relations entitled *History of the Savage Peoples who are Allies of New France*, based on the writing of Nicolas Perrot, a French officer who was familiar with the western tribes. La Potherie's writings describe Sault Sainte Marie as the primary residence of the

Ojibway on Lake Superior in the 1690s. The Dakota were eventually forced to allow the Saulteurs (Ojibway) to hunt and trade farther west for it was only through them that they obtained French goods.

14. Harold Hickerson, "Ethnohistory of Mississippi Bands and Pillagers and Winnibigoshish Bands of Chippewa," in *Chippewa Indians II* (New York, 1974), pp. 43, and 66-67; and Warren, *History of the Ojibway*, chap. 8. Hickerson noted three stages of Ojibway occupancy west of Lake Superior. Before 1680, the Sioux (Dakota) lived on the rice lakes west of Lake Superior, but the Chippewa (Ojibway) competed with them for game. From 1680 to 1736, the Sioux continued to occupy the region but the Ojibway were allowed to hunt and trade with them. There were some brief ruptures in the peace in 1683 and 1720, but the alliance held. Finally, from 1736-1751, the region west of the lake was the scene of conflict as both sides competed for game.

15 Justin Winsor, *Narrative and Critical History of America*, 8 vols. (New York, 1967), vol. 4, p. 216.

16. Helen E. Knuth, "Economic and Historical Background of Northeastern Minnesota Lands: Chippewa Indians of Lake Superior," in *Chippewa Indians III* (New York, 1974), pp. 62-63, states the *Ouacé* or *Auwausee* band of Ojibway had settled near the mouth of the Kaministiquia River and another Ojibway band was located on the Vermilion River in 1737. There is some disagreement regarding the exact date the Ojibway occupied their village site at the entrance to the St. Louis River. Alexander Henry, The Elder, commented about a group of Ojibway at Fond du Lac in 1765 in Alexander Henry, *Travels & Adventures In Canada and the Indian Territories Between the Years 1760 and 1776*, ed. by James Bain (1809, reprint ed., Boston, 1901), p.188. Ojibway settlement followed a pattern of selecting islands or points as village sites because of their defensibility as well as proximity to sources of food and travel routes. On Ojibway fisheries, see Matti Kaups, "Ojibway Fisheries on St. Louis River, Minnesota: 1800-1835," *Journal of Cultural Geography*, vol. 5, no. 1 (Fall-Winter, 1984), pp. 61-83.

17. Hickerson, *Chippewa Indians III*, p. 27; Warren, *History of the Ojibway*, pp. 127-129 and 176-177; and, Clifford Greer, *Twelve Poses West* (McGregor, Minnesota, 1967), pp. 26-27. Cf. Greer with Hickerson and Schaefer. Hickerson describes the commandant of Fort Beauharnois, Jacques le Gardeur, Sieur de Saint Pierre, reporting the slaying of an Ojibway family near the head of Lake Superior in 1737. The attackers came from a village near the French post on Lake Pepin, and it was not long before a retaliatory raid was undertaken by the Ojibway against that Dakota village. See also Francis J. Schaefer, "Fort Beauharnois," in *Acta et Dicta*, vol. 2, no. 1 (July, 1909), p.108. In this more detailed version, Sieur de Saint-Pierre, learned that an Ojibway man, woman, and two children were killed and scalped near the western end of Lake Superior by thirty Dakota on about March 20th, 1737. The Ojibway organized a war party shortly thereafter to attack the Dakota village near the French fort. The murder of the French at Massacre Island took place on June 6th, 1737, several months after the murder of the Ojibway family.

18. Fort Beauharnois was established by Réné Boucher, Sieur de La Perrière, in September, 1727. The Mission of St. Michael the Archangel was founded by two Jesuit missionaries, Michael Guignas and Nicolas de Gonner. See William Watts Folwell, *A History of Minnesota*, 4 vols. (1921; reprint ed., St. Paul, 1956), vol. 1, pp. 45-47; Newton H. Winchell, *The Aborigines of Minnesota* (St. Paul, 1911), p. 530; and Schaefer, "Fort Beauharnois," pp. 94-133.

19. For information on the trading posts and explorations of Sieur de la Vérendrye and his sons see Lawrence J. Burpee, *Journals and Letters of Pierre Gaultier de Varennes de la Vérendrye and His Sons* (Toronto, 1927); and Martin Kavanagh, *La Vérendrye, His Life and Times* (Brandon, Manitoba, 1967).

20. Francis J. Schaefer, "Fort St. Charles, The Massacre in the Lake of the Woods, and the Discoveries Connected Therewith," *Acta et Dicta*, vol. 2, no. 1 (July,1909), pp. 114-133. All the French were decapitated. Curiously, the heads of La Vérendrye's son and Father Aulneau were never found. Schaefer suggests they were retained by the Dakota as war trophies. A more recent study of this gruesome practice is included in Victor G. Hopwood, *David Thompson: Travels in Western North America, 1784-1812* (Toronto, 1971), pp. 184 and 195. An enemy's scalp was a significant war trophy since it represented his soul. Whoever killed an enemy and scalped him could send his soul to be the slave of a lost relative in the other world. Decapitation was resorted to if there was no time to properly scalp an enemy.

21.   Hickerson, *Chippewa Indians II*, pp. 31-32. Of the two main northern "war roads" used by the Dakota, the first extended from the Mississippi to Red Lake, thence via the Red River and War Road River to Lake of the Woods. The second war road led up the St. Louis River, thence by portage to the Pike River and eventually intersected the chain of lakes along the northern Minnesota border. Ojibway occupation of Fond du Lac and Sandy Lake effectively cut both of these routes.

22.   Warren, *History of the Ojibway*, pp. 176-177 and 183; and Clifford Greer, *Twelve Poses West* (McGregor, Minn., 1967), pp. 26-27. Both accounts contain information regarding Biaswa II. Note the lengthy references to battles and warfare in Warren's index. The traditional account of the man and woman who stumbled upon a Dakota village at Sandy Lake has an oddly familiar ring when compared with the recorded events mentioned in Francis J. Schaefer, "Fort Beauharnois," p.108.

23.   Hickerson, *Chippewa Indians II*, pp. 69-70, and 246 highlights economic ties to the French and the problem of obtaining adequate subsistence. The Ojibway became increasingly dependent on access to big game–especially southwest of Sandy Lake in territory claimed by the Dakota. Hickerson believed the conflict that resulted was driven largely by competition for subsistence.

24.   Warren, *History of the Ojibway*, p. 126, and Winchell, *Aborigines*, p. 585, mention the growing prevalence of firearms among the Ojibway and their close relationship with the French. Hickerson, *Chippewa Indians II*, p.15, notes the advance of the Chippewa west of Lake Superior took place after 1736, with the help of French weapons and influence.

25.   See Francis Parkman, *The Conspiracy of Pontiac* (10th edition, New York, 1966), pp. 159-163, for a description of Indian warfare. For example, it was difficult for the Indians to conduct a siege of a fortified post. Parkman describes the sieges of Detroit during the Outagami War in 1712, and during Pontiac's Conspiracy in 1763-1764.

26.   Winchell, *Aborigines*, p. 583.

27.   Ibid., p. 582, lists the fall of Sandy Lake prior to the loss of the villages at Mille Lacs in 1744; Warren, *History of the Ojibway*, pp. 184-185, described the first attempt by the Dakota of Leech Lake to retake Sandy Lake but gave no date in his narrative.

28.   Ibid., pp. 177-178.

29.   Ibid., pp. 175-176; Mentor L. Williams (ed.), *Schoolcraft's Narrative Journal of Travels* (East Lansing, 1992), p. 152.

30.   Warren, *History of the Ojibway*, p. 184.

31.   Ibid., p. 222. Warren gave no specific date for the second attack at Sandy Lake, but the year 1768 has been inserted in his narrative to mark the second campaign by the Dakota to regain their lost village at Sandy Lake. Warren's map lists a battle in 1758. The selection of the year 1768 was made by Warren's publisher based on when the narrative was completed (1852).

32.   See Greer, *Twelve Poses*, p. 32 for the story of Battle Island.

33.   Irving H. [Harlow] Hart, "The Story of Beengwa, Daughter of a Chippewa Warrior," *Minnesota History*, vol. 9, no. 4 (December, 1928), pp. 324-326.

34.   No notes exist for Hart's interview, and the present location of Greer's manuscript and notes is unknown.

35.   A favorite aboriginal tactic involved ambushing an enemy force fording a stream or strung out along a line of march.

36.   Parkman, *Pontiac*, pp. 47-48; and Warren, *History of the Ojibway*, pp. 106-107.

37.   What Hart referred to as "Moose Gut Island" did not exist prior to the completion of the Sandy Lake Dam in 1895. The so-called "island" was formerly part of a long peninsula, known appropriately as Long Point or Big Point, which extended into the lake. A small island located northeast of Moose Gut Island was formerly known as Moose Island but is now referred to as Battle Island. None of these names appear on early maps of the lake.

38.   See Parkman, *Pontiac*, pp. 160-161, for his opinion of the Indian as a soldier. Parkman observed, "To twist a rope of sand would be as easy a task as to form a permanent and effective army of such materials."

39.   Archaeological investigation of Moose Gut Island (known officially as site AK 23) has not disclosed any physical evidence of a battle.

40. The indecisive nature of ritual warfare, and of the tactics of ambush or hit-and-run, is evident to anyone who studies the long series of frontier wars. The European method of waging war stressed the destruction of the enemy's forces and his capability to wage war. If the ponderous armies fielded by the English and French could not catch the nimble Indian war parties, they more than made up the difference by destroying villages, crops, and orchards. The prospect of facing a harsh northern winter without adequate food, clothing, or shelter soon convinced even the hardiest tribe that long-term conflict with a more powerful but clumsy adversary eventually meant destruction.

41. Several reasons why the Ojibway prevailed where other tribes failed are cited in Edmund Jefferson Danziger, Jr., *The Chippewas of Lake Superior* (Norman, 1979), p. 37.

42. Warren's map shows 1746 as the date of the Sioux (Dakota) attack on the Ojibway village at Sandy Lake. This date appears consistent with the movements of other tribes such as the Assiniboine and Cree as noted by Arthur J. Ray, *Indians in the Fur Trade* (Toronto, 1974), pp. 23. Ray states both the Assiniboine and Cree were initially drawn eastward toward Lake Superior in the period before 1670, and then rapidly reversed direction to the northwest following the establishment of trading posts on Hudson Bay. The Ojibway merely filled the vacuum created by the withdrawal of these two tribes, but historians do not agree exactly when the first French traders or explorers were able to use the Northwest Trail. For a differing view see Tanner, *Atlas*, p. 97, who notes the spread of Ojibway villages north and west of Lake Superior after 1768, was tied to the rapid expansion of the British fur trade.

43. Ibid., pp. 169-174. Tanner has listed epidemics in the aboriginal population from 1630-1880, but refers to the period from 1633-1733, as "the century of pestilence."

44. Ibid., p. 46, Tanner mentions Charles Michel de Mouet Langlade, a trader of French-Ottawa ancestry, who led the Great Lakes tribes against Fort William Henry during the French and Indian War. After the battle, the Indians encountered a smallpox epidemic. Tanner estimates approximately two thousand contracted the smallpox from the English garrison. The resulting epidemic spread from southern Labrador to the Great Lakes.

45. Louise Phelps Kellogg, *The French Régime in Wisconsin and the Northwest* (Madison, 1925), p. 432. The smallpox was rife among the garrison and the Indians quickly became infected with the disease which followed them back to Mackinac and Lake Superior. See also Francis Parkman, *The Seven Years War*, ed. by John H. McCallum (3rd printing, New York, 1968), p.159.

46. See Parkman, *Pontiac*, pp. 297 and 344, for plans to weaken the Indians. During the initial phase of Pontiac's Conspiracy, British General Jeffrey Amherst pondered the idea of deliberately spreading smallpox among the hostile Indian population. Amherst's letter on the subject can be found in the collections of the British Museum, Bouquet and Haldiman Papers, no. 21,634. Parkman, also quotes a letter to Amherst from Major Gladwyn, commandant at Detroit, who suggested weakening the native population "...by permitting a free sale of rum, which will destroy them more effectually than fire and sword." Tanner, *Atlas*, p. 49, claims Captain Simeon Ecuyer at Fort Pitt gave the Delaware blankets from the smallpox ward.

47. Warren, *History of the Ojibway*, pp. 257-260.

48. Reuben Gold Thwaites (ed.), "The French Régime in Wisconsin, 1743-1760," *Collections of the State Historical Society of Wisconsin* (Madison, 1902), vol. 16, p. 104, defines the expression "covering the dead."

49. Warren, *History of the Ojibway*, pp. 260-262.

50. Tanner, *Atlas*, p. 173.

51. Warren, *History of the Ojibway*, p. 262; Hickerson, *Chippewa Indians III*, p. 47.

52. Richard Glover (ed.), *David Thompson's Narrative, 1784-1812* (Toronto, 1962), p. 236; Ray, *Indians*, pp. 105-106, quotes Thompson and points out that those afflicted with the disease were abandoned by their comrades thus assuring their demise. Ray mentions those suffering from the disease had a "fatalistic outlook" and were resigned to their death.

53. See Tanner, *Atlas*, p. 170 for a map showing the extent of the various epidemics. The smallpox epidemic at Fond du Lac in 1770, is cited on page 173.

54. For Dr. Douglass Houghton's report on the vaccination of northern Indians in 1832, see Philip P. Mason (ed.), *Schoolcraft's Expedition to Lake Itasca* (East Lansing, 1993), pp. 299-304.

COUREUR DU BOIS

AFTER FREDERIC REMINGTON

"They Passed This Way"

EAH

Sketch of a coureur de bois by Evan A. Hart
after Frederic Remington. Author's collection

Chapter 5 ❧ The Pathway of the Voyageur

General references to the presence of French voyageurs and traders, operating along the Northwest Trail, are not unusual. However, references to specific traders using the route during the French regime in Canada are sparse. Early historical accounts sometimes vaguely refer to "the French" without really clarifying that the people simply spoke French or were indeed subjects of the King of France.

Like the Ojibway, who followed an east to west route, the early French explorers and traders also sought a direct route to the west. They searched from Lake Michigan via Green Bay and the Fox-Wisconsin rivers to the Mississippi, and due west, either by way of the Northwest Trail or along the Boundary Waters from Lake Superior. It became apparent the east to west route through Lake Superior was more direct, shortening what was already a long trip from the bases of French power at Montreal and Quebec. Who were these people in the vanguard of exploration and trade?

French Traders in the La Pointe Dependency

Whether he worked for an outlaw or unlicensed *coureur de bois* operating at large in the West or a licensed French trader, it was the voyageur who mastered the intricacies of the network of waterways connecting east to west. These men became indispensable guides to all future travelers or officials regardless of nationality. Knowledge of the country west of Lake Superior, however, is largely traceable through the records of explorers and traders who penetrated that unknown land. Their written records reveal where they went and who they traded with.[1]

For example, traders operating under the French colonial system were required to obtain a royal license, which identified each individual trading in the West. The license system was later superseded by the practice of "farming" or leasing a western post, such as the fort at La Pointe, to the commandant of the post. He in turn recovered the expense of manning the post through a monopoly of the trade within the surrounding territory or "dependency." Gradually the leasing system became less associated with a territory and more with specific tribes. For example, the country occupied by the Ojibway, which included the south shore of Lake Superior and the Northwest Trail, was considered within the "La Pointe Dependency." It is possible to determine who might have been operating along the Northwest Trail at a given date by observing who "farmed" the post at La Pointe.[2]

Some documentary evidence, archaeological remains, and traditional accounts suggest that French subjects were indeed in the area known as the *Fond du Lac.* Such being the case, they undoubtedly used the Northwest Trail to travel to the Mississippi and other locations in search of furs.

The first recorded use of the Northwest Trail was discussed in Chapter 3 in connection with the journey to the Dakota undertaken by Daniel Greysolon, Sieur du Lhut in 1679. Du Lhut's choice of route has been questioned by some writers, but the Northwest Trail afforded him the quickest way to the nearest Dakota village (Sandy Lake) and by water to his historic rendezvous with the Dakota at their village, which the French called *Issati*. A glance at any map of the rivers of Minnesota shows the probable route of this famous explorer was up the St. Louis River, across the height of land on the Savanna Portage to Sandy Lake, down the Mississippi from the Sandy Lake River to the Muddy River (present Ripple River), thence up that stream and across a short portage to Mille Lacs. This typical all-water route was exactly what Du Lhut was looking for.[3]

Du Lhut accomplished a number of objectives during his travels in the west. He not only visited the Dakota, but also claimed their land for King Louis XIV. He was interested in the rivers flowing into Lake Superior. It is noteworthy that Du Lhut ultimately found a water connection to the west not on the St. Louis, but far to the north. Unfortunately, the hostility of the Dakota toward their northern neighbors, and the fact that both the St. Louis and Mississippi rivers were their main "war roads," discouraged Du Lhut from further exploration of these waterways. Although he was able to explore to the northwest of Lake Superior, a series of events interrupted Du Lhut's plans. The intermittent war between the French and the Iroquois compelled him to turn his attention to the defense of Canada and he never resumed his search.

Those who immediately followed Du Lhut all proceeded north up the Mississippi seeking the same elusive water route to the West. Even though explorers who approached from the south were unsuccessful in finding a route to the western sea, their efforts are worth reviewing since they presumably ventured at least as far as Sandy Lake, the site of the western terminus of the Northwest Trail. The first of these explorations occurred shortly after Du Lhut's visit.

A small expedition commissioned by Robert Cavalier, Sieur de la Salle, was sent to find the source of the Mississippi. While La Salle was certain the route to the South Sea or Pacific Ocean lay somewhere down the Mississippi and to the southwest, he was curious where the great river originated. In 1680, La Salle sent Michael Accault, sometimes referred to as Sieur Ako, the Récollet missionary Father Louis Hennepin, "four Frenchmen, two Savages," necessary supplies, and a stock of trade goods to find the source and report back to him.[4]

Two sources, both of which barely acknowledge the other, note the Accault expedition up the Mississippi River. Father Louis Hennepin published an account complete with map showing the scenes of his adventures along the Mississippi. Unfortunately, Hennepin's narrative hardly mentions Accault, with whom he could not get along, nor Du Lhut, who rescued him from the Dakota, who in turn had taken the good Father and some of his party prisoner.[5]

The second account of Accault's journey was supposedly written by La Salle's lieutenant, the Italian soldier and cousin of Du Lhut, Sieur Henri de Tonti (also spelled Tonty). Tonti of the iron hand, sometimes referred to as the Chevalier de Tonti or simply Henri de Tonti, was a skilled professional soldier who had lost his hand in war. To the Indians, Tonti's iron prosthesis was a curiosity, and they referred to him in French as the *Bras Coupé* (Cut Arm). His account of the discovery of the source of the Mississippi River, made by the leader of the expedition named Dacan (a variation on the name of Accault, or d'Accault), was reportedly published in 1679, one year earlier than the date given for the expedition described by Father Hennepin.[6]

Dacan's story reportedly described the location of the northernmost source of the Mississippi. It originated in a lake located at the headwaters of the Turtle River in substantially the same spot as later noted by another Italian adventurer, Giacomo Beltrami. Whether or not d'Accault, or Dacan, ever heard of the Northwest Trail or of Sandy Lake is not certain, but to ascend the Mississippi to its northern source would have taken him right past the lake and a major Dakota village. Following d'Accault's journey, Pierre Le Sueur recorded his visit to the headwaters.

Charles Pierre Le Sueur reportedly ascended the Mississippi River at least as far as Sandy Lake in 1690 before turning back. Le Sueur reportedly traveled one hundred leagues above St. Anthony Falls and was told he would have to travel yet another one hundred leagues through very dangerous and difficult country to reach the sources of the river. He remarked, "I say sources, because there are many of them, according to the report of the Savages." Again, some early writers suspect Le Sueur only reached as far north as Sandy Lake in pursuit of his goal, but no further mention was recorded of his journey and the whole adventure has been largely overlooked.[7]

Shortly after Le Sueur's trip up the Mississippi, other French traders found the great river to be a promising source of fur. As early as 1719, Paul de la Margue (or Malgue), Sieur Marin, became interested in establishing permanent posts on the upper reaches of the Mississippi with connection to Canada by way of the *Baye de Puants* or "Bay of the Stinkers," (modern Green Bay, Lake Michigan) and the portage between the Fox and Wisconsin rivers. He did not apparently know about the passage from Lake Superior to the Mississippi River at Sandy Lake. The exploits of Paul de la Margue and his son Joseph on the Mississippi not only show French activity on the river but suggest they may have reached as far north as Sandy Lake.[8]

A brief sketch of the activities of the de la Margues, father and son, and of the clash with one of the sons of Pierre Gaultier de Varennes, Sieur de la Vérendrye, will help to put the advantages of using the Northwest Trail in perspective. In 1729, Paul de la Margue was sent to the upper Mississippi to subdue the western tribes by Charles de la Boische, Marquis de Beauharnois, Governor-General of Canada. La Margue's mission involved the establishment of permanent posts to control the Dakota and insure a greater flow of furs from the region through Green Bay. The elder Marin was apparently successful for a time in keeping the peace and in maintaining a French presence in the region.

In 1749, Paul de la Margue's son, Joseph de la Margue, also known as Sieur

Marin or Marin *fils* (Marin, Junior), was placed in command of La Pointe, a position he held until 1750. Following the elder La Margue's death on October 29th,1753, Marin Junior was given command of his father's posts on the Mississippi.

Meanwhile, during Marin Junior's absence, command of the post at La Pointe was purchased by Louis-Joseph Gaultier, or as he was commonly known, "the Chevalier," the youngest son of Pierre Gaultier de Varennes, Sieur de la Vérendrye. The elder La Vérendrye died in 1749, and the western posts were placed under the command of Jacques le Gardeur, Sieur de Sainte-Pierre, thus leaving La Vérendrey's three surviving sons without any benefit from a string of trading posts they had constructed while searching for a route to the Sea of the West.

The usual story is that the sons of La Vérendrye sank into poverty and obscurity following their father's untimely death. The story, however, was given a new twist by the careful research of the late Professor Grace Lee Nute. Nute's investigation disclosed that far from becoming an impoverished colonial officer, the youngest son of La Vérendrye became enormously successful in the fur trade, especially along the Northwest Trail.

In 1752, Louis-Joseph Gaultier, Chevalier de la Vérendrye, commanded the post at La Pointe. The regular commandant, Pierre Hertel de Beaubassin, did not arrive to assume his duties until 1756. In his absence, the trading area or dependency of La Pointe was "farmed"(leased) to Louis-Joseph by the government for eight thousand *livres* (pounds). On February 18th, 1752, the Chevalier formed a three year partnership with Sieur de St. Luc de la Corne to trade in the La Pointe, or *Chagouamigon* (Chequamegon), dependency with the Chevalier's younger brother, François Gaultier Du Tremblay, serving as interpreter. The estimated return from this post amounted to two hundred and fifty packs of furs.[9]

Professor Nute found the Chevalier's name on a number of *engagements* or employment contracts signed during the 1750s by voyageurs together with information stating which posts and territories the men were to work in. One such contract was for a voyageur named Pierre St. Paul, "*dit.* (alias) Montauban," who became an *engagé* on May 18th, 1752, to Joseph écuyer Chevalier de la Vérendrye for Chagouamigon.[10]

A clash between Marin Junior and the Chevalier over the boundary of their respective trading areas was inevitable because of the limited knowledge of the extent of the country. As Marin Junior expanded his trading operation with the Dakota bands along the Mississippi, he came ever closer to Sandy Lake and the Northwest Trail.

According to Nute, Marin Junior had three major posts, all named for Canadian governors. They stretched along the Mississippi from the mouth of the Wisconsin River (Fort Vaudreuil) to the vicinity of Sturgeon Lake near the confluence of the Mississippi and St. Croix rivers (Fort La Jonquière), and at last to the confluence of the Crow Wing and Mississippi rivers (Fort Duquesne).[11]

In October of 1753, in obedience to earlier instructions from the Governor of New France, Pierre Jacques de Taffanel, Marquis de la Jonquière, Marin Junior sent his trading partner Paul Lacroix with two canoes and enough men to man them to find the source of the Mississippi and if possible "...any knowledge of the Sea of the West and the means of getting there." He also sent a man named Houl or Hout with three canoes to travel among the Dakota as far as the mouth of Crow Wing River and distribute a considerable number of presents in return for maintaining peace on the frontier.

On October 21st, 1753, about a day's journey north of Sandy Lake, Lacroix was stopped by the Chevalier, who informed him he was in the La Pointe Dependency, ordered him to turn back, and seized his goods. Shortly thereafter, the Chevalier and his men met Houl and his party. Likewise, he also ordered them to turn back and confiscated their trade goods. Furthermore, Houl was told not to stop at Fort Duquesne but instead to winter lower down river at Fort La Jonquière.[12]

Sieur Marin Junior was furious over the actions of the Chevalier de la Vérendrye and reported what had taken place to the governor-general, but to no avail. A new governor, the Marquis Duquesne de Menneville, had apparently given the Chevalier de la Vérendrye not only permission to trade in the Mississippi headwaters but also the authority to establish two small posts even though the Chevalier's new territory infringed on territory claimed by Sieur Marin. The dispute over the boundaries of the La Pointe and Green Bay dependencies was not resolved during the remaining years of the French regime in Canada.[13]

Chevalier de la Vérendrye continued to operate from La Pointe and repeatedly traveled west along the Northwest Trail in 1753-1754 to oversee trade. In 1756, he was appointed commandant of La Mer de l'Ouest for three years provided he pay an eight thousand livre gratification. The records of voyageur engagements preserved in Montreal continued to bear the name of the Chevalier de la Vérendrye up to 1759. In that year he was summoned, with Charles de Langlade and "twelve hundred Cree, Sioux, Sauk, Folles Avoines (Menominee), Chippewa, and Foxes," to assist in the defense of Canada. He reportedly gave his wife a power of attorney to manage his trading business while he was busy on active military duty.[14]

After the conclusion of the French and Indian War, the Chevalier intended to remain in Canada and pursue the fur trade, but he apparently had business to settle in France. On October 15th, 1761, he sailed from Quebec on the ship *Auguste*. A last reference to Louis-Joseph Gaultier, Chevalier de la Vérendrye, is included in the work of historian Francis Parkman:

> After the fall of Canada, the Chevalier de la Vérendrye, he whose eyes first beheld the snowy peaks of the Rocky Mountains, perished in the wreck of the ship *Auguste*, on the coast of Cape Breton [Island], in November, 1761.[15]

While it seems clear that the Chevalier de la Vérendrye and his men used the Northwest Trail to reach the Mississippi River at Sandy Lake, the question naturally arises: Did the Chevalier build trading posts on Sandy Lake or near the source of the Mississippi? Accounts indicate he actively traded in the area and he was authorized to build two small posts. Given his previous exploration and experience in the fur trade, the Chevalier de la Vérendrye might indeed have built two wintering cabins.

The presence of French traders along the Northwest Trail goes without saying. The engagements mentioned in regard to the La Pointe Dependency, the names of specific traders, and the accounts of men involved in the trade are convincing evidence. In addition to documentary evidence, physical remains of trade goods and traditional accounts of trader's establishments, point to a significant French presence.

French Trade Goods

Several historical artifacts recently found at Sandy Lake offer some compelling evidence of the presence of French traders in the area. Unearthed among scattered fur trade relics within what appeared to be the outlines of a building of some type was an eighteenth century French trade pistol. The chance discovery of the pistol within an early structure lends some credence to the presence of French traders in the region. To find a relic pistol in conjunction with a possible habitation site is significant, but the information that this single artifact disclosed is even more revealing. How old was the French trade pistol? How did it get to Sandy Lake?[16]

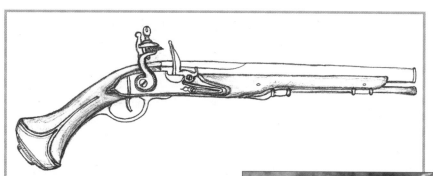

Sketch of a French trade pistol found at Sandy Lake and a photograph showing engraved panoply of arms on the pistol's brass sideplate.
Sketch and photo by Larry Luukkonen

The French trade pistol began its journey to North America in the first half of the eighteenth century. Tracing its journey requires an understanding of how the early French colonial system worked and where different types of goods were manufactured. For instance, the French colonies were under the jurisdiction of the Minister of Marine and Colonies. From the 1690s through the 1740s, arms for the French Navy and for the fur trade were purchased from manufacturers in the city of Tulle. This fact may explain the similarity between the design of weapons used by the French Navy and trade guns found on the frontier. The trade pistol closely resembles a French pistol, Model 1733.[17]

Given the circumstances, it is very likely the trade pistol was manufactured in Tulle. Furthermore, unique markings on the pistol indicate it was made for export sometime in the mid 1740s. Once completed, the pistol was shipped from Tulle to the port of Rochefort, located on the west coast of France near the Isle d'Oleron. From there, it was sent to Quebec and ultimately Montreal.

Once they arrived in North America, trade goods destined for posts in the interior were carefully repacked in portage pieces or bales. The goods were then transported by cargo canoe or bateau from Montreal to Lachine where they were temporarily stored awaiting shipment up the Ottawa River and by a series of portages to Georgian Bay on Lake Huron. From there, the trade pistol probably traveled to Michilimackinac, then to Sault Sainte Marie and most likely to the French fort at La Pointe, which supplied trade goods for the residents at Sandy Lake by way of the Northwest Trail.[18]

There are a number of other possible scenarios whereby the French trade pistol arrived at Sandy Lake. It could have been the personal weapon of a trader. It may have been purchased or given to an influential tribal leader. There is also the possibility that it may have been acquired in battle, stolen, or merely bartered. Whatever the origin of the Sandy Lake pistol, it is well-known that the French traded weapons and ammunition to the Ojibway, and they in turn resold some of these items to tribes farther west in their capacity as middlemen.

The discovery of the Sandy Lake pistol nonetheless provides much useful information about French trade guns in general. It also represents a trade item that had its origins in a specific French manufacturing center. The pistol was one of thousands of weapons traded on the frontier. Based on extensive research, the noted historian Doctor Carl P. Russell determined the French exported an estimated two hundred thousand weapons, including pistols, to trading posts in North America. Given more recent research, Doctor Russell's figure may be a very conservative estimate.[19]

The French pistol was just one type of firearm used at Sandy Lake during the long history of the fur trade. Many different types were traded judging from fragments found at fur trade sites. Unfortunately, no complete specimen of these other types of trade guns has been found at Sandy Lake.[20] In contrast, the French pistol is remarkably complete and constitutes a good example of one type of trade gun used in the region. Aside from its significance as undoubtedly the earliest item of proven European manufacture discovered thus far in the area, its association with what appears to be the remains of some form of habitation sheds new light on two stories about a trader's cabin or trading post in the vicinity of the western end of the Northwest Trail, where the pistol was originally found.

There is a persistent story about a trader's cabin located in conjunction with part of the Northwest Trail. First discussed in 1926 by Professor Irving H. Hart, various versions of the story of the trader's cabin have appeared in both published works and oral accounts. The obvious question arises: Was the cabin or the trading post built by the owner of the French trade pistol?[21]

Archaeological surveys of the Savanna Portage sought to identify the actual site of a reported trader's cabin within the present boundaries of Minnesota's Savanna Portage State Park. Thus far, the only promising evidence recovered consists of relatively few artifacts most likely dropped at posés along one of the presumed routes of the portage, but no conclusive evidence of a trader's cabin in the park has been reported.

The stories regarding the existence and location of the trader's cabin come from several sources. The first can be traced to a translation of an account of the trading adventure of Montreal trader Jean-Baptiste Perrault. Perrault's original narrative was written in French and subsequently translated into English in the 1830s by Henry Schoolcraft. Unfortunately, Schoolcraft mistakenly placed Perrault's 1784 wintering cabin on the west end of the Savanna Portage, instead of its proper location on the Prairie Portage.[22]

A more recent account of the trader's cabin is contained in *Twelve Poses West*, originally written in 1940 by Clifford Greer. Greer, who was mentioned earlier in connection with the Battle Island story, placed Perrault's cabin somewhere on the Prairie River. Exactly where is not mentioned.

In addition to the two stories of a trader's cabin on or near the Savanna Portage, information regarding an early trading post on Northeast Bay of Sandy Lake exists in the form of an oral account by a Sandy Lake Ojibway woman named Niby-na-gaunce. Her story of the trading post is also included in Clifford Greer's *Twelve Poses West*.

In the story, the trading post was located near the end of the overland extension of the Savanna Portage. The unidentified post was situated at the base of a prominent hill facing east across Northeast Bay toward what appears to have been a habitation where the French trade pistol was found.

Greer's statements concerning the unidentified post on Northeast Bay include a reference to certain fur trade artifacts that were unearthed at or near the site, however, the present location of these relics is not known. A detailed examination of the site and of the relics, if they can be located, may provide a connection between the French trade pistol and the alleged existence of the French trading post on Sandy Lake. Very likely one or more wintering houses or cabins might have been built on the lake during the French regime, but the subject requires further research.[23]

Suffice it to say evidence in the form of early written records, fur trade artifacts, and oral accounts of a trading establishment strongly suggest that traders routinely followed the Northwest Trail to Sandy Lake during the closing years of the French regime in Canada.

Professor Nute's findings indicate there was a small but steady number of French traders visiting the area from the 1750s through the 1760s. The trade conducted in the Great Lakes and west of Lake Superior by established traders, such as the Cadotte, Campion, and Trottier-Desrivières families, continued after the conquest of Canada with only a brief interruption. From 1763 to 1764, the general Indian revolt in the west, commonly identified with the Ottawa chief Pontiac, put a temporary stop to trade on the Great Lakes. Following this incident, the old line French traders were joined by new traders from the English colonies such as Peter Pond and Alexander Henry, the Elder.

Northwest by the South Side of Lake Superior

Any recitation of the history of the Northwest Trail and the development of the fur trade immediately after the conquest of Canada must of necessity include a trader named Alexander Henry, since he was known to have traded at Fond du Lac. Known as "the Elder," to distinguish him from his nephew, Alexander Henry "the Younger," he followed the British forces that invaded Canada under General Jeffrey Amherst. Henry, a New Jersey native, began his commercial career on the Great Lakes in 1761, with the backing of a leading French trader named Etienne Campion. Shortly thereafter, Henry was granted a monopoly to trade in Lake Superior by the commandant of Michilimackinac.[24]

In 1764, following the end of Pontiac's insurrection in the Great Lakes region, Henry began trading along the south shore of Lake Superior. Before departing for his trading adventure, he established a partnership with Jean Baptiste Cadotte of Sault Sainte Marie. Cadotte, a well-known trader whose family had lived at the Sault since 1671, was an excellent choice because of his connections with local Ojibway bands. Henry chose Chequamegon Bay as the destination for his trading adventure in Lake Superior. While stationed there during the winter of 1764-1765, he first heard of Fond du Lac, which was the gateway to the Northwest Trail and the vast wilderness west of Lake Superior.[25]

Henry's Chequamegon Bay adventure was so successful, he exhausted his credit and was forced to forgo the opportunity to acquire an additional thousand beaver skins. Other traders, seeing Henry's immense profit, protested to General Thomas Gage, the new Commander-in-Chief of British forces in Canada. Ultimately, the British government issued a proclamation ending the old French practice of granting territorial trade monopolies, after which, trade was open to all subjects provided they obtained a license.[26]

A list of trade licenses for 1767 mentions Henry and four traders he employed to actually conduct his affairs. One of the four traders, a man named Bartie (Barthe?) was sent with two canoes of trade goods to Fond du Lac. It is not known for certain if Bartie simply traded somewhere near the entrance to the St. Louis River or actually used the Northwest Trail to trade with Ojibway hunters at Sandy Lake and other points in the interior.[27]

From the time of Alexander Henry's first adventure to Fond du Lac, various independent Lake Superior traders sought to exploit the fur trade along the south shore of the great lake. Most of the traders operated independently and competed fiercely with one another, but cutthroat competition was injurious to the trade.

By the 1770s, the traders who operated in the same general geographic area began to combine in temporary partnerships for a single season.[28]

With the outbreak of the American Revolutionary War (1775-1783), fear of attack, in addition to ruinous competition, prompted the Great Lakes traders to eventually combine forces. In 1779 they formed what was referred to as the "General Company of Lake Superior and the South" or the "General Store." To further safeguard the route west, in 1778 a small guard of British troops from Michilimackinac temporarily occupied the Grand Portage post.

Following the end of the war, trade increased to the Northwest via Grand Portage while independent traders moved into the Fond du Lac area. The latter followed the south shore of the lake to the mouth of the St. Louis River, and from there proceeded along the Northwest Trail to Sandy Lake and the Mississippi. Known by their contemporaries as the "South Traders" because of the route they followed, these independent traders found the region highly profitable. Also, the river route provided a shortcut to trading areas in the west. Although some writers believe that the route to the west via the Northwest Trail was completely closed to trade until approximately 1792, it does not seem plausible given the accounts of traders who used the trail to the northwest long before the 1790s.[29]

South Traders such as Joseph Réaume, his cousin Alexander, John Baptiste Cadotte, Gabriel Atina Laviolette, John Hay, one named Cazelet (or Cazalai), Alexander Kay, and Jean Baptiste Perrault all used the Northwest Trail. They traded on the Mississippi headwaters or traversed the many lakes and streams which connected them by portage with tributaries of the Red River of the North and other trade routes west.[30]

Every year these men would meet at Mackinac and form a partnership. They pooled their trade goods for which each received proportional shares. Then, proceeding west along the south shore of Lake Superior and over the Northwest Trail, they held a general rendezvous at Sandy Lake. All final arrangements having been made, they dispersed in pairs to their respective trading areas. In the spring, once navigation commenced on inland lakes and streams, the traders rendezvoused again at Sandy Lake. Here they divided the furs they received in trade according to the contribution of goods made in the previous fall and dissolved the partnership. The recollections of these traders provide a detailed picture of what was involved in undertaking a typical fur trade enterprise, or as it was commonly referred to, "an adventure."

Certainly one of the most interesting and colorful of the South Traders to travel the Northwest Trail was the French Canadian fur trader Jean-Baptiste Perrault. He is perhaps best remembered as the author of one of the most detailed accounts of the fur trade in the country west of Lake Superior.[31] In fact, few accounts of the early fur trade contain so much information and thrilling adventure. It is worthwhile to follow the narrative of Perrault's first real adventure along the Northwest Trail as a "winterer" or one who spent a season in the wilderness trading.

Jean-Baptiste Perrault was born at Three Rivers, Quebec, on March 10th, 1761, to a well-known Canadian family. He received a good education for the time at the Collége de Québec beginning in 1774. He remained at the Collége until 1782-1783, when he began a career in the fur trade. It was a pursuit he followed with few interruptions for the next thirty-eight years.

Perrault's first experience in the fur trade was brief, lasting for a year (1783-1784), and involved working as a clerk at Cahokia (Illinois) for a trader named Marchesseaux, a friend of his father. His first real wilderness experience, however, began in the spring of 1784, at Mackinac Island where Perrault stopped while en route home following his work at Cahokia.[32]

Mackinac Island, or "Mackinac" as it was commonly referred to, replaced the settlement and trading center of Michilimackinac, located on the south shore of the Straits of Mackinac, in 1781. Seeing the shortcomings of the settlement and the old wooden fortifications that surrounded it, the new commandant of the post, Henry Sinclair, moved the entire community to the more defensible island.[33]

Mackinac Island with its trademark Mackinaw boat moored along the waterfront. Library of Congress

Mackinac Island was a focal point of the western Great Lakes fur trade, and it was there, in July of 1784, that Perrault agreed to accompany an old acquaintance, Alexander Kay, on a trading adventure into the country west of Lake Superior. Kay intended to follow the Northwest Trail to the Mississippi and trade at *Lac de la Sangsue* (literally "Lake of the Leech" or Leech Lake).[34]

Alexander Kay had worked for the British Indian Department as an interpreter during the Revolutionary War. During his service, he participated in the abortive British attempt to capture the Spanish frontier settlement of St. Louis (Missouri). Discharged from the Indian Department in 1782 as an economy measure, Kay sought to recoup his fortune in the fur trade.[35]

Whatever experience Alexander Kay had as a trader, it is evident from Perrault's account that the mission was risky from the outset. Perrault noted, "His (Kay's) intention Was to go in late in order to Avoid making Credits." By starting late in the season, Kay hoped to avoid having to advance supplies to Indian trappers on credit. The practice of "making credits" was a risky business, especially for one not used to the country or familiar with the reputation and reliability of the various trappers.

Instead, Kay intended to profit at the expense of other traders by waiting until the trappers had completed their seasonal hunt and then purchase any available pelts on a straight barter basis. To carry out his plan, Kay sent another trader William Harris ahead of the main party to purchase necessary food supplies for the winter. Harris was to wait for the rest of the party at Fond du Lac.

Perrault, Kay and his Indian wife, along with a crew of fourteen voyageurs, left Mackinac Island on August 29th, 1784, in two canoes loaded with trade goods. They had no guide and no one in the crew knew the route. Instead, they had to navigate carefully along the south shore of Lake Superior during the worst part of the year. Unfamiliar with the shoreline of Lake Superior, Perrault's party wasted valuable time. For example, they were forced to go around the Keweenaw Peninsula since they were unaware of the portage across that formidable obstacle:

> We were compelled to go around Kiweonanning [Keweenaw], where at that season the wind Blew continuously (this joined with a downpour of rain). It took us a considerable time to reach La Pointe. We reached there on the 1st of november all saint's day, about noon.[36]

Perrault noted everyone at La Pointe was drunk as it was a *fête* or "feast day," so Kay's party set out the next day "with a light wind at Our Backs." The "light wind" soon became a November gale and buffeted the canoes so fiercely they could not land.

By the time Kay and his crew reached the mouth of the St. Louis River, the men were nearly frozen and barely able to control the canoes as they approached the narrow passage at the entrance to the river. In the early morning gloom, the dark unbroken shoreline of towering pines was marked by foaming white combers that crashed against a desolate sandy beach littered with driftwood. Caught in opposing currents at the entrance to the bay, Kay, his men, and their baggage were all flung into the icy surf as the canoes capsized. Sodden and freezing in the face of the raging gale, the survivors staggered ashore, salvaged some belongings, and tried to warm themselves in the shelter of the woods:

> About two hours before day, being unable to enter the rivière du fond du Lac, we were compelled to cast ourselves on the Coast, where we were wrecked in the bay at the left of the river. Our Canoes were broken up; our goods thrown here and there along the beach, at least Ten *arpents* on either Shore. We were all soaked and chilled with cold. It was at that time I deplored my fate.[37]

Breakers along Lake Superior's shore.
Photo by Marlene Wisuri

The next day, still soaked to the skin, Perrault and the men repaired their two canoes and collected what remained of the baggage and trade goods. They proceeded into the relative shelter of St. Louis Bay and there met a resident trader named Dufaut, who worked for the North West Company. Dufaut welcomed the unfortunate travelers and offered them his hospitality, a custom invariably practiced on the frontier even among rival traders. Perrault observed that Alexander Kay, in spite of his party's obvious distress, treated Dufaut rudely, for which conduct Perrault admonished him severely.

Perrault advised the party to wait at Fond du Lac and go into the interior in the spring when the hunters had returned to their villages with their stock of furs. Alexander Kay, however, would have none of it and was determined to winter in the interior. Kay at one point became intoxicated and even threatened his men with a pistol if they did not do as he said. To make matters worse, Kay's party of seventeen was joined by the trader Harris and three men. The total stock of provisions consisted of part of a keg of salt pork for the men; and a sack of flour, a keg of butter, and a keg of sugar for Mr. Kay.

Alexander Kay resolved to take half of the men and Mr. Harris and winter in the interior on the Pine River (in present-day Crow Wing County, Minnesota). He would attempt to gather sufficient provisions for himself and the rest of the party. Perrault was to take the trade goods and what was left of the baggage and store them at Prairie Portage.

It took Perrault and his men eleven days to travel along the Northwest Trail from Fond du Lac to the Prairie Portage. Over six inches of snow had fallen. It was cold and with almost no provisions, the men experienced great hardship. Once at the Prairie Portage, Perrault remarked, "We lived on the Seed-pods of the wild rose, and the Sap of trees."

Perrault's party lived in an oilcloth tent and foraged as best they could off the land. About Christmas, 1784, they could stand it no longer and set off over the remainder of the Northwest Trail toward Sandy Lake in hope of finding Alexander Kay and a source of food. Scant relief awaited them at Sandy Lake:

> We saw there in a bay the poles of a lodge, where the savages had Camped before The snow. I went and investigated and found by Chance a Frame where the savages had left the edges of moose skin, which they had dried there; and as we were very hungry we did not pamper ourselves by boiling it but ate it roasted...[38]

From Sandy Lake, Perrault's party continued on foot down the frozen Mississippi River until they reached the *Rivière Vaseuse* or the "Muddy River" (present-day Ripple River). Finding the river open, the men had no choice but to swim across the open water. Shortly after this experience, they met Big Marten, a hunter from Mr. Kay's party, who guided them to Kay's post on Pine River. On the way, they took a shortcut across *Lac du Lièvre* (Rabbit Lake) and met a rival trading party of the North West Company led by Pierre Pinault.

Kay decided that Perrault should return to Prairie Portage, wait until the opening of the rivers and then bring the trade goods to the general rendezvous at Sandy Lake. Doubtless Kay heard about the presence of Pinault's Nor' Westers and wanted to conceal the true extent of his supply of trade goods. Perhaps he also feared that his unguarded cache of trade goods might be plundered if Perrault remained at Pine River.

Perrault, now loaded with a supply of provisions, returned to Prairie Portage where he commenced to build a ten by twelve foot storehouse. Kay had promised to send a hunting party and more provisions, but it was only through the efforts of the trader Harris that Perrault got any supplies at all.

In the spring the Indians came to make sugar near Perrault's Prairie Portage cabin followed by a visit from Kay, who was curious about the fate of his trade goods. On April 25th, 1785, Kay decided it was time to bring the trade goods to Sandy Lake; so, the entire party left Prairie Lake by way of Prairie River, which was in full spring flood, for the two day journey to Sandy Lake. While en route Kay, true to form, declined to portage around the Pine Rapids and instead tried to run them. In the process, he swamped his canoe, lost his baggage, and nearly lost his life in the rushing water.

Kay's party arrived at Sandy Lake on April 27th, 1785, and camped on a sand-bar near the entrance to the lake. At first the Indians were not aware of their presence and were busy at the south end of the lake building canoes. When word of Kay's arrival reached the chief, he sent presents and indicated he would join them as soon as they completed the canoes then under construction.[39]

Kay was not the first trader to reach Sandy Lake. Traders and Indian hunters had already begun to arrive and soon the general rendezvous was underway. Kay and Perrault anxiously awaited the arrival of Mr. Harris with the winter's catch of furs from Pine River. On May 2nd, 1785, the sound of gunfire on the south end of Sandy Lake announced the arrival of his partner William Harris over the short portage from Sandy Lake Rapids on the Mississippi to the southwest end of the lake. Kay, who had been refreshing himself with rum, went to meet his partner by canoe complete with a flagon full of rum from his liquor case as a special treat for Harris.

Perrault related how the general carousal at the trader's rendezvous progressed with more of the participants requesting rum and becoming increasingly intoxicated by the moment. Harris and Kay returned both feeling very merry, and it was at this moment that an Indian named le Cul-blanc (the White Tail) plotted to revenge himself against Kay for some fancied insult.

Alexander Kay was not only disliked by his own men but "mortally hated," to use Perrault's words, by some of the Indians. All winter le Cul-blanc had nursed a grudge against Kay and sought to convince another Indian named le Cousin (the Cousin or the Friend) to assassinate Kay. In the midst of the bacchanal, le Cousin feigned friendship to get close to Kay and then without warning stabbed Kay in the back of the neck. Kay, realizing that he had been stabbed in the back seized a knife and ran after le Cousin. The latter's mother, thinking that Kay meant to murder her son, walked up to him and stabbed Kay in the side. Pandemonium gripped the camp.

Kay's friends took him to his tent and one of their number, an Indian hunter named le Petit Mort (the Little Death) grasped his own knife and, realizing that le Cul-blanc was the true culprit, seized him and stabbed him in the breast, although he begged for mercy. With three deadly assaults having taken place in the camp, the women poured the remaining rum on the ground and began making preparations to break camp. Le Petit Mort's wife brought roots which were made into a poultice for Kay's wounds and the chief, le Bras Cassé (the Broken Arm), was summoned for his skill in the art of healing. The next day the chief gave Alexander Kay a medication which was very effective, and Kay began to show signs of improvement. He resolved to return to Mackinac Island with a small party of men and instructed Perrault and Harris to conclude the season's trade.

Kay sufficiently recovered from his wounds to address the business of the trade. He learned that the Indians of Leech Lake, his original destination, were about to return from their hunt and advised Perrault to go to there. He remarked, "Pinault has too small a stock of goods to compete with you." Perrault followed Kay's advice and made a very favorable trade in spite of having to keep Mr. Harris sober.[40]

After completing the trading venture, Perrault and his men returned to Sandy Lake and proceeded to Lake Superior over the Northwest Trail. They were low on provisions and hoped to reach a food cache on the St. Louis River. To their dismay, they found their cache had been eaten by a *carcajou* (wolverine). They resolved to continue to Fond du Lac and purchase provisions there.

While traveling down the St. Louis River, Perrault noted several changes in the weather. At the Grand Portage of the St., Louis, a great hail storm struck with hail stones weighing up to a pound raining down until the ground was covered to a depth of six inches. Arriving at Fond du Lac on June 7th, Perrault learned Alexander Kay was apparently a little better and "there was a chance of his recovery." He also learned the entrance to the St. Louis River was blocked with ice. He was forced to wait seven days before venturing out on Lake Superior. Finally, he departed in a large Mackinaw boat with his crew and winter's stock of furs.[41]

On the 26th of July, Perrault reached Mackinac Island. There he found that Alexander Kay's condition had suddenly worsened. Kay left the island shortly after meeting with Perrault to seek medical attention at Montreal. Alexander Kay reached the Lake of the Two Mountains on the Ottawa River, but his old wounds were too much for him. He died August 26th, 1785.

Jean Baptiste Perrault continued his career in the fur trade. For a time he worked for the General Company of Lake Superior and the South. Later he joined the North West Company as a clerk; and in 1793, under instructions from John Sayer, he built Fort St. Louis near the mouth of the river of that name. He continued to have many adventures in the interior of Minnesota. For example, in 1797, while returning from a season's hunt, one of his men named St. Louis was mysteriously poisoned and died on the west end of the Savanna Portage.[42]

Perrault continued to trade until 1805, when he left to attend to his sick father. He never returned to northern Minnesota. Instead, he taught school for two years. Following that experience, he once again worked as a fur trader on the northeast shore of Lake Superior near the Michipicoten River. Perrault finally left the trade for good in 1821, after the amalgamation of the Hudson's Bay Company and the North West Company.

Perrault remained in Sault Sainte Marie for the rest of his life. It was there, at the urging of ethnologist Henry Schoolcraft, that Jean Baptiste Perrault, near seventy, wrote his narrative of the fur trade. His story and eleven sketch maps were based on diaries and his own recollections of experiences in the wilderness. But his first trip into the country west of Lake Superior and the record of his first rendezvous at Sandy Lake, remain the most thrilling of all his many adventures.

Perrault's account not only contains a glimpse of what a trader's life was like but also highlights some important points in the history of trade along the Northwest Trail. His journal notes the presence of the North West Company (e.g., the traders Dufaut and Pinault) prior to the establishment of permanent stations by that company in the region. Also, the description of the loose associations formed by the South Traders and Perrault's career with the General Company of Lake Superior and the South organized in 1785 are indicative of both the large number of traders going into the country by way of the Northwest Trail and efforts to reduce ruinous competition through the formation of associations or partnerships by those same traders.

Jean Baptiste Perrault's account contains a great deal of valuable information about the fur trade, individual traders, the route(s) they traveled, and the location of their operations. There are, however, other records which tell how these traders traveled from Mackinac Island to the site of the general rendezvous at Sandy Lake.

A Voyage From Mackinac

Paul Beaulieu, voyageur, interpreter, and government farmer for the Ojibway.
Minnesota Historical Society

Among those who passed over the Northwest Trail and later wrote about it was a veteran trader named Paul Hudon Beaulieu. Beaulieu's account of his journey from Mackinac Island to Sandy Lake is of particular interest and includes many brief and colorful insights. Although his work has been quoted by fur trade historians such as Professor Grace Lee Nute, his experiences traveling along the south shore of Lake Superior and along the Northwest Trail have been largely overlooked.[43]

Paul H. Beaulieu, the youngest son of former Mackinac trader Bazil Hudon de Beaulieu, wrote a description of the progress of an American Fur Company brigade from Mackinac to Sandy Lake and captures the essence of a typical voyage. Although Beaulieu's trip was more recent than any similar activity discussed thus far, it is worthwhile to recount his experiences to understand what was involved in such an undertaking. Paul Beaulieu, who was born on Mackinac Island, was in a unique position to write about the fur trade since his family had a long association with it. Historian Elliott Coues, writing in the last quarter of the nineteenth century, noted the Beaulieu family was in the vanguard of trade and exploration:

> Beaulieu is a very old name in these annals. A half-breed family of that name was found on slave river when the Northwest [sic] Fur Company first reached it in or about 1778, showing prior presence of the French so far as this. Francois Beaulieu, one of the family born in the region, was one of the six voyageurs who accompanied sir Alexander Mackenzie on his exploring expedition across the Rocky Mountains to the Pacific coast, in 1793, from the place where they had wintered on the Peace River.[44]

Paul's older brother, Clement Hudon Beaulieu, was also active in the fur trade, first on Lake Superior, then at Sandy Lake, and finally, at the village of Crow Wing on the Mississippi River situated nine miles below the present-day city of Brainerd, Minnesota.

Paul Beaulieu's narrative, written in his own inimitable style late in life (c.1880), was never published, but contains considerable information relating to the everyday operation of a fur trade brigade. The account consists of three parts: a description of a trader's outfit, or stock of goods; the voyage along the shore of Lake Superior and the Northwest Trail; and the landfall at Sandy Lake.[45]

Beaulieu begins his narrative with a description of the types of trade goods brought into the country and some of the well-known traders who worked for the American Fur Company; such as John H. Fairbanks, William A. Aitkin, Samuel Ashmun, Augustine Bellanger, and Eustache Roussain. Beaulieu remarked that such veteran traders knew from experience the types and amount of trade goods required by their clientele. He described the preparations for a trading expedition, or adventure, into the interior and the assembly of an outfit for each post and for each trapper.

All of the items used in the trade were packed in bales known as "portage pieces," which were cleverly assembled so that no space was wasted. "...dry goods were baled in packages of 75 to 80 pounds in weight being 3 feet in length by 20 inches to 24 in width and tied with bed cord in three places...."[46] Small notions were folded into three point blankets or bolts of cloth. Each fold of the cloth contained such items as silver ornaments, yarn, beads, thimbles, "papers" (small envelopes) of Chinese vermilion, and needles. Once the bale was complete, it was covered with coarse sheeting and tied.

The next item of importance to Beaulieu was ammunition. Superfine gunpowder (FFFg) was packed in fifty pound kegs. Lead musket balls and shot of various sizes were packed in twenty-five pound bags. Three sacks of shot in a canvas bag constituted a portage piece.

Two of the most awkward items to "pack" or carry over a portage were also two of the most desirable trade items for the Indian trapper or hunter. Axes and trade muskets, commonly referred to as "Northwest Guns," were shipped in a way calculated to vex even the most complacent voyageur. The ax heads were shipped without handles, the heads simply being strung on a cord which was placed around the packer's neck and carried in that fashion over the intervening portages:

> ...axes commonly called indian axes of a very clumsy pattern...was also a staple article in trade and were made in three sizes. they were strung through the eye for transportation and the feeling of the Packer was far from comfortable with a string of such ornaments as they were wont to [be] named by those whose turn it was to wear them.[47]

Eight to ten trade muskets or trade rifles were packed in heavy wooden crates that resembled coffins. They were extremely difficult to carry over portages because of their shape. Beaulieu remarked of them:

> Next came the dead as the boxes containing the Norwest guns imported from England or the Leman Lancaster rifles was named on account of the shape of the boxes in which they were packed these Packages were the curse of the voyageur, as they were tied with the Portage Strap [tumpline] 3/4 from the end and resting on the Packers rump and back of the head and in stepping over a log would by the lower part touching the log give the poor devil a rap on the head or by touching a limb the other way would serve him the same way...but as a general thing, they got these troublesome burdens through if their lower extremities held out.[48]

Basic provisions were also a vital part of the cargo carried inland for both the trader and the voyageurs. Beaulieu mentioned the close attention given to providing only what was absolutely essential:

> A No 1 trader & family was allowed 2 barrels of flour 2 keg of Pork 66 lbs to the Keg 20 lb Butter 12 lb Tea. Sugar was made in the country from the Sugar Maple and a sufficiency was always on hand, at the trading Posts. A Wintering Station Clerk was allowed half to a no 1 trader, this allowance to last for 10 months.
> Next for the class called Voyageurs & Packer. Corn hulled with lye...together with tallow to season the same was put up and the daily ration issued as soon as the different parties left the borders of civilization.[49]

The food did not always agree with the men, and the "found" or daily ration of one quart of hominy (corn) and an ounce of grease or tallow was served twice a day. A steady diet of this nutritious but bland food led to complaints by the men of being "distressed" (constipated). Beaulieu commented:

...and every now & then a party will be heard saying as his bowels are not regular he is compelled in order to make them all right, or to appease his present hunger to be obliged to swallow the ounce of grease and let the corn go without seasoning which feat generally creates great merriment amongst that class of men.[50]

With the loading of the trade goods, ammunition, and provisions, the brigade was ready to embark. Beaulieu described the boats used to transport the American Fur Company's men and supplies. Large wooden six-oared Mackinaw boats had largely replaced the birch-bark "North" or freight canoes by the time he penned his description of the trade. The Mackinaw boat had certain advantages, such as strength and longevity. More importantly, they were routinely equipped with both oars and sails. Accounts of the fur trade credit the oar with being three to four times as efficient as the voyageur's paddle when it came to propelling large craft through the rough waters of Lake Superior.[51]

After the traders left Mackinac Island, they proceeded to Sault Sainte Marie. Here they visited the revenue officer. According to the provisions of the act regulating trade with the various Indian tribes, liquor was prohibited in "Indian Country." The trader could only take in a small amount for personal use, but some enterprising souls found ways to circumvent the regulation.

The boats left Sault Sainte Marie loaded to the gunwales with tons of goods, provisions, and ten to twelve persons on board. For the first few miles, the traders kept a sharp eye so that none of their boatmen deserted. Once the flotilla of Mackinaw boats rounded Whitefish Point, the traders relaxed their vigilance. The men toiled at the oars in fair weather or foul for periods of about an hour. The boats averaged about three miles between rest breaks. The breaks were referred to as "pipes," since the men relaxed for a few minutes and smoked their clay pipes. Whenever a favorable breeze stirred, the sails were set and the men rested.

To encourage a favorable breeze to ease their labors, offerings of small pieces of tobacco were tossed on the water accompanied by short incantations uttered by the superstitious voyageurs such as, *Souffle, souffle, la vielle* ("Blow, blow old woman"). Beaulieu noted the results when la vielle, or "the old woman of the wind," favored the men with a breeze:

> ...and when their prayers are heard and their sacrifices are accepted by the old woman or the She Neptune of Lake Superior the masts are fastened and keyed in position the canvass spread...with mild breeze these boats will sail from 60 to 70 miles per day, while they cannot be propelled with oars more than one half that distance...[52]

Finally, after days of coasting along the south shore of Lake Superior, the flotilla of Mackinaw boats reached the St. Louis River. Arriving at the entrance to St. Louis Bay, the heavily laden boats were carefully brought from Lake Superior over the shifting sand bar into the calm waters of the bay formed by Minnesota and Wisconsin points. After crossing the bar, the craft proceeded about twenty miles upstream to the head of navigation at the Fond du Lac post of the American Fur Company. Prior to 1817, the boats would have stopped at Fort St. Louis, a major supply depot established by the North West Company in 1793, approximately two and a half miles from the river's mouth. By the time of Beaulieu's account, however, old Fort St. Louis had been abandoned by traders for over thirty years in favor of a new post near the foot of the Grand Portage of the St. Louis.

Upon reaching the post at Fond du Lac, the men unloaded some of the goods for storage in the company's warehouse. All of the remaining supplies needed in the interior were packed over the Grand Portage of the St. Louis, which generally took about three days. The men and supplies re-embarked at the head of the Grand Portage and slowly poled their way upstream against the powerful current. During the crossing of the Grand Portage and other carrying places along the Northwest Trail, two men were usually charged with carrying the canoes. Beaulieu describes how the canoes were carried, "...and off they go on a keen trot, which is conceded the easiest way to carry canoes as the spring of the canoe at every step helps the carrier on his way."[53]

Three days were necessary to cover the distance between the head of the Grand Portage and the entrance to the East Savanna River. At the junction of the St. Louis and East Savanna rivers, the traders bound for Lake Vermilion left the main party and continued up the St. Louis, where they portaged to the Pike River and on to Lake Vermilion. The main party paddled and poled their canoes up the winding East Savanna until they reached the beginning of the Savanna Portage.

Once at the Savanna Portage, a full day was needed to carry the canoes and goods across to the West Savanna. Launching their canoes on the river, "...down current they go to Sandy Lake fort as it was termed Headquarters of Fond du Lac outfit..."

Arrival at the trading post offered a welcome rest for the voyageur and the chance to enjoy different food: "Here the voyageur enjoys a feast of 1 lbs. flour and 1/2 lb. Pork...for the poor Jack...has been fed on Corn since leaving Sault St. Marys."

Paul Beaulieu's narrative ended at Sandy Lake. With all of the preparation completed, the brigades split up and the men traveled to their assigned wintering posts. He concluded by describing how the men prepared for the coming winter: "...forming plans of the various and different trips...talking of old Supernatural beliefs, [and] How to manage in the divers situations that a voyageur may be placed in...."[54]

After reading the narrative, one can imagine how the voyageurs looked forward to their arrival at Sandy Lake. Although their work did not end, the prospect of profits to be made in the fur trade not to mention better food, made the long journey from Mackinac worthwhile.

Chapter 5 - The Pathway of the Voyageur
Notes

1.   The classic work on the French voyageurs or boatmen is Grace Lee Nute, *The Voyageur* (1931; reprint ed., St. Paul, 1955). For a good general discussion of the early French explorers see John Bartlet Brebner, *The Explorers of North America, 1492-1806* (3rd printing, Cleveland, 1968).

2.   Hamilton Nelson Ross, *La Pointe, Village Outpost* (St. Paul, 1960) provides an overall history of the post and the surrounding country. A detailed contemporary description of the various western posts including La Pointe was made in 1757 by Louis Antoine de Bougainville (see chap. 3, n. 32 above).

3.   Williams Watts Folwell, *A History of Minnesota*, 4 vols. (1921; reprint ed., St. Paul, 1956), vol. 1, pp. 22-23.

4.   Newton H. Winchell, *The Aborigines of Minnesota*, (St. Paul, 1911), pp. 524-525.

5.   In 1683, Father Louis Hennepin, published *Description de la Louisiane, nouvellement découverte au sudoüest de la Nouvelle France*. For an early assessment of Hennepin's work see John Gilmary Shea, *Discovery and Exploration of the Mississippi Valley* (New York, 1853).

6.   Winchell, *Aborigines*, pp. 524-525. Tonti's account was published in Amsterdam in 1720, as *Relation de la Louisiana et du fleuve Mississippi*. For a biographical sketch of Henri de Tonti (also spelled Tonty) see Reuben Gold Thwaites (ed.), "The French Régime in Wisconsin, 1634-1727," *Collections of the State Historical Society of Wisconsin*, vol. 16 (Madison,1902), p. 165.

7.   For a discussion of Le Sueur's exploits see Winchell, *Aborigines*, pp. 527-530; and also Harold Hickerson, "Ethnohistory of Mississippi Bands and Pillager and Winnibigoshish Bands of Chippewa," in *Chippewa Indians II* (New York, 1974), pp. 27-28. Hickerson relies on a translation of Pierre Margry, *Découvertes et établissements des Francais dans l'ouest et dans le sud de l'Amerique septentrionale (1614-1754). Mémoires et documents originaux* 6 parts (Paris, 1875-1886), vol. 6, pp. 191-193; see Brebner, *Explorers*, p. 249, for comments on Margry's reliability.

8.   Historian Grace Lee Nute spelled Sieur Marin's name *de la Margue* while others spell it *de la Malgue*. For details on the Marins, father and son, see Emma Helen Blair, *The Indian Tribes of the Upper Mississippi Valley and the Region of the Great Lakes*, 2 vols. (Cleveland, 1912), vol. 2, pp. 216-217; see also Kenneth P. Bailey (ed.), *Journal of Joseph Marin*, (Irvine, California, 1975); and *Dictionary of Canadian Biography*, 15 vols. (Toronto, 1974), s.v. "Marin de la Malgue, Paul," (by William J. Eccles); Dictionary of Canadian Biography, 15 vols. (Toronto, 1979), s.v. "Marin de la Malgue, Joseph." (by Donald Chaput).

9.   *Dictionary of Canadian Biography, On Line*, s.v. "Gaultier de la Vérendrye, Louis-Joseph," (by Antoine Champagne), http://www.biographi.ca. Accessed March 7th, 2006; For an older but interesting study by A. H. de Trémaudan see "Who Was the Chevalier de la Vérendrye?" *Canadian Historical Review*, vol. 1 (September, 1920), pp. 246-254.

10.   Champagne, "Louis-Joseph," n.p.; For details on the leasing of the post by St. Luc, see Reuben Gold Thwaites (ed.), "The French Régime in Wisconsin, 1743-1760," *Collections of the State Historical Society of Wisconsin*, vol. 18 (Madison, 1908), p. 191; Bailey, *Joseph Marin*, pp. 150 and 157; and Louis Phelps Kellogg, *The French Régime in Wisconsin and the Northwest* (Madison, 1925), p. 384. The prices for the various trading posts were given in *livres* (pounds). The livre was a unit of weight and a unit of currency. Both measurements were greater than their English counterparts. The *livre* coin used in New France was equal to twenty *sol*, and one *sol* was equal to twelve *denier*.

11.   For the clash between the Chevalier de la Vérendrye and Sieur Marin over trade districts see Grace Lee Nute, "Marin versus La Vérendrye," in *Minnesota History*, vol. 32, no. 4 (December, 1951) pp. 226-238; Ross, *La Pointe*, pp. 54-55; and Bailey, *Joseph Marin*, pp. 72-73, 149-152; and 157.

12.   Ibid., pp. 229-233.

13.   Champagne, "Louis-Joseph," n.p.

14.   Ibid.

15. Francis Parkman, *A Half-Century of Conflict* (3rd printing, New York, 1966), p. 279.

16. Carl P. Russell, *Guns on the Early Frontiers* (Berkeley, 1962) p. 297, n. 31. French era fur trade artifacts appear to be extremely scarce in spite of the volume of trade conducted in the region as well as the distribution of presents to various Indian tribes during the seventeenth and eighteenth centuries. Presents, including huge quantities of arms and ammunition, were annually distributed to France's Indian allies. In 1759, the Intendant for New France, François Bigot, complained he spent four hundred million francs on presents for Indian allies. See Wilbur R. Jacobs, "Presents to Indians Along the French Frontier in the Old Northwest, 1748-1763," *Indiana Magazine of History*, vol. 44 (September, 1948), p. 249 and n. 20.

In the case of the French trade pistol, it was accidentally unearthed on private property near Sandy Lake by residents installing a swing set. The author was contacted by the owner and made a positive identification of the remains of the piece as being manufactured in the 1740s in Tulle, France, for trade in North America.

17. For details and photographs of French arms see Russel Bouchard, *Les Fusils de Traite en Nouvelle-France, 1690-1760* (Chicontimi, Quebec, 1976); Jean Boudroit, *Armes a Feu Françaises*, 2 series: Systemes 1728-1734 (Paris, 1963); T. M. Hamilton, "Firearms on the Frontier: Guns at Fort Michilimackinac 1715-1781," in *Reports in Mackinac History and Archaeology*, number 5 (Williamston, Michigan, 1976); and, T. M. Hamilton, *Colonial Frontier Guns* (Chadron, Nebraska, 1980).

18. Careful records were kept of the number and kinds of trade goods sent into the interior by every merchant involved in the fur trade. See Hamilton, *Colonial Frontier Guns*, pp. 12 -19 for several examples of trade invoices listing French goods.

19. Carl P. Russell, *Firearms on the Frontier*, p. 23; and Hamilton, Colonial Frontier Guns, p. 21.

20. Photographs of trade gun lockplates and related parts found on or near the supposed site of the North West Company's Sandy Lake post were taken by Irving H. and Evan A. Hart. No complete specimen of a trade gun has been reported in the vicinity.

21. See Irving H. Hart, "The Old Savanna Portage," in *Minnesota History*, vol. 8, no. 2 (June, 1927), pp. 117-139. Hart's report was followed by a claim to have found the site of a trading post; Richard R. Sackett, "An Unidentified Trading Post on the Portage la Savanna," in *The Minnesota Archaeologist*, vol. 7, no. 4 (October, 1941), pp. 75-77; Clifford Greer, *Twelve Poses West* (McGregor, Minnesota, 1967), p. 40. Greer mentioned Jean Baptiste Perrault's "Prairie River cabin." More recent archaeological work within the boundary of Savanna Portage State Park has failed to identify the site of the trading post. No known sources from the fur trade era exist to support the assertion that there ever was such a post on the portage. Furthermore, the proximity to Sandy Lake and the need to be close to dependable sources of food precluded the existence of a permanent establishment on either the Prairie or the West Savanna rivers.

22. The origin of the trader's cabin story can be traced back to the 1830s, and an error in translation by Henry Rowe Schoolcraft. The small cabin built by Perrault during the winter of 1784-1785, was located on the north side of Prairie Lake in present-day St. Louis County, Minnesota.

23. Greer, *Twelve Poses*, p. 62.

24. Alexander Henry, *Travels and Adventures in Canada and the Indian Territories Between the Years 1760 and 1776*, ed. by James Bain (1809, reprint ed., Boston, 1901). Henry was fortunate to receive the assistance and financial backing of experienced French trader Étienne Campion as noted in Brebner, *Explorers*, p. 360.

25. Kellogg, *French Régime*, p. 384.

26. Alexander Henry, *Travels*, pp. 184-185.

27. One of the earliest lists of traders and merchants, who operated in the Lake Superior region following the British conquest of Canada, was discovered in an assortment of Colonial Office papers (C. O. 42, 14) in the Record Office in London. See Charles E. Lart, "Fur Trade Returns, 1767," *Canadian Historical Review*, vol. 3 (December, 1922), pp. 351-358. The value of the merchandise provided Alexander Henry's traders, Cadot, Bartie, and Chinn, was the largest of all those listed bound for Lake Superior. The specific destinations of his traders were: "St. Mary's, Du Fond du Lac, and la Poine [Pointe]." For additional names and locations of independent traders who used the Northwest Trail see "Abstract of Indian Trade Licenses, 1768-1774," in the collections of the Minnesota Historical Society.

28. For a brief history of the formation of the fur trade partnership see Wayne Stevens, "Fur Trading Companies in the Northwest, 1760-1816," in *Proceedings of the Mississippi Valley Historical Association*, vol. 9 (1916-1917), pp. 283-291. The most famous of these partnerships was the North West Company. Although a major factor in the fur trade, the North West Company was actually a series of partnerships which were renewed annually. See Marjorie Wilkins Campbell, *The North West Company* (Vancouver, 1957), for an in-depth history of the company. For information on the military threat to the Lake Superior traders during the American Revolution, see David A. Armour and Keith R. Widder, *At The Crossroads: Michilimackinac During The American Revolution* (Mackinac Island, Michigan, 1978). To secure the area, the commandant of Michilimackinac sent Lieutenant Thomas Bennett, Sergeant Amos Langdon, and five privates of the King's 8th Regiment of Foot to Grand Portage as a temporary garrison in the summer of 1778.

29. The exploits of fur traders along the Northwest Trail have been known since the first publication of the *Narrative of Jean Baptiste Perrault*, translated by Henry Schoolcraft. In the 1920s, attention was once again focused on the route and the traders with the publication of Charles Napier Bell's, "The Earliest Fur Traders on the Upper Red River and Red Lake, Minn. (1783-1810)," in *The Historical and Scientific Society of Manitoba*, Transaction no. 1, n.s., (Winnipeg, Manitoba,1926), pp. 2-16; Harry W. Duckworth, "The Last Coureurs Des Bois," *The Beaver*, outfit 314, no. 2 (Spring, 1984), pp. 4-12. Among those who claim the area west of Lake Superior was "an uninhabited war zone'" are Tanner, *Atlas*, pp. 42-43; Innis, *Fur Trade*, p. 254, n. 297; and, Hickerson, *Chippewa Indians II*, p. 8. Hickerson cites Alexander Henry and Jonathan Carver, as authorities for his statement, but neither person actually visited the area in question. Carver only visited the village of Fond du Lac briefly before proceeding to Grand Portage. Both Alexander Henry and Jonathan Carver relied on the opinions of others regarding the contested territory. Hickerson devotes an entire chapter to the subject of "Warfare and the Debatable Zone West of the Mississippi," in *The Chippewa and Their Neighbors: A Study in Ethnohistory* (1970; rev. ed., Prospect Heights, Illinois, 1988), chap. 7, but his bibliography is noticeably lacking in French sources from the period before 1763. Nute's researches regarding the La Vérendrye family, the lists of traders bound for Fond du Lac, and the fact that Jean Baptiste Perrault encountered other traders including Nor'Westers along the Northwest Trail in 1784-1785 indicate the area was hardly a no man's land.

30. Duckworth, "Last Coureurs Des Bois," p. 6.

31. Jean Baptiste Perrault, "Narrative of the Travels of a Merchant Voyageur In The Savage Territories of Northern America Leaving Montreal the 28th of May, 1783," ed. by John Sharpless Fox, in *Historical Collections and Researches Made by the Michigan Pioneer and Historical Society*, vol. 37 (Lansing,1909-1910), pp. 508-619 (see also chap. 2, n. 26 above).

32. Ibid., pp. 509-510.

33. Armour and Widder, *At The Crossroads*, pp. 120-122.

34. Hickerson, *Chippewa Indians II*, pp. 63-64, nn. 107-108.

35. Armour and Widder, *At The Crossroads*, pp. 130, 138, and 180.

36. Perrault, *Narrative of Travels*, p. 518.

37. Ibid., p. 519. The *arpent* (also known as the *arpent de Paris*) referred to by Perrault was a unit of linear measurement equal to one hundred and eighty feet.

38. Ibid., pp. 521-522.

39. Ibid., pp. 525-526. The Sandy Lake Ojibway had a canoe yard on the southern end of the lake near the portage connecting Sandy Lake with Great Wild Rice Lake to the southeast. Perrault, *Narrative of Travels*, p. 570, mentioned purchasing two canoes from *Kâwè-mitticouche-imon* a local builder Perrault nicknamed *pierro le pânis*.

40. Ibid., p. 530.

41. Ibid., p. 534.

42. Ibid., p. 574. The voyageur St. Louis may have succumbed to blood poisoning or a burst appendix.

43. Alvin H. Wilcox, *A Pioneer History of Becker County Minnesota* (St. Paul, 1907), pp. 221, 240-241, 244 and 247.

44. Elliot Coues (ed.), *New Light on the Early History of the Greater Northwest. The Manuscript Journals of Alexander Henry, fur trader of the Northwest Company, and David Thompson, official geographer and explorer of the same company, 1799-1814. Exploration and Adventure among the Indians on the Red, Saskatchewan, Missouri, and Colombia Rivers*, 3 vols. (1897; reprint ed., Minneapolis, 1965), vol. 1, p.266, n. 4.

45. Beaulieu's observations and description of travel and trade have been largely overlooked by writers. A brief reference to him as "an erstwhile voyageur" was made by Grace Lee Nute, who nonetheless used his account in *The Voyageur* (1931; reprint ed., St. Paul, 1955), p. 268, n. 27. See Paul Beaulieu, untitled manuscript, n.d. in Henry M. Rice Papers, Minnesota Historical Society (hereafter referred to as Paul Beaulieu, ms.).

46. Paul Beaulieu, ms., p. 2.

47. Ibid., p. 4. The shape of the trade ax head evolved from an old French style. See Arthur Woodward, *Denominators of the Fur Trade: An Anthology of Writings on the Material Culture of the Fur Trade* (Pasadena, 1970), pp. 81-107.

48. Ibid., pp. 3-4. The Northwest gun was a distinct type of firearm developed to meet the needs of the Indian hunter. For a detailed discussion see Charles E. Hanson, Jr., *The Northwest Gun* (Lincoln, 1955).

49. Paul Beaulieu, ms., p. 4; Ross, *La Pointe*, pp. 59-60, states the wages for the voyageurs included the "found," or the standard individual food ration, which consisted of one bushel of corn and two pounds of fat per man per month.

50. Paul Beaulieu, ms., p. 5.

51. Both David Thompson (1798) and Lieutenant James Allen (1832) mention fitting a large cargo canoe with oars.

52. Paul Beaulieu, ms., p. 8.

53. Ibid., p. 10.

54. Ibid., p. 14. Beaulieu's narrative ends when the brigade arrives at Sandy Lake. He closed his account by describing in detail the various preparations made for the winter hunt.

A view of the end of the Northwest Trail at Sandy Lake.
Photo by Larry Luukkonen

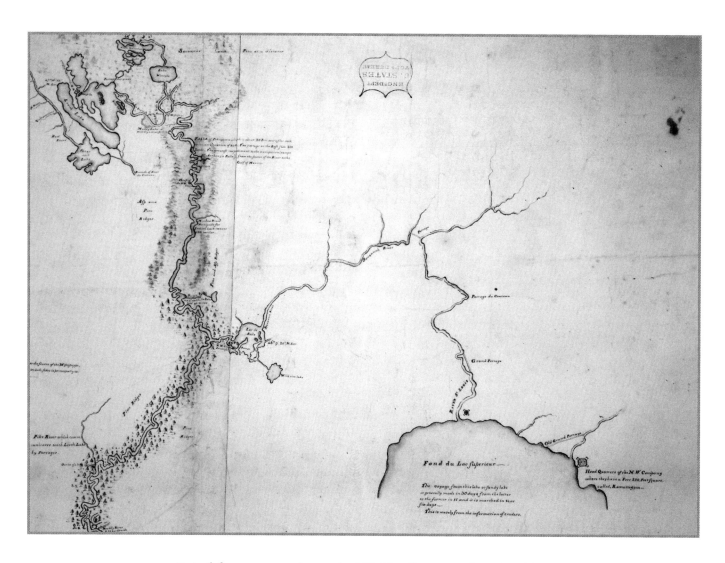

Detail from a map drawn in 1806 by Sergeant Antoine Nau
under the direction of Lieutenant Zebulon Pike. National Archives

Chapter 6 ❧ Government Expeditions

In addition to being a major migration and trade route from Lake Superior, the Northwest Trail also served as a path for various explorations undertaken by the United States. The benefit of exploration was apparent in Lieutenant Zebulon Montgomery Pike's reconnaissance of 1805-1806, which included charting the course of the Mississippi River to its main source, fixing the location of trading posts, and showing the route of the Northwest Trail to Lake Superior. In fact, each of the government expeditions that followed Pike's had a number of important objectives including the gathering of further geographical information and the reconciliation of the local Indian tribes. Most of the government expeditions sought in one way or another to deal effectively with the incessant warfare waged between the Dakota and Ojibway, but it continued in spite of elaborate councils, solemn treaties, and the distribution of countless presents.

Zebulon Pike's Contribution

Zebulon Pike's role in mapping the course of the Mississippi was discussed in Chapter 3, but his expedition involved more than gathering geographic information. Although the area including Lake Superior and the Northwest Trail was considered part of the United States, there was no effective American presence west of the little garrison at Fort Mackinac. To assert that presence, Pike was instructed to note the population and residence of the various Indian tribes and conciliate them, select sites for military posts and trading houses, and gather information on trading and other activities in the area around the headwaters of the Mississippi. Pike was to inform British traders that the provisions of Jay's Treaty, which allowed them to trade along with Americans in the Northwest Territory, did not extend to the former French colony of Louisiana, which had been recently purchased by the United States (1803).[1]

Pike faced enormous difficulties, but he persisted. Toiling up the frozen Mississippi in the dead of winter was very taxing. Thin ice and harsh weather required the men stop and build fires to warm themselves. Pike commented:

Zebulon Pike
Library of Congress

We made but Eleven points, and then had to send ahead and make fires every three miles—notwithstanding which, the cold was so intense, that some froze their noses—some their fingers and some their toes—even before they felt the cold sensibly. Very hard days march.[2]

His manuscript map and his accompanying report to General James Wilkinson at St. Louis showed the major fur trading posts and the water routes which connected them including the Northwest Trail. His report is filled with data regarding the trade, the number of traders, the types of trade goods and prices, the annual harvest of furs, the types of skins, and other useful information to measure the extent of the traffic in furs. Pike concluded his report with a recommendation that the government establish a custom house with a garrison of one hundred men at Fond du Lac to enforce the customs duties on goods imported into the country.[3] While Pike did not actually follow the Northwest Trail eastward, his manuscript map clearly shows the common route to Lake Superior and the trading posts at Fond du Lac and Kaministiquia.

Pike's travels through the headwaters region of Minnesota in 1805-1806 established an American presence in a region that it had rightfully claimed by treaty since 1783. His exploits, however, were not followed up by further exploration for another fifteen years. In the interval, the outbreak of the War of 1812 proved the United State's claim to the Northwest Territory was tenuous at best. In a sweeping move, the British and their Indian allies effectively drove United States forces back to their positions at the conclusion of the Revolutionary War.

As for Zebulon Pike, his exploration on the northern frontier in 1805-1806, followed by an extensive journey through the southwest, earned him not only notoriety but also advancement in the army to the rank of colonel of the Fifteenth Infantry Regiment. Pike's account of his first trip was published in 1806. A later version of his explorations, which included his adventures in the southwest and Mexico was printed in 1810. In 1813, Pike was promoted to brigadier general. On April 27th, 1813, Zebulon Montgomery Pike, one of the few successful commanders on the Northwestern frontier, was tragically killed by the explosion of a powder magazine while leading a successful assault on Fort York (Toronto).

Following the War of 1812, the United States realized it must take appropriate action to safeguard the frontier; and after 1815 plans were implemented to secure the territory northwest of the Ohio River with a series of strategic military posts. None of the proposed posts, however, insured control of Lake Superior and the routes west, nor was anything done to win the allegiance of the Ojibway. An expedition was needed into the very heart of the country to secure a site for a northern post and meet with the indigenous population. That objective was not accomplished until 1820, five years after the end of the United States' second war with Great Britain.[4]

In the summer of 1820, Michigan Territorial Governor Lewis Cass led an expedition up the Great Lakes and across the Northwest Trail into the very heart of the wilderness to meet with the Ojibway of the Mississippi at Sandy Lake. The residents of Sandy Lake had no idea they would be playing host to a major government enterprise.

The Northwestern Expedition of 1820

Thursday, July 13th, 1820, began like any other typical sultry summer day at the American Fur Company's Sandy Lake post. An early morning shower changed to bright sunshine; and by midday, the heat and humidity—not to mention the mosquitoes—were unbearable. Situated at the crossroads of major watersheds in the remote northwestern corner of the newly created Michigan Territory, the post was usually visited by fur traders and trappers. This day, however, would be different. An advance party arrived at the post about two p.m. with news that an expedition was on its way to Sandy Lake from the St. Louis River by way of the Savanna Portage. It was headed by no less a person than the Territorial Governor himself—Lewis Cass.

Such was the setting at Sandy Lake for the arrival of the Northwestern Expedition, perhaps the most significant exploring party to ever pass over the Northwest Trail. What makes the event even more interesting is that Governor Cass chose Sandy Lake to be the expedition's base camp for exploring the Mississippi River headwaters and the setting for a council with the Ojibway of the Mississippi.

Michigan Territorial Governor
Lewis Cass
Library of Congress

From a national perspective, the Northwestern Expedition was one of three expeditions undertaken during the years 1819-1820. It was the intention of the government following the War of 1812 to redouble its efforts to establish an American presence both in the Northwest Territory and in the newly acquired Louisiana Territory. Secretary of War, John C. Calhoun, planned to erect a series of military posts at key locations to secure the frontier, counteract British influence among the Indian tribes, and establish peace between various warring bands. The expeditions were the first stage of his plans. Given the continued close relations between the Canadian traders and the Ojibway of Lake Superior, it is not hard to see why Cass used the chance to assert an American presence at a major treaty negotiation at the crossroads of the Northwest Trail. Cass' objective was quite clear in a letter of November 18th, 1819, to Secretary of War Calhoun:

> In addition to these objects [six reasons to undertake the Northwestern Expedition of 1820], I think it very important to carry the flag of the United States into those remote regions, where it has never been borne by any person in a public station.[5]

Although endorsed by Secretary Calhoun, the Northwestern Expedition was the brainchild of New Hampshire native Lewis Cass. Cass, a former attorney turned army officer, had been appointed governor of Michigan Territory in 1813. With his experience in the War of 1812, he had knowledge of the country. Concerned for the future growth of Michigan, Cass clearly saw the need for the expedition. He believed the expedition would encompass more than just a military maneuver. As a scientific undertaking, it would gather valuable information about the region. Furthermore, such a project would also acquire information about the fur trade, the size and distribution of Indian tribes in the Northwest, the existence of minerals (e.g., copper) and other resources vital to the future development of the territory. The expedition also complemented Calhoun's plans by negotiating with the "Chippewa," as they were known officially, and establishing a fort at Sault Sainte Marie to secure trade and communication from Lake Superior to Detroit.

Mindful of the broad importance of his mission, Cass embarked with the expedition from Detroit on Wednesday, May 24th, at four o'clock in the afternoon, bound for Mackinac Island and the unknown country west of Lake Superior. The Northwestern Expedition was a model for future trips. It was the largest United States expedition thus far and the most comprehensive scientific undertaking since Lewis and Clark's trip in 1804-1806. It was also the first to proceed at least part way west on a steamboat called the *Walk in the Water*. The progress of the group was chronicled by several of its members—Henry Schoolcraft, Captain David Bates Douglass, James D. Doty, Charles C. Trowbridge, and Doctor Alexander Wolcott all kept notes or journals describing the trip.[6]

Schoolcraft and Douglass were supposed to take notes on the trip and co-author an account of the adventure. Of the two, Douglass, having been trained as a mathematician, was very well-qualified for the task. He held a faculty position at West Point, where he taught himself to read French so he could translate French military engineering texts into English for use in his classes. Schoolcraft's experience was limited to a tour of Missouri lead mines.

The route of the expedition lay west from Detroit to Mackinac Island, then to Sault Sainte Marie, and along the southern shore of Lake Superior to the mouth of the St. Louis River. From that point, the expedition had to pass over the familiar yet difficult series of portages to Sandy Lake and the Mississippi, where the group established its base of operations. The return route lay down the Mississippi River to meet the military contingent dispatched to build a fort (Fort Snelling) at the confluence of the Mississippi and St. Peter's (Minnesota) rivers. The expedition continued downstream to the mouth of the Wisconsin River, then up that stream and by portage to the Fox River and finally into Lake Michigan, returning by way of Mackinac Island and finally ending at Detroit.

The Northwestern Expedition reached Sault Sainte Marie on the evening of June 14th. Here a parcel of land was set aside for a fort fronting on the St. Mary's Rapids (Fort Brady). During a meeting with local tribal leaders, a dissident chief walked out of the conference and hoisted a British flag over his tent in open defiance of Cass. The enraged Governor marched up to the tent alone, seized the flag and threw it in the dust before the astonished crowd. Then Cass "expostulated pretty warmly" with the multitude. A show of firmness by Cass and the timely diplomatic intervention on behalf of the Americans by Susan Johnston (O-shaw-gus-co-day-way-quah), wife of respected trader John Johnston, brought about a peaceful end to a meeting initially marred by open hostility to the Americans.[7]

On June 18th, the expedition left Sault Sainte Marie and coasted along the south shore of Lake Superior. The coastline was charted as the expedition continued westward and the area was periodically examined for minerals, such as copper, which was known to exist in the Keweenaw Peninsula. Schoolcraft, the expedition's geologist and mineralogist, recorded the various types of minerals found and visited copper mines worked by the Indians. He also kept a table of places and distances traveled.

On July 5th, the expedition finally reached the mouth of the St. Louis River. Now the hardest part of the journey began—the trek along the Northwest Trail. After a brief stop at the newly established (1817) American Fur Company post at the village of Fond du Lac, the expedition exchanged some of their large lake canoes for smaller canoes typically used in the interior by the fur company. Cass hired two guides and arranged for the services of local Indians to assist the party in carrying their baggage over the Grand Portage of the St. Louis. The crossing took four days to complete. Schoolcraft wrote:

> Every thing around us wears a wild and sterile aspect, and the extreme ruggedness of the country—the succession of swampy grounds, and rocky precipices—the dark forest of hemlock and pines which overshadow the soil—and the distant roaring of the river, would render it a gloomy and dismal scene, without the toil of transporting baggage, and the saddening influence of one of the most dreary days.[8]

On Sunday, July 9th, the expedition passed Fortress Island, at the foot of the Knife Portage and camped at the head of the portage near Knife Falls. Because of low water in the river, Cass was advised by his guide, a Mr. Defour (Dufaut?), to send part of the expedition ahead by an overland trail to Sandy Lake. By reducing the number of passengers, the draft of the canoes would be decreased and the extra men could provide assistance once Cass and the main party arrived at the Savanna Portage.

Hardly had Cass gotten underway on the St. Louis River when his own canoe was dashed against a rock in the rapids near what Captain Douglass called the *Isle au Plaie* or "Island of the Plague" (*Paw-paw-sco-me-me-tig* or Plain Island). Six miles farther upstream, the scene was repeated at the *Isle au Pins* (Island of Pines near Pine Rapids) and within two and a half miles, at the Grand Rapids of the St. Louis, another canoe broke. It was not until the main party reached calm water above the Cloquet Rapids that the men could make reasonable headway without fear of puncturing the delicate birch-bark hulls of the canoes.[9]

Meanwhile, the overland party consisting of Henry Schoolcraft, Charles C. Trowbridge, James Doty, Alexander Chase, Lieutenant Aeneas Mackay, eight soldiers, two guides, and an interpreter struck out along a trail leading in a westerly direction. Equipped with provisions consisting of ham and sea biscuits to last five days, the party left the head of Knife Portage at six o'clock, Monday, July 10th. The men followed a path from the head of the Knife Portage that led west for two miles parallel with the course of the river, until it intersected a well-traveled trail leading from Plain Island (cited above) to the interior. All was well until the two guides lost the trail west of Perch Lake in present-day Carlton County; and the trip, which should have taken two days, instead took four.

The overland party stumbled through dense tamarack swamps and at times sank up to their knees in mud. Schoolcraft commented:

> While toiling our way through this dreary and inhospitable region, the remark of the Baron La Honton [sic], respecting the northwestern region of Canada, that it is "the fag end of the world," came forcibly to mind.[10]

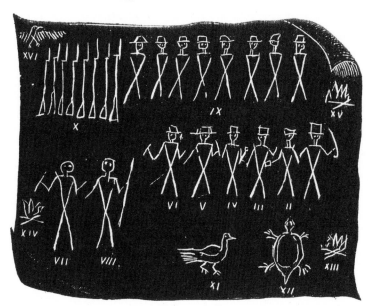

Ojibway pictograph mentioned by Henry R. Schoolcraft in 1820. Found near Perch Lake, Carlton County.
Winchell's, *Aborigines of Minnesota*

One item of interest encountered on the four day trip was a pictograph inscribed on a piece of birch-bark left by one of the Indian guides at the beginning of the second day's march. Schoolcraft admitted he had "no previous idea of the existence of such a medium of intelligence among the northern Indians."[11]

Late on the afternoon of July 13th, the weary travelers arrived at Sandy Lake. James Doty remarked, "We struck the Lake about 50 rods below the mouth of the Little Savanna [Prairie River]." Schoolcraft observed the setting sun on the water of Sandy Lake resembled "burnished gold." The arrival of the advance party of the expedition at Sandy Lake caused quite a sensation among the Indians. Shots fired to alert the trading post of their arrival were mistaken for an attack by the Dakota. Presently, two clerks, Samuel Ashmun and John H. Fairbanks, set out by canoe to investigate. The two clerks cautiously approached the bedraggled group of strangers on the beach. Ashmun and Fairbanks hesitated before coming closer. Suddenly, they noticed a group of men clad in mud-stained white cotton uniforms line up along the beach. The clerks realized the strangers were Americans. Henry Schoolcraft remarked:

...at last two were descried in a canoe, cautiously approaching. They appeared to be in doubt whether we were white men or Indians,—friends or foes,—but we soon convinced them by parading our soldiers upon the beach...[12]

The overland party was conducted to the trading post where they were fed and refreshed. Charles Christopher Trowbridge, the expedition's assistant topographer, noted the hospitality extended to the men upon their arrival at the trading post:

Immediately after our arrival at the post we were invited to take supper; welcome news to us for our provisions were exhausted before our arrival at the Lake. We found on the table a plate for each person, containing each a Boiled [broiled ?] Duck and a large slice of Buffalo meat, dried in the sun. The quantity seemed repelling, but we had learned to eat as well as the Indians, and we were astonished at looking at our plates in a little time, to find them all empty.[13]

Early on the morning of Friday, July 14th, the men of the advance party, joined by sixteen Indians from Sandy Lake, left the fort to assist the main expedition in crossing the Savanna Portage. Cass, fondly referred to as "Big Belly," in reference to his corpulence, was almost overcome by the heat and fatigue experienced during the crossing. The men camped on the west end of the Savanna Portage. At five a.m. the next morning they started for Sandy Lake.

With great difficulty Cass and his group descended the river. Since the water was low, some of the men elected to walk to Sandy Lake on the overland extension of the Savanna Portage which paralleled the West Savanna River. The governor proceeded slowly downstream with the canoes. At one point his large canoe was pierced by a sharp rock and had to be unloaded and repaired before the party could continue.[14]

About four o'clock in the afternoon, a flotilla of canoes carrying Cass and his men appeared on Sandy Lake. As the heavy laden canoes approached the post, colorfully dressed French voyageurs strained at their red-tipped paddles in one last burst of speed. Such a display of prowess with a canoe was calculated to impress the crowd of onlookers that had gathered on the beach.

Along the shore and near the stockaded trading post, cottony puffs of white smoke drifted lazily upward in the thick humid air, followed by the distant reports of musketry. Small geysers of water erupted around the canoes prompting Schoolcraft to remark:

We were received with a salute from the Indians *a la mode de saváge*, with balls. The custom of firing a salute was introduced into this region by the North West Company, who were in the habit of receiving their agents & clerks, on their annual return from Montreal, with this mark of respect. But the Indians never use blank cartridges on these occasions, the precise reason for which I did not learn. The balls dropped in the water all around us, and it would seem as if they were apparantly [sic] trying [to see?] how near they could strike to the canoes without endangering our lives.[15]

As the canoes gently approached the shore, the scene probably resembled the arrival of a typical fur trade brigade. Orders given to the men were mingled with greetings and shouts from old acquaintances. Those spontaneous acts were punctuated with the cries of children and the barking of dogs, of which there were many. And, over all the excited babel, the incessant banging of musketry continued as the men fired a *feu de joie*, or "volley of joy."

The clerks, being without news from the outside world, quizzed their guests from the moment of their arrival. Captain Douglass wrote:

We are much amused at the enquiries of these gentlemen about the news. They get it ordinarily about once a year and as the time of its arrival is now near at hand they have been almost a year without hearing it.[16]

Shortly after the arrival of the entire expedition, Cass met with tribal leaders in the clerk's quarters. The next day, Sunday, July 16th, 1820, he held a formal council to acquaint the Indians with his mission. Cass requested a delegation from the tribe to accompany him to the mouth of the St. Peters River to hold a peace conference with the Dakota. The tribal leaders agreed to his proposal, and the council ended with an elaborate distribution of gifts by Governor Cass.

Following the conclusion of the meeting, Cass and a small party made a side trip up the Mississippi River in search of the source of that stream. Schoolcraft and Captain Douglass were part of a select group chosen to accompany Cass. Both men kept a detailed record of the journey. Because of exceptionally low water in the river, Cass proceeded only as far as Upper Red Cedar Lake. He was informed that a source of the Mississippi lay ahead at *Lac la Biche* (Elk Lake). Satisfied he could go no farther, Cass ordered the party to return to Sandy Lake. To commemorate the trip, Henry Schoolcraft suggested the name of Upper Red Cedar Lake be changed to "Cassina Lake." The name of the lake was later changed to simply Cass Lake.[17]

While the expedition to the headwaters was absent, the rest of the men busied themselves gathering information about the country, the trading post, and the lake. Charles Trowbridge and James Doty recorded their impressions of the country and obtained vital information about trade and the surrounding territory by interviewing the two clerks, Ashmun and Fairbanks.

Doty later provided Cass with an elaborate report on the Indians of Sandy Lake. He noted three principle places of residence for the Indians of the region: Leech Lake, Sandy Lake, and Fond du Lac. The population of Leech Lake was estimated at two hundred men, three hundred and fifty women, and eleven hundred children. Sandy Lake's population was estimated at eighty-five men, two hundred and forty-three women and children, plus thirty-five half-breeds. Fond du Lac's population was forty-five men, sixty women, and two hundred and forty children.[18]

The Sandy Lake population was further divided into three groups. The largest group was located at Sandy Lake proper. A second group was situated at Pokegama Lake (near present-day Grand Rapids, Minnesota); and, according to Doty, a small group at *Pauc-quan-meno-min-ic-con*, or what is today called Rice Lake, located approximately fifteen miles south of Sandy Lake.

Among the many things recorded by Charles Trowbridge at Sandy Lake was the large number of mosquitoes:

> ...we are obliged not only to use our nets, but to keep a smoke [smudge] in our room during the night...in the day time if we walk toward the woods it is necessary to use veils.[19]

Trowbridge also commented on the nature of the fur trade and the kinds of goods traded at Sandy Lake: "One very necessary article to the Indian hunter he never fails to pay for; this is his axe...his best skins are selected and given to the trader for this instrument..."[20]

He also wrote about efforts by the expedition commissary, Alexander Ralston Chase, to map Sandy Lake:

> Mr. Chase who has been out to survey & delineate Sandy Lake... returned, and has probably the most correct chart that was ever made of it. The shape is very singular: its width is in no one place more than 4 or 5 miles, but there are many deep indentations, and its circumference cannot be less than 30 miles. The shores are not generally sandy as has been supposed, but gravely, abounding in the most beautiful cornelians [carnelians] and agates...[21]

While Trowbridge and Chase recorded information, the voyageurs worked to complete a bateau, a type of boat having a sharp prow and propelled by oars. When Cass rejoined the expedition at Sandy Lake on July 24th, the bateau was finished and all was in readiness for departure.

The Northwestern Expedition left Sandy Lake without much fanfare on the afternoon of July 25th, 1820. Although the expedition passed into history as the last canoe faded from view down the Mississippi River, the legacy of Cass' trip to the country west of Lake Superior lives on in the stories of the people, places, and events encountered along the Northwest Trail. Henry Schoolcraft rushed an account of the trip to the press. His version proved to be quite popular with a reading public that craved stories of adventure. In so doing, he alienated David Bates Douglass, with whom he was supposed to co-author an official record of the Northwestern Expedition. In disgust, Douglass abandoned any further work on the project and returned to his teaching position at West Point. His complete account of the 1820 expedition was not published until 1969.[22]

Efforts to expand on the accomplishments of the Northwestern Expedition were hampered by the continued enmity between the Dakota and the Ojibway. Although Cass persuaded a delegation of Ojibway leaders from Sandy Lake and the headwaters to talk peace with their Dakota counterparts, nothing substantive resulted from the meeting. This council, near the site of the new military establishment being built on the bluff commanding the confluence of the Mississippi and St. Peter's rivers, did not accomplish the long-term outcome everyone hoped for. Peace on the frontier was short-lived. What was clearly needed was a formal agreement between the tribes and an agreed upon boundary separating the two tribes within the contested lands lying west of the Mississippi River.

A treaty negotiated at Prairie du Chien in 1825 addressed the problem of keeping the peace among the tribes, but all of the Ojibway were not present in the deliberations and treaty signing. In an effort to complete the negotiations that had been started at Prairie du Chien, a second treaty council was planned with the "Chippewa of Lake Superior and the Mississippi" bands who were not signatories to the 1825 agreement. The location picked for the treaty deliberations was at the village of Fond du Lac at the entrance to the Northwest Trail. Once again, Michigan Territorial Governor Lewis Cass visited the area. This time, however, he was accompanied by the new Superintendent of the Indian Department, Thomas L. McKenney. To impress all who attended, Cass employed all the pomp and ceremony he could muster for the event.

The Grand Council of 1826

Lithograph of the bower for the Grand Council of 1826.
McKenney, *Sketches of a Tour to the Lakes*

The residents of the American Fur Company post at the village of Fond du Lac had never seen anything like it before. A large flotilla of flag bedecked boats, stretching for a quarter of a mile, slowly rowed up the St. Louis River toward them. The oars of the boats flashed in the sunlight as they dipped and rose in unison from the dark coffee-colored river water.

Such was the scene on Saturday, July 29th, 1826, as the procession of boats carrying the United States delegation to "The Grand Council of the Lake Superior and Mississippi Chippewa" approached the site of the meeting. For several days word had spread that a large number of boats were coasting along the south shore of Lake Superior bound for Fond du Lac. Now, for the first time, all could see for themselves.

A message had been sent by the territorial governor for all the Ojibway to meet at Fond du Lac at the end of July. Many had already arrived before the government delegation. They too, joined in witnessing the spectacle unfolding before them.

The boats skimmed over the calm surface of the river like giant six-legged water bugs. The onlookers waiting on shore could observe the territorial governor's barge bedecked with flags and the portly governor himself in the bow. Preceding Cass was a freight canoe carrying the new Superintendent of Indian Affairs, Thomas L. McKenney. Following in perfect order were other boats filled with men and supplies. The voyageurs strained at their oars and paddles. Their distinctive garb of red woolen caps or lace trimmed hats, gaudy shirts, sashes, and Indian leggings set them apart from the military escort with their unmistakable visor caps, white fatigue uniforms, and cross belts. Flanking the boats were Indian canoes ten to twelve abreast filled with tribesmen in all their colorful finery bound for the Grand Council.

Suddenly the stillness was broken by the sound of a military band. A group of red-coated musicians struck up *Hail Columbia.* The shrill whistle of the fifes and the rattle of the rope and tug snare drums reverberated across the river valley. The music added a thrilling element to the dramatic arrival of the official procession. Thomas McKenney described the scene:

> Our canoe in the lead some fifty yards—the Governor's barge next, flanked by the Indians, some ten or twelve canoes of them on either side; then the barges, Capt. Boardman and his military, first, and the rest in order, all with flags flying, and martial music. The barges were thrown at such distances as to make a line of a quarter of a mile. The sight was truly interesting; while the music filled the valleys and rose over the mountain's tops, for the first time since their formation.[23]

As the canoes and boats approached the landing in front of the trading post, the resident voyageurs and Ojibway hunters saluted the new arrivals with a customary *feu de joie.* In response, the band played the national air *Yankee Doodle.* Governor Cass clearly meant to impress everyone with as much pageantry as possible.

Shortly after their arrival at Fond du Lac, Cass and McKenney met with a delegation of chiefs. During the meeting, the chiefs lit their pipes and, according to McKenney, "almost smothered us with smoke." He remarked, "The Governor and I neither of us make out in a fog of this sort, as neither of us use tobacco in any way."

These small but colorful details of the council at Fond du Lac were recorded by Thomas McKenney and later published in a book entitled *Sketches of a Tour to the Lakes*, which was printed in Baltimore in 1827. In his book, McKenney wrote each chapter in the form of a letter to his wife. McKenney documented some incredibly interesting accounts of not only the events at Fond du Lac, but also observations of the people and the country which he passed through on the way to the treaty grounds.

Unlike McKenney, Lewis Cass had visited the remote region at the head of Lake Superior before, which is probably why he chose the eastern terminus of the Northwest Trail as the site for the Grand Council. It was a location of great symbolic importance to the Ojibway of Lake Superior and of the Mississippi.[24]

According to the Ojibway historian Warren, Cass chose the location because it was the most central point in the lands occupied by the Ojibway. Cass may have had another motive as well. In 1826, the remote region west of Detroit was only nominally controlled by the United States. Unsettled boundary questions still existed between the United States and Great Britain because of vague language in the peace treaty ending the American Revolutionary War. The chief issue concerned the customary route west of Lake Superior previously discussed in Chapter 3. The British negotiators proposed the boundary follow the course of the St. Louis River to its headwaters and by portage to Rainy Lake. To that end, they sent out a survey party headed by the well-known geographer David Thompson to survey the proposed route along the St. Louis River in 1825. In view of the activity along the Northwest Trail, it is understandable that Cass wanted to show the flag.

As it turned out, a boundary question was a major issue to be decided at the Grand Council, but not the boundary between the United States and Canada. Cass and McKenney hoped to bring about a cessation of the ongoing hostilities between the Ojibway and Dakota. A treaty with the Northwestern tribes, concluded by Cass and Indian Agent William Clark at Prairie du Chien on August 19th, 1825, included an agreement on a boundary line separating the tribes to be surveyed by the government. Hopefully, the Ojibway of Lake Superior and the Mississippi would join with the other tribes and consent to the provisions of the treaty agreed to at Prairie du Chien.[25]

The Grand Council was one of the most elaborate ceremonies ever held in the Lake Superior region. Representatives of twelve different bands attended the week long session. The chief goal was to persuade the assembled Ojibway to accept the boundary settlement of the Northwestern tribes at Prairie du Chien. Cass and McKenney also hoped to conclude an agreement among the Ojibway, the Winnebago, and the Menominee tribes recognizing each group's territorial claims. To achieve the agreement they proposed another council to be held during the summer of 1827.

Details of the Grand Council–from July 29th, to the conclusion of the meeting on August 8th–were faithfully recorded by McKenney. The daily proceedings, the ordinary events in the camp, and the text of the final agreement were recorded and submitted to Congress and President John Quincy Adams.[26] The site of the Grand Council was on the grounds of the American Fur Company's Fond du Lac post on the banks of the St. Louis River. Each council session was announced by the firing of three guns. The meetings, which took place in a specially constructed bower or awning, were filled with ceremony and speeches as each participant voiced his opinion. The speeches and ceremonies were interrupted by frequent intermissions. A contemporary sketch of the scene shows the assembled delegates seated underneath the shade of the bower with the military escort standing in the rear dressed in their blue uniform coats and shakos crowned by cockades, tassels, and plumes. McKenney wrote:

> Our bower, or awning, with its covering of leaves, under which we shall hold our council, has been put up today. We have taken down the tents in front of the buildings [trading post], and erected it on the ground where these stood. It is sixty feet by eighteen. We wait only for the first of August to commence our council. I have engaged Mr. Lewis to take a sketch of this bower when the Indians are assembled, and while we are engaged in council.[27]

McKenney noted the many details of everyday life during his visit to Fond du Lac. In the evening he sat in his camp chair surrounded with mosquito netting. While being serenaded by countless frogs and the constant humming of insects, he drafted a letter by candlelight. On August 1st, 1826, he wrote the following lines:

> My Dear
> I find my mosquito net invaluable at this place. I have it fixed permanently, and am quite delighted to hear the singing of this biting tribe, while I feel secure from their attacks.[28]

He noted the arrival of various bands of Indians and the circumstances surrounding the initial distribution of presents that preceded the beginning of the treaty session:

> A slight shower of rain fell last night; but the morning is fine, and the elements are all composed. I had not risen before I heard in the distance the thump of the Indian drum, and now and then a yell. It turned out to be the Sandy Lake band, on their way from their encampment to pay their visit of ceremony.[29]

McKenney had very strong reservations about the use of liquor in the Indian territory; however, it was a long-standing custom, even at treaty ceremonies, to provide each arrival with a taste of the vile brew, "We made the same kinds of presents. Whiskey is the great object. Their love of this poisonous draught is without bounds." He added, "we give them only an occasional drink, out of a wine glass, and that we dilute, and firmly reject their application for more."[30]

The purpose for the Grand Council was achieved after days of ceremony. The final result was a treaty embodying several issues. The first article of the treaty held that the "Chiefs and Warriors of the Chippewa tribe" agree to the treaty concluded at Prairie du Chien, "and engage to observe and fulfill the stipulations thereof." The second article provided that a delegation from the Chippewa tribe would attend a treaty session at Green Bay in 1827 to address boundary issues with the Winnebago and Menominee.

The third article included a provision allowing the government of the United States the "right to search for, and carry away, any metals or minerals from any part of their country." Although the French and British governments had heard about the existence of copper deposits in the Lake Superior region, neither colonial power developed copper mines. Because of the strategic importance of copper, the United States government investigated reports of deposits of this metal as evidenced by this specific article included in the treaty.

Among the provisions of the treaty were two articles (IV and V) calling for the allotments of land to certain "half-breeds" at Sault Sainte Marie and an annual annuity of two thousand dollars. These two provisions were eliminated from the final draft approved by Congress. A sixth article providing for the establishment of a school was approved.

The last significant article of the treaty stipulated that "The Chippeway tribe of Indians fully acknowledge the authority and jurisdiction of the United States, and disclaim all connexion [sic] with any foreign power." This last provision meant to stop the annual visits by Ojibway bands to British posts to receive gifts and other tokens of goodwill.[31]

With the conclusion of the Grand Council, lavish presents and provisions were distributed from stores previously brought for that purpose. McKenney noted, "Everyone was told he should have as much as he could carry; and the promise was literally fulfilled." The storehouse was so full of materials that the remainder of the provisions and goods were distributed the next day.

> This great store was not quite disposed of this evening, the residue is to be given out in the morning, when the drink of whiskey is to be distributed. This is the last gift—and never before was a gift so long coming. This is my last night at the Fond du Lac. Thermometer, sundown, 66.°[32]

So the Grand Council ended on a hopeful note. The delegation prepared to embark on August 8th:

> Everything was put in motion this morning. The military in their fatigue dress—the voyageurs by the sides of their canoes, with little fires near them at which the gum is melted, send up their smoke into the brightness of the morning. The noise of hammers and saws, and the splitting

up of boxes and making of others, in which to pack away our supplies, all indicate a speedy embarkment.[33]

Lastly, McKenney toured the trading post and visited the Ojibway camp located on the island in the river opposite the post. Then all were in readiness to leave.

The squeal of the fife and the roll of the drum were signals to break camp. The musical code was understood by the troops; and once it was played, they sprang into action. McKenney noted, "The company is in motion–the military are playing "strike your tents," &c.–they fall while I write. Our voyageurs are seated, and the Governor calls.   Ever yours."[34]

So ended the most elaborate assemblage yet seen at the head of Lake Superior. The Grand Council at Fond du Lac set the pattern for future councils and treaty negotiations in the region. Eleven years later, on July 29th, 1837, the Ojibway signed their first land cession in what would later become the Territory, and finally, the State of Minnesota. As far as the fate of the provision establishing a boundary between the Ojibway and Dakota was concerned, the outcome was predictable. Time passed and nothing was done to establish a line. When the government finally appropriated funds for the survey in 1835, members of both tribes destroyed the boundary markers as fast as the surveyors set them. Old deep-seated animosities between the tribes continued to spark controversy; but as long as the Ojibway were firmly ensconced in their villages at Fond du Lac and Sandy Lake, travelers and traders along the Northwest Trail were secure.

Schoolcraft's Odyssey

Events in the country west of Lake Superior had not changed materially four years after the conclusion of the Grand Council. In 1830, Governor Cass instructed Henry Schoolcraft, by then Indian Agent for the "Chippewa at Sault Sainte Marie," to travel to the Fond du Lac to settle the ongoing Dakota-Ojibway hostilities. The expedition was delayed until May of 1832, when Schoolcraft was ordered to proceed to the Mississippi headwaters and "visit as many Indians ... as circumstances will permit." His official instructions included promoting peace, overseeing the fur trade, gathering information about the country and vaccinating the Indians against smallpox. His group included a missionary, Reverend William Thurston Boutwell; a "surgeon," Doctor Douglass Houghton; and a military escort under the command of Lieutenant James Allen.[35]

From all appearances, the real objective of Schoolcraft's 1832 expedition was to search for the source of the Mississippi River, which was said to originate in Lac la Biche ("Elk Lake"). Only extraordinary low water had prevented Lewis Cass from reaching Elk Lake, which the local Indians believed to be one of the sources of the great river. This time, leaving nothing to chance, Schoolcraft even created the name "Itasca," which he intended to apply to Elk Lake, once "discovered."[36]

Schoolcraft's pace on this trip into the interior was phenomenal and further reveals his true purpose–that of finding the source of the Mississippi. He left Sault Sainte Marie on June 7th, 1832, and reached Sandy Lake by July 3rd. While coasting the south shore of Lake Superior, he met a party of Ojibway from Cass Lake bound for the Sault, one of whom, named Ozawindib, or the "Yellow Head," he persuaded to accompany him.

Schoolcraft's whirlwind speed frequently left the military escort behind, a circumstance which did not endear him to Lieutenant Allen. James Allen was supposed to keep a journal and draw a map of the country he passed through to include in a final report on the expedition. A glance at Allen's map—at least that portion covering the St. Louis River—discloses very little detail. In fact, Allen's notes indicate he was having a dreadful time negotiating the river and rapids with an inexperienced crew and no guide.[37]

One notable achievement of the expedition was the passage over the notorious Savanna Portage without any serious casualties. The men floundered along in waist deep mud while beset by hordes of ravenous mosquitoes. Reverend William Boutwell, the missionary Schoolcraft had requested be sent along, remarked rather laconically about the conditions encountered at this immemorial carrying place: "The musketoes here are voracious, long billed and dyspeptic. They gore me until the blood runs. Landed at 9 and breakfasted in their midst."[38] Later, while crossing the Savanna Portage, he continued:

> July 2, 1832. Rose at 6. Pleasant sun this morning, but the musketoes are smoke and fire proof. Was almost devoured while attempting to mend my pantaloons, which suffered a sorry rend in the mud on Saturday. Much bickering and dissatisfaction among the soldiers this morning about carrying their baggage. Not a little profanity.[39]

Toward the end of the portage, Boutwell once again lamented the clouds of mosquitos:

> To all the other severity's of this portage, is yet to be added, that of being half devoured by musketoes. They exceed all description for being voracious, as if they never saw a human being, and were fully determined he should not escape till they had made a meal off him, at least. They are, if possible, more numerous than frogs, locusts or lice of Egypt, rising in clouds from the grass and underbrush.[40]

After enduring the rigors of the Savanna, Schoolcraft's party continued on to the American Fur Company post at the confluence of the Sandy Lake and Mississippi rivers. It was while the expedition halted there, that Lieutenant Allen had the company workmen fit his canoe with oars. Allen realized that the soldiers who manned the canoe could propel the craft better by oars than paddles.[41] After celebrating the national holiday on July 4th, the expedition departed Sandy Lake and swiftly proceeded upstream.

The expedition passed familiar landmarks as it toiled against the current of the Mississippi. Soon Schoolcraft's party arrived at Cass Lake where his guide Ozawindib secured additional canoes and guides. From Cass Lake the party now ascended the Mississippi to its east fork. Leaving the river to wind its way through dense growth, Schoolcraft's party portaged overland and arrived at Lac la Biche, which he officially named "Lake Itasca."

An exploration of the lake lasting about an hour was sufficient for Schoolcraft, and after a brief ceremony and flag raising on Schoolcraft Island, so named by Lieutenant Allen, the "discoverer" embarked with his entourage and guides for the return trip. The rest of Schoolcraft's journal records how the expedition crossed over a series of portages to avoid retracing their steps down the Mississippi. Eventually, the expedition rejoined the Mississippi and proceeded to Fort Snelling. After a day at the fort, Schoolcraft departed for Sault Sainte Marie by way of the St. Croix River. He left Lieutenant Allen to follow him without a guide or benefit of direction.

In spite of its rapid transit of the Northwest Trail, the Schoolcraft Expedition of 1832 left a considerable written record of observations of the route. Aside from Lieutenant James Allen's official report, other members, such as Reverend Boutwell and Doctor Houghton, also left journals and letters describing the trip. Schoolcraft later published a book setting forth his adventures as he had done following the Northwestern Expedition twelve years before. It too, was popular with the public. Lieutenant Allen submitted an official report to Congress and a map of the area detailing the events of the expedition. Nowhere in his official account does Allen ever mention "Lake Itasca."[42]

Schoolcraft's search for the source of the river was later followed by a thorough examination of the area around Lac la Biche and the discovery of the actual source of the Mississippi River in 1836 by the French mathematician and explorer Joseph Nicollet. Further exploration of the interior of what is now Minnesota continued with other groups following the old Northwest Trail over the same rapids, rivers, and portages in quest of knowledge about the region. Most of these expeditions were rather small, and most were either concerned with geology or with surveying the public domain.

Doctor Norwood's Survey

On the afternoon of June 24th, 1848, a small but determined band of men struggled through knee-deep mud as they trudged east over the rugged Savanna Portage. Unmindful of the great events of the time, they were focused instead on the need to complete the daunting task that lay before them—the first comprehensive geological survey of northern Minnesota.

Few heeded their exploration in a far off corner of the wilderness west of Lake Superior. Far from garnering headlines for their pioneering work in the relatively new science of geology, their story was eclipsed instead by word of revolutions rocking Europe and headlines with news that United States military forces were poised to withdraw from Mexico.

Undeterred, the geological survey party under the direction of Doctor Joseph Norwood moved along the route separating the Mississippi River from the Great Lakes. They studied the layers of soil that lay bare along the riverbank, and looked for rock formations that might yield new clues as to the earth's origin.

Commissioned by the United States Treasury Department under the overall direction of United States Geologist, Doctor David Dale Owen, the geological survey was charged with mapping the basic geological structure of Wisconsin, Minnesota, Iowa, and part of Nebraska. Begun in 1847, the project took five years to complete. The map and report produced by the geological survey contained not only information about the types of rocks found in the region, but also extensive information about various geological formations, some of which were thought to contain deposits of copper. In addition to information useful to future miners, the map and report also contained descriptions of the country traversed by the survey teams.[4s3]

The base map used for the survey was the product of Joseph N. Nicollet, who explored the area in the 1830s. In addition to his skills as a geographer, Nicollet was an amateur geologist and faithfully recorded rock and mineral formations that he felt were of scientific interest. Nicollet and fur trader William Aitkin, traveling over the Northwest Trail, measured distances, noted elevations, and recorded physical features during the summer of 1837. Nicollet's map, first published by the United States Army Bureau of the Corps of Topographical Engineers in 1842, was followed by a scale-down version, which accompanied the report of his explorations in 1843. These documents were by far the most accurate depiction of the country west of Lake Superior.[44]

Even with the best of maps, however, the geological survey was no easy task. The risk of running out of food, getting lost because of faulty directions, lacking adequate guides or no guides at all were all serious considerations. Added to the normal risks of travel in rugged terrain was the threat of disease. Asian cholera had been reported in certain locations on the frontier in 1848. As if to underscore the risks, other early explorers were known to have suffered violent deaths in the wilderness. Michigan State Geologist, Doctor Douglass Houghton, who had accompanied Schoolcraft's expedition of 1832, drowned in Lake Superior near Eagle River in October of 1845. The canoe in which he and four companions were riding was swamped by high waves. Only two men were rescued from the frigid water.

Mindful of the many risks involved, Doctor Joseph Norwood, consulted with fur traders about the most effective way to explore the vast wilderness of northern Minnesota. It was decided that the most productive course was to follow the major rivers and observe the layers exposed by the deep cuts along the stream banks. He also decided to explore the basins of the large lakes in the region including the north shore of Lake Superior. Doctor Norwood was assigned the Mississippi River, the St. Louis River, the Red, Leech, Cass, Winnibigoshish, and Vermilion lakes and the north shore of Superior.[45]

In June of 1848, Norwood and his assistant, Colonel Charles Whittlesey, traveled up the Mississippi to the village of Crow Wing, a small trading settlement located at the confluence of the Crow Wing and Mississippi rivers. Crow Wing was a starting point for anyone traveling into the interior; and it was there Norwood sought to procure supplies, canoes, and experienced voyageurs. Most importantly, Norwood needed the services of a capable guide:

But before we could reach that place, most of the clerks had come in and made their "returns," and nearly all the voyageurs acquainted with the section of country I was directed to explore, had left the post. My only chance, therefore, was to wait for the arrival of Mr. Chaboeuliez [sic], who, with several men, was daily expected to arrive from Red Lake.[46]

Norwood was delayed for a week at Crow Wing as he awaited the arrival of voyageurs and Chaboillez. Finally, on the 13th of June, the voyageurs and their guide arrived. Chaboillez agreed to join Norwood's "corps" at Fond du Lac in July.

At nine o'clock on the morning of June 16th, Norwood left Crow Wing after he had obtained two "half-worn canoes" and four of the best voyageurs in the Northwest for his "reconnoissance [sic]." The expedition traveled eleven miles the first day. As the expedition slowly ascended the Mississippi, the nature of the surrounding landscape changed. Norwood noted that above Rabbit River "good second-rate pine occurs on the ridges on both sides of the river."[47] The geological features of the Mississippi were recorded in the form of cross sectional drawings showing strata.

Norwood's party reached the western end of the Northwest Trail at the mouth of the Sandy Lake River six days after leaving Crow Wing:

We entered the outlet of Sandy Lake on the morning of the 22nd of June, at half past eight o'clock, and pitched our tents on the island nearest to, and immediately opposite the Indian Village.[48]

As Norwood passed through the country, he noted items of not only geological interest, but also natural and cultural features. For example, at the mouth of the Sandy Lake River, he observed an infestation of tent caterpillars which had cleanly stripped the trees and bushes of leaves. "The caterpillar—was very abundant here, where it was first seen on the 19th. The trees, bushes, and shrubs, were literally covered with them."

Shortly after their arrival, the expedition members met the resident Methodist missionary, Reverend Samuel Spates and his family. The missionary was very hospitable and gave Doctor Norwood information about the country surrounding Sandy Lake. Spates also gave valuable information about the route from Sandy Lake to Fond du Lac. The geologists described the products of the mission garden, which consisted of corn, potatoes, turnips, and "a generality of garden vegetables." Apparently the crops grew very well in the sandy loam.

After resting two days at Sandy Lake, the geological survey left by way of the Prairie and West Savanna rivers. Norwood commented that they traveled by "the route over which the fur companies have transported their goods toward the far Northwestern posts for many years" in reference to the Northwest Trail. He described the route up the West "Savannah" River:

West Savannah River enters Prairie river about a mile and a half above Sandy Lake. It is twenty feet wide at its mouth, but soon contracts to ten or twelve feet, which general width it retains throughout its course. It is extremely crooked, and winds through extensive swamps covered with aquatic grasses. It is very shallow, becoming quite rapid towards its source, with a pebbly bottom, and, as the portage is approached, is obstructed by boulders.[49]

Little Savanna Lake as seen from a branch of the Savanna Portage. Photo by Larry Luukkonen

High hills on either side of the West Savanna were crowned with a luxuriant growth of aspen, birch, and pine. As Norwood neared the portage between the East and West Savanna rivers, he observed a large boulder on top of a hill immediately south of, and overlooking Little Savanna Lake. According to his published report, the flat rock measured sixty-eight feet in circumference and was exposed at least three and a half feet above ground. The rock, which is situated near the overland trail from the west end of the Savanna Portage to Northeast Bay on Sandy Lake, occupies a prominent position on a hillside and, although partly obscured by brush, is visible today from the road leading into Savanna Portage State Park. "Norwood's Rock" is noteworthy because it represents one of the very few historically identified natural features, other than waterways, that still exists within the present boundaries of the park.[50]

As the expedition crossed the Savanna Portage, many details of the country were recorded and later included in the official report. These remarks offer a glimpse of what the countryside looked like in 1848, long before homesteaders and land developers transformed the area:

> The distance from the mouth of the river to the beginning of the portage, is about ten miles. The portage is six miles long, and leads over the highlands which divide the waters of the Mississippi from those of Lake Superior. The dividing ridge is composed of ranges of drift hills, the highest of which, on the portage, is by barometric measurement, one hundred and thirty-nine feet above the level of Sandy Lake.[51]

Norwood noticed a marked change in the country as his group crossed the Savanna Portage:

For the last four and a half miles, the portage is dry and passes over ridges covered with young birch, maple, and pine. On some of the ridges, the pine may be considered first-rate. The east end of the portage for the distance of a mile and a half, runs through a tamarack swamp, which is flooded with water, and next to impassable. It is generally considered the worst "carrying place" in the Northwest, and, judging from the great number of canoes which lie decaying along this part of it, having been abandoned in consequence of the difficulty experienced in getting them over, its reputation is well deserved.[52]

Arriving at the east end of the portage, the expedition found the East Savanna River to be quite navigable. The stream was five yards wide with a slow current. The country around the head of the East Savanna was generally characterized as bog with small islands or knolls that were crowned with stunted tamarack, aspen, and birch.

As the expedition approached the St. Louis River, the banks of the East

Rough going on the East Savanna River. Obstructions such as this were encountered in 1983 during a canoe trip tracing the historic trade route. Author's collection

Savanna became steeper. They also observed a more luxuriant growth of aspen, maple, ash, elm, birch, hemlock, pine, and fir. In places the current, undercutting the clay banks, caused trees and brush to fall into the stream. The debris collected at bends and constrictions and created the "rafts" or obstructions that countless travelers associated with the East Savanna.

Finally, on June 26th, the men reached the junction of the East Savanna and St. Louis rivers. Norwood intended to retrace his steps and explore the upper reaches of the St. Louis. He did not describe his journey downstream to the village of Fond du Lac other than mentioning he reached Fond du Lac in two days. He calculated the distance between Sandy Lake and the "Trading-Post by way of the Savannah Rivers" to be ninety-six miles. Here, at the head of navigation on the St. Louis, he rested, replenished his provisions, and explored the surrounding country.

Two men were sent by canoe to La Pointe to obtain supplies. Meanwhile, Colonel Whittlesey remained at the trading post to observe latitude and longitude, measure elevations, and explore the range of hills north of the village (Spirit Mountain and Bardon's Peak). Norwood and two voyageurs set off by canoe to explore the Left Hand (Nemadji) and Black rivers. After a brief reconnaissance, before heading back up the St. Louis River, he returned to Fond du Lac and began preparations for a survey of the north shore of Lake Superior.

Reuben B. Carlton, government blacksmith at Fond du Lac from 1846 to 1863.
Carlton County Historical Society

The exploration of the Lake Superior's north shore occupied an important part of Joseph Norwood's report. A considerable amount of useful geological information including sketches, diagrams, and detailed maps was compiled in the final published version of the report. One of the most interesting episodes in the exploration along the shore was the discovery and naming of Carlton Peak.

As the survey party set out from the trading post at Fond du Lac to explore the shore, it was accompanied by the government blacksmith stationed there, Mr. Reuben B. Carlton. Exactly what function Carlton provided is not certain, but he was included in the exploring party that went as far as the mouth of the *Kawimbash* (present-day Temperance) River. All along the shore, the party investigated the rock formations and explored the mouth of each stream.[53]

From Fond du Lac to the Pigeon River, a chain of low mountains extend parallel to the shore of Lake Superior. Because of their irregular shape, they are known as the Sawtooth Mountains. As Norwood's survey party neared the mouth of the Kawimbash River, they noticed a prominent peak looming over the shore to the north. The Ojibway referred to this impressive feature as *Ga-nijike-pikwadinag*, meaning "lone hill." The expedition paused about half a mile from the entrance to the river to examine the promontory.

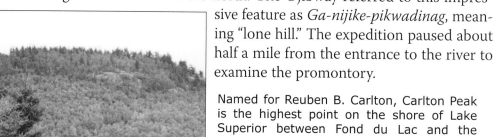

Named for Reuben B. Carlton, Carlton Peak is the highest point on the shore of Lake Superior between Fond du Lac and the Pigeon River. Photos by Marlene Wisuri

Colonel Whittlesey and Reuben Carlton walked inland about a half mile to get a closer look. Their curiosity ultimately took them to the base of the mountain; then they climbed it. Later, Colonel Whittlesey proposed that the mountain be named "Carlton's Peak." The name has remained to the present day.

The following year, a second geological survey team returned to resume the exploration of the rest of the north shore. One of the members of the new party, Major Richard Owen, climbed Carlton Peak and measured the elevation with a mercury barometer. He found it to be nine hundred and thirty-seven feet above lake level. Modern sources give the distance as nine hundred and twenty-four feet above lake level and one thousand five hundred and twenty feet above sea level. Although higher mountains exist inland, Carlton Peak holds the honor of being the highest point along the shore from Fond du Lac to Pigeon River.

With the completion of the survey as far as the Kawimbash River, Norwood returned to Fond du Lac and the old American Fur Company post to resupply his expedition. From there, he set off for a reconnaissance of the St. Louis River. He portaged from the upper reaches of the St. Louis River to waters draining into Lake Vermilion. From there he followed the ancient trade route along the border lakes. His party proceeded as far west as the mouth of the Big Fork River.

The expedition also visited Red Lake and followed the old trade route down Turtle River to Cass Lake and the Mississippi. Proceeding downstream, Norwood examined Lake Winnibigoshish and continued to Sandy Lake. On October 6th, Norwood's party reached the mouth of the Muddy, or as he called it the "Mud" (Ripple) River, where the expedition divided. Norwood, Whittlesey, and one voyageur canoed up the Muddy River, then crossed by a short portage to the north shore of Mille Lacs. After examining rock formations on the lake, Norwood canoed down the Rum River and joined the rest of his party at St. Paul on October 16th, 1848.[54]

Doctor Norwood's portion of the geological survey, published in the final report in 1852, provides a wealth of information about the geology of the region and interesting facts about the people and places he visited. Norwood's voyage of discovery along the Northwest Trail has also preserved a very complete picture of travel in the interior of Minnesota in the summer of 1848.

Chapter 6 - Official Expeditions
Notes

1. William Watts Folwell, *A History of Minnesota*, 4 vols. (1921; reprint ed., St. Paul, 1956), vol. 1, pp. 90-101, includes Pike's instructions; Donald Jackson (ed.), *The Journals of Zebulon Montgomery Pike*, 2 vols. (Norman, 1966), includes a detailed biographical account of Zebulon Pike.

2. Ibid., vol. 1, p. 78.

3. Ibid., vol. 1, pp. 182-183.

4. For a discussion of the frontier defense program of John C. Calhoun see Mentor L. Williams (ed.), *Schoolcraft's Narrative Journal of Travels* (East Lansing, 1992), pp. 7-8.

5. Ibid., pp. 302-304.

6. Ibid., pp. 21-22, includes copies of the journals of James Duane Doty and Charles Christopher Trowbridge in appendices F and G; For the complete journal of David Bates Douglass see Sydney W. Jackman (et al., eds.), *American Voyageur: The Journal of David Bates Douglass* (Marquette, 1969).

7. Ibid., p. 39.

8. Williams (ed.), *Schoolcraft's Narrative Journal*, pp. 141-142.

9. Jackman (ed.), *American Voyageur*, p. 74.

10. Williams (ed.), *Schoolcraft's Narrative Journal*, p. 146.

11. Newton H. Winchell, *The Aborigines of Minnesota* (St. Paul, 1911), pp. 607-608. Winchell cited as his source Schoolcraft's, *The American Indians: Their History, Condition, and Prospects* (Rochester, New York, 1851).

12. Williams (ed.), *Schoolcraft's Narrative Journal*, p. 148.

13. Ibid., p. 483. For an earlier version of Trowbridge's account see Ralph H. Brown, "With Cass in the Northwest in 1820: The Journal of Charles Christopher Trowbridge, May 24th-September 13th, 1820," *Minnesota History*, vol. 23, nos. 2, 3, and 4 (June, September, and December, 1942), p. 250.

14. Jackman (ed.), *American Voyageur*, p. 79.

15. Williams (ed.), *Schoolcraft's Narrative Journal*, p. 152.

16. Jackman (ed.), *American Voyageur*, p. 79.

17. Williams (ed.), *Schoolcraft's Narrative Journal*, p. 168. Here one finds the first reference to "Cassina" or present-day Cass Lake.

18. James Doty's report to Cass can be found in Williams (ed.), *Schoolcraft's Narrative Journal*, pp. 436-445.

19. Brown, "With Cass," p. 333. Charles Christopher Trowbridge's remarks can also be found in Williams (ed.), *Schoolcraft's Narrative Journal*, pp. 461-500.

20. Brown, "With Cass," p. 333.

21. Ibid., p. 334.

22. For Douglass' reaction to Schoolcraft's decision to publish see Williams (ed.), *Schoolcraft's Narrative Journal*, p. 22.

23. Thomas L. McKenney, *Sketches of a Tour to the Lakes* (1827; reprint ed., Minneapolis, 1959), pp. 274-275.

24. William Whipple Warren, *History of the Ojibway People* (1885; reprint ed., St. Paul, 1984), p. 392.

25. For the detailed text of the various treaties see Charles J. Kappler (ed.), *Indian Treaties: 1778-1883* (New York, 1973).

26. McKenney, *Sketches of a Tour*, pp. 479-481. The author makes several references to McKenney in the text.

27. Ibid., p. 297.

28. Ibid., p. 299.

29. Ibid.

30. Ibid.

31.   Ibid., pp. 479-484. McKenney noted on page 479, "This work not being published until after the ratification of the treaty, it is inserted here in its ratified form."

32.   Ibid., p. 343.

33.   Ibid., p. 337.

34.   Ibid., p. 345.

35.   Philip P. Mason (ed.), *Schoolcraft's Expedition to Lake Itasca* (East Lansing, 1993), includes the journals and letters of Lieutenant James Allen, Doctor Douglass Houghton, and Reverend William Thurston Boutwell are included in appendices C, D, and E.

36.   Ibid., pp. xxi-xxii, 97, n. b., 350-351, 352, 356, and 358.

37.   Ibid., pp. 192-195.

38.   Ibid., p. 321.

39.   Ibid., p. 322.

40.   Ibid., p. 323.

41.   Ibid., p. 198.

42.   Ibid., pp. 205 and 235-236. Neither Lieutenant Allen nor Doctor Houghton mentioned Lake "Itasca" in their report or correspondence. As for Reverend Boutwell, it was not until many years after the 1832 expedition that he described his small part in providing Schoolcraft with the Latin words *verum* or *veritas* and *caput* from which "Itasca" was formed.

43.   David Dale Owen, *Report of a Geological Survey of Wisconsin, Iowa, and Minnesota; and Incidentally of a Portion of Nebraska Territory* (Philadelphia, 1852).
For information on the geological survey and of Doctor Norwood's activities, the author has relied on the geologist's detailed contemporary report.

44.   Nicollet's map was originally published in 1842. See chap. 3, nn. 59-60.

45.   Colonel Charles Whittlesey, who accompanied Doctor Norwood, was responsible for fixing the geographic locations of important points by astronomical observations with sextant and chronometer. Owen, *Geological Survey*, p. 293. The author quotes Norwood several times in the text.

46.   Ibid., p. 296.

47.   Ibid.

48.   Ibid., p. 298.

49.   Ibid., p. 300.

50.   Ibid., p. 310.

51.   Ibid., p. 300.

52.   Ibid., pp. 300-301.

53.   Ibid., p. 380. For an account of Reuben B. Carlton and the naming of Carlton Peak, see Larry Luukkonen, *Reuben B. Carlton: Frontier Blacksmith and Visionary* (Cloquet, Minnesota, 2005).

54.   Owen, *Geological Survey*, pp. 329-332.

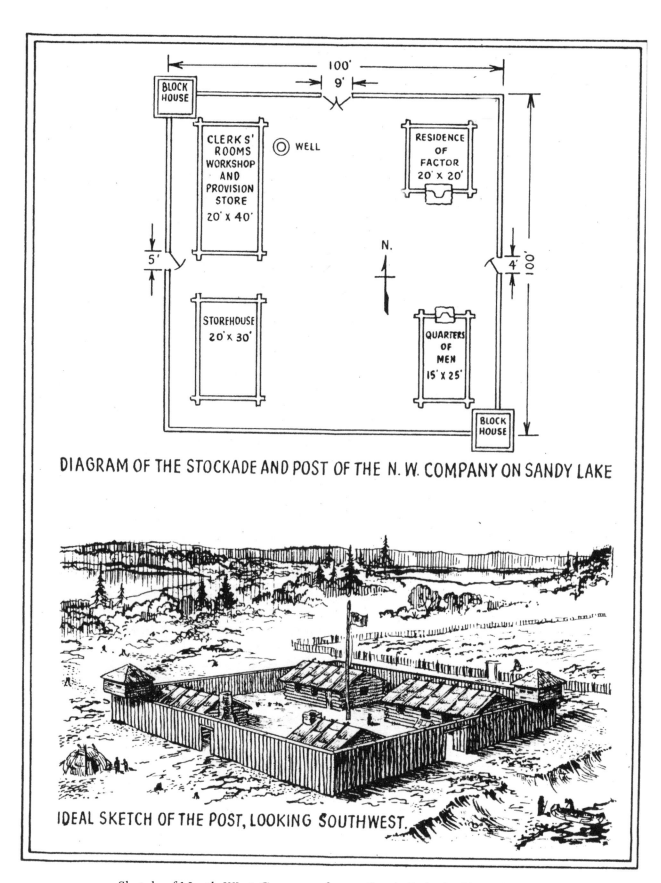

DIAGRAM OF THE STOCKADE AND POST OF THE N.W. COMPANY ON SANDY LAKE

IDEAL SKETCH OF THE POST, LOOKING SOUTHWEST.

Sketch of North West Company fort at Sandy Lake by Evan A. Hart.
Author's collection

Part III ⤙ The Quest for Fur

Chapter 7 ✄ Frontier Outposts

Thus far, the journey along the Northwest Trail has led across portages, along rushing rivers, and over winter roads from Lake Superior to the Mississippi River. Along the way not only features and place-names have been identified, but also some of the people who used the route and left a record of their passage through the wilderness. Most of the earliest travelers were connected in some way with the fur trade. In fact, the first major economic endeavor which brought people to the region was the fur trade.

The era of the large-scale exploitation of the fur-bearing resources of North America began in the seventeenth century and progressed through the nineteenth century. Starting as individual barter, the trade in rich furs grew to become a global enterprise with huge economic ramifications for both the individuals and the countries that were involved in it.

Building and Supplying a Trading Post

In addition to exploration and mapping, previous chapters have shown how the Northwest Trail became known as a migration route and trade artery long before the end of the French regime in Canada. By the mid-eighteenth century, a gradual increase in traffic occurred as a growing number of the independent, or "South Traders," sought to either reach the Northwest by way of the south shore of Lake Superior and the St. Louis River-Savanna Portage-Mississippi River route, or tap the rich furs in what is now northern Minnesota. By the last quarter of the eighteenth century, records show a significant increase in the number of independent traders wintering west of Lake Superior.[1] It was not long before they faced stiff competition from the North West Company, which built large permanent supply bases or depots at either end of the Northwest Trail.

A key element in the trade was the establishment of trading posts or depots where trade goods could be stored and where the harvest of furs could be tallied, examined, and packaged for the long voyage to the markets of Europe and Asia. The fact that major trading establishments existed, first at Fond du Lac and second at Sandy Lake, underscores the importance of the route as an avenue of the North American fur trade. By comparing accounts of these two trading houses, one can acquire a fairly complete picture of their appearance and their importance.[2]

In reviewing the South Trader's experiences on the route, contemporary accounts first mention the site of a general rendezvous of traders at Sandy Lake followed by the establishment of seasonal trading cabins. The wintering house or trader's cabin ultimately gave way to larger establishments capable of a high degree of self-sufficiency. This section will examine the qualities of major trading sites, the trading houses, the men who built them, and the the number and location of trading posts at Fond du Lac and Sandy Lake.[3]

The establishment of permanent trading posts often occurred after the repeated use of a given location as a camp or rendezvous point. The trading posts located at Fond du Lac and Sandy Lake are good examples of such prior usage. Situated astride junctions of major streams and trails, the sites were natural points where travelers congregated. In addition to being at the hub of travel networks, these sites were—and are still—attractive even today for the establishment of dwellings or businesses.

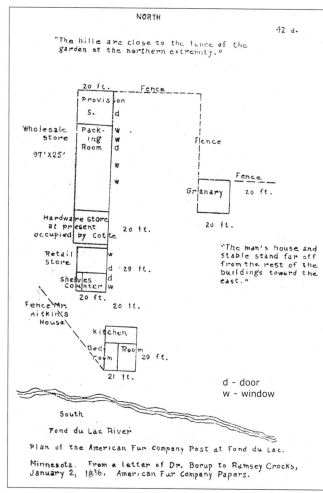

The plan of the American Fur Company Post
at Fond du Lac 1836.
Ellworth Carlstedt, *A History of the Fond du Lac Tradings Posts with Some Mention of the Fond du Lac Department*

The building of a trading post involved expense and labor; therefore, a number of conditions had to be met for the post to be profitable. The location of a prospective trading house was crucial to its long-term success and was the first matter to be considered. Fur trade etiquette required the trader be "invited" to live among the band he traded with. It is commonplace to find references to chiefs asking officials that a trader be sent to live amongst a certain band. If the invitation was accepted, the first step involved construction of a trading house. To that end, the trader consulted with the elders of the tribe concerning the most advantageous place for the building. Site requirements included a dry location with sufficient timber for construction and fuel, ease of access, and abundant sources of food in the area such as wild rice, maple sugar, fish, fowl, and big game.

Sometimes posts were mistakenly built on what later proved to be a flood plain. For example, the third American Fur Company post at Sandy Lake, was submerged under several feet of water during a particularly high flood in the spring of 1850. A quick spring thaw or heavy rains turned normally serene rivers into raging torrents and flooded the surrounding countryside. Alexander Henry the Younger described his experiences on the Red River of the North during a spring thaw which, flooding the country, turned the prairie into a huge lake. Ice dams routinely form on the the Red River of the North, since the mouth of the stream is usually still frozen even though its headwaters and tributaries are not.[4]

Generally flooding of trading post sites along the Northwest Trail was not a problem; however, there were times when the countryside was submerged. Although the Mississippi flowed south into a warmer climate, floods occurred because of the meandering nature of the stream. The winding course of the river slowed the volume of flow, thus backing water up and flooding the land. Sandy Lake rose to great heights as the Mississippi backed up into the Sandy Lake River eventually causing huge areas on the margin of the lake itself to be inundated. Lieutenant James Allen noted such an occurrence at Sandy Lake.[5]

The St. Louis River presented yet another unique problem. It flowed east into Lake Superior whose great depth kept the water temperatures so cold that frequently the mouth of the river was frozen or at the very least blocked with ice flows well into the spring of the year. In such circumstances, location of a post free from potential flooding was extremely important to the eventual success of a trading adventure.[6]

Original American Fur Company building at Fond du Lac in foreground. The photo shows the wholesale store being demolished c. 1917. Russell Photo Co., Carlton County Historical Society

The availability of wood for the construction of a trading house or post was crucial. Good supplies of this material were available at both Fond du Lac and at Sandy Lake. Not only were substantial quantities of wood used in building shelters and storage facilities, but also tremendous quantities were consumed for heating and cooking, especially if the post was used for several years. Very few trading establishments appear to have had metal stoves, although such appliances were widely used in Europe and in parts of America. Most trading establishments used primitive fireplaces as sources of heat and for cooking. The fireplaces were usually wooden structures carefully plastered on the inside with clay to keep the wood framing from igniting and burning the attached structure to the ground. Fire was a constant threat. For example, Jean Baptiste Perrault mentioned in his *Narrative* how sparks from his chimney set the thatch on the roof of his wintering cabin on fire in 1791.[7]

Normally, buildings housing trade goods or stores where they were exchanged had no provision for heat whatsoever. The materials used in construction, especially for the roofs of the buildings, were highly combustible. Depending upon availability, either cedar bark, elm bark, split cedar shingles, or thatch was used to cover the buildings. If the storehouse caught fire, one risked not merely the loss of trade goods, but the loss of food supplies which could spell starvation for the trader and his employees. The storehouse and trade room usually had numerous windows to let in an abundance of natural light, but no candles or oil lamps were allowed for the very same reason given for the prohibition of heating and cooking equipment. Surviving photographs of the Fond du Lac trading post retail store and warehouse show no provision for a chimney but several openings for windows and doors.[8]

Of all the commodities stored at trading posts, gunpowder was the most dangerous. Shipped in barrels of various sizes, it was routinely stored far away from buildings housing people, furs, trade articles, and open flames of any kind. Usually it was either secured in a detached building or kept in a special fire proof magazine with a protective berm of earth constructed to shield the structure on all sides. The berm was also meant to direct the force of an explosion upward and away from other structures should the magazine's contents accidentally ignite.

Aside from the location of the post and the availability of wood from which to construct the buildings, another important consideration in the siting of a trading post was a dependable food supply. For both indigenous people and trader, the need to have adequate supplies of food, or as they termed it—subsistence—was vital to survival. Anyone who ventured into the interior had to allow for subsistence. Northeastern Minnesota was a sparsely populated wilderness, and there is every indication from early travelers' accounts that game was not as plentiful then as now. In addition, seasonal and climatic variations affected the availability of wild plants, fish, and game, or efforts to grow crops.

Long ago the indigenous people had located at both Fond du Lac and Sandy Lake for the same reason that later fur traders selected the sites. They faced the same set of challenges for survival. Fortunately, both locations were blessed with ample supplies of several types of food they could depend on.[9]

Wild rice (*manomin*), sometimes referred to as "marsh rye," "wild oats" or *folle avoine*, was harvested from area lakes in late summer. Each family was assigned a specific area of the rice bed from which they harvested on average twenty-five or more "fawnskins" of rice. The term "fawnskin" referred to the material from which the rice bags were manufactured and not the capacity. The standard dry measure of volume was the *minot*, an old French measure of grain roughly equivalent to a bushel. Fur trade accounts invariably list the number of minots of rice purchased or on hand at Sandy Lake and other trading posts. In fact, Perrault purchased rice at Sandy Lake in 1790 on his way into the interior to trade.[10]

Wild rice was a major staple for the Ojibway as well as other tribes who lived within its natural range. As mentioned previously, the Menominee, or "wild rice men," even took their name from the popular grain. Most tribes that harvested wild rice used the surplus to barter for trade goods, and each trader purchased as much rice as he could upon arriving in the region. James D. Doty mentioned the purchase of rice in an article published in the Detroit *Gazette* on January 19th, 1821. "Their rice, and the best meat they can obtain, are generally sold to the traders for tobacco and personal ornaments."[11]

Another important food item was fish, especially whitefish and tullibee. A number of men at the fur posts were annually assigned to provide a continuous supply of fish for the trading posts. Charles C. Trowbridge recorded the type of fish caught at Sandy Lake in his journal entry for Monday, July 17th, 1820:

> Some other kinds of fish are caught, among which are Pike, Carp, Blk Bass [Black Bass], Catfish, and a kind resembling the whitefish in colour and shape, but smaller, called the Telibee [sic]. Without these..., together with the wild rice, the trade could not be conducted in this country, for it would be utterly impossible to transport provisions from the South. The whitefish are taken in autumn & the Telibees in the spring of the year, in nets of 60 to 100 fathoms in length.[12]

Nets were also used in winter for various kinds of fish. They were stretched under the ice and hauled in and examined daily.

It is interesting to note the post fishermen were also the custodians of the sled dogs used by the traders during the long northern winters. Part of the catch was reserved and all winter the dogs were fed on frozen or dried fish. Evidence of a fish *cache*, or "storage place," was found at a village and trading post site on Sandy Lake. The accumulation of fish scales found buried on the site was several inches thick.[13]

A third type of food used by Indians and traders alike was maple sugar. This natural product was gathered in the spring and represented a mainstay in the diet of local Indians. The French voyageurs called maple sugar *sucre sauvage*, or "wild sugar," and it was an important commodity in the fur trade. Some of the traders referred to maple sugar as "Indian sugar" to differentiate it from the

Boiling maple sugar at an Ojibway camp.
Minnesota Historical Society

cane sugar grown in the West Indies. Each type of sugar in its natural or unrefined state has a very distinct flavor as opposed to the refined sugar commonly used today.

Maple sugar was stored in birch-bark containers or "mococks," which varied in weight from thirty to eighty pounds. The word "mocock" is a corruption of the Ojibway word *makuk* or *makak* meaning "box" or *makakossag*, meaning "tub." Although great quantities of maple sugar were purchased by traders and shipped east, most of the product was consumed or sold along the way, and very little, if any, reached eastern cities. The maple was not the only source of wild sugar.[14]

Sugar was also made from the sap of the birch tree. Abundant birch groves on *Grand Lac du Folle Avoine* (Great Wild Rice Lake), located by a short portage southeast of Sandy Lake, provided not only sugar for the local inhabitants, but also birch-bark, which furnished material for lodges, canoes, and even the very mococks the sugar was stored in. Evidence the Ojibway also had a sizable canoe yard on the south end of Sandy Lake is found in remarks in Perrault's *Narrative* and in other accounts. On one of his trips inland, Perrault purchased two canoes at Sandy Lake built to his specifications. Given the variety of useful products that it provided, it is easy to see why the versatile birch tree was much revered by the Ojibway for its many gifts.[15]

Ojibway canoe construction. The Ojibway had extensive canoe yards at Fond du Lac and at Sandy Lake.
Photo by T.W. Ingersoll, Minnesota Historical Society

Interestingly enough, even in the midst of plenty there can be problems. The consumption of too much maple sugar caused tooth decay. The Methodist missionary Reverend Alfred Brunson described his experience as a frontier dentist:

In former intercourse with Indians I had learned that it was necessary for an agent, a missionary, or even a trader or visitor among them, to have some surgical instruments, and especially such as are used for pulling teeth [dental forceps]. Both Indians and white men...came from ten to twenty miles to me to pull their decayed and aching teeth. As 'practice makes perfect' I soon became an adept at the business, and received many thanks, but no pay.[16]

During his visit to Minnesota in 1832, Henry Schoolcraft also mentioned the problem of tooth decay due to too much maple sugar.

In addition to the three commodities mentioned, wild game such as bear, woodland caribou, moose, bison, ducks, geese, and rabbits were hunted. Some of the hunters obtained both meat and hides from their quarry. Bison were found close to Sandy Lake in 1820. According to Henry Schoolcraft, "The only part of the country east of the river [Mississippi], where the buffalo now remains, is that included between the falls of St. Anthony and Sandy Lake, a range of about six hundred miles."[17] A scant decade later, Indian hunters from Sandy Lake had to pursue them to the southwest near the present city of Little Falls, Minnesota. Such a hunting trip involved a two day journey downstream by canoe into what some referred to as the "contested ground," or the hunting lands claimed by the Dakota and Ojibway.[18]

Ojibway hunters with snowshoes, and what appears to be a Lancaster trade rifle, pose for the camera.
Photo by C.A. Zimmerman, Minnesota Historical Society

One of the more exotic foods mentioned at Sandy Lake was beaver tail. David Thompson indicated he had four beaver tails as part of his provisions when he left Sandy Lake bound for Lake Superior in the spring of 1798. In 1806, Lieutenant Zebulon Pike stayed at the North West Company's Sandy Lake post while recovering from his winter journey up the frozen Mississippi River. During that time he dined on frontier cuisine:

> While I was at this Post, I eat [sic] Roasted Beavers, dressed in every respect as you would dress a Pig for that purpose. I could not discover the least taste of Des Bois [wood]; on the contrary, found it excellent; Also, a boiled Mooses Head, which, when well boiled, I consider equal to the tail of the Beaver; and in taste and substance is very similar.[19]

Members of the Northwestern Expedition who visited Sandy Lake in the summer of 1820, found the local menu was even more intriguing than they expected. James Doty described a dish being prepared by a group of local inhabitants, "I saw them yesterday cooking a skunk, but when it was prepared for the table, it was impossible to approach the lodge except to the windward."

Charles Trowbridge of the same expedition was astonished to find some of the Ojibway did not eviscerate their game before cooking it. He remarked, "They eat every animal and every part of it..."[20]

Maple sugar was the only seasoning readily available to the Indians and voyageurs alike. Henry Schoolcraft observed, "The Indians of this region subsist wholly without the use of salt with their provisions." Zebulon Pike noted that salt was too expensive for the ordinary voyageur. Normally the voyageur's only source of this condiment was heavily salted pork mixed with their ration of pea soup or corn porridge.[21]

In addition to food supplies purchased from local sources, each of the various trading posts at Fond du Lac and Sandy Lake maintained a garden and grew such crops as potatoes and cereal grains. According to contemporary witnesses, they also imported livestock including cattle, pigs, and horses. What could not be gathered, grown, caught, or shot for food had to be brought into the country on the sturdy backs of the voyageurs.[22]

Very little space for the transportation of food was allotted in the canoes or Mackinaw boats used by the fur traders. The organization of the waterborne transportation system developed by the fur traders required the men who manned the canoes be constantly resupplied with food as they journeyed inland; and, at the same time, the individual trading posts were encouraged to be as self-sufficient in the production of foodstuffs as possible. In fact, the posts at Fond du Lac and Sandy Lake were expected not only to provide for the needs of their own residents, but also to function as provision posts for fur trade contingents passing through the country bound for places further inland.[23]

In spite of the spartan fare accorded the ordinary voyageur, some luxuries were shipped to the distant trading posts. Examples of imported foodstuffs included flour and salt pork shipped in barrels and butter shipped in small kegs called "firkins." Other items such as tea, coffee, salt, chocolate, ham, cheese, peas, raisins, and prunes were shipped in special containers or in sacks. Most of these items were considered luxuries and reserved for the use of chief traders and clerks. In addition, items such as sacks of dried prunes were distributed to the voyageurs if they became "distressed" (constipated) because of their usual diet on the trail of parched corn (hominy) and grease, or their home fare, a type of corn stew called "sagamity."[24]

Certain supplies at first deemed "luxuries" over time became "necessities." Chief among these commodities was wheat flour. Every year traders consumed more and more flour, mostly in the form of bannock. Bannock, sometimes referred to as "fry bread" or "Indian fry bread" was actually a type of biscuit or scone that was introduced into the country by Scotch traders.[25]

Although the Indians made bread from ground corn, the recipe did not include the necessary ingredients to make the dough rise. Yeast was not in common use at northern trading posts. In fact, a reference to baking bread at a local trading post first appears in the diary of Reverend Edmund Franklin Ely. Ely, who was a missionary at Sandy Lake in 1833 before moving to Fond du Lac in 1834, mentioned yeast and baking bread for his own consumption. He noted the local custom of making unleavened bread, but he observed, "...the people of this country know nothing of making fermented bread, & consequently waste flour."[26]

Food stored at the trading posts was usually kept in an elevated storehouse set above the ground on posts. These buildings were sometimes referred to as "magazines" or "granaries." The reason for placing the building on posts was to ensure a flow of air on all sides of the storage containers and to prevent animals, chiefly rodents, from getting into the boxes, barrels, and bags where the food was stored. A diagram of the post at Fond du Lac shows the location of the granary, and a photograph of a corner of one of these elevated structures at a fur post near Sandy Lake shows the lengths people went to to protect perishable items.[27]

In addition to food pilferage by animals, food spoilage was a constant problem. In spite of careful attention, provisions could be damaged by moisture, mildew, weevils, maggots, and a host of other causes. Food, whether carried on the trail or kept at trading posts, was carefully watched for any sign of spoilage. Even with the best of care, food often spoiled and the unexpected loss of vital provisions threatened the very survival of trader and Indian hunter alike.

The small lone bands of hunters were particularly vulnerable. The specter of starvation regularly haunted the isolated lodges. If the provisions were depleted for any reason, the hunter had to somehow obtain more from the trading post or head for the nearest sugar bush and hope for an early sap flow. Once at the sugar bush, the hunter and his family existed on the raw sap to regain strength.[28]

For the isolated trader, the prospect of starvation was also very real. In extreme cases hides, leather moccasins, and other skins were boiled to the consistency of glue and eaten to sustain life. Failing the receipt of any relief supplies from neighboring posts or a break in the weather to allow fishing or hunting, death by starvation was certain.

> Oh the long, the dreary winter!
> Oh the cold and cruel winter.
> Ever thicker, thicker, thicker,
> Froze the ice on lake and river,
> Ever deeper, deeper, deeper,
> Fell the snow o're all the landscape,
> Fell the covering snow, and drifted
> Through the forest-round the village;
> Hardly from his buried wigwam
> Could the hunter force a passage;
> With his mittens and his snow-shoes
> Vainly walked he through the forest,
> Sought for bird, or beast, and found none,
> Saw no track of deer or rabbit,
> In the snow beheld no foot-prints,
> In the ghastly, gleaming forest
> Fell, and could not rise from weakness-
> Perished there from cold and hunger.
>
> "The Famine," from *The Song of Hiawatha*, by Henry Wadsworth Longfellow

Fort St. Louis and Fond du Lac

The existence of permanent trading posts along the Northwest Trail can be documented as far back as the 1790s. In 1793, the North West Company, acknowledging the serious competition provided by the South Traders, built a depot near the mouth of the St. Louis River to service what was called the Fond du Lac Department. The headquarters of the department was situated at the new fortified trading post. The decision to build a depot probably came none too soon, for Perrault noted the traders Charles Bousquet and Michael Marchard (or Machar) had constructed a wintering house by the entrance to the St. Louis River sometime during the 1791-1792 season. From their position, they could interdict the trade by enticing Indian trappers or traders bound for La Pointe or Mackinac to dispose of their furs rather than risk the long and dangerous trip east on Lake Superior.[29]

The narrative of Perrault, a former South Trader himself, disclosed the presence of North West Company traders on the Mississippi during his first visit in 1784-1785. The company's decision to build the depot was undoubtedly influenced by competitors. By his own account, Perrault more than met the competition of the Nor'Westers at Leech Lake back in the spring of 1785, since at that time the company men had no special advantage when they opposed the independent traders one on one.[30]

From a practical standpoint, the establishment of a secure trade depot gave the North West Company an enormous advantage over the small independent trader in terms of the sheer volume of goods available close to the actual trading location. The company could ship large quantities of trade goods by sailing vessel from Sault Sainte Marie or Grand Portage to the new fortified trading post at the entrance to the St. Louis River. This could be done cheaper and faster than the South Traders, who had to transport their trade goods all the way from Mackinac or Sault Sainte Marie using freight canoes. Once Fort St. Louis was completed, fourteen large lake canoes or *canot du maitre* filled with four hundred and two bales or packs consisting of one third provisions and two thirds trade items were dispatched to supply the company's traders in the Fond du Lac Department.[31]

The location of Fort St. Louis was about two and a half miles upstream from the mouth of the St. Louis River. David Thompson recorded the exact location of the site when he visited the post in the spring of 1798:

Near the mouth of the river [St. Louis] is a Trading House of the Northwest Company under the charge of Mons. [monsieur] Lemoine... This House is in Latitude 46° 44' 33 n, Longitude 92° 9' 45" w, variation 41/2 degrees East.[32]

He included the latitude and longitude of the fort in his journal, as he did with all company establishments. The location was included on a map he prepared for the North West Company (1812) and on a later map of the St. Louis River (1826).

Some accounts place Fort St. Louis on the south side of a narrow passage now called "Connor's Point," where two low points of land jut out toward each other leaving only a narrow passage separating Superior Bay from St. Louis Bay. The basis for the Connor's Point location is a statement by trader Michael Curot, who visited Fond du Lac in 1803 and 1804. He noted the fort's location as being three miles from the mouth of the river. Henry Schoolcraft observed the same location in 1820 while en route to Sandy Lake with Governor Cass. Either site was ideal since anyone passing up or down river could be seen from the trading post.[33]

Although the Ojibway historian William Warren credited the construction of Fort St. Louis to his granduncle, Jean Baptiste Cadotte, in truth it was Perrault, who was engaged by John Sayer, a partner in the North West Company, to build a trading depot in 1793 for "80 Livres [pounds] current value of the province." On August 18th, 1793, Perrault began the construction with two men sawing boards and four men squaring timbers. The plan for Fort St. Louis consisted of two houses of forty feet each and a shed of sixty feet. Within a month Sayer and his family moved into the first house, which was half completed. Over the course of the next few months, Perrault's men completed the second house, and by spring they had finished the warehouse and the stockade. These few comments represent the extent of the description of the post as given by the man who built it. The historian Warren added that the stockade surrounding Fort St. Louis consisted of "strong cedar pickets."[34]

Later accounts of Fort St. Louis provide a picture of the establishment's appearance, but may describe a different trading post. United States government surveyor and fur trader George Riley Stuntz recorded the following description of a second fort site on Conner's Point in the 1850s:

> At the base of Connor's Point were mounds where there had been dirt chimneys, parallel heaps representing the banking around the houses, several feet of cedar posts that had been burned down to the sod, and a clearing of several acres. This clearing was partially covered with second growth timber. Within the lines made by the decay of the log houses were trees seventy-five years of age.[35]

Contemporaries of Stuntz, such as August Zachau, an early settler and the builder of the first home in the city of Superior, Wisconsin, found remains of a dock constructed of cedar logs on a bay to the west of Connor's Point proper, now referred to as "Howard Bay" or "Howard's Pocket." He also found similar remains on the shore of Superior Bay. The second fort and dock was perhaps that of the competing XY Company known to have been located near Fort St. Louis.[36] Another contemporary, a voyageur named La Suisse La Mure, who lived in Superior shortly after the platting of the town, said the voyageurs had no "sleeping-house" on Connor's Point after 1831. His account differs from a statement attributed to Thomas M. Fullerton, that the old fort was retained until 1840, when the goods stored there were removed and the buildings supposedly burned so opposition traders could not use them. This story may account for the charred timbers noticed by Stuntz. Other sources indicate the fort was in existence until 1842 or 1843.[37]

To the Indians, the act of burning a trading establishment was very symbolic. In effect, it meant the establishment was closed forever and would no longer be used for trade. As a practical matter, burning the buildings not only denied the use of the structures to others, but also allowed the owners to quickly salvage hardware such as bolts and nails.

A description of Fort St. Louis, attributed to Superior, Wisconsin, pioneer Colonel Hiram Hayes, mentioned twenty foot stockade walls with two double-ribbed gates, stores, magazine, workshops, and,"...dwellings of heavy timber, mortised Canadian fashion and painted white," and, on one corner of the enclosure, a two-storied log tower, "bristling with port holes [sic] and cannon." No mention was made by Perrault that Fort St. Louis included defensive measures such as flanking bastions or cannon, but it is perhaps safe to say that bastions were part of the overall design given the known layout of other interior posts.[38]

Pike's map of his exploration in 1805-1806 shows the locations of Fort St. Louis and Fort William even though Pike never included either place on his expedition itinerary. He delineated both installations on his manuscript map in the same manner that he did the fortified trading posts he visited at Lower Red Cedar, Sandy, and Leech lakes. The fortified trading houses at Leech and Sandy lakes each had two flanking bastions to protect the walls, with the additional provision at the Leech Lake post for a future block house mounting a small piece of artillery (swivel gun?) over the main entrance.[39]

In addition to various structures mentioned by visitors, descriptions of Fort St. Louis included the activities and persons associated with the place. In fact, many of the accounts of Fort St. Louis center solely around the clerk or factor in charge and provide little if any further information concerning the location or construction of the post itself. In 1807, North West Company clerk George Henry Monk included such things as the post's livestock in his description of the place. Altogether, two horses, a cow, a bull, and a few pigs were duly noted by Monk.[40] Also mentioned were three acres under cultivation which yielded two hundred and twenty bushels of potatoes. Although surprisingly not mentioned, the fort's location near a superb fishery in the St. Louis River and Lake Superior insured an ample supply of fish for the men and their sled dogs.

Connor's Point itself has an interesting link to the fur trade apart from the construction of Fort St. Louis. The point was ostensibly named for Benjamin Henry Connor, who arrived at Fond du Lac in July of 1852 on the schooner *Algonquin.* Connor was an employee of the fur trading firm operated by the Ewing brothers of Fort Wayne, Indiana. The Ewings, who had a reputation for being totally unscrupulous, had long been ardent foes of the American Fur Company and probably sensed the trade opportunity in the region following the sale of American Fur's assets in 1847.[41]

Connor married a local Ojibway woman and in 1853 moved to the future site of the city of Superior, Wisconsin. Biographical sketches of Connor indicate he had eight children and was fluent in "French, Chippewa, Ottowa [sic], and English." One of his children, Z. B. Connor, lived to a ripe old age. On the occasion of his eighty-seventh birthday in 1946, Z. B. Connor was featured in a local newspaper interview and recounted his experiences in Superior. Five years later, at age ninety-two, he was still sharing tales about the early years.[42]

There is another story concerning the naming of Connor's Point that is also rooted in the fur trade. Reverend Norris C. Dickey, in a history of Connor's Point published in 1941, maintained the point was named not for Benjamin H. Connor, but for Thomas Patrick Connor, an Irish immigrant who first came to Fond du Lac in 1802 and settled on Rice's Point opposite what he believed to be Fort St.

Louis. Records show there was a Thomas Connor employed by the XY Company, which was in direct competition with the North West Company. The XY Company reportedly operated a trading post on Rice's Point. According to Dickey, Connor later worked for the North West Company at Fort St. Louis. Other records, however, show Thomas Connor was employed in 1802 by the XY Company in the Athabaska country. Dickey states Connor married an Ojibway woman and had three children: Patrick, Peter, and Elizabeth.[43]

Thomas Patrick Connor supposedly worked for the North West Company for a time on the Snake River and was active in the fur trade in the St. Croix region throughout the 1830s and 1840s. He apparently returned to Fond du Lac in 1848, and later settled in the new town of Superior, Wisconsin. According to Dickey, Thomas Connor was known to have kept a diary of his experiences to which other early settlers referred. Unfortunately, Reverend Dickey's story does not include his sources of information or other corroborating materials. Furthermore, it is not clear if Thomas Patrick Connor was related to Benjamin H. Connor, whose existence in the area can be proven.[44] Regardless of the authenticity of the story, it is certain the landmarks in the vicinity of Fort St. Louis are well steeped in the lore of the fur trade.

After the completion of Fort St. Louis, John Sayer remained in charge of the post as an associate of the North West Company from 1793 until 1798, when he became a partner in the company. He was succeeded by Jean Baptiste Cotton, who was a clerk and interpreter in the department after 1798. While Sayer managed the Fond du Lac Department, it appears most of the traders and clerks working for him remained where they were originally stationed in 1794. For example, Charles Bousquet was at Sandy Lake from 1794 until at least 1804, when he was replaced by James Grant. Pike remarked in his journal that the post at Sandy Lake was formerly under the direction of "Mr. Brusky."[45]

As noted earlier, historian William Warren credits Jean Baptiste Cadotte as having built Fort St. Louis and being in charge of the post. It is well known that Cadotte worked for the company. Historian Harold L. Innis cited a five year agreement, concluded with Jean Baptiste Cadotte in 1796, to carry on trade in the Fond du Lac Department. Records also show Cadotte was apparently employed as a clerk and interpreter in the Fond du Lac Department after 1798, but there is no evidence other than Warren's statement that Jean Baptiste Cadotte either built or was in charge of Fort St. Louis.[46]

Warren indicated that Cadotte was present at Fort St. Louis in the 1790s and officiated at a dramatic trial held there concerning an unnamed Indian who murdered a *coureur du bois* at "Lac Shatac [Chetek]." The victim was employed by a clerk named Coutouse at Lac Courte Oreilles. The details of the story are sketchy but the Indian supposedly surrendered to Cadotte at Fort St. Louis. A "council or jury" consisting of company clerks was convened to examine the evidence. In spite of a willingness by relatives of the accused to "cover the dead," the clerks found clear evidence of guilt and decreed the Indian must be executed in the same way in which he murdered his victim. Accordingly, the clerk Coutouse was selected to strike the fatal blow with a scalping knife.[47]

Warren's account is quite vivid. The murderer was taken outside the fort and his bonds loosened. He was about to dash for freedom when Coutouse struck him in the side with his knife. The blow did not stop his attempt to escape, but a second and apparently fatal blow was delivered by another clerk named Landré. Bleeding profusely, the murderer ran away from the fort and along the sandy shore for some distance before he expired thus ending the episode. Warren's story of frontier justice is strikingly similar to the proceedings at Michilimackinac, described by Sieur Du Lhut, when he ordered two murderer's "heads broken" in a public execution witnessed by four hundred Indians and Frenchmen.[48]

The idea that Cadotte was involved with the construction and operation of the trading post has persisted and found its expression in the name "Fort Cadotte," given to the establishment by some later writers. Reverend Dickey not only credited Jean Baptiste Cadotte with building Fort St. Louis, but also that the post was later called "Fort Cadotte" and more recently "The Old Fort." As if to further confuse the issue, a newspaper clipping from 1870 refers to the location as "Fort Vincent Roy," and states the post was built by "French fur traders in 1797." A trader named Vincent Roy worked in the area in 1799, but records show he neither built Fort St. Louis nor managed the post.[49]

Various accounts show that whoever was in charge of the Fond du Lac Department selected his own site for company headquarters, and the location of the headquarters post changed with each chief trader. By the time of Pike's visit in 1805-1806, the North West Company's headquarters had moved from Fort St. Louis to Leech Lake, where chief factor Hugh McGillis resided. Fort St. Louis continued to be a major depot regardless of the location of the headquarters. In the same manner, the fort at Sandy Lake retained its importance as a distributing center and rendezvous point as it had ever since the first traders visited the area.

Proof that Fort St. Louis and the surrounding department were of major importance to the North West Company can be seen in 1805 with one hundred and nine men employed at a wage of sixty-three thousand nine hundred thirteen livres. Returns for 1807 indicate that the production of furs in the Fond du Lac Department was second only to Athabaska. This record production was followed by a sharp decline when the local beaver population was stricken with disease. Of course, the returns from the department were also influenced by competition from the South Traders.[50]

No sooner was Fort St. Louis completed than opposition traders aligned with Alexander Henry the Elder established themselves in the region. Michael Cadotte the Elder, Michael Cadotte the Younger, and two traders named L'etang and Marchard joined with Henry to oppose the Nor' Westers in all quarters of the Fond du Lac Department. The competition undoubtedly prompted the North West Company to have Perrault construct a second fortified depot at Leech Lake in 1794.[51]

It is clear the North West Company intended to meet the competition by erecting a string of depots stretching into the interior. Following the construction of Fort St. Louis, posts were built at Leech Lake, Sandy Lake, Lake Winnibigoshish, Red Lake, Vermilion Lake, and Upper and Lower Red Cedar lakes. The size of the posts differed. The large posts at Fort St. Louis, Sandy Lake, Leech Lake, and Lower Red Cedar Lake were surrounded by palisades and flanked by bastions. The smaller trading posts consisted of merely a single cabin or group of cabins. Based on Pike's detailed description, the post at Leech Lake appears to have been the largest inland establishment built by the North West Company in the area and was well fortified with a double row of palisades, musket-proof walls, and window shutters.[52]

Situated near the contested ground and the Dakota, the Leech Lake post included measures to defend against possible attack. In contrast, during the twenty-three years (1793-1816) that Fort St. Louis served as an active trading post, there is no known record of an attack on the installation by the neighboring Ojibway or any other tribe.

When the trading posts were transferred to the American Fur Company in 1817, the logistical problems associated with operating Fort St. Louis became apparent. Transferring trade goods from vessels on Lake Superior to Fort St. Louis, was a waste of effort since they had to be transferred again at the head of navigation. The extra handling of trade goods and furs undoubtedly contributed to the American Fur Company's decision to move the location of the supply depot upstream. Sometime during 1817, a site for a new depot was selected on the north bank of the St. Louis River opposite the Ojibway village of Fond du Lac located on *Nikig* (Otter) Island.[53]

There are very few comments respecting the actual layout of the new American Fur Company post at the village of Fond du Lac. Certainly the site was superior to that occupied by old Fort St. Louis from the standpoint of handling the transfer of cargo.[54] Here, at the head of navigation, the river passes between two high hills. Approaching the site up the St. Louis River, the traders saw afar off blue peaks rising above lush pine forests that frame the river valley. The narrow commanding spot occupied by the new trading post afforded a convenient vantage point from which all who entered or left the interior could be observed.

The various buildings erected by the American Fur Company faced the river and, according to early drawings, were parallel to the course of the St. Louis River. Certain discrepancies exist, however, between the drawings and later descriptions which suggest the buildings were either expanded or replaced over the years from 1817 to 1836.

The Fond du Lac post consisted of a clerk's quarters, warehouses, a granary, an enclosed garden, and men's quarters. In addition, a boat yard for construction of canoes existed close to the river. According to a scale drawing of the post in 1836 by Doctor Charles William Wulff Borup, the arrangement of the clerk's house, retail store, a combination warehouse and wholesale store, and an elevated granary differs from earlier accounts.[55]

Surviving photographs from the beginning of the twentieth century show three of the buildings exactly as Borup described them in 1836. Local accounts claim the buildings were demolished in 1917, exactly a century after the post was first established.[56]

Twenty years after the demolition, remnants from one of the buildings were used in the construction of a replica of what was purported to be the original post. The reconstructed trading post opened to the public in 1937. The author remembers touring the replica as part of a school field trip and seeing a sign on the inside wall of the trading post building proclaiming the pedigree of the ancient timbers.[57]

Unfortunately, the replica containing the original timbers was allowed to gradually deteriorate until the structure was finally torn down. The present location of the original timbers is unknown. Thus, part of an historic structure that stood at the east end of the old Northwest Trail for a century or more was, after an attempt at restoration, allowed to slip away unnoticed.

Of all the early trading posts built along the Northwest Trail, only two surviving buildings remain, and they are located near the confluence of the Mississippi and Sandy Lake rivers. The two buildings are the last of several trading establishments built by the rivers. It is ironic that although the location of the two buildings is well-known locally, travelers, who pass by them everyday, have no idea of their history. Those who exhibit any curiosity at all about the location of trading posts on Sandy Lake search instead for the location of the North West Company post.

The North West Company's Sandy Lake Post

Ever since the 1920s, the question of the location of the first trading post on Sandy Lake has excited the curiosity of scholars and laymen alike. Although a relatively large number of travelers visited and described the post while it was in operation, its date of origin and exact location have eluded seekers.[58]

The exact date for the construction of the North West Company's post should be fairly easy to determine, but existing accounts disagree about its location and when it was built. Warren dates the construction of the post at Sandy Lake to 1796. Pike lists the fortified trading post at Sandy Lake as being built twelve years before his visit in 1806 (1794). Perrault mentions an earlier establishment in his narrative. He states he initially decided to winter at Sandy Lake late in the fall of 1791, but on arriving at the lake, found Mr. Meniclié de Morachon "who had already built there." He continued up the Mississippi River to the vicinity of *la pointe aux chêne* (Oak Point), where he established a wintering post.[59]

Perrault's statement regarding Mr. Morachon having "already built there" seems to imply he had constructed a trading house on Sandy Lake. It is not entirely clear whether or not there was more to the establishment built by Mr. Morachon than merely a wintering cabin. Perrault's sketch map of Sandy Lake, which accompanies his printed *Narrative*, shows a post on the west side. On the other hand, a map accompanying John Hay's account of his 1794 journey along the Northwest Trail denotes a "camp" on the actual site of the of the Northwest Company establishment at the south end of Sandy Lake but no mention of a permanent trading post.[60]

Clearly the growing number of wintering posts constructed in the interior by opposition traders was indicative of a commitment to trade in the region, but the exact layout of these trading posts and their location is not clear. Thus far, Pike's estimate of the date of construction as 1794, seems closest to the exact date. Most likely the post was started in the fall of 1794 and completed in time for the 1795 season.

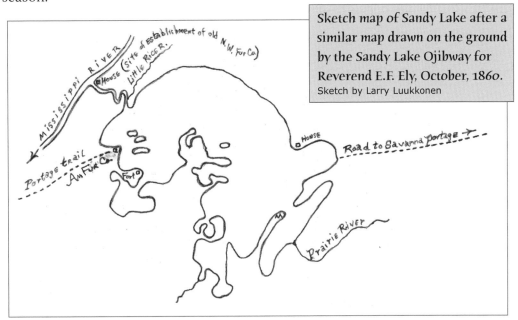

Sketch map of Sandy Lake after a similar map drawn on the ground by the Sandy Lake Ojibway for Reverend E.F. Ely, October, 1860.
Sketch by Larry Luukkonen

Charles C. Trowbridge, who visited Sandy Lake in 1820, remarked that the North West Company built the post on a point in the lake and employed expert builders. The ten men sent from Grand Portage with Perrault to the site of Fort St. Louis in 1793, may in fact have been experienced builders who erected other trading posts in the interior.[61]

Finding the exact location of the North West Company post on Sandy Lake has excited great curiosity among scholars and laymen alike. The story of the search for the lost trading post goes back at least to the second half of the nineteenth century. In the 1860s an English draftsman and antiquarian, Mr. Alfred J. Hill, gathered information concerning various historic locations in Minnesota including several sketch maps of the Sandy Lake area.

One of Hill's sources of information about early villages and trading posts was a former missionary at Sandy Lake, Reverend Edmund Ely. Hill wrote to Ely several times in the 1860s requesting specific information about the lake and surrounding area. In 1860, Ely sent Hill a crude sketch based on a map drawn on the ground for him by the Sandy Lake Ojibway. The Indian map, although rudimentary, accurately depicted the true location of three posts: the North West Company's first post, a later post built by William Aitkin erroneously marked as belonging to the North West Company, and a third trading post constructed c.1838 by the American Fur Company in the northwest quadrant of Sandy Lake. The third post was located midway on a point known locally as "Brown's Point" after an early homesteader. For the sake of convenience we shall call it American Fur Company Post Number 3. Unfortunately, Alfred J. Hill never completed his proposed map of these historic fur trade sites.[62]

Apparently Hill did not agree with the Indian map because the word "Wrong" appears written briskly over the spot where William Aitkin's post was identified as belonging to the North West Company. It is not clear if Hill ever visited the site or that he knew the location he marked was also the site of the general rendezvous for the Nor'Westers, which antedated the construction of Aitkin's post. Apparently Hill had decided about the original location of the North West Company post and simply corrected what he believed to be conflicting information. In this respect, he was not alone. Professor Irving H. Hart also reviewed Hill's maps. Hart concluded the site of the North West Company post must be on Brown's Point even though the location of the post shown on Hill's copy of the Indian map was clearly marked "American Fur Company." It is clear that Hart and in all probability Hill were not aware that a second American Fur Company post existed at one time on Sandy Lake. Both men probably believed there should only be one trading post at the confluence of the rivers and one on the lake, not two.[63]

Aerial photo of the west side of Sandy Lake showing the actual location of the North West Company post.
U.S. Department of Agriculture photo, 1939

Other writers also mentioned the North West Company trading post. Historian Elliott Coues, who edited Lieutenant Zebulon Pike's journal of the 1805-1806 expedition up the Mississippi River, actually retraced Pike's trip by canoe in the 1890s. Strangely, he did not bother to stop and investigate Sandy Lake, where Pike spent twelve days in January of 1806. Instead, Coues continued upstream. His later edition of Pike's journals contain elaborate footnotes and a detailed "Historico-Geographical" map of Pike's entire voyage. Unfortunately, the scale of Coues' map is too small to determine the precise location of the trading post on Sandy Lake.[64]

Archaeologist Jacob Vandenburg Brower also traveled through the area by canoe in 1894, in search of prehistoric sites. Brower entered Sandy Lake and paddled right past the site of the old North West Company post while on his way to investigate prehistoric Indian mounds on the Sandy Lake River. Brower casually mentioned the ruins of the post and believed the surrounding "wasteland" would undoubtedly be inundated by the rising water of the lake caused by the construction of the new government dam.[65]

Both Brower and Coues had a perfect opportunity to provide an exact location and description of the trading post, but for unknown reasons both failed to do so. Nothing further was done to investigate the site until the 1920s.

In 1926, Professor Hart and William P. Ingersoll, a local resident and amateur historian, announced they had found the North West Company post midway on Brown's Point. Professor Hart published an article in *Minnesota History* in December of 1926, which described their excavation of the supposed site. The article included a map of the area, a sketch of the post site, and a drawing by Ingersoll of what the post probably looked like.

Professor Hart's description of the trading post relied largely on Pike's 1806 account for details concerning the buildings and their location within the stockade. He also offered evidence from Pike and later visitors, such as Reverend Ely and fur trader William Johnston, about the supposed location. Interestingly, Hart's strongest piece of evidence was the Indian map of the lake drawn for Alfred J. Hill and Reverend Ely, but Hart identified the site marked American Fur Company as the original North West Company location.[66]

Hart followed his article about the discovery of the trading post with other publications including an interview with an elderly Indian woman in the summer of 1927. Mrs. George Curtis, also known as Beengwa, was the former wife of fur trader and early Sandy Lake pioneer Joseph Wakefield. Although no notes or other evidence survive from the interview, Hart claimed in an article published in 1928 in *Minnesota History* that Mrs. Curtis' response confirmed the correct location of the North West Company post.[67]

Professor Hart's interview with Mrs. Curtis stated she positively identified the trading post site on Brown's Point. Hart quoted his witness, who recalled visiting the post when she was a young girl. Based on the questions Hart asked Mrs. Curtis, the interview did not clearly establish whether or not the post identified by her was in fact the former North West Company establishment. The North West Company had merged with the Hudson's Bay Company in 1821, long before Mrs. Curtis was born. Furthermore, the North West Company had not operated at Sandy Lake since 1816. It seems highly doubtful that, as a child growing up in the mid-nineteenth century, Mrs. Curtis ever had any dealings with the North West Company or that the name really meant anything to her. The existence of a later post on Brown's Point in Sandy Lake, built in 1838 by the American Fur Company, was perhaps what Mrs. Curtis meant as "the trading post" when she was interviewed by Professor Hart in 1927.

For thirty years after his first article was published about the lost trading post, Professor Hart continued to pursue his research and publishing. His last article, published in 1956 in *Minnesota Archaeologist*, was accompanied by a sketch drawn by his artist son Evan A. Hart. In the article, Irving Hart essentially recounted his earlier experiences at Sandy Lake. Two years later, Irving Hart died still believing that he had indeed found the lost trading post.[68]

In 1960, an archaeological excavation of the supposed North West Company site was undertaken by Evan Hart. The surviving site map and photographs show evidence of structures extending beyond the walls of the post identified by Irving Hart. In addition, the nearby site of what was once a blacksmith's shop suggests more recent occupancy.[69]

There are three major sources of information giving the exact location of the North West Company's post on Sandy Lake. The first is provided by David Thompson, the noted geographer for the North West Company, who visited the post in May of 1798. The second source is provided by Zebulon Pike, who stopped at the trading post on Sandy Lake in January of 1806; and the last major source is the sketch map drawn by the Sandy Lake Indians for Reverend Ely in 1860. All three sources plus a host of observations by other contemporary travelers confirm the North West Company post was situated at the tip of a point projecting into Sandy Lake from the southwest side and not from Brown's Point as commonly believed by Hart and others.

Of the three major sources, David Thompson's rough track survey notes from 1798, give three sets of measurements. The first are the observations for latitude and longitude of the post site. As noted earlier, Thompson used his four foot achromatic telescope to observe the eclipse of Jupiter's moons to get the most accurate possible fix on his position. Comparing the differences between known points recorded by Thompson and the differences between these same points today using modern instruments provides a reasonably good picture of the location of the post.[70]

Secondly, Thompson took a bearing toward the southeast from the point at which he entered Sandy Lake to where the trading post was located. Prior to the construction of the government dam, the entrance to the Sandy Lake River extended farther east than at present. With the same bearing today, and adjusting for the change in depth of the lake and the resulting location of the entrance to the river, the course of an air line in the lake points toward the actual site of the North West Company post.[71]

Thirdly, Thompson recorded his course in the lake after leaving the trading post bound for the "Savannah Brook" (Prairie River), as he called it. By tracing Thompson's rough track survey notes backward from the entrance to the "Savannah Brook," and comparing the other two observations just discussed, the focus of all three measurements centers on the southwest quadrant of Sandy Lake. In all three cases, there is some small degree of error, due to the Earth's ever-changing North Magnetic Pole and the difference in the instruments and navigation tables used in 1798, from those of today. Adjusting for these factors, however, the lines of all three measurements converge reasonably close to the actual post site.[72]

Zebulon Pike's notes and manuscript map also furnish valuable information regarding the location of the North West Company post. Pike 's journal contains a detailed account of his march up the frozen Mississippi River. When he reached the vicinity of the Sandy Lake Rapids, Pike turned right and proceeded along the old portage that led from that point on the river in an almost straight easterly direction to a bay on the southwest corner of Sandy Lake. Professor Hart assumed that Pike veered off course and drifted toward the northeast, striking Brown's Bay and then the site he discovered in 1926.[73]

Hart's assumption that Pike drifted off course and crossed Brown's Bay overlooks several facts including the description in Pike's journal, where he remarks about striking the shore of Sandy Lake in the evening during a snow storm. Thinking he could see the opposite side, Pike kept a straight course in the lake until he observed a light and found the trading post. Pike was obviously an experienced army officer who knew how to use a compass, hence his reference to keeping a straight course. Secondly, if he in fact had veered northeast toward the site Professor Hart claimed to be that of the North West Company post, he did so over dry land and not over an arm of the lake. Brown's Bay, located south and west of the site found by Professor Hart, did not exist before the completion of the Sandy Lake Dam in 1895.

Pike's manuscript map and his journal are valuable sources of information regarding the exact location of the North West Company post. The map was drafted by Sergeant Antoine Nau, mentioned in Chapter 3. Unlike all of the later maps published with Pike's account, the Nau map was created under the direct supervision of Pike and clearly shows the North West Company post on the tip of a point extending southeasterly into Sandy Lake. During his stay at Sandy Lake, Pike made a tour of the lake and had a reasonably good understanding of the general geography of the place.[74]

Lastly, an important piece of information is the hand drawn map provided to Reverend Ely in 1860 by the Sandy Lake Ojibway. It shows the site of the North West Company post on the same long point extending into the lake as shown on Pike's manuscript map. In addition, the Indian sketch map clearly indicates a post marked "Am Fur Co" (American Fur Company Post Number 3) on the site where Professor Hart claimed the North West Company establishment stood.[75]

Hart's assumptions about the true location of the so-called North West Company post on Brown's Point simply did not take into account these key documentary sources or the eyewitness accounts of the post during the period in which it was an active trading center. All of the available information taken collectively presents a far different picture from that described by Professor Hart or any other writer to date.

In addition to the manuscript sources, which show the post site, a collection of Northwest trade gun lockplates found by Hart within the outlines of the post on Brown's Point—all date from after the period of North West Company activities in the area. Earlier examples of trade gun lockplates were found, but they were recovered east of the location Professor Hart claimed was the original North West Company site.[76]

The 1860 Indian sketch map provided by Ely shows a trading house at the confluence of the Mississippi and Sandy Lake rivers that is erroneously marked as the North West Company's post. This mistake, as noted earlier, may be attributable to the fact that the site at the confluence of the Sandy Lake and Mississippi rivers was the location of the general rendezvous held every spring and fall before the construction of the North West Company's permanent depot on Sandy Lake. It was at this location, during the general rendezvous in the spring of 1785, that Alexander Kay met his fate. It was not until 1822, that the first trading post was built at the junction of the rivers by William Aitkin. A second trading post was established in the 1850s, further away from the rivers and the Aitkin site. All of the fur trade activity at the confluence of the two rivers may have resulted in the mistaken location of a fur post where an earlier campsite was located.[77]

Indian maps contained useful information about post sites, but they were not highly recommended by some explorers. There is evidence, however, that explorers copied them for cartographers. For example, the French explorer La

Veréndrye copied Chief Ochagach's map of the three river systems west of Lake Superior, even though he was disappointed with the quality of the information obtained from local sources. He noted, "These people are great liars but every once in awhile they tell the truth."[78]

A view of the reliability of information obtained from the Indians was expressed by archaeologist Jacob Brower, whose collective writings espoused opinions on a vast array of subjects with or without documents to back them up.

> The time is past when aborigines are needed, or their aid required for reliable geographic facts; indeed, as a rule, Indian maps have always been but distortions. When first known in history, the banks of the Mississippi were peopled nearly its entire length. Those people had stamped upon their countenances the color of their origin, and as they probably floated across the Pacific Ocean and reached the coast of the New World, that color indicating their mental capacity precluded the possibility of their grasping opportunities, not yet fully availed by the Anglo-Saxon race.[79]

A number of accounts written by members of the Northwestern Expedition of 1820 contain information about the North West Company trading post site gleaned from personal observation. For example, Charles C. Trowbridge mentioned the post was located on a point of land extending into the lake. James D. Doty, also a member of the same expedition, noted a hill behind the post that he climbed from which he could see several other lakes. No hill of sufficient height as mentioned by Doty ever existed on Brown's Point.[80]

George Henry Monk, who described Fort St. Louis, also mentioned the post at Sandy Lake as being on the south side of the lake. Fur trader William Johnston, Henry Schoolcraft's brother-in-law, stated the post was situated at the end of a long point, as did Doctor Douglass Houghton.

The most complete description of the North West Company post was given by Lieutenant Pike. With the practiced eye of an army officer, Pike recorded the dimension of the stockade, how it was constructed, its height, and the location of the gates. He also noted the fact there were covered towers or bastions at the northwest and southeast corners, which protected the stockade with an enfilading fire should the place be attacked. He listed the purpose and size of the four buildings sheltered within the walls. In addition, he noted the existence of a two and a half acre post garden on the north and west sides of the stockade that was protected by pickets. Pike described a unique vault or root cellar complete with a hidden compartment for storage within the garden enclosure. Later travelers added details about the old post, but none ever described it so completely as Zebulon Pike.[81]

The old North West Company post on Sandy Lake, like its eastern counterparts Fort St. Louis and the American Fur Company's stores at Fond du Lac, stood for many years after it ceased to be used as a fur trading post. At first it was taken over from the South West Company by the American Fur Company in

1816-1817. The Sandy Lake post served its purpose well until the company, by mutual agreement, decided to transfer operations to William Aitkin's post at the confluence of the Mississippi and Sandy Lake rivers. After the American Fur Company moved out of the old establishment, competing traders moved into the fort and used it for several seasons.[82]

There is a traditional story that the North West Company post on Sandy Lake was burned, but accounts indicate that from 1840 until 1855, the post was used as a Methodist mission. Whatever limited use the buildings or timbers of the old fort provided, following the evacuation of the site by the Methodist missionary Samuel Spates and his family, is unknown. It is certain that the missionaries left in such haste they neglected to burn the structure. If anything was done to erase the site, it was done at the hands of local people as a sign to future missionaries. After 1855, there is no further mention of the existence of the original stockaded post of the North West Company other than Brower's casual comment.

In all, there are references to what appear to be nine different trading post sites that existed at one time or another on Sandy Lake. Of this number, the North West Company post was used for a variety of purposes in addition to serving as a major inland depot for the fur trade. Of the other remaining establishments that have been cited, three posts have sufficient documentation to verify with certainty their location. The remaining five sites require further documentation to prove their precise location or authenticity (See Appendix A).

The construction and location of the original trading posts by the North West Company at Fond du Lac and at Sandy Lake were influenced by the people who used them. Fort St. Louis and the post at Sandy Lake were built to withstand an attack, because they were located on the fringes of what was termed "the contested ground." Later trading establishments did not have the elaborate defenses of these first posts.

The various accounts describing the original trading posts have collectively contributed a great deal of significant information. These descriptions determine the location of the posts with reasonable certainty, however, the most intriguing question is who were the men who built them?

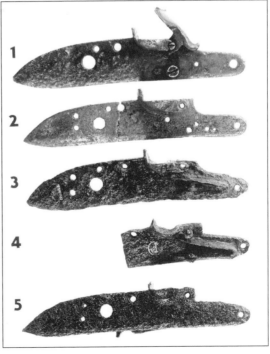

Trade gun lockplates found on Brown's Point, Sandy Lake, in 1960. Photo, author's collection

Chapter 7 - Frontier Outposts
Notes

1. Charles E. Lart, "Fur Trade Returns, 1767," *Canadian Historical Review*, vol. 3 (December, 1922), pp. 351-358.

2. The manuscript journals of David Thompson and Jean Baptiste Perrault, contain valuable information regarding the location and design of the first trading post at Fond du Lac. In the same way, the journals of Thompson and Zebulon Pike provide details for the post at Sandy Lake (see chap. 2, n. 26 above for Perrault; chap. 3., n. 37 above for Thompson; and chap. 3, n. 54 above for Pike).

3. *Collections of the State Historical Society of Wisconsin*, vol. 12 (Madison, 1892), p. 82.

4. Elliot Coues (ed.), *New Light on the Early History of the Greater Northwest. The Manuscript Journals of Alexander Henry, fur trader of the Northwest Company, and of David Thompson, official geographer and explorer of the same company, 1799-1814. Exploration and Adventure among the Indians on the Red, Saskatchewan, Missouri and Columbia Rivers*, 3 vols. (1897; reprint ed., New York, 1965), vol. 1, p. 275.

5. Philip P. Mason (ed.), *Schoolcraft's Expedition to Lake Itasca* (East Lansing, 1993), p. 198.

6. Jean Baptiste Perrault, "Narrative of the Travels and Adventures of a Merchant voyageur in the Savage Territories of Northern America Leaving Montreal the 28th of May 1783 (to 1820)," ed. by John Sharpless Fox in *Historical Collections and Researches Made by the Michigan Pioneer and Historical Society*, vol. 37 (1909-1910), p. 534. See page 519 for a copy of Perrault's Map 1, which traces the Northwest Trail from Lake Superior to Sandy Lake.

7. Ibid., p. 563.

8. John Fritzen, *The History of Fond du Lac and Jay Cooke State Park* (Duluth, Minnesota, 1978), pp. 16-17.

9. William Whipple Warren, *History of the Ojibway People* (1885; reprint ed., St. Paul, 1984), pp., 263, 266, and 282.

10. Perrault, "Narrative of Travels," p. 557.

11. Mentor L. Williams (ed.), *Schoolcraft's Narrative Journal of Travels* (East Lansing, 1992), p. 448.

12. Ibid., p. 485.

13. For comments on voyageur sled dogs see Grace Lee Nute, *The Voyageur* (1931; reprint ed., St. Paul, 1955), pp. 93-98.

14. Perrault, "Narrative of Travels," p. 574. In 1797, Perrault traded two eight gallon kegs of rum for forty tubs of sugar during his trading adventure in the Fond du Lac Department. The following year he traded eighteen packs of furs and made six kegs of sugar.

15. Ibid., p. 570.

16. Alfred Brunson, *A Western Pioneer*, 2 vols. (New York, 1872), vol. 1, p. 147.

17. Williams (ed.), *Schoolcraft's Narrative Journal*, pp. 187 and 342.

18. Harold Hickerson, "Ethnohistory of Mississippi Bands and Pillager and Winnibigoshish Bands of Chippewa," in *Chippewa Indians II* (New York, 1972), p. 108.

19. Donald Jackson (ed.), *The Journals of Zebulon Montgomery Pike, with Letters and Related Documents*, 2 vols. (Norman, 1966), vol. 1, p. 82.

20. See Williams (ed.), *Schoolcraft's Narrative Journal*, pp. 448 and 487.

21. Jackson (ed.), *Zebulon Montgomery Pike*, pp. 79-80.

22. See chap. 5, n. 49 above; Nute, *Voyageur*, pp. 51-56.

23. Eric W. Morse, *Canoe Routes of Canada! Then and Now* (Ottawa, 1969), pp. 24-26.

24. Reuben Gold Thwaities (ed.), *Collections of the State Historical Society of Wisconsin*, vol. 16 (Madison, 1902), p. 355, includes a definition of "sagamity."

25. Nute, *Voyageur*, p. 53.

26. Edmund Franklin Ely, Journal No. 5, Tuesday, September, 16th, 1834, p. 11. The original documents are in the Northeast Minnesota Historical Center, Duluth, Minnesota (hereafter referred to as NEMHC). Typescript copies of the diaries are in the collections of the Minnesota Historical Society.

27. Ellworth T. Carlstedt, "A History of the Fond du Lac Trading Posts With Some Mention of the Fond du Lac Department," unpublished manuscript, University of Minnesota, December 9th, 1933, p. 42, includes a map of the American Fur Company post at Fond du Lac. Carlstedt's drawing is based on one made by Dr. Charles William Wulff Borup in a letter to Ramsay Crooks, dated January 2nd, 1834, in the American Fur Company Papers, New York Historical Society, N.Y. Microfilm copies available at the Minnesota Historical Society.

28. Perrault, *Narrative of Travels*, pp. 521-522. Perrault described his own desperate circumstances during the winter of 1784-1785.

29. Ibid., p. 564.

30. Ibid., p. 530.

31. Ibid., pp. 568-569. Perrault stated his trade goods and supplies were brought by Captain Maxwell on the North West Company schooner *Otter*.

32. There is some disagreement about the location of Fort St. Louis. David Thompson's 1826 map of the St. Louis River clearly shows the post located approximately two and one half miles northwest from the entrance to the estuary on the left side (see chap. 3, n. 37 above). In Williams, *Schoolcraft's Narrative Journal*, p. 139, Schoolcraft indicates the post was situated three miles northwest from the entrance. Warren, *History of the Ojibway*, p. 292, locates the post "about two miles within the entry of the St. Louis River."

33. Perrault, *Narrative of Travels*, p. 568; Carlstedt, "A History of Fond du Lac," pp. 19-22.

34. Warren, *History of the Ojibway*, p. 288; for John Sayer see *Collections of the State Historical Society of Wisconsin*, vol. 19 (Madison, 1910), pp. 173-174, n. 41; see also *Dictionary of Canadian Biography*, 15 vols. (Toronto, 1983), s.v. "John Sayer" (by Douglas A. Birk), for information on Sayer's career in the Fond du Lac Department and in the North West Company.

35. See the description of the site of Fort St. Louis by surveyor George Riley Stuntz in "Early History of Superior" unpublished manuscript, Superior Public Library, Superior, Wisconsin, n.d., p. 5.

36. Ibid.

37. Frank A. Flower, *The Eye of the North-west: First Annual Report of the Statistician of Superior, Wisconsin* (Milwaukee, 1890), p. 43. Flower quotes a number of witnesses including Reverend Thomas M. Fullerton who stated Fort St. Louis was used as as a storage facility until 1840, when the remaining goods were removed and the buildings burned. Compare Flower's story with the description of missionary Florantha Sproat who was stormbound at the old fort for two days in April of 1842; See Florantha Thompson Sproat, "La Pointe Letters," *Wisconsin Magazine of History*, vol. 16, no. 2 (December, 1932), p. 207. Reverend Alfred Brunson also described Fort St. Louis during a visit in 1843. See Brunson, *Western Pioneer*, vol. 1, pp. 179-181; Allan Morrison, "History of the Fur Trade in the Northwest," unpublished manuscript, p. 6, Minnesota Historical Society, n.d. Brunson's rather dramatic description of the fort included an armament of two "six pounders" which he claimed were used against the local Indians on at least one occasion. Morrison states that "Each fort [Fond du Lac and Sandy Lake] had a small cannon mounted." There is no documentary proof, outside of these statements, of artillery being present at Fort St. Louis or any other North West Company post in the area now comprising Minnesota with the sole possible exception being the fort at Leech Lake. Zebulon Pike mentioned plans to place a small piece of artillery over the main gate but no actual description of the proposed armament has come to light. Perhaps the company intended to mount a rampart or swivel gun, but that is only conjecture. Any larger piece of ordnance would have required a crew of six men to man the gun and that was frequently more men than were normally present at the Fond du Lac posts.

38. Early Superior, Wisconsin, resident Colonel Hiram Hayes' account of Fort St. Louis is quoted in Fritzen, *History of Fond du Lac*, p. 12. In this account, as in the description given by Brunson, Fort St. Louis is erroneously depicted as bristling with armament.

39. Jackson (ed.), *Zebulon Montgomery Pike*, pp. 184-185.

40. George Henry Monk, "A Description of Northern Minnesota by a Fur Trader in 1807," ed. by Grace Lee Nute, in *Minnesota History Bulletin*, vol. 5, no. 1 (1923-1924), pp. 28-39.

41. By the 1840s, competition between the American Fur Company and the Ewing brothers of Fort Wayne, Indiana, proved ruinous to both companies. See, David Lavender, *The Fist in the Wilderness* (1964; reprint ed., Albuquerque, 1979), pp. 418-419.

42.   The story of Benjamin Connor is told in an article by Joanne Gidley, "Connor's Point 'Then,'" in *The Connection* (May, 2002), n.p.; see also, "Connor's Point First Settler's Son Now 87, Recalls Early History of Territory, Special to the Telegram," *Superior Evening Telegram* (1946), Dateline, Cumberland, Wisconsin. Both articles can be found in Clippings Collection, Superior Public Library, Superior, Wisconsin.

43.   Michel Curot, "A Wisconsin Fur Traders Journal, 1803-1804," *Collections of the State Historical Society of Wisconsin*, vol. 20 (Madison, 1911), pp. 396-471. Carlstedt credits Curot with the first mention of a trading post operated by the XY Company on Connor's Point. Carlstedt, "A History of Fond du Lac," pp. 23-24; Norris C. Dickey, *A Brief History of Connor's Point, Its Rise and Decline: Compiled for the Superior Public Library by WPA Project # 11068* (Superior, Wisconsin, 1941), pp. 9-11.

44.   Ibid., pp. 9-11; Charles M. Gates (ed.), *Five Fur Traders of the Northwest*, 2nd ed. (1933; reprint ed., St. Paul, 1965), pp. 245-278. The first edition of Gates' book was printed in 1933, eight years before Dickey's study was completed. Dickey mentions Connor's diary, but apparently did not know Connor was illiterate. For more on the controversy surrounding Connor's diary see Douglas A. Birk and Bruce M. White, "Who Wrote the Diary of 'Thomas Connor'? A Fur Trade Mystery," in *Minnesota History*, vol. 46, no. 2 (Spring, 1979), pp. 170-188.

45.   Jackson (ed.), *Zebulon Montgomery Pike*, p. 79.

46.   See Carlstedt, "A History of Fond du Lac," pp. 17-20, for the background on Fort St. Louis; Harold A. Innis, *The Fur Trade in Canada: An Introduction to Canadian Economic History* (1930; rev. ed., New Haven, 1962), p. 186, cites a copy of Cadotte's agreement; and Charles Napier Bell, "The Earliest Fur Traders on the Upper Red River and Red Lake, Minnesota (1783-1810)," *The Historical and Scientific Society of Manitoba*, Transaction no. 1, n.s. (Winnipeg, 1926), pp. 5-6, also mentions Cadotte's agreement.

47.   Warren, *History of the Ojibway*, pp. 295-296; Brunson, *Western Pioneer*, pp. 180-181.

48.   See also chapter 3, n. 25 above, for comparison with Du Lhut's report.

49.   Various names were given to Fort St. Louis. For example, in an 1870 newspaper account of a speech by Mrs. W. C. Loundsbury of Superior, Wisconsin, Fort St. Louis was referred to as "Fort Vincent Roy," after a French fur trader who supposedly built the post in 1797. Her source for this statement was apparently an old settler named Colonel Hiram Hayes. See Hiram Hayes, "Early History," n.d. in Clippings Collection, Superior Public Library, Superior, Wisconsin.

50.   See n. 40 above.

51.   Carlstedt, "A History of Fond du Lac," pp. 20-21.

52.   Jackson (ed.), *Zebulon Montgomery Pike*, pp. 184-185.

53.   Williams (ed,), *Schoolcraft's Narrative Journal*, p. 139.

54.   Ibid.

55.   A comparison of the descriptions and illustrations in McKenney's book with the map and letter of January 2nd, 1836, from Dr. Borup to Ramsey Crooks, American Fur Company Papers, shows a different arrangement of the post buildings. Reconstruction of some of the post buildings undoubtedly occurred sometime between 1826 and 1836.

56.   Fritzen, *History of Fond du Lac*, pp. 16-17.

57.   From August 4th through the 7th, 1935, the reconstructed trading post was the scene of a huge dedication ceremony and historical pageant celebrating the fur trade. Although several of the seven episodes of the pageant had nothing whatsoever to do with the actual history of Fond du Lac, the pageant received an enthusiastic response from an estimated audience of fifteen thousand people. See the following news articles: "Pageant Opens at Fond du Lac, Sunday, Aug. 4th," in the *Pine Knot*, August 2nd, 1935; "Fond du Lac Had Thousands Attend Historical Pageant," in the *Carlton County Vidette*, August 7th, 1935, in Clippings Collection, Carlton County Historical Society, Cloquet, Minnesota.

58.   The first effort to relocate the North West Company post on Sandy Lake was made by Alfred J. Hill in the 1860s. The supposed site was later described by Irving H. Hart in "The Site of the Northwest Company Post on Sandy Lake," in *Minnesota History*, vol. 7, no. 4 (December, 1926), pp. 311-325.

59.   Perrault, *Narrative of Travels*, pp. 561-562.

60.   John Hay, "Journal in the N.W. by S. side of L. Superior," in "Extracts from Capt. McKay's

Journal-and Others." *Publications of the State Historical Society of Wisconsin. Proceedings of the Society at the Sixty-Third Annual Meeting, October 21st, 1915* (Madison, 1916).

61. Perrault, *Narrative of Travels*, pp. 568-569; Williams (ed.), *Schoolcraft's Narrative Journal*, p. 483.

62. Hart, "Northwest Company Post," pp. 316-317. Hart cites a map drawn for Edmund F. Ely by the Sandy Lake Indians in 1860, a sketch map by Alfred J. Hill in 1884, and a map drawn by Lieutenant James Allen in 1832, as proof of the location of the post, but he does not provide a copy of the maps so the reader can draw his or her own conclusion. Unfortunately, Allen's map is so small it is virtually useless for determining the exact location of the site. Apparently Hart did not know about the manuscript map drafted by Antoine Nau under Pike's supervision, which clearly shows the location of the North West Company post on Sandy Lake.

63. Ibid.

64. Elliott Coues, *The Expeditions of Zebulon Montgomery Pike* (1895; reprint ed. Minneapolis, 1965). See pp. 137-138, n. 49 for a description of the Mississippi River and Sandy Lake.

65. Jacob Vandenburg Brower, "Prehistoric Man at the Headwaters of the Mississippi River" *Collections of the Minnesota Historical Society*, vol. 8 (1896), p. 238.

66. For maps and drawings, see Hart, "Northwest Company Post," pp. 313, 318, 322, and 324.

67. Irving H. Hart, "The Story of Beengwa, Daughter of a Chippewa Warrior," *Minnesota History*, vol. 9, no. 4 (December, 1928), pp. 319-330.

68. Irving H. Hart, "An Amateur Archaeologist in Northern Minnesota," in *The Minnesota Archaeologist*, vol. 21, no. 2 (April, 1956), pp. 1-20.

69. Evan A. Hart, "North West Company Post, Sandy Lake, 1794: Minnesota Historical Society Dig, September, 1960," unpublished notebook in author's private collection. Hart's original copy of the notebook contains maps, site diagrams, and correspondence relating to what the participants called "The Big Dig." According to Evan Hart's letters, the project was supposed to be a joint endeavor with the Minnesota Historical Society and the State Archaeologist. Unfortunately, both organizations were unable to participate so Hart and his crew proceeded with the site excavation.

70. For Thompson's latitude and longitude measurements at Sandy Lake see Richard Glover, *David Thompson's Narrative, 1784-1812*, (Toronto, 1962), p. 209.

71 David Thompson, Notebook No. 9, May 6th, 1798. Thompson's rough track survey notes read: "Course in the Sand Lake S 14° E 1 1/4 mi. to the House." .

72. Ibid. Thompson's rough track survey notes include his course in the lake after leaving Sandy Lake House.

73. Cf. Jackson, *Zebulon Montgomery Pike*, p. 78, and Hart, "Northwest Company," p. 312.

74. Jackson, *Zebulon Montgomery Pike*, p.81. See copy of Nau's map made under Pike's direction.

75. See Alfred J. Hill Papers, Minnesota Historical Society, for a copy of a map of Sandy Lake drawn for Ely in October of 1860 and the 1884 sketch map showing Sandy Lake and vicinity; also, the Edmund F. Ely Papers, 1840-1854, in the collections of the Minnesota Historical Society, contain several letters to Ely from Hill requesting information on a proposed historical aboriginal map. For example, see letter from Hill to Ely dated May 21st, 1860, Hill to Ely, January 18th, 1861, and Hill to Ely, September 28th, 1861.

76. Evan A. Hart, "Catalog of Antiquities," unpublished manuscript in the author's private collection, n.d., n.p. The "Catalog" contains Hart's original photographs and drawings showing a collection of trade gun lockplates recovered from the supposed site of the North West Company and a nearby blacksmith shop. The pictures of the lockplates found within the outline of the fort, exhibit several characteristics found on trade guns manufactured after the North West Company ceased operation on Sandy Lake.

77. See Perrault, *Narrative of Travels*, p. 519, Map 1 "Western Lake Superior."

78. Francis Parkman, *A Half-Century of Conflict* (New York, 1962), p. 258.

79. Jacob Vandenburg Brower, "The Mississippi River and Its Source, " in *Collections of the Minnesota Historical Society*, vol. 7 (1893), p. 109.

80. For Doty's comments see Williams (ed.), *Schoolcraft's Narrative Journal*, p. 429.

81. Jackson (ed.), *Zebulon Montgomery Pike*, p.184.

82 See entry for Ely Journal No. 2, October 12th, 1833, p.7 in Edmund F. Ely Papers, NEMHC.

A view of the overland trail extension of the Savanna Portage.
photo by Larry Luukkonen

Chapter 8 ✖ Headwaters Traders

Prior to the War of 1812, different trading companies operated along the Northwest Trail. In 1806, the partners of the North West Company formed the Michilimackinac Company as a way of maintaining their trade monopoly in United States territory, while the North West Company continued to operate north of the border as before. Subsequently, the new American Fur Company, formed in 1808, faced stiff competition from the Canadian-owned Michilimackinac Company. Finally, in the face of growing anti-British sentiment in the United States, the Canadian traders formed a partnership with the American Fur Company in 1811, as a way of securing their operations within American territory. The new company, known as the South West Company, operated from 1811 until 1812.

Following the War of 1812, legislation expressly prohibited Canadian traders from participating in the fur trade within territory claimed by the United States, but allowed American traders to hire experienced Canadian voyageurs and interpreters. That legislation did not stop independent Canadian traders from using creative means to circumvent the law. In fact, trading companies like the American Fur Company needed experienced employees including traders. To solve the shortage of experienced men, veteran traders were hired as "interpreters" or "boatmen."

Many of the Canadian traders who operated in the United States eventually became prominent in the trade and changed citizenship. A few traders actually held important leadership positions in the American Fur Company, especially in the Fond du Lac Department. Who were these men and how did they attain their positions in the trade? Their stories begin with the organization of the fur trade in the years before the War of 1812.

The Domain of American Fur

Although the trading posts first constructed along the Northwest Trail have generally been thought of as belonging to the North West Company, in the years before the War of 1812, two new companies were formed and operated these posts. The first of these companies took over operation of the posts at Sandy Lake and at the mouth of the St. Louis River after 1806. Known as the Michilimackinac Company, the company was an offshoot of the North West Company and traded exclusively in the territory claimed by the United States. The North West Company retained its operations in the territory north of the border, and certain partners in the North West Company also had a business interest in the

Michilimackinac Company. Both companies purchased their supplies of trade goods from the same Montreal merchants.[1]

The Michilimackinac Company's aim was to monopolize the American fur trade. Its objective, however, fanned growing resentment in the West against Great Britain as well as the Canadian traders in general. To counteract American opposition, an agreement was reached in 1811 between the Michilimackinac Company and the recently chartered (1808) American Fur Company, a New York corporation headed by John Jacob Astor. The two companies formed the South West Company. Although the new company was meant to overcome opposition, American hostility toward anything British continued in various ways. For example, some American customs officials strictly interpreted various regulations on goods imported for use in the United States to the disadvantage of the Canadians.

Historian David Lavender points out an example of how rigorous enforcement of the laws respecting the importation of liquor worked against the Canadian traders. Importation of "High Wine" (straight grain alcohol) had traditionally been in eight gallon kegs, which were easy for the men to carry on the portages. American regulations, however, required the liquor be imported in thirty-two gallon casks, which were too heavy for a single man to portage.[2]

The passage of the Embargo Act in December of 1807, and other subsequent restrictive trade measures, almost completely interdicted American trade with Canada and Great Britain. In spite of the creation of the jointly owned South West Company the fur trade west of Lake Superior languished. Meanwhile, Astor developed trade with the Orient and solidified the position of the American Fur Company by purchasing trade goods and operating on his own in other parts of the West. Astor 's arrangement with the South West Company in 1811 was merely one aspect of his growing business empire.[3]

The new South West Company traded south of the border in the Fond du Lac Department. Astor, as a United States citizen, secured the license to trade and the Nor' Westers received a share of the profits. Unfortunately, the War of 1812 ended the arrangement. With the outbreak of hostilities, the North West Company moved into the South West Company posts and operated them during the war.[4]

Meanwhile, competition escalated between the Hudson's Bay Company and the North West Company. The establishment of a colony on the Red River of the North by Thomas Douglas, fifth Earl of Selkirk and Governor of the Hudson's Bay Company, was perceived by the Nor' Westers as a threat to their operation that had to be dealt with. Tension finally led to armed conflict on the banks of the Red River of the North. A skirmish between employees of the rival companies at a place called Seven Oaks resulted in the deaths of some twenty-two of the Hudson's Bay Company's employees including the colony's governor, Robert Semple.[5]

In retaliation, Selkirk and a contingent of former Swiss mercenaries, recently mustered out of British military service, captured the North West Company's main depot at Fort William in 1816. This action was followed by seizing the posts in the Fond du Lac Department.

Selkirk's particular reason for taking the Fond du Lac posts may have stemmed from the alleged participation of Sandy Lake men in the skirmish at Seven Oaks. Furthermore, a messenger sent by Semple to Selkirk over the Northwest Trail had been waylaid at Fond du Lac by Nor' Westers, which may also have motivated Selkirk to retaliate against the trading posts belonging to the South West Company.[6]

Lord Selkirk did not distinguish between posts owned by either the South West Company or the North West Company, since he knew both concerns were operated by the same individuals. In the process, Selkirk's men detained eight of Astor's clerks and approximately forty of his voyageurs at Fort William and confiscated trade goods totaling more than ten thousand dollars, including seventy kegs of High Wine. Hudson's Bay Company men occupied the South West Company posts including Fort St. Louis and the post at Sandy Lake with the intention of operating them. Selkirk responded to protests from Astor and his employees by citing the fact the international boundary west of Lake Superior was not settled; furthermore, he maintained that the Hudson's Bay Company's charter of 1670 extended the company's authority to the sources of the rivers draining into Hudson Bay, a claim publicized in the writings of Sir Alexander MacKenzie.[7]

Selkirk could not occupy the posts at Sandy Lake and Fond du Lac in land claimed by the United States indefinitely. He had already aroused the ire of the Nor' Westers, who involved the Earl in protracted and expensive litigation. If that was not enough trouble, Astor had complained loudly to his government; and it was rumored there was a contingent of American troops at the mouth of the St. Croix River en route to the Fond du Lac Department. Hoping to appeal to American authorities for assistance, Sandy Lake trader William Morrison lost little time in sending a messenger to them.[8]

In retrospect, operation of the posts in the Fond du Lac Department by the Hudson's Bay Company was unthinkable, especially after Congress passed legislation in 1816 excluding foreigners from the American fur trade. Furthermore, diplomatic work was underway to establish a permanent boundary through the offices of a boundary commission established by a provision in the Treaty of Ghent ending the War of 1812. With the passage of the new law in April, 1816, known as the "Exclusion Act," the North West Company partners sold their interest in the South West Company to Astor in 1817. In the meantime, rather than sue Selkirk for the confiscated trade goods and the expenses incurred by the crews, who drew wages but were unable to trade, Astor's business manager Ramsay Crooks favored negotiating with Selkirk. Diplomacy worked and Selkirk returned the company's goods and indemnified Astor for his losses. On the surface, it appeared Astor had his long hoped for monopoly, but there were other traders to contend with.[9]

Since only American citizens could pursue the fur trade within the United States, the practical outcome of the new law was the wholesale application for American citizenship by former Canadian traders employed with the North West and the South West companies. Many of these men, including experienced former Nor'Westers like William Morrison, James Grant, Pierre Cotté, and Eustache Roussain worked for John Jacob Astor's American Fur Company. The new Exclusion Act included a provision that allowed Canadian voyageurs and interpreters to work for American traders, but prohibited foreign traders from obtaining a license to operate in the United States.[10]

Astor's American Fur Company needed experienced traders and resorted to a novel means of training them. A cadre of Americans, mostly all young men recruited from the Lake Champlain area of New York State, was nominally in charge of the fur company's operations. Actually, these young men served as apprentices under veteran Canadian traders who occupied supposedly subordinate positions in the American Fur Company hierarchy. In reality, the company was "American" in name only; the method of operation followed the time-honored pattern first developed by the French.

The new clerks names that appeared on the American Fur Company's roster of employees were far outnumbered by the experienced personnel who actually managed the trade. Familiar names and faces comprised the annual brigade sent west along the Northwest Trail with a supply of new trade goods in the spring of 1818. The only difference was in the leadership. Two of these clerks, Samuel Ashmun and John H. Fairbanks, were assigned to the American Fur Company's establishment at Sandy Lake according to the roster of men employed by the company for 1818-1819.[11]

Ashmun and Fairbanks were present at Sandy Lake when Governor Lewis Cass' Northwestern Expedition arrived in the summer of 1820. Life in a remote trading post far removed from the comforts of civilized life was difficult for the two young men. Although both men wrote letters home, the mail was slow and uncertain. Judging from the remarks of Cass and his men, the two apprentice clerks not only craved news from their respective families, but also were eager to know what was happening in the world at large.[12]

Of these two clerks, only Fairbanks stayed in the wilderness after his apprenticeship. Ashmun later moved to the American settlement on the south side of the St. Mary's River, where he continued to participate in the lucrative fur trade but still enjoyed some of the comforts not found at a frontier outpost. Eventually he rose to prominence in the frontier town. Today, the main street of Sault Sainte Marie, Michigan, bears the name of the Sandy Lake fur trader Samuel Ashmun.[13]

John H. Fairbanks, unlike Samuel Ashmun, chose to stay in the West. He was one of that generation of men who saw in the fur trade not only a promising livelihood, but also a way of life. He was born in Champlain, New York. While still very young, he was pressed into service as a teamster for the British Army during the War of 1812 and witnessed the battle of Plattsburg and Commodore McDonough's victory over the British fleet on Lake Champlain.

In June of 1818, Fairbanks arrived at Mackinac Island as one of several new clerks hired for the American Fur Company. He was engaged for a term of five years for a salary of thirteen hundred dollars, and was assigned to Sandy Lake. He served for several years at different posts in the headwaters including Leech Lake, Lake Winnibigoshish, and Red Cedar Lake. Fairbanks married a local Ojibway woman *à la façon du pays*, or "in the fashion of the country." "Taking a country wife" was a common practice, if not in fact expected of a promising young trader on the frontier, even if he was already married. Fairbank's descendants are still to be found throughout Minnesota where the scion of the family first began his career.[14]

If Ashman and Fairbanks were the clerks at Sandy Lake, the real power behind the trading company's operation there was William Morrison. Morrison's career is typical of the kind of men Astor chose to run his far-flung operations.

A Scottish Trader's Story

William Morrison was born March 7th, 1785, at Montreal. At some point in his early career, a second "r" was mistakenly added to Morrison's name on the roster of employees of a fur company, and apparently he never bothered to change it. His father, Allan Morison, Senior, came from Stornoway on the Island of Lewis, one of the Hebrides or Western Isles. William's mother was a French Canadian lady named Jane Wadin (also known as Jessie Waden). Her father, a Swiss trader named Jean Etienne Waden, was one of the first to trade near Lake Athabaska in the very heart of the richest fur country in the Northwest.[15]

Waden was allegedly murdered in 1780 by his partner, a Yankee trader named Peter Pond. Waden was buried at *Lac le Ronge* and no charges were ever brought against Pond. William never forgot the murder of his father-in-law and referred to Pond as "Pierre pont" and his accomplice as "Lesiur." Memories of this incident probably hardened him because he eventually became one of the most formidable traders on the frontier.[16]

William received a common school education and started work as a clerk in a store in Montreal when he was just fifteen years old. Montreal was the major location for merchants who supplied the North West Company and independent traders with trade goods in exchange for furs. It was perhaps natural that William Morrison gravitated toward a career in the fur trade given his proximity to the great merchant houses of Montreal.

In January of 1802, William Morrison signed an engagement with the "New North West," or "XY Company," an organization operating in competition with the North West Company, comprised of former members of the old company including the famous explorer Sir Alexander MacKenzie. Morrison's first trip into the interior was over the Northwest Trail to Leech Lake and later to a wintering post on the Crow Wing River.

Photograph of Sandy Lake fur trader William Morrison taken late in life.
Crow Wing County Historical Society

The following year, Morrison was sent to a trading post on the Wild Rice River. While en route to that place, he passed by *Lac la Biche* or "Elk Lake," (Lake Itasca). Interestingly, in 1856, William Morrison sent a letter to his younger brother Allan. It described his visit in 1804 and again in 1811-1812 to Lac la Biche–the lake that Henry Schoolcraft claimed to have discovered as being the source of the Mississippi River. Allan Morrison subsequently sought support for his brother's claim to have discovered the true source of the river thirty years before Schoolcraft ever set foot on its shores and sent the letter to Territorial Governor Alexander Ramsey. How many other veteran traders also knew about the lake is unknown, but Schoolcraft received the publicity and those who preceded him have largely been forgotten.[17]

In 1804, Simon McTavish, the principal partner in the North West Company, died and shortly thereafter the disaffected partners who had left the concern and created the rival XY Company merged with the old North West Company. William Morrison continued with the Nor'Westers as a clerk and a "summer man" (caretaker) at Leech Lake. In 1811, he was employed by the South West Company. With the outbreak of the War of 1812, the North West Company assumed operation of the Fond du Lac Department. Morrison continued working at Sandy Lake as a clerk for the department at a salary of twelve hundred livres.

On September 9th, 1816, Morrison was arrested by Hudson's Bay Company men as part of Lord Selkirk's retaliation against the North West Company for the attack at Seven Oaks. This incident occurred while Morrison was operating the post at Sandy Lake. He was taken from there to Fort William and then transported by Lord Selkirk's men to Sault Sainte Marie, where he later escaped his captors.[18] He returned to Sandy Lake and as previously noted sent a messenger to find a United States Army contingent, which was said to be near the mouth of the St. Croix River. His messenger carried a letter addressed to fellow trader William Alexander Aitkin, then operating a trading post in the Folle Avoine country near the headwaters of the St. Croix, asking for his aid as well as his support for the messenger.

Morrison stayed on at Sandy Lake after the War of 1812 and was employed by Astor's American Fur Company in 1817 as an "Interpreter" with a salary of one thousand dollars per year. Although ostensibly under the direction of the two clerks Ashmun and Fairbanks, in reality Astor hired the experienced Morrison to superintend the operations of the Fond du Lac Department. In this new capacity, he proved to be quite successful. On July 19th, 1820, William Morrison became a naturalized United States citizen. With his new status, Morrison now openly assumed the reins of management for the department.[19]

Morrison's change of allegiance came just before the amalgamation of the Hudson's Bay Company and the North West Company in 1821. When the two companies merged, the union created a surplus of experienced workers including traders who later found work in the United States. Most of these men eventually applied for American citizenship to circumvent the prohibition contained in the Exclusion Act of 1816 against employing Canadian fur traders.

In 1821, Morrison signed an agreement with the American Fur Company to formally manage the Fond du Lac Department with his headquarters at Sandy Lake. The four year contract specified an annual salary of fourteen hundred dollars. The following year, he reached an agreement with Astor, whereby he agreed to operate the Fond du Lac Department on half shares. This lucrative arrangement continued while he was employed by the American Fur Company and possibly reflected his effectiveness in meeting all competition.[20]

Part of William Morrison's success may have been due to his marital arrangements. Various accounts state he had either three or four wives. As one might expect, Morrison took a country wife *à la façon du pays*. His first wife was an Ojibway woman who belonged to the Pillager Band, with whom he had three children. She died after bearing their third child. His second wife, Anne Roussain, was the daughter of his clerk Eustache Roussain. One of their four children from the marriage later took part in John C. Fremont's famous western expedition. Morrison's third wife was Elizabeth Ann Kittson, the elder sister of "Commodore" Norman W. Kittson, for whom Kittson County, Minnesota, is named. The steamboat king's sister bore Morrison four children, all daughters.

William Morrison retired from the American Fur Company in 1826, while still a comparatively young man. He returned to Canada and bought an island in the St. Lawrence River opposite the settlements of Sorel and Berthier-en-Haut. There, Morrison established a farm and carried on a business. He once again became a Canadian citizen and was elected judge of the local county court. Morrison died at his country estate on August 7th, 1866.[21]

During his lifetime, William Morrison was said to have had great influence over the local Indian people and was well-respected by the voyageurs for whom he had responsibility. From his headquarters at Sandy Lake, he ruled the wilderness; and he was fearless in his pursuit of independent American traders operating in his territory. Many were allegedly starved out of the country due to his business practice of undercutting the competition. Known among the Ojibway as *Sha-gah-nansh-eence* or "The Little Englishman," Morrison had a reputation for cunning and ruthlessness unrivaled in the Northwest, but there were some traders that defied even his best efforts to eliminate their competition.

Competition From A Swiss Adventurer

The annals of exploration and trade are filled with the names of French, English, Scottish, and Swiss traders. Out of this number, there were several notable figures who regularly traveled the Northwest Trail and traded with impunity under the very noses of Astor's best traders. One of these men was a Swiss trader, Charles Oaks Ermatinger.

Ermatinger, the son of a Swiss gunsmith turned fur trader, became extremely successful in the trade. He was the last of seven children born to Laurenz and Jemima (Oaks) Ermatinger. Laurenz had been a gunsmith in his native country of Switzerland. Shortly after moving to Canada (c. 1761), he entered the fur trade in partnership with his future father-in-law, Forrest Oaks, a Montreal merchant.[22]

It is not completely clear exactly when Charles began his career in the fur trade, but it was an activity that would occupy his attention for thirty years. The first mention of Charles Ermatinger came in 1798, when his initial adventure into the Northwest as an independent trader took him to Sandy Lake. The North West Company already had a trading post and supply center on the lake with experienced trader Charles Bousquet in charge. Unlike the other departments of the North West Company, Fond du Lac clerks such as Bousquet did not regularly rotate from post to post. As long as John Sayer was in charge of the department, he apparently chose to keep his experienced traders at assigned posts and Bousquet had been at Sandy Lake since the post was built. As a consequence, he undoubtedly knew his trappers and their habits very well. During his first trading adventure the young Charles Ermatinger astutely moved to counteract the advantage of his rival. Not having an established trading post or an especially large stock of trade goods, he chose to live or "winter" with the local band of Ojibway.[23]

Sometime during the winter of 1798-1799, Charles opted to "take a country wife." He married a fifteen year old Sandy Lake woman by the name of Mananowe, also known as Charlotte Katawabeda. He was twenty-one years old. Charlotte was the daughter of Chief Katawabeda, so the marriage may have been motivated by true affection as well as mutual convenience. Wilderness marriages did not carry any social stigma and many traders later celebrated their nuptials with benefit of clergy to protect the legitimacy of their resultant offspring. Such was the case with Charles and Charlotte. Although married sometime during 1798, they finally solemnized their relationship on September 6th, 1832, one year before Charles died.[24]

It is worth noting that wilderness marriages were looked upon by some people as business arrangements. That attitude may account for the tolerance afforded such unions. Unfortunately, some of the marriages were strictly marriages of convenience; and when a particular trader decided to "rotate" or return east, he simply abandoned his country wife to her own resources. It was probably as a result of this all too common practice that Jane Johnston Schoolcraft, the talented wife of Indian Agent Henry Schoolcraft, was inspired to write the song, "The Ojibway Maid." (See Appendix B)[25]

Charles and Charlotte's marriage proved to be lasting and mutually beneficial. Through the marriage, Charles acquired enhanced status in the band as Charlotte was the daughter of a prominent chief. Chief Katawabeda was well-known, and his name appears in several early journals. In fact, Charles' grandson, Charles Henry Catawabiddy Ermatinger, was named in honor of the chief.

For her part, Charlotte Ermatinger enjoyed the social prestige accorded a trader's wife. She was also well-provided for by the "trader's allowance" of goods and provisions customarily furnished to her husband at a discount.

It is worth noting that unattached young men from outside the local community were looked upon with suspicion by Ojibway hunters and trappers who frequently spent much time away from home. Not to arouse the suspicion of a jealous husband, the wise trader showed he was above reproach from his own men by taking a country wife.

Shortly after they were married, Charles and Charlotte decided to leave Sandy Lake. One account has them traveling northwest in the spring of 1798. They followed the customary route by way of the Mississippi River to Upper Red Cedar or Cass Lake, then crossed the height of land by way of the Turtle and Mud rivers to Red Lake, paddled downstream on the Red Lake River, thence to the Red River of the North. By the fall of 1798, they were established in a new wintering station near Fort George on the Saskatchewan River. Charles' trading activities in that location were very lucrative. There is no evidence that either of them ever returned to Sandy Lake, although they continued to have commercial contacts in the area.

References to Charles' career as a trader after he and Charlotte left Sandy Lake are fragmentary. Apparently he worked as an independent trader and later joined Alexander Mackenzie's New North West or XY Company, in opposition to the North West Company. In 1800 he joined the Nor' Westers as a clerk and later traded at Lake Winnipeg, eventually becoming a partner in the company. After 1804, his share of the profits declined due in part to the amalgamation of the North West and XY companies. In 1808, Charles left the North West Company and established himself as an independent trader at Sault Sainte Marie, Upper Canada (Province of Ontario).[26]

From his new base at Sault Sainte Marie, Charles outfitted traders who operated in the Fond du Lac Department. His success, in spite of stiff competition from his old partners in the North West Company, was due to his connections in the interior of what is now Minnesota. His main route of trade lay along the Northwest Trail by way of Sandy Lake, where his his father-in-law, Chief Katawabida evidently cooperated with Charles' trading activities and shared in the enjoyment of the fruits of that trade. During the years preceding the outbreak of the War of 1812, Congress and the President attempted to regulate foreign involvement by traders such as Charles in the United States as part of a larger policy meant to punish France and Great Britain for interfering with American commerce on the high seas or in foreign ports.

The North West Company and Astor formed the South West Company to avoid trade restrictions imposed by the government. Meanwhile Charles simply kept on supplying trade goods to his father-in-law in exchange for furs. He probably used the simple expedient of declaring the trade goods destined for western Canada and not for use within the territory claimed by the United States. Charles also had Charlotte and her father secure the necessary trade license and post bond. At other times, he used the good offices of American merchants who obtained the required trade license and posted bond in their own names, thus allaying any suspicion that Charles meant to subvert the intent of the trade laws. Regardless of the method used, there was obviously no one at Sandy Lake to report to American authorities what was really happening.[27]

While the large companies jockeyed for position in the face of changing government regulations, Ermatinger's profits as an independent trader continued to grow. When war finally broke out in June of 1812, Charles joined the expedition that surprised and captured the American occupied fort on Mackinac Island.

Old Block House, Fort Mackinac on Mackinac Island.
Photo by Detroit Publishing, Library of Congress

When United States forces retaliated the following year with a raid against Sault Sainte Marie, incredibly Ermatinger's property on the south (American) side of the river was not sacked or burned, but the commercial property and house of fellow trader John Johnston was burned to the ground along with commercial property on the north (Canadian) side belonging to the North West Company. Somehow, Charles convinced the American commander, Major Holmes, to spare his home and commercial property.[28] Much to the relief of the Canadian traders at the Sault, British forces managed to retain control of the vital trade route connecting Lake Superior with Montreal and the East.

Toward the close of the war, in 1814, Charles decided to build a permanent home on the Canadian side of the St. Mary's River. The construction of the Ermatinger home at Sault Sainte Marie involved painstaking craftsmanship and evidently took some time to build. The result was a splendid two story stone edifice thirty-five by forty feet modeled after similar homes built in Quebec. The "Old Stone House" as it is now called, still stands in Sault Sainte Marie, Ontario. It has been restored to its original appearance after having served as a residence, a hotel, the Algoma District's first courthouse, sheriff's residence, Y.W.C.A., a social club, and an apartment building. Today visitors can tour the elegant structure and marvel at the great beams, hand forged nails, solid flooring, and three foot thick stone walls that have survived the rigors of northern winters since 1814.[29]

Charles and Charlotte's grand home was a symbol of their growing prosperity as much as it was a home for their thirteen children. The Ermatinger house was a favorite stopping point for travelers, both American and Canadian, passing through Sault Sainte Marie. It was also a favorite of the permanent residents of the area, particularly during the holidays. Henry Schoolcraft, who lived just across the river on the American side wrote:

Visiting from house to house is the order. The humblest individual is expected to make his appearance in the routine.... The French custom of salutation prevails. The Indians are not the last to remember the day. To them it is a season of privileges....[30]

The American poet and journalist William Cullen Bryant described the Ermatinger house as:

...a large mansion built of stone by a former agent of the North West or Hudson's Bay Company who lived here in a kind of grand manorial style, with servants and horses and hounds, and gave hospitable dinners in those days when it was fashion for the host to do his best to drink his guests under the table.[31]

Charles Oakes Ermatinger's "Old Stone House," Sault Sainte Marie, Ontario, an enduring symbol of wealth gained from trade along the Northwest Trail. The house was built in 1814 by Charles for his wife Charlotte Katawabeda, daughter of Sandy Lake Chief Katawabeda.
Photo by Larry Luukkonen

With the end of the war, the South West Company prepared to resume trade south and west of Lake Superior, and Charles Ermatinger's competition was not appreciated by the partners of that concern. In fact, Charles was the bane of not only the Nor'Westers, but of the United States government as well.

Lingering animosity and the desire to preserve the fur trade on American soil led, in 1816, to the passage of the Exclusion Act mentioned previously. In spite of the new law, Charles continued to trade in the Sandy Lake area. His strategy had not changed since before the War of 1812, and it seemed he was always able to find someone to obtain a trading license on his behalf.[32]

Indian Agent Henry Schoolcraft noted that Charles even had his father-in-law Chief Katawabeda, apply for an American license. In 1820, Captain David Bates Douglass commented about Ermatinger after reaching Sandy Lake with

Governor Lewis Cass' Northwestern Expedition:

> There is an opposition trade [at Sandy Lake] carried on by Mrs. Armatinger [sic] from the Sault St. Marys in which report says the British Armatinger [Charles] is the capitalist—while the name only of the American one is used. I remember what Mr. Johnson [John Johnston] said at the Sault, but suspect some collusion in the Indian trade on all hands. Perhaps the North West and South West have an understanding still, but I have no good ground for believing so.[33]

One of the outlets for Charles Ermatinger's trading operations on American soil was a newly established trading post built in 1822 at the junction of the Mississippi and Sandy Lake rivers by independent trader William Aitkin. In an affidavit signed by Aitkin in 1824, he stated he purchased half of his trade goods from Charles Ermatinger and the remaining half from the American Fur Company. Although Aitkin was an independent trader, the American Fur Company gladly sold him trade goods. This arrangement may seem strange as both the concerns were in competition for essentially the same furs, but such practice was quite common on the frontier. American Fur operated both retail outlets and a wholesale business.[34]

Aitkin continued to receive supplies of trade goods from Charles Ermatinger until 1828, when Charles decided to retire from the fur trade. Robert Stuart, the American Fur Company agent at Mackinac, remarked to Astor's business manager Ramsay Crooks that, "Ermatinger has resigned to us all his interests in the Superior trade."[35]

Any references to an Ermatinger trading west of Lake Superior after 1828 refer to Charles' brother George Ermatinger or George's son James Rough Ermatinger. George lived on the south side of the St. Mary's River within the United States and also pursued a career in the fur trade. Although both brothers engaged in the trade, there is little evidence they cooperated in any way. One exception occurred when Charles asked George to obtain an American trade license for him.

Ramsay Crooks was John Jacob Astor's business manager and later president of the American Fur Company.
Minnesota Historical Society

George's son, James Ermatinger, was also an active trader along the Northwest Trail. He not only was an American citizen but also joined an old line fur trade family when he wed Charlotte Cadotte Warren. James Rough had a large family, but he lost two sons in the American Civil War. Although Charles Oaks and his siblings were part of a extensive family, unlike so many other fur trade families in the Northwest, all of the Ermatinger family died out after four generations.

James Ermatinger and his brother-in-law James Abbott traded at Sandy Lake and Leech Lake in the 1830s in opposition to William Aitkin. Ironically, Aitkin, who was one of Charles best customers, proved to be too much of an adversary for James Rough and James Abbott. By the 1830s, Aitkin was the chief trader for the American Fur Company in the old Fond du Lac Department, and he used every stratagem to squeeze his competition.

Some historical accounts maintain William Aitkin married a daughter of Charles Oaks Ermatinger, but that assertion is unsubstantiated. In spite of the story being repeatedly included in accounts of Aitkin's career, there is no factual basis for the claim since all of Ermatinger's thirteen children can be accounted for. Furthermore, at least nine of his children were without issue, and his oldest daughter Ann died less than a year after Aitkin's oldest child, Alfred was born. Ann Ermatinger never married.[36]

Charles and Charlotte left Sault Sainte Marie in 1828 and resided near Montreal at Elmwood, one of six farms owned by Charles. Strangely, while he still retained ownership of the property at the Sault, Charles never had a clear title to the stone house. He petitioned the government for title, but, in spite of his service during the War of 1812, he never received title to his land. In 1857, his son quitclaimed any remaining interest in the property at Sault Sainte Marie, and the last vestiges of ownership passed out of family control.

Charles Oaks Ermatinger died on September 4th, 1833. Funeral services were held at Christ Church in Montreal, and he was supposedly buried in Mount Royal Cemetery. Charles had executed several wills before his death. His final testament provided an annuity of sixty pounds a year for Charlotte, but transferred no real property to her.

Charlotte outlived her husband by seventeen years, dying in July of 1850, at age sixty-five. She was supposedly buried near Charles, although the exact location of both of their graves is questionable since Mount Royal Cemetery was only opened after both died.[37]

In death as in life, Charles Oaks Ermatinger proved to be something of a mystery. Many aspects of his career are not as clear as they could be, but maybe that was by his own design. Like so many other figures who traveled along the old Northwest Trail, Charles Oaks Ermatinger played a role in both American and Canadian history. He was a highly successful fur trader who married the daughter of an important chief and left an imposing monument in the form of the "Old Stone House" of Sault Sainte Marie.

Clerks and Voyageurs

Fur traders like William Morrison and Charles Oaks Ermatinger left a lengthy record of their service at trading posts along the Northwest Trail, but what of the other clerks and voyageurs? Many did not leave any records at all except an "X" on an *engagement* or employment contract. What we know of the ordinary folk who worked in the fur trade is largely dependent on the descriptions of them furnished by contemporaries or from fur company records that have survived the ravages of time.[38]

Some of the lessor known clerks working for the American Fur Company at Fond du Lac are mentioned in company records. For example, Pierre Cotté started his career with the North West Company as an interpreter in the Fond du Lac Department. In 1817 he was listed as working for the South West Company, still stationed at Fond du Lac. In 1818, he was listed as working as an interpreter for the American Fur Company and later as a clerk at the same post. He remained at Fond du Lac until 1836, when he was transferred to the company's fishing station at Grand Portage. We last hear of Pierre Cotté in 1839.[39]

Cotté was succeeded at Fond du Lac in 1836 by James P. Scott. Scott, a young newcomer to the fur trade, married Anna Aitkin, the daughter of William Aitkin, at the La Pointe mission church on August 7th, 1836. He was twenty-one and she was seventeen. The marriage was performed by Father Frederic Baraga, with Lyman Marquis Warren and Pierre Cotté as witnesses. Scott apparently only served for a year as clerk at Fond du Lac.[40]

Peter Crebassa was listed as clerk for 1836-1837, followed by John Fairbanks in 1837 and John Aitkin and another clerk named Landrie in 1838-1839. They in turn were succeeded by Francis Roussain, who apparently served at the post until the company was sold. The Roussain family had a long association with the community of Fond du Lac and the American Fur Company.

Charles H. Oakes, fur trader who succeeded William A. Aitkin as chief trader in the Fond du Lac Department. Oakes was stationed at Sandy Lake.
Minnesota Historical Society

The clerks at Sandy Lake were comparatively fewer in number than those serving at Fond du Lac. Charles Bousquet was employed by John Sayer & Company from 1795 through at least 1799. There is a reference to a boatman named Bousquet on the Red River of the North in 1804, which may be the same person. Bousquet could have fallen victim to staff reduction or simply retired from the trade. Zebulon Pike's reference to Charles Bousquet in the winter of 1806 seems to imply that he had just recently left Sandy Lake and that he was sufficiently well-known in the region.[41]

Bousquet was followed by another Nor' Wester, James Grant, who was the clerk at Sandy Lake in 1806. Following the transfer of the old North West Company's post to Astor's American Fur Company in 1817, the duties of post clerk were shared by two young men from New York, Samuel Ashmun and John H. Fairbanks, as mentioned earlier. Both men were recruited by American Fur and signed a five year contract or engagement.

Ashmun and Fairbanks were succeeded by William Morrison and later by William Aitkin. Aitkin's long tenure with American Fur was spent in part at his trading post near Sandy Lake. He also lived for a time at Fond du Lac. Following Aitkin's withdrawal from the company in 1838, the clerk in charge at Sandy Lake was Charles H. Oaks. For a time Allan Morrison, William Morrison's younger brother, also served in that capacity at a new establishment built by the company on Sandy Lake. Aitkin's post, which formerly served as company headquarters, reverted to his ownership.

Less is known about the voyageurs and trappers employed by the company. Church records and fur company papers are filled with the names of employees. Some of these records capture a little of the lives of the ordinary people who made the American Fur Company prosper. For example, numerous voyageurs and not a few clerks took country wives. Some of the records of these unions are preserved in church records such as those at St. Joseph Mission at La Pointe, where Father Frederic Baraga meticulously recorded marriages, baptisms, and deaths. In the church register can be found the Latinized names of voyageurs and their Ojibway wives carefully witnessed and recorded.

Marriages and baptisms were sometimes solemnized in groups. In fact, it is not unusual to see the marriages of several people from Sandy Lake or other inland trading posts recorded on the same day. The La Pointe church register for August 16th, 1835, shows two group weddings from different locations: One group of three couples from Lac Courte Oreilles and a second group of three couples from Sandy Lake. This suggests the participants traveled together on the long journey to La Pointe to say their marriage vows. The three couples from Sandy Lake who were wed included: Carolus Chalout, age 28 who married Isabella DuFault, age 22; Ludovicus DuFault, Junior, age 25, who married Josepha Goneville, age 16; and Josephus Belanger, age 22, who married Anna Pitawigijigokwe, age 20.[42]

It was important to the devout voyageurs to say their marriage vows before a priest or to have a son or daughter baptized. Some were also brought to the church to be buried in sanctified ground. Sometimes siblings who died from childhood diseases were brought to holy ground and interred in the same grave.

Of course fur company records also contain important information about some of the early residents along the Northwest Trail. One of the more well-known figures was also the first Swede in Minnesota. Jacob Falstrom, whose son was born at Sandy Lake, was recorded on both the roster of American Fur Company employees in 1817 and for subsequent years as "Jacob Falstraw."[43]

Jacob Falstrom had originally sailed from Sweden for England only to be shipwrecked off the English coast. He traveled with an uncle to London. There he became separated and wandered the streets of the city alone, unable to communicate with anyone. Through a strange twist of fate, he found himself in the employ of the Hudson's Bay Company on a ship bound for Canada. No sooner had he arrived at the company's depot at York Factory than he wandered too far away from the post and became lost. He survived among the Cree and gradually wandered south to what is now Minnesota. In 1823, he married Margaret Bonga, of the mixed Indian–African Bonga family before settling into the life of a headwaters fur trader. Of course Falstrom's story is just one of thousands.[44]

Steven Bonga was a decendent of a former West Indian slave and an Ojibway mother. His father was freed by his owner Captain Daniel Robertson, British commander of Fort Mackinac. The Bonga familiy was well-known throughout Minnesota. Carlton County Historical Society

The last names of five ordinary fur company employees working for Charles Bousquet at Sandy Lake in 1795 are given in North West Company records. While the family names of a few of these men are familiar in the Great Lakes trade, most are unknown. The men include a Mr. Beaudry, a Mr. Cotté, a clerk named JN (Jean?) Lemoine, a Mr. Montreuil, and a Mr. Rhiell (Rheil?).[45]

The names of three men are given as being employed by the North West Company's rival, the XY Company at Sandy Lake in 1805. These men are listed as Bazil Durand or Durant, Amable Durocher, and Berthy (Barthelemy?) Lapoitre.

There are at least two serious questions concerning references to these XY Company employees assigned to Sandy Lake. First, the obvious problem is the lack of an identifiable XY Company trading station on or near Sandy Lake in 1805. Zebulon Pike left a very detailed description of the lake, which he toured in January of 1806, and he did not mention the XY Company's presence on the lake. The XY men may have stayed at *Le Vieux fort* marked on one of Nicolett's sketch maps of Sandy Lake or at some other location, but there is little evidence to support the idea.[46]

A second problem with the references to XY men at Sandy Lake in 1805 concerns the timing of their employment. The North West Company and the XY Company merged in November of 1804. Anyone assigned to Sandy Lake by the XY Company prior to the amalgamation would have been either reassigned for 1805 or paid off.

Following the amalgamation of the XY and North West companies in 1804, a number of boatmen and clerks were either demoted or discharged. The new united concern did not need men as much as it needed an ever increasing amount of capital for operations.[47]

Chapter 8 - Headwaters Traders
Notes

1. Marjorie Wilkins Campbell, *The North West Company* (2nd ed.,Toronto, 1983), pp. 159 and 167.

2. David Lavender, *The Fist in The Wilderness* (1964; reprint ed., Albuquerque, 1979), pp. 42-43.

3. Ibid., pp. 109-113, Provides details on the formation of the American Fur Company.

4. Ibid., pp. 148-150.

5. Campbell, *North West Company*, pp. 216-217; At the time of the skirmish between the Hudson's Bay Company men and the Nor'Westers at Seven Oaks (June 17th, 1816), Selkirk was proceeding west through the Great Lakes with the veterans of the Regiment de Meuron. His intended course was by way of the Northwest Trail; however, on hearing the news of the clash at Seven Oaks, he changed course and followed the customary route along the northeast shore of Lake Superior to Fort William.

6. Ibid., p. 229.

7. Lavender, *Fist in the Wilderness*, pp. 247-248.

8. Ibid., p. 248. Astor contemplated military action to expel Selkirk's men. The government also knew of the incursion by Selkirk, but decided not to send troops. The mere rumor of American troops on the St. Croix had the desired effect as evident in Morrison's actions and Selkirk's eventual withdrawal. See William Morrison to William Aitkin, January 25th, 1817. Henry Hastings Sibley Papers, in the collections of the Minnesota Historical Society. Microfilm copy, roll 1.

9. Lavender, *Fist in the Wilderness*, p. 248.

10. Edgar B. Wesley, *Guarding the Frontier: A Study of Frontier Defense From 1815-1825* (Minneapolis, 1935); Henry Putney Beers, The Western Military Frontier, 1815-1846 (Philadelphia, 1975); Information on the Exclusion Act of April 29th, 1816, and some of the practical difficulties surrounding its enforcement, were outlined in a letter dated January 22nd, 1818, from Governor Lewis Cass to Colonel John Bowyer, Indian Agent at Green Bay. For a copy of this letter see *Collections of the State Historical Society of Wisconsin*, vol. 20 (Madison, 1911), pp. 16-17.

11. The names of Ashman and Fairbanks can be found on a roster compiled by Dwight H. Kelton, "American Fur Company Employees–1818-1819," in *Collections of the State Historical Society of Wisconsin*, vol. 12 (Madison, 1892), pp. 154-155 and 160-161.

12. A series of letters written by Ashman and Fairbanks describing their experiences on the frontier can be found in *The Moorsfield Antiquarian*, vol. 2, no. 1 (May, 1938), pp. 5-24; According to Captain David Bates Douglass, both clerks were apparently starved for news from the outside world. For Douglass' reaction see Sydney W. Jackman (et al., eds.), *American Voyageur: The Journal of David Bates Douglass* (Marquette, 1969), p. 80.

13. A short biography of Samuel Ashman can be found in Joseph E. and Estelle Bayliss, *River of Destiny: The Saint Marys* (Detroit, 1955), pp. 285-286.

14. Biographical information about John H. Fairbanks can be found in Warren Upham, "Minnesota Biographies, 1655-1912," *Minnesota Historical Society Collections*, vol. 14 (June, 1912), p. 214; references to John Fairbanks as well as other members of the Fairbanks family are listed in Alvin H. Wilcox, *A Pioneer History of Becker County* (St. Paul, 1907).

15. Sir Alexander MacKenzie, *Voyages From Montreal on the River St. Lawrence Through the Continent of North America to the Frozen and Pacific Oceans in the Years 1789 and 1793* in Master Works of Canadian Authors (Toronto, 1927), p. 22, includes a brief biographical sketch of Etienne Wadin.

16. Ibid., pp. 23-24. There is a brief mention of the death of Wadin in Warren, *History of the Ojibway People* (1885; reprint ed., St. Paul, 1984), pp. 378-381; See also Harold A. Innis, *Peter Pond: Fur Trader and Adventurer* (Toronto, 1930). Innis discounts the idea that Pond deliberately murdered Etienne Wadin.

17.   For a biography of William Morrison by his nephew George A. Morrison, see Wilcox, *A Pioneer History*, pp. 226-232. A more recent biographical sketch of William Morrison can be found in the *Morrison County Historical Society Newsletter* (Spring, 1994), p. 5. Further information regarding the Morrison brothers can also be found in Warren Upham (et al.), *Minnesota in Three Centuries: 1655-1908*, 4 vols. (Mankato, 1908), vol. 1, pp. 316-317; Newton H. Winchell, Edward D. Neill, and J. Fletcher Williams, *History of the Upper Mississippi Valley* (Minneapolis, 1881), p. 174; Warren Upham (comp.), "Minnesota Biographies, 1655-1912," in *Minnesota Historical Society Collections*, vol. 14 (June, 1912), p. 526; and Warren Upham, Minnesota Geographic Names: Their Origin and Historic Significance (1920; reprint ed., St. Paul, 1969), p. 350.

18.   Lavender, *Fist in the Wilderness*, pp. 247-248.

19.   *Collections of the State Historical Society of Wisconsin*, vol. 12 (Madison, 1892), pp. 164-165.

20.   See n. 17 above for details of Morrison's agreements with the American Fur Company.

21.   See n. 17 above regarding Morrison's obituary.

22.   Gladys McNeice, *The Ermatinger Family of Sault Sainte Marie* (Sault Sainte Marie, Ontario, 1984), is the most complete account of the life of Charles Oakes Ermatinger; Bayliss, *River of Destiny*, pp. 218-219, includes a short biographic sketch of Charles Oakes Ermatinger.

23.   McNeice, *Ermatinger*, p. 5.

24.   Ibid., pp. 8 and 75.

25.   The story of the "country wife" is aptly told in Jennifer S. H. Brown, *Strangers in Blood: Fur Trade Company Families in Indian Country* (Vancouver, 1980). For the relationships among fur trade families see Sylvia Van Kirk, *Many Tender Ties* (Winnipeg, 1980). The Ermatingers frequently invited Henry and Jane Johnston Schoolcraft to their elegant home, where guests undoubtedly heard the tune played on the piano by Mrs. Schoolcraft. The melody is based on "The Minstrel Boy," an old Irish tune. An arrangement of "The Ojibway Maid" can be found in Appendix B; see also Thomas L. McKenney, *Sketches of a Tour to the Lakes* (1885; reprint ed., Minneapolis, 1959), pp. 187-189.

26   McNeice, *Ermatinger*, pp. 9-11. The author quotes McNeice several times in the text.

27.   Ibid., pp. 13-15.

28.   Ibid., pp. 17-18.

29.   Ibid., pp. 19-22.

30.   Ibid., pp. 50-51.

31.   Ibid., p. 51.

32.   Warren (ed.), *History of the Ojibway*, p. 384.

33.   Jackman, *American Voyageur*, p. 41.

34.   Lavender, *Fist in the Wilderness*, p. 458, n. 7.

35.   McNeice, *Ermatinger*, p. 55.

36.   Ibid., Appendix II, "Ermatinger Family Genealogy."

37.   Ibid., pp. 60-62.

38.   See Grace Lee Nute, *The Voyageur* (1931; reprint edition, St. Paul, 1955), pp. 13-20. Note the description of the employment contracts, or *engagements*, on page 36; Alfred Brunson, *A Western Pioneer*, 2 vols.(New York, 1872), vol. 1, p. 175; and Allan Morrison, "History of the Fur Trade in the Northwest," unpublished manuscript in the collections of the Minnesota Historical Society, n.d.

39.   Anna M. Keeton, "Pierre Cotté," in *Acta et Dicta*, vol. 6, n.1(October, 1933), pp. 86-96. Cotté is also mentioned frequently in the Journals of Edmund Franklin Ely.

40.   Linda M. Bristol (comp.), *St. Joseph Mission and Holy Family Catholic Church: Marriage Records, 1835-1880* (Bayfield, Wisconsin, 1993), p. 4.

41.   See Donald Jackson (ed.), *The Journals of Zebulon Montgomery Pike*, 2 vols., (Norman, 1966), vol. 1, p. 79, n. 141, for Pike's mention of "Mr. Charles Brusky." Bousquet may have spent his last years at Red River colony. A reference to a Charles Bousquet appears in a petition for a priest from the inhabitants of the colony to the Bishop of Quebec. Bousquet signed the petition with an "X" indicating he was illiterate. See Grace Lee Nute, *Documents Relating to Northwest Missions* (St. Paul, 1942), pp. 16-17.

42.   Bristol, *St. Joseph Mission*, p. 1.

43.   Kelton, "American Fur Company Employees," pp. 160-161.

44.   For more information on Falstrom see Theodore A. Norelius, "The First Swede in Minnesota," in *Swedish Pioneer Historical Quarterly*, vol. 8 (October, 1957), pp. 107-115.

45.   Bruce M. White (comp.), *The Fur Trade in Minnesota: An Introductory Guide to Manuscript Sources* (St. Paul, 1977), Appendix 2, pp. 30-57.

46.   Jackson (ed.), *Zebulon Montgomery Pike*, pp. 78-82; Grace Lee Nute, "Posts in the Minnesota Fur-Trading Area, 1660-1855," *Minnesota History*, vol. 11, no. 4 (December, 1930), pp. 383-385.

47.   Harold A. Innis, *The Fur Trade in Canada: An Introduction to Canadian Economic History* (1932; rev. ed., New Haven, 1962), p. 259.

Retail store and office of the American Fur Company post at Fond du Lac. It is possible that trade goods were passed through the small opening to the left of the doorway. A similar arrangement was used by the Hudson's Bay Company in Canada. Northeast Minnesota Historical Center, Duluth S2386 B13f1

Photo of the site of William A. Aitkin's trading post at the confluence of
the Sandy Lake and Mississippi rivers.
Photo by Larry Luukkonen

Chapter 9 ❧ William Alexander Aitkin

Of the various fur traders who passed along the Northwest Trail, perhaps the one who best symbolized the very essence of the headwaters trader in the old Fond du Lac Department was William Alexander Aitkin. In fact, no historical account of the fur trade in Northern Minnesota would be complete without a reference to him. One can also argue that Aitkin's career in the fur trade was the history of the American Fur Company in Minnesota, because he played such a large role in its operation, at least during the years 1829 to 1838.

The Beginnings of an Independent Trader

William Alexander Aitkin began his career as an independent trader in the same fashion as Charles Ermatinger, with whom he associated for many years. Like Ermatinger, very little is known about Aitkin's early years. For example, it is not certain exactly when and where William Aitkin was born. Charles H. Oaks stated he believed William A. Aitkin: "...was a Canadian by birth of British descent." Some sources list his birthplace as Edinburgh, Scotland. Church records, however, indicate he was baptized on May 14th, 1792, by his uncle Reverend Roger Aitken in Aberdeen, Scotland. Aitkin's uncle spelled his last name "Aitken."[1]

William Alexander Aitkin's father, also named William Aiken (spelled without the "t"), was from Dumfries, Scotland, and served as a Bombardier (Corporal) in the 4th Battalion of the Royal Regiment of Artillery stationed at Fort Mackinac. His father-in-law, Sergeant John McDonald, was the Barrack Master for the King's (or 8th) Regiment of Foot and also served at Mackinac. McDonald's daughter Elizabeth and William Aiken met and were later married at the fort on May 10th, 1787.[2]

Due to a dispute over the terms of the peace treaty ending the Revolutionary War (1783), the British continued to occupy the post. Both William A. Aitkin's father and his future father-in-law remained as part of the British garrison at Fort Mackinac during the 1780s. It was customary for British military authorities to allow a limited number of the soldiers in each regiment to marry and keep their wives at the various military posts. The wives followed the regiments as they moved from post to post and performed many useful services for the army, even assisting on the battlefield at times. Aitkin's parents may have stayed in the regular barracks, where their only privacy consisted of a blanket hung from the ceiling as a screen.[3]

There is some question regarding the spelling of Aitkin's name. His father spelled his name "Aiken," whereas other records show it spelled "Aitken" or "Aitkin." Many of the people who knew William Alexander Aitkin spelled his name Aitkin, including the noted geographer and mathematician Joseph Nicollet, referred to earlier. Nicollet spelled the name Aitkin in his notes and correspondence and even named a lake north of Aitkin's trading post at the junction of the Sandy Lake and Mississippi rivers, "Aitkin Lake."

Many years after the death of William Alexander Aitkin, his son Roger insisted his father spelled the family name Aitkin. William Aitkin had beautiful penmanship and his signature at times appears as "Aitkin" and at other times the tail of the "t" obscures any effort to dot the second "i," thus seemingly vindicating the spelling "Aitken." The official spelling in Minnesota is "Aitkin," even though some authors stubbornly insist on retaining the spelling utilizing an "e." Of course, the spelling of the family name is not the only mystery surrounding this famous frontier figure.[4]

A copy of William A. Aitkin's signature.
Benton County Historical Society

Estimates of the date of William Aitkin's birth vary considerably. His obituary, which appeared in *The Minnesota Democrat* one month after his demise, stated he was sixty-six at the time of his death on September 16th, 1851.[5] That would put his birth date in 1785–two years before his parents were married. Aitkin himself stated in the census taken at his residence on September 18th, 1850, that he was fifty-eight years old. That would place his birthday in 1792, which is consistent with the existing church records and some five years after his parents were married at Fort Mackinac. Aitkin also affirmed for the census that he was born in Scotland.[6]

William Aitkin's papers reveal he maintained close family ties. Surviving letters from his mother Elizabeth, brother David, and sister Violet offer insights into his family life. Other relatives, such as his cousin Roger, also contributed interesting facts about his life and the time in which he lived. For example, correspondence from his cousin Roger Aitkin, who was an officer in the Royal Navy, described his experiences during the Napoleonic Wars. Roger, it seems, was captured by the French and spent nine years in prison. William's cousin wrote to him from Lunnenburg near Halifax, Nova Scotia, where many of Aitkin's relatives lived following the Revolutionary War. One of William Aitkin's sons was named Roger, but whether or not there was any connection to his cousin is not clear. It is certain, however, that William named his children after his siblings. The same names were frequently repeated from one generation to the next.

William Aitkin's parents later settled in the town of Sandwich, Upper Canada (Ontario), where William's father was listed as a manufacturer. Records indicate he was a "Tobacconist." Whether he processed tobacco or merely sold it is not clear. William's mother apparently wrote to him often while he was pursuing a career in the fur trade. In one letter, written after a visit to Nova Scotia in 1815, she told of several problems that had beset her and of her physical condition. The letter, which is barely legible and badly faded, was sent to William in care of the Dousman family on Mackinac Island. Elizabeth Aitkin's sister Jane had married Michael Dousman, the descendent of a Dutch nobleman.[7] Their first child, Hercules Louis Dousman, began his career in the fur trade at Prairie du Chien, Wisconsin, and later became prominent in the transportation business on the Mississippi River. William Aitkin had close business relations with Hercules; and, later in his fur trading career, William received financial backing from his cousin for various ventures. The Dousman family was also associated with the settlement and development of Milwaukee, Wisconsin.

Throughout his career, William Aitkin employed his relatives as clerks or sought to improve their lot through recommendation to influential people. For example, his younger brother David Aitkin, born in 1804 at Amherstberg, Upper Canada, later served for a time as the clerk of the American Fur Company post at Pembina. Aitkin's sons, Alfred, John, and Roger were all employed at different trading posts throughout Aitkin's department.

Familiar relations with friends and relatives often brought about reciprocity of favors as can be seen in a letter dated March 12th, 1842, wherein Henry Sibley and Hercules Dousman recommended David Aitkin to Michigan Senator William Woodbridge for the vacant post of Collector of Customs at Mackinac. David later secured the post of Indian Sub-Agent at Sault Sainte Marie in 1851, possibly through the same good offices.[8] Several of William Aitkin's daughters also married fur traders. It was typical of the time that fur trade families maintained very close relations, both familial and commercial, with their kin.

Close family relations also carried over into the fur trade for William Aitkin. Like so many other fur traders of his time, he "took a country wife" early in his fur trading career. He married an Ojibway woman named Bay-ji-quod-equa, also known as "Striped Cloud," or Madeline Aitkin. Some sources say they married on Mackinac Island before he even began his career as a trader.[9]

Aitkin may very well have met his wife at Mackinac, but records show it was not until many years later that they had their marriage solemnized with the benefit of clergy. On July 28th, 1829, William and "Magdelene" Aitkin were married by the Presbyterian missionary, the Reverend William Ferry, at Mackinac Island.[10] Aitkin had been boarding his three eldest children—Alfred, Nancy, and John—at Reverend Ferry's mission school and undoubtedly wanted to legitimize his children through formal marriage vows. This concern over legitimacy was common among traders who cared about the future legal status of their children and their right to inherit property and other important matters.

There is a persistent story that William Aitkin married the mixed-blood daughter of the Sault Sainte Marie trader Charles Ermatinger. Several accounts refer to "Madeline Ermatinger;" however, all of Ermatinger's children can be accounted for as mentioned earlier.[11] Furthermore, he never had a daughter named Madeline. Ermatinger was very proud of his family and it is highly unlikely that he would not have recognized any of his own offspring.   There was a possible relationship between William Aitkin and Charles Ermatinger through marriage, but the exact arrangement is not clear. The most important relationship between Aitkin and Charles appears to have been a commercial one.

Like so many other aspects of William Aitkin's long career, there are questions as to exactly when he began operating as a fur trader. He gave several hints in his correspondence. In a letter to Ramsay Crooks, dated September 25th, 1834, Aitkin stated, "I have been in the Indian trade since the age of sixteen and never one year free from opposition in all forms...." So, assuming he was born in 1792, Aitkin would have begun trading in 1808.[12]

In yet another letter to Crooks on January 26th, 1835, Aitkin remarked that, "as our returns stand at present they are better than I have known them at this season for the last twelve years that I have been in this country...."[13] This statement seems to refer to the commencement of Aitkin's operations at Sandy Lake (1822-1823), and not necessarily to when he first began trading.

The date 1802 has been given as the year William Aitkin began his career in the fur trade, and is based on an assumed birth date in 1785-1786. Other sources are not so helpful. One respected fur trade historian even ventured to say Aitkin was "a veteran of the old North West company." This statement is remarkable since it implies Aitkin was an "experienced" trader while barely in his teens!

More reliable and consistent with other known facts was a report by Aitkin's son-in-law, the historian William Warren. Warren gave a sketch of Aitkin in his *History of the Ojibway People*, wherein he stated Aitkin began his career in 1815, as a servant to a trader named John Drew.[14]

John A. Drew was a resident of Mackinac Island and later a justice of the peace, who undoubtedly knew William Aitkin. Drew was an independent trader who operated exclusively on Lake Michigan, chiefly in the Grand River area. An invoice for four hundred and twenty dollars worth of trade goods belonging to Drew, dated December 1834, was printed in the *Historical Collections and Researches Made by the Michigan Pioneer and Historical Society* and contained a notation that Drew began trading in 1815.[15] The date coincides with Warren's statement concerning the year Aitkin began trading, and it is indeed likely that Aitkin clerked for Drew at Mackinac before venturing into the field on his own. There is no evidence that indicates John Drew ever operated on the south side of Lake Superior or on the Mississippi headwaters. Instead, annual lists of trade licenses issued show that he traded in the Lake Michigan area and he remained active in the fur trade well into the 1830s.[16]

The earliest we hear of William Aitkin trading on Lake Superior is in 1817. He was operating in what was known as the Folle Avoine country near the headwaters of the St. Croix River on the south side of Lake Superior. Aitkin's appearance in the St. Croix area seems to indicate he may have been in partnership with Charles Oaks Ermatinger. Ermatinger, it will be recalled, wanted to get into the lucrative Fond du Lac trade in 1817; however, as a Canadian trader, he was barred by the Exclusion Act. He also faced formidable opposition from some former Nor'Westers now working for John Jacob Astor's American Fur Company.

Ermatinger circumvented the law excluding foreigners from the fur trade by getting Oliver Bostwick of the firm of David Stone & Co. to obtain a trading license for him. David Stone & Co. had recruited most of the experienced traders in the country as a way of competing with Astor's company. Charles Oaks, writing in 1872, stated that Aitkin and Ermatinger were both trading in American territory but neither were citizens. Due to the citizenship requirement, imposed as a condition of licensure after 1816, Aitkin and a number of other traders took the oath of allegiance to the United States in 1820.[17]

Aitkin's trading post at the junction of the rivers

Burial grounds

Last trading post on the Northwest Trail →

White square is Aitkin's Field
←

Aerial photo of the site of Aitkin's trading post. Aitkin's fields are still being cultivated. Several buildings belonging to a later trading post and the pioneer cemetery and Indian burial ground can be seen.

U.S. Department of Agriculture photo, 1940

By 1822, William Aitkin was trading at Sandy Lake. His new trading post, situated at the junction of the Sandy Lake and Mississippi rivers, was first noticed by the Italian explorer, Giacomo Beltrami in 1823.[18] Beltrami stopped at the post on his trip down the Mississippi after having "discovered" the northern source of that river. Aitkin's new post was also described by Lieutenant James Allen and Doctor Douglass Houghton, who stopped there with the Schoolcraft Expedition on July 3rd, 1832. Dr. Houghton wrote about Aitkin's post:

> This situation has long been regarded as an important one for the Indian trade. It was occupied by the old Northwest Company, and subsequently by the American Fur Company to the present time. Mr. Aitkin, the present agent of the company, makes this his residence, and the central depot for the great district over which he has charge; the posts and trade of which have been described in another part of this journal. His establishment, at present, consists of a large comfortable dwelling, several storehouses, and barns, stables, &c.; he raises corn and potatoes in fields near the house, and has a good stock of cattle.[19]

Aitkin had made a major commitment by opening the new post, and it is evident he intended to succeed. A license granted to him on July 25th, 1822, at Mackinac Island by Indian Agent George Boyd, showed he had two to three times the merchandise of any other trader in the region.[20]

Aitkin's Sandy Lake post was one of several that served as his headquarters during his career as a fur trader. The others were located as follows: at the new American Fur Company post at the village of Fond du Lac, where Aitkin had a residence; on the Crow Wing River, which he first visited in 1827; and, at the junction of the Swan and Mississippi rivers, which was his last residence.

Aitkin's trading posts were also recognized by the government. In fact, in 1824, Congress passed additional requirements regarding trade license information, commonly known as the "Location Law," for traders operating in Indian Territory. The measure required all traders to specify where they intended to operate for a specified period when applying for a license, in addition to the usual declaration of the value of trade goods brought into the interior and the posting of a performance bond.[21]

Indian Agent Lawrence Taliaferro, headquartered at Fort Snelling, included Aitkin's Sandy Lake post as one of seventeen recognized "forts" on a list he prepared in 1826. Apparently, Taliaferro thought the post was in his jurisdiction, since he also gave it the name "Fort Benton," after the famous United States Senator from Missouri, Thomas Hart Benton.[22]

Taliaferro's was the only official reference to the post as a "fort." Very shortly thereafter the army required the term "fort" be eliminated from the description of recognized trading posts. Apparently, officials did not wish to refer to trading establishments with a term usually reserved for military installations. Regardless of the official action, most posts in the interior were called "forts" or "trading houses" by the persons doing business there.

The period of Aitkin's association with the American Fur Company is one of the best documented parts of his life. Extensive correspondence by or about him exists. Also, it was a period when many travelers, explorers, and missionaries passed through the region, and almost all of them commented on William Aitkin's trading establishments.

The post at Sandy Lake was described not only by the explorers Beltrami, Allen, and Houghton as previously mentioned, but also by Reverend William Boutwell, who visited the place several times in the course of his missionary work.[23] Reverend Edmund Ely was another missionary whose diary records a day by day view of life at Aitkin's trading post. Ely spent several months during 1833-1834 teaching at the trading post and traveling about the country visiting other posts. During his time at Sandy Lake he stayed in Aitkin's house. Later, he resided at the American Fur Company post at the village of Fond du Lac and worked with Aitkin for a time as a clerk.[24]

Ely's diary records daily events at Fond du Lac in much the way he did while at Sandy Lake. In addition to Ely's descriptions of life at Fond du Lac, there is a scale drawing of the post prepared by Doctor Charles William Wulff Borup in

1836, which shows the company buildings and Aitkin's house. Visiting explorers in the 1840s recorded other views of the trading post.[25]

Comments about Aitkin's later Crow Wing River post, however, were not very flattering. In the summer of 1846, traveler Robert Clouston referred to that post as, "...two or three wretched houses called 'the fort'—an abominable hot-bed of bugs and fleas...." The next day he met William Aitkin and recorded that Aitkin was actually headquartered at the Little Rock River further downstream:

> On the following morning we started early and about 5 miles from "the Fort" met Mr. W. Aitkin, to whom this splendid "fort" belongs, but he resides at another called "Fort des Petites Rochers," about 50 miles further down the Mississippi....[26]

The contrast between Aitkin's residence at Sandy Lake and the post on the Crow Wing River must indeed have been remarkable. Clouston did not have the opportunity to compare the two places, but others certainly did.

Aitkin and the American Fur Company

The 1820s proved to be a profitable period for the fur trade, and William Aitkin began to expand his operations. On July 25th, 1827, Aitkin obtained a trading license for the Crow Wing River from Indian Agent George Boyd at Mackinac Island. Later, on August 8th of the same year, he received a trading license for Sandy Lake from Henry Schoolcraft at Sault Sainte Marie.[27]

In 1826, William Morrison, veteran trader and superintendent of Astor's operations in the old Fond du Lac Department, retired. Aitkin and Eustache Roussain, another old Nor'Wester and Morrison's clerk and father-in-law, managed the department. Each received one-sixth of the profits from 1826 to 1829.[28]

On July 22nd, 1830, Aitkin concluded a four year agreement with Robert Stuart, Astor's agent at Mackinac. The agreement, which placed Aitkin solely in charge of the Fond du Lac Department, provided for a share of the profits but no salary. He also received a trader's allowance and could purchase goods from the company at a modest markup. Aitkin received three hundred dollars for the use of his post at Sandy Lake. Additional money would be paid for any future improvements of the post at the conclusion of the agreement. Furthermore, the contract provided for an annual payment to Aitkin of one hundred dollars to keep Roussain out of the trade. Under the terms, Aitkin was to buy out Roussain. Aitkin would receive one-third share of the profits for the remainder of the 1830-1831 season and one half share annually thereafter for the duration of the contract. The agreement was to be effective in full in 1831.[29]

As a trader for the American Fur Company, Aitkin had the responsibility of overseeing the largest and potentially most profitable part of the Northern Outfit. The old Fond du Lac Department covered an enormous area ranging from Pembina, in the west, to the Rum River, in the south, including part of the watershed of the St. Croix River, then north to Rainy River and Lake Vermilion.

The period from 1828 to 1834 saw increasingly higher numbers of furs harvested in the Fond du Lac Department. Several factors determined the availability of furs. Fire, drought, disease, hunting pressure, individual hunter's needs, and the presence of alcohol all exerted an influence that could not be accurately forecast by Aitkin or other traders. The availability of liquor was a particularly vexing problem for American fur traders.

The United States government's official policy was to restrict the sale of alcohol to the Indians. Rival Canadian traders, however, were not subject to the same restrictions within their own country and freely provided liquor to Indian trappers in exchange for their furs. Many trappers as far south as Leech Lake availed themselves of the opportunity and carried their annual harvest of fur north to the Hudson's Bay Company post at Rainy Lake.[30]

Although American traders complained about the unfair advantage, all the various Indian agents could do was to allow a limited amount of alcohol to enter into those areas along the border where the use of liquor by the Hudson's Bay Company men was most flagrant.[31] Another stratagem practiced by traders confronted with the use of alcohol by their rivals was to "give" the liquor gratis to their respective trappers prior to any trading. The rules restricted the sale of alcohol to the Indians, but nothing was said about a "free" drink. So widespread was the practice of giving a free drink prior to serious trading that it even carried over to treaty negotiations. Thomas McKenney mentioned giving the Indians a diluted glass of spirits at the beginning of treaty negotiations and another upon the completion of business.

The use of alcohol by competing traders was not the only problem confronting Aitkin. Beaver, the standard of value by which all other pelts were valued, fluctuated in price per pound. In periods of high prices, the trader had to be on alert for deceptive practices. Clever trappers knew how to treat the skins to make them weigh more. Practices such as storing the skins in damp cellars or cache pits and rubbing grease into the fur to increase the weight were just a few tricks hunters were willing to play on the inexperienced or unwary clerk.

To guard against competition, William Aitkin had to be everywhere. Despite having experienced men manning the far-flung trading posts, he still had to travel enormous distances to oversee his clerks and deal with any competing traders. The annual activities of the fur trade continued under Aitkin's supervision. Sandy Lake had long served as the general rendezvous point for traders, and each spring the clerks from the scattered posts gathered at Aitkin's post to assess the results of the season's trading before beginning the long journey over the Northwest Trail to Fond du Lac and Mackinac Island.

The timeless routine of the fur trade, however, changed in 1834. In that year, Astor who was in bad health, retired from the fur trade; and the company was sold to his former business manager, Ramsay Crooks. As president of the concern, Crooks kept the old name but instituted several changes. He reorganized the company into six "outfits," or departments, and created two outfits on Lake Superior.[32] One was based at Sault Sainte Marie and a second, which Crooks called the "Northern Outfit" located at La Pointe on Madeline Island under the control of Chief Factor Lyman Marquis Warren, the father of historian William Warren. Although the old Fond du Lac Department comprised the largest part of the Northern Outfit, Aitkin had to report to Warren for instructions regarding the company's business.

Early sketch of Fond du Lac showing fur company buildings and Aitkin's house by the St. Louis River.
Oliphant, *Minnesota and the Far West*

In an attempt at diversification, Crooks embraced the idea of establishing fisheries on Lake Superior to not only supply company personnel and sled dogs with fish, but also sell the surplus catch to residents of the Ohio Valley. Crooks was also interested in land speculation and shipping, both potentially profitable businesses on Lake Superior. The company kept three schooners busy hauling furs, trade goods, general freight, and copper ore. One change, however, meant a marked departure from the customs of the past.

Customarily each Indian trapper drew on the stores of the company for his annual supply of necessary items, or as they called it, his "outfit." Trade guns, blankets, knives, hatchets, and other assorted goods were all supplied in advance of each season's hunt. The entire system operated on credit with records kept on each man in book entry form. Beaver was the unit of exchange, and prices for all of the trade goods were denominated in beaver. Other skins were also converted into beaver for ease in accounting. By the late 1820s, however, beaver was no longer the dominant fur. Raccoon had replaced beaver in terms of market demand.

Crooks changed everything. He wanted to replace the old credit system with a cash-and-carry operation–the cash being the furs gathered after each fall and winter trapping season. No goods were to be given out on credit in advance of the season. Aitkin was critical of the change in policy and informed Crooks of the hostility the new method of trade engendered, but Crooks was determined to cut expenses and make American Fur a very profitable concern. With little viable competition, the company could impose its will. In fact, an arrangement previously concluded between Aitkin and the Hudson's Bay Company pertaining to trade along the border, gave American Fur a virtual monopoly farther south in the Mississippi headwaters region. The trappers had little choice but to acquiesce.[33]

With respect to other plans, Aitkin supported the fisheries proposal. The American Fur Company post at Fond du Lac was ideally suited for a fishing station. Aitkin wrote to Crooks regarding the location of fishing stations on Lake Superior, and had little doubt the venture would in time become more valuable than the fur trade.[34]

By 1836, regular fishing stations had been established at Grand Portage and at Knife River. Aitkin ordered barrels of salt to preserve the catch, chiefly white fish and trout, and employed a cooper at Fond du Lac to make additional barrels in which to ship the fish. Over time, the returns from the fishing operation appeared promising, and Crooks urged Aitkin to relocate his headquarters from Sandy Lake to Fond du Lac. Aitkin had a house on the river front at Fond du Lac, but divided his time between that location and his former residence at Sandy Lake.

In 1836, Fond du Lac shipped three hundred barrels of fish, second only to La Pointe's three hundred twenty barrels. Aitkin's operations thus far had been profitable, and the new president of the company apparently approved of his management. The year 1836, however, marked a turning point in Aitkin's business fortunes and in his personal life.

During the years from 1830 to 1836, William Aitkin's luck seemed to follow that of the American Fur Company. Where he experienced success, he also encountered enmity and jealousy from those who were his rivals in the fur trade. He also undoubtedly was aware of men even within his own company who felt threatened by his success. Perhaps this is why he surrounded himself with family whom he knew, or who were expected to be loyal to him in much the same way as a highland chief's men were loyal to him above all others. The bonds that united the men in such a chain of authority were strongest at the local level and grew progressively more abstract as one advanced through the hierarchy. Given his Scottish background, such an outlook would seem natural. The notion of clan loyalty was reinforced by the people he dealt with on a daily basis, the structure of the fur trade companies, and the Ojibway, who also felt a measure of clan loyalty in their own way.

To Aitkin, the fur trade was more than kith and kin or a mere commercial venture; it was a way of life. The rhythm of activity associated with the business rituals of the fur trade changed with the coming of each new season. During his association with the American Fur Company, his successes and shortcomings were reflected in the correspondence of the company. While it was customary for traders to malign each other as scoundrels, Aitkin received considerable criticism from his associates. In many ways his personal experiences simply reflected the same problems faced by the company.

A good example of the similarity between charges against Aitkin and the American Fur Company can be seen in the hostility exhibited toward both in the writings of William Johnston, the mixed-blood son of the famous Sault Sainte Marie trader John Johnston. William Johnston's sister Jane was the wife of the newly commissioned Indian Agent at Sault Sainte Marie, Henry Schoolcraft.

While on a trading adventure in 1832 along the Northwest Trail with Samuel Abbott, George Ermatinger and James Rough Ermatinger, Johnston wrote a series of letters to his sister describing his experiences in the wilderness. In the letters, William Johnston was critical of the American Fur Company and extremely hostile toward anyone who appeared to be in league with William Aitkin. Johnston's enmity even extended as far as the missionary Reverend Ely, whom Johnston denounced not only to his sister but to the local trader at Fond du Lac, Pierre Cotté.[35]

It is easy to understand Johnston's hostility toward the company since he was in competition with it, the case against Aitkin may be harder to fathom. The particular reason for William Johnston's dislike of Aitkin can be traced back to an incident in 1827, when Aitkin and several other traders swore in an affidavit that his brother, George Johnston, then employed as a Sub-Agent at La Pointe, had confiscated the goods of a trader on trumped-up charges and subsequently used the merchandise for his own purposes. The charge was later proven and Johnston dismissed. William apparently never forgot Aitkin's role in the affair and used every opportunity to focus official attention on his actions.[36]

While Johnston's sister and Henry Schoolcraft undoubtedly saw through his schemes, William Johnston persisted. Among his accusations were charges that Aitkin used liquor in the fur trade. This is particularly interesting since Schoolcraft himself authorized Aitkin to take a quantity of liquor into Indian territory to offset the use of alcohol as an inducement to trade by agents of the Hudson's Bay Company.

William Johnston's charges that Aitkin used liquor in the trade were somewhat ironic since George Johnston, ever the black sheep of the family, was subsequently dismissed from his job as superintendent of the Indian dormitory on Mackinac Island for drunkenness. After that episode he ceased to have any meaningful influence with Schoolcraft.[37]

Aitkin was not the only one accused of using liquor in the trade. Critics accused the American Fur Company of the same action. Ironically, after Ramsay Crooks assumed leadership of the company, he began a campaign to eliminate the use of liquor in the trade. For decades traders had lamented the introduction of "ardent spirits" into the Indian country because of the misery it caused, but they reluctantly went along with the practice because the local people would either trade with competitors who used liquor or they would simply go to locations where they knew they could buy liquor.

Another bitter foe of William Aitkin was the Indian Agent at Fort Snelling, Major Lawrence Taliaferro. Taliaferro resented the fact that Aitkin's trading area was under the jurisdiction of his rival, the bookish Henry Schoolcraft, a man whom he not only personally despised because of his notoriety, but also felt was out to ruin his work with the Dakota and Ojibway Indians. At one point Taliaferro's intense dislike of Schoolcraft led him to send a written challenge demanding satisfaction. Schoolcraft apparently discarded the invitation to a duel as ridiculous. Taliaferro reserved his strongest dislike for William Aitkin because he saw him as an instrument of the American Fur Company.[38]

The most spiteful remarks about Aitkin, however, were directed at his marital status. Although married to Madeline for several years, Aitkin appears to have suspected her of infidelity. Reverend Ely noted in his diary that he had been informed Aitkin had offered her, "...a form of divorce–but she refused it." Ely remarked that Aitkin told him, "...when last here [at Fond du Lac], that he had determined to throw her away. He can prove nothing against her...." Shortly after Ely's remarks, Aitkin took a second country wife.[39]

Very little is actually known about either of Aitkin's wives. Documents from the time of Aitkin's death mention a Julia Quatince needing money to support Aitkin's minor children while his estate was being probated. In 1843, the same Julia Quatince appeared on annuity rolls as a resident of Sandy Lake with three children. Other documents show that Aitkin married O-be-be-won-o-quay, the granddaughter of chief Katawabeda.[40]

That Aitkin should be criticized for taking a country wife sounds on the surface highly hypocritical given the widespread record of acceptance of the practice among men who were already married. Aitkin had seven children with each of his two wives and openly acknowledged all of them (See Appendix C).[41]

The remarks about Aitkin's marital status reached Ramsay Crooks, who inquired of Aitkin about the matter. Once again, it seems a bit hypocritical to even broach the subject since Crooks had taken a country wife. His illegitimate but talented, mixed-blood daughter Hester later married Reverend William Boutwell in a ceremony at the Fond du Lac mission with Reverend Ely.[42]

All of the jealousy expressed in the various attacks on Aitkin did little to diminish his ability as a trader. The stories about his wives continued unabated till the day he died. In fact, there was one story reportedly told by Aitkin himself. Domestic difficulties and other petty innuendo whispered about Aitkin did not undermine his standing with Crooks so much as other factors.

The years from 1836 to 1838 were difficult ones for both William Aitkin and the American Fur Company. With Crooks firmly in control, the company launched several innovations including the development of the fisheries, noted earlier. Aitkin was placed in charge of the fishing operations at Fond du Lac and along the north shore of Lake Superior. He did not know much about the commercial fishing business, but tried to carry out the necessary supervisory functions of the operation while at the same time managing the primary business of the department, namely fur trading. Mistakes were undoubtedly made in handling the fishing enterprise of which Aitkin was to blame, but some of the company's agents also erred. William Brewster, Crook's factor at the Detroit Department, let fish spoil on the docks while he dickered for a higher price.[43]

The year 1836 ended on a sad note for Aitkin. On December 6th, 1836, his eldest son Alfred was murdered at Upper Red Cedar Lake (Cass Lake). Alfred had just taken over the management of the trading post on the lake after having operated the Fond du Lac post under his father's watchful eye. The circumstances of Alfred's sudden and untimely death, the pursuit of his assailant, the resulting trial, and even his final resting place are surrounded with uncertainty.

Frontier Calamity: The Murder of Alfred Aitkin

There are numerous contemporary references to Alfred Aitkin's death. Some writers have speculated that his demise made a lasting impression on his father from which he never recovered. Whatever effect that horrific act had on William Aitkin, the story of Alfred's murder has gone largely unreported. Who was Alfred Aitkin?

Very little is known about Alfred's early years. He was born in 1816 at Fond du Lac, the first child of William and Madeline Aitkin. He was educated, along with two younger siblings, at the mission school on Mackinac Island run by the Presbyterian missionary Reverend William Ferry. Alfred entered the fur trade at an early age and worked with his father at various locations throughout Minnesota in the old Fond du Lac Department. As noted earlier, the elder Aitkin presided over an extensive area that stretched from Lake Superior to parts of the Red River Valley, including approximately two-thirds of what is now the State of Minnesota.

By the fall of 1836, Alfred had sufficient experience in the practical management of a trading post so that his father could entrust him with the position of clerk at the post on Cass Lake. As a clerk, Alfred had the responsibility of maintaining the post and overseeing the activities of the resident voyageurs and local trappers. It was there, on December 6th, 1836, that he met a violent death.

There are several contemporary versions of the incident and the personalities involved. One account stated that Alfred was murdered by the jealous suitor of another man's wife for interfering in the affair. Another version maintained that he was killed by an irate husband whose wife he had stolen. Both stories leave something to be desired, for Alfred had just taken over the management of the post and barely knew the parties to the affair.[44]

On the day of his murder, an Ojibway named Pashkwewozh, also referred to as Che-ga-wa-skung, was reportedly trying to break into the trading post storehouse with an ax. One of the voyageurs reported the act to Alfred, who, on hearing of this, went to the storehouse and told the man to stop. He was ignored by Che-ga-wa-skung. Alfred took the ax away from the man and ordered him out of the post. The murderer turned as if to leave but instead picked up a loaded musket that he had hidden and shot Alfred in the breast killing him instantly. The murderer fled and sought refuge with his relatives on Grand Island (present Star Island) in Cass Lake.

Word of the murder spread quickly. William Aitkin, who had just arrived at Sandy Lake, heard the news and immediately set off by dog sled in pursuit with a posse of clerks, voyageurs, an Indian hunter, and the missionary Reverend Boutwell. William Aitkin later wrote to Indian Agent Henry Schoolcraft that, "Our friend Mr. Boutwell joined the party with his musket on his shoulder as a man and as a Christian for he knew it was a righteous cause."[45]

The reaction to the news of Alfred's death was also noted by the missionary Reverend Edmund Ely. Ely, who was living near the Fond du Lac trading post at the time, made the following notation in his journal:

About 9 o'clock as I was sitting with Miss Cook I heard a strange sound as of many voices crying out–but concluded it was some Canadians singing, again resumed my conversation–but in a few minutes Coteque and her daughter Jane rushed in, in an agony of distress, saying that Mr. Aitkin's oldest son was killed and pointed toward the houses. I stepped to the door and the air resounded with a most dreadful wail. I immediately went over, and found Mrs. Aitkins and her whole family in the snow by the side of the fence near the stable–surrounded by Indian women–in an agony of wailing.[46]

Before leaving to pursue the murderer, William Aitkin sent out word from Sandy Lake to all the northern trading posts to cease operations. Not one ounce of powder or a single musket ball was to be sold until the murderer was apprehended. The fur trade in the Northwest ground to a halt.

Aitkin's posse moved rapidly through the snow toward Leech Lake. Each sled, pulled by a team of panting dogs, raced through the gleaming forest following the frozen trail leading northwest from Sandy Lake. They paused only long enough at Leech Lake to gather more men. Aitkin then set off toward Cass Lake. As the afternoon shadows lengthened into evening, the posse approached the lake and the Indian encampment on Grand Island. Soon it was dark and Aitkin realized that his quarry might use the cover of night to slip away if his men were seen crossing the lake to the island. Instead, the posse waited for nightfall before closing in on the sleeping camp. Cautiously Aitkin's men approached the camp in the predawn darkness. He posted his men at a distance around the camp to insure that no one escaped.

At the first gleam of daylight, Aitkin's men with leveled muskets rushed the sleeping encampment. So thoroughly overwhelmed were the occupants that they gave up without a fight. All guns, knives, and hatchets were gathered lest anyone have second thoughts regarding resistance. The murderer was taken into custody and sent back to the fur company's post at Leech Lake under guard. Somewhere on Leech Lake, the murderer escaped in broad daylight with the aid of his two brothers. Aitkin, who stayed behind with the rest of his men at the encampment, learned of the escape and sent a second party under the leadership of Francis Brunet to recapture the fugitive.[47]

After six days and nights of unrelenting pursuit, one of Brunet's men, the trader George Bonga, succeeded in tracking down the desperate fugitive and his brothers. At the time of his capture, Che-ga-wa-skung was in deplorable physical condition and had to be carried by his two brothers. This time he was sent to Aitkin's post at Sandy Lake by dog sled with, what one observer termed, "a perfect network of ropes and cords about him."

After a short stay at Sandy Lake, the murderer was once again lashed to a dog sled and taken by William Aitkin's son John and Allan Morrison to Fort Snelling for trial. The men arrived at the fort on February 20th, 1837, only to be informed that court would not convene until May. Furthermore, the trial would have to take place at the nearest courthouse which was located at Prairie du Chien, the county seat for Crawford County, Wisconsin Territory. Accordingly, the murderer was confined in irons in the fort guardhouse.

In the meantime, Aitkin wrote to his friend Henry Hastings Sibley, "Do see that the wretch is well secured, as he made his escape once since I took him, and it cost us a pursuit of six days to retake him."[48] The imprisonment of the murderer at the fort was noticed by the mixed-blood population, the Dakota, and the Ojibway, who were interested in the outcome of the trial. In a letter to Governor Henry Dodge, Indian agent Lawrence Taliaferro appeared more concerned about his reputation with the tribes than with the murder. He believed the presence of the murderer at the fort, "...will add to the unpleasantness of my situation."[49]

The legal proceedings for Alfred Aitkin's murderer in the United States District Court at Prairie du Chien proved to be a very protracted process. The case dragged on into the fall of 1837, when the counsel for the defense succeeded in having the trial postponed until the next term of court. William Aitkin, confident that he had made all the necessary arrangements, wrote, "I have engaged the best lawyer in the territory and have taken every precaution....The wretch remains in chains for eight months more in a dungeon."[50]

The decision in the Alfred Aitkin murder case in 1838 had many implications, especially for Minnesota's mixed-blood population. Although Alfred was the product of a mixed marriage, he was regarded by his contemporaries as a "white man." Therefore, if an Indian committed a crime against him, the perpetrator must stand trial in criminal court. The proceedings at Prairie du Chien, however, decided differently. In spite of careful instruction, it was determined that Alfred was an Indian and, since he was murdered by another Indian, the court did not have jurisdiction. The murderer was set free.

The decision caused a furor among the mixed-blood population who were concerned about their status as citizens of the United States and the legitimacy of their offspring. A lengthy correspondence ensued about the decision of the Alfred Aitkin murder case. The mixed-bloods even threatened to use their influence to undo the 1837 treaty recently concluded between the Chippewa, as they were officially known, and the United States, which ceded the tribe's title to certain lands in Minnesota.[51]

Meanwhile, the friends and family of the murderer were enraged at the proceedings and the possibility their relation might be executed. George Bonga, the company trader at Leech Lake, was harassed. His canoe was broken and he was threatened with dire consequences if a guilty verdict was returned. Bonga wrote to Reverend William Boutwell at Sandy Lake about his situation. Aitkin responded to the unrest by threatening to close the posts northwest of Sandy Lake and concentrate his men to defend the company's property. Crooks pondered the drastic move, but Aitkin insisted that firmness was necessary in the face of threats.[52]

David Aitkin, William's younger brother, stayed at Prairie du Chien during the proceedings and informed him of the outcome. William Aitkin was furious. United States District Attorney Thomas Pendleton Burnett wrote to Aitkin "...to advise you as counsel and friend to let the matter rest." As for the murderer, he reportedly never set foot in the northern wilderness out of fear that Aitkin and the mixed-bloods would seek revenge.[53]

The events surrounding the murder of Alfred and the decision rendered by the court were both blows to William Aitkin. At least he was spared the knowledge of the eventual disappearance of his son's remains. After the murder at Cass Lake, Alfred's remains were taken to the American Fur Company post at Leech Lake. They were examined by Reverend Boutwell, who made a report of his findings and forwarded it to the Indian Agent at La Pointe. Alfred was interred near the post.

In February of 1837, it was decided to move Alfred's body to his birthplace at Fond du Lac. He was to be buried in the cemetery that was reserved for traders and their families. The funeral on February 25th at Fond du Lac was witnessed by Delia Cook, a missionary assistant to Reverend Ely:

> This afternoon I followed the remains of poor Alfred Aitkin to the grave. The wretched father arrived with them yesterday. It is impossible to see and not to pity him. He is the picture of distress and almost of despair. By his request the church burial service was read at the house. The scene at the grave was impressive and affecting.[54]

Sometime later, William Aitkin purchased a gray (granite?) tombstone to mark his son's grave. The inscription on the stone was recorded by the missionary Reverend Samuel Spates in 1841. It read:

> Sacred to the memory of Alfred Aitkins, who fell a victim to a treacherous assassin Dec. 6th, 1836. Aged 20 years, 10 months and 26 days.[55]

Several early visitors to Fond du Lac commented about Alfred's stone. The missionary Florantha Sproat noted the forlorn grave during a tour of the Fond du Lac mission in 1842:

> After a breakfast of boiled sturgeon we all went for a walk, visiting first the grave-yard. There we saw the stone marking the grave of the young man who had been murdered by an Indian—a horrid murder.[56]

In 1854, another visitor described Alfred's grave. Mary Clara Post arrived in the frontier town of Superior, Wisconsin, with her parents on June 10th, on board the schooner *Algonquin*. In the days and weeks following her arrival, she wrote about her impressions of the area including a visit to the settlement of Fond du Lac and Alfred's grave:

> Just at the base of the hills, is an Indian grave yard, and the first mound we reached, was covered by a slab of gray stone which told the tragic story, that a white man who slumbered beneath it, was slain by an assassin.[57]

The old traders' cemetery and an adjoining Indian cemetery were moved to make way for the Lake Superior & Mississippi Railroad after 1869. Some families arranged for the relocation of their deceased family members, but no one mentioned Alfred Aitkin. Instead, Alfred's grave with its heavy stone marker has completely disappeared. Some graves were accidentally uncovered in 1937 during a nearby road construction project, but there was no further mention of Alfred's grave after the description given by Mary Clara Post in 1854. Furthermore, there is no record of Alfred's remains being moved to another site. Chances are, if the railroad construction did not disturb the site, the heavy stone has probably sunk beneath the ground due to the natural settling of the grave. The lost tomb of this unfortunate man adds merely another unsolved mystery in an already tragic story.

Competition and Conflict to the End

While the trial of Alfred Aitkin's murderer was underway, William Aitkin was busy presenting a trader's claim to be included in a pending treaty with the Chippewa. Aitkin succeeded in meeting the stringent claims criteria for submission of a claim for twenty-eight thousand dollars inserted in Article Four of what was officially known as the "Treaty with the Chippewa at St. Peter's," concluded in 1837.[58]

Other traders' claims for payment of outstanding debts from treaty money such as Lyman Warren's for twenty-five thousand dollars, and Hercules Dousman's claim for five thousand dollars, were part of a larger sum of seventy thousand dollars appropriated by the government to satisfy legitimate demands, but Aitkin's claim was by far the largest individual claim.

The matter of Aitkin's claim soon became a bone of contention between Aitkin and Ramsay Crooks. Aitkin undoubtedly believed the money was intended as reimbursement for losses he sustained due to bad debts over the years. Crooks, on the other hand, probably felt the money rightfully belonged to the American Fur Company. To what extent other traders in the company undermined Aitkin in the eyes of Crooks over the treaty money is problematical. Lyman Warren wrote to Aitkin advising, "We have no friends here (at La Pointe)."[59]

A considerable exchange of correspondence resulted from Aitkin's claim. One can trace Crook's movements and his desire to be present at the payment. Initially, Aitkin was cooperative, but he soon cooled to the idea of transferring the money to the company. Unable to get Aitkin to agree to a final settlement, Crooks tried to negotiate as the payment neared. Instead, Hercules Dousman, who acted as Aitkin's fiscal agent, was given power of attorney over his claim.[60]

During the maneuvering for Aitkin's treaty claim, Crooks probably tipped his hand regarding his plan to replace Aitkin and reorganize the Fond du Lac portion of the Northern Outfit. This may explain Aitkin's sudden change of heart concerning the final disposition of his claim.

Some writers who have traced Aitkin's career claim he, like Lyman Warren, was dismissed from the American Fur Company at the end of 1838 for mismanagement. No one, however, appears to have investigated the extent to which the issue of the trader's claim influenced Crooks' decision to ask William Aitkin to "withdraw" from the company. The mismanagement story is also interesting in light of the correspondence from Crooks to Aitkin on August 29th, 1837, wherein Crooks approved of Aitkin's management of his territory. Crooks' statements in the letter stand in stark contrast to the later claim of mismanagement—especially given his frequent detailed instructions to Aitkin concerning the operation of the department.[61]

In actuality, an agreement was reached between Aitkin and Crooks whereby the former withdrew from the company and agreed not to interfere in the trade or in the operation of the fisheries. Aitkin was to receive his share of the profits from the 1838 season and his house at the confluence of the Mississippi and Sandy Lake rivers. Aitkin wanted his house and root cellar, but his wife claimed she was entitled to the house. Crooks' new manager at La Pointe, Doctor Borup, instructed Charles H. Oaks and Allan Morrison to take over operations at Sandy Lake but avoided any mention of Aitkin's post.[62]

Apparently, in the face of the dispute between Aitkin and his wife over the ownership of the buildings, the company decided to establish a new trading post on Sandy Lake proper. This new trading post represented the third location of the American Fur Company and was located on Brown's Point–the supposed location of the old North West Company post according to Professor Hart cited earlier.

An interesting account by Lucy Lewis, the wife of a headwaters missionary, provides a clue to where the post was situated since a light shown from a high hill near Northeast Bay on the lake could be seen from the post. The light was used at night, or a smoky fire was kindled during the day, to signal the post that a party had arrived over land from the Savanna Portage and required boats to reach the post. There is only a limited area on the western side of Sandy Lake where such a light could be seen. This narrows the search for the site of the third American Fur Company post to the western end of the lake near Brown's Point. The post was used from 1838 until trading operations ceased by the company in 1847. Several of the buildings in the complex were apparently used when the Sandy Lake Indian Sub-Agency was established c. 1850.[63]

With Aitkin out of the company and a new post established on Sandy Lake, Crooks felt confident that there would be no interference with the trade; nonetheless, he warned Borup to keep a lookout for Aitkin. By August of 1839, Aitkin was back at his old post. Correspondence and trade license records indicate that on September 30th, 1839, Indian Agent Daniel Bushnell issued Aitkin a license to trade at Sandy Lake. Upon hearing the news, Crooks was angry and suspected Aitkin would try to compete in the trade. Oaks, however, assured Crooks that Aitkin only had a small store of goods at his post and did not constitute a threat.[64]

Real opposition to American Fur came in 1840. Apparently Aitkin was not satisfied with his share of the 1838 returns. He resumed serious trading at Sandy

Lake in the fall of 1840. This time he had the financial backing of Crooks' former chief factor at La Pointe, Lyman Marquis Warren. In October of 1840, Borup frantically wrote Crooks that "Aitkin has a large assortment of goods at Sandy Lake." Aitkin not only occupied his old post at Sandy Lake, but also had men at Leech Lake, Swan River, and on the Chippewa River (Wisconsin). By November, Borup was certain that Aitkin would get a considerable return from the trade.[65]

Some idea of the scope of the threat posed by Aitkin's resumption of trade is contained in the correspondence between Crooks and George Simpson of the Hudson's Bay Company. There was talk that Aitkin would even try to station men near the Canadian border. Both companies discussed measures to overcome any serious competition in the region. Meanwhile, Aitkin's trade rivalry with American Fur intensified. Finally, Borup and Oaks met with Aitkin at La Pointe in January of 1841, to try to reach an agreement.

Borup, in a letter to Crooks, gave a glowing account of the settlement with Aitkin, but James McKay, a disgruntled company clerk at La Pointe, wrote to William Brewster, the company's factor at Detroit, complaining that Borup had paid Aitkin three thousand eight hundred dollars for his remaining merchandise. McKay believed this was too much and suggested Aitkin had inflated his accounts and soundly trumped Borup. The true value of the trade goods only amounted to eight hundred dollars. The terms of the new agreement stated Aitkin would be supplied by American Fur and have the exclusive trade in the Crow Wing River area. Part of Aitkin's new territory was below the 1837 treaty line in an area not subject to the same stringent trade rules that applied in "Indian Territory."[66]

Aitkin had no sooner been brought back into the fold than disaster struck. On May 24th, 1841, a Dakota war party attacked the Ojibway mission established by the Presbyterians at Lake Pokegama (Pine County, Minnesota). Ojibway hunters and their families scattered. Many fled north to Sandy Lake and Leech Lake. The Lake Pokegama disaster in 1841 was only the beginning of a series of events that finally overwhelmed the American Fur Company in 1842.

In July of 1841, Aitkin traveled to La Pointe to collect old debts at the annual annuity payment so he in turn could pay his friend Henry Sibley.[67] By August, Aitkin was back at Sandy Lake waiting for the arrival of his promised trade goods from American Fur. He was still waiting for his trade goods in October. We next hear of Aitkin in the spring of 1842, at his former trading post just below the confluence of the Mississippi and Crow Wing rivers.

Aitkin's involvement in the fur trade shifted away from the Northwest Trail toward the Mississippi River and its tributaries below the mouth of the Crow Wing River. His story, as far as it relates to the route from Lake Superior to the Mississippi River at Sandy Lake, for the most part ends after 1842. He did not completely neglect his old trading post at Sandy Lake. His sons or other employees continued to work at that location during the late 1840s, often in competition with American Fur or other traders.

By 1847, Aitkin undoubtedly saw the handwriting on the wall concerning the future of the fur trade. Traveling over the Northwest Trail for the last time to attend a treaty signing at Fond du Lac in 1847, he noticed the steady decline in the amount of traders' claims. There was also a growing competition in the field from new settlers on the fringe of the Indian Territory who increasingly supplemented their farmstead earnings with trapping on the side. In 1848, William Aitkin opened a commercial center, ferry, and a new townsite located near the confluence of the Mississippi and Swan rivers. Designed to serve not only travelers along the Red River Trail, but also nearby Fort Gaines (later Fort Ripley) and the newly established Winnebago Reservation at Long Prairie, Aitkin's new town was named appropriately "Aitkinsville." He operated it successfully until his death in 1851.[68]

As for American Fur, the company encountered continuing competition from small traders which it in turn attempted to either buy out or crush with ruthless price wars. With competition heating up on the Mississippi, Crooks continued to wage a price war with the Ewing brothers of Fort Wayne. Unfortunately, the European fur market collapsed while the company was overextended on several fronts. When the returns for the year proved poor, Crooks resorted to selling off part of the company's trading area to the Chouteau Fur Company of St. Louis, Missouri. That move, however, was not enough.

By September of 1842, the American Fur Company's hopes of remaining financially stable rested on recovering outstanding debts through traders' claims contained in a pending treaty with the Dakota. Unfortunately, the treaty was rejected by Congress. On September 10th, 1842, with three hundred thousand dollars in outstanding debts, the company was forced to suspend payments. It took the next five years for Ramsay Crooks to pay off creditors. The company finally sold all its assets and went out of business in 1847, thus ending a thirty year history of trade along the Northwest Trail.[69]

> Reverend William Boutwell's description of Aitkin's post at Sandy Lake, 1832:
> Mr. Aitkin has a large establishment here, a two-story dwelling house, from 40 to 48 feet by 30, I should judge: a store house still larger, besides a small house for his men. One or two other small out houses, besides stables for 30 head of cattle, 3 or 4 horses, and 15 swine.... Mr. A's post is located on a point of land where the Savannah unites with the Mississippi. It faces the former on the east, and the latter on the west, elevated 15 or 20 feet above either, and perhaps 3 to 5 rods from each.

Chapter 9 - William Alexander Aitkin
Notes

1.   Charles H. Oakes to J. Fletcher Williams, August 9th, 1872, J. Fletcher Williams Papers, Minnesota Historical Society. Oakes was writing in response to William's "Aitkin Memoranda" or questionnaire sent out by the society to gather biographical information on Aitkin. William Alexander Aitkin's baptism was recorded on May 14th, 1792, in the County of Aberdeen Parochial Register, St. Nicholas, Aberdeen, Births 1771-1798, p. 195.

2.   Information about William Aitkin's father, father-in-law, and wife during their residence at Fort Mackinac can be found in Dwight H. Kelton, *Annals of Fort Mackinac* (Chicago, 1882), p. 63.

3.   See Francis Parkman, *The Conspiracy of Pontiac* (10th ed., New York, 1966), pp. 132-133, n. 9; and David A. Armour and Keith R. Widder, *At The Crossroads: Michilimackinac During the American Revolution* (Mackinac Island, Michigan, 1978), p. 34, for conditions confronting soldiers and their wives at frontier posts.

4.   The spelling of the family name was the subject of a letter dated January 3rd, 1898, from Roger B. Aitkin of Beaulieu, Minnesota, to a Mr. Hungerford in Aitkin, Minnesota. The letter was later printed in the *Aitkin Independent Age*, June 28th, 1951, under the heading "Son Spelled it 'Aitkin.'" Aitkin's father spelled the family name "Aiken" and that spelling was used in Minnesota until the present spelling "Aitkin" was established by an act of the legislature in 1872. A short biographic sketch about William A. Aitkin, can be found in Warren Upham (et al.), *Minnesota in Three Centuries, 1655-1908*, 4 vols. (Mankato, 1908), vol. 1, p. 317. A similar sketch appears in Warren Upham, *Minnesota Geographic Names: Their Origin and Historic Significance* (1920; reprint ed., St. Paul, 1969), p. 14.

5.   *The Minnesota Democrat* (October, 1851), p. 2.

6.   Letter from Ernestine and Roderick J. Henry [direct descendants of William A. Aitkin] to author, October 30th, 2004. The correspondence contained photo copies of church records showing William A. Aitkin was indeed baptized in Scotland; see also United States Census, 1850, Sauk Rapids District, Benton County, Minnesota Territory. Microfilm copy 432.

7.   Details regarding the Dousman family can be found in "Writing and Research Notes, 1935-1942," Federal Writer's Project, Works Progress Administration, State Historical Society of Wisconsin; Virginia Dousman Bigelow, "Ancestry of Hercules L. [Louis] Dousman," unpublished manuscript in the collections of the Wisconsin State Historical Society, c. 1950); and Henry H. Sibley, "Memoir of Hercules L. Dousman," in *Minnesota Historical Collections*, vol. 3 (1880), pp. 192-200.

8.   Letter from Henry H. Sibley and Hercules L. Dousman to Senator William Woodbridge, March 12th, 1842. Henry Hastings Sibley Papers, Minnesota Historical Society.

9.   Aitkin's first wife is mentioned in Newton H. Winchell, *The Aborigines of Minnesota* (St. Paul, 1911), p. 708. Information about Aitkin's second wife can be found in Ransom J. Powell Papers, vol. 6, Minnesota Historical Society.

10.   Stella L. Obesaw, *Mackinac County Marriage Records, 1821-1868* (St. Ignace, Michigan, 1993), p. 3, n. 65.

11.   See chapter 8, n. 36 above.

12.   William A. Aitkin to Ramsay Crooks, September 25th, 1834. American Fur Company Papers, New York Historical Society (hereafter referred to as AFC Papers). Microfilm copies of the papers can be found in the collections of the Minnesota Historical Society.

13.   Letter from William A. Aitkin to Ramsay Crooks, January 26th, 1835. AFC Papers.

14.   William Whipple Warren, *History of the Ojibway People* (1885; reprint ed., St. Paul, 1984), p. 383.

15.   "Invoice of Goods and Merchandise Taken by John A. Drew in His Trade With the Indians at Grand River—December 12th, 1834," in *Historical Collections and Researches Made by the Michigan Pioneer and Historical Society*, vol. 37 (1909-1910), p. 309-310.

16. *House Document No. 41*, 21st Congress, 2nd Session. "Abstract of Licenses to Trade with the Indians for the Year Ending Sept. 30th, 1830," transmitted by Secretary of War, John H. Eaton, January 7th, 1831.

17. David Lavender, *The Fist in the Wilderness* (1964; reprint ed., Albuquerque, 1979), pp. 268-269. Aitkin, and most other experienced traders operating along the Northwest Trail, took the oath of allegiance to the United States by 1820, as noted in the *Collections of the State Historical Society of Wisconsin*, vol. 20 (1911), p. 177, n 37.

18. For a complete account of Beltrami's journey, see Giacomo Constantino Beltrami, *A Pilgrimage in Europe and America Leading to the Discovery of the Sources of the Mississippi and Bloody* [Red] *Rivers, with a Description of the Whole Course of the Former, and of the Ohio* (London, 1824), pp. 301-482. For a summary of Beltrami's travels see William Watts Folwell, *A History of Minnesota*, 4 vols. (1921; rev. ed., St. Paul, 1956), vol. 1, p. 111, nn. 50 and 51; and Warren Upham, *Minnesota Geographical Names: Their Origin and Historical Significance* (1921; reprint ed., St. Paul, 1969), pp. 34-35.

19. Philip P. Mason (ed.), *Schoolcraft's Expedition to Lake Itasca* (East Lansing, 1993), pp. 197-198.

20. *House Document No. 7*, 18th Congress, 1st Session. "An Abstract of all Licenses Granted by Superintendents of Indian Trade, &c. &c.," December 15th, 1823.

21. An act passed May 25th, 1824, allowed Indian agents to designate the locations of trading posts within their respective jurisdictions. See "Regulation Concerning Trading Stations [Location Law]," in *Collections of the State Historical Society of Wisconsin*, vol. 20 (1911), p. 339.

22. "Fort Benton" was the name for trading post "Number 17" on the list included in Lawrence Taliaferro's circular issued in April, 1826. See Letter Book, p. 36, Lawrence Taliaferro Papers, Minnesota Historical Society.

23. Mason (ed.), *Lake Itasca*, pp. 323-324.

24. Edmund Franklin Ely's Diaries record daily events at Sandy Lake from his arrival on September 19th, 1833, until his departure, March 4th, 1834. The original documents are in the Northeast Minnesota Historical Center, Duluth, Minnesota (hereafter referred to as NEMHC). Typescript copies of the diaries are in the collections of the Minnesota Historical Society.

25   Ellworth T. Carlstedt, "A History of the Fond du Lac Trading Posts With Some Mention of the Fond du Lac Department," unpublished manuscript, University of Minnesota, December 9th, 1933, p. 42.

26. Robert Clouston, "Sketches of a Journey Between RRS [Red River Settlement] and St. Peter's in the United States, 1846," unpublished manuscript, dated 1846, in the collections of the Minnesota Historical Society.

27. *House Document No. 140*, 20th Congress, 1st Session. "Licenses granted to trade with the Indians, &c.," February 12th, 1828.

28. Warren, *History of the Ojibway*, pp. 382-383.

29. Contract between William A. Aitkin and Robert Stuart of the American Fur Company, dated July 22nd, 1830. Henry Hastings Sibley Papers, Minnesota Historical Society.

30. John S. Galbraith, "British-American Competition in the Border Fur Trade," *Minnesota History*, vol. 36, n. 3 (September 1959), pp. 241-249.

31. See letter from Schoolcraft to Aitkin dated August 2nd, 1824, authorizing the importation of ten kegs of ardent spirits. Henry Hastings Sibley Papers, Minnesota Historical Society. The "ten kegs letter" strictly limited the use of liquor to the American Fur Company border posts.

32. Lavender, *Fist in the Wilderness*, p. 417.

33. Ibid., p. 418.

34. Letter from Aitkin to Crooks, October 11th, 1836, in AFC Papers.

35. William Johnston, "Letters on the Fur Trade," in *Historical Collections and Researches made by the Michigan Pioneer and Historical Society*, vol. 37 (Lansing, 1909-1910), pp. 157 and 204. Johnston's letter is dated Fond du Lac, August 27th, 1833. Johnston apparently harbored the same negative thoughts about Reverend Boutwell as he expressed earlier about Ely.

36. See undated affidavit signed by Aitkin before a justice of the peace, c. 1826-1827, in Henry Hastings Sibley Papers, Minnesota Historical Society.

37. Indian agent Lawrence Taliaferro also complained about Johnston's drunkenness. See Lavender, *Fist in the Wilderness*, p. 376.

38. Letter from Major Lawrence Taliaferro to Wisconsin Territorial Governor, Henry Dodge, July 24th, 1837, in John Porter Boom (ed.), *The Territorial Papers of the United States*, vols. 27-28 (Washington, D.C., 1969), vol. 27, p. 830. Taliaferro denounced Aitkin as: "a Scotch man, and only one out of the Many Foreign Agents attached to the Am. Fur Company."

39. Edmund Franklin Ely, Journal No. 5, Friday, September 26th, 1834. Edmund F. Ely Papers, NEMHC.

40. Powell, Papers, vol. 6.

41. See Appendix.

42. Edmund F. Ely Journal No. 9, Monday, September 15, 1834. Edmund F. Ely Papers, NEMHC. Ely accompanied Boutwell and his new bride as far as the foot of the Grand Portage of the St. Louis and bid them farewell.

43. Grace Lee Nute, "The American Fur Company's Fishing Enterprises on Lake Superior," in *Mississippi Valley Historical Review*, vol. 12 (March, 1926), p. 496.

44. For details on Letters from Aitkin to Crooks, January 4th, 1837; and Boutwell to Crooks, January 19th, 1837, see AFC Papers; Boutwell's Diary, December 8th, 1836, in the collections of the Minnesota Historical Society. For a printed version of Boutwell's Diary, see Edward D. Neill, "Memoir of William T. Boutwell, The First Christian Minister Resident Among the Indians of Minnesota," in *Macalester College Contributions*, 2nd series no. 1 (St. Paul, 1892), pp. 35-37; Henry R. Schoolcraft, *Personal Memoirs of a Residence of Thirty Years with the Indian Tribes on the American Frontier* (Philadelphia, 1851), pp. 553-555. Schoolcraft quotes from a letter he received from William A. Aitkin concerning Alfred's murder at Cass Lake; Another contemporary comment on Alfred's death came from Martin McLeod, who visited with Alfred Aitkin on November 27th, 1836. "The Diary of Martin McLeod," ed. by Grace Lee Nute, *Minnesota History Bulletin*, vol. 4, nos. 7 and 8 (August-November, 1922), p. 387 and n. 51. McLeod noted: "In the evening dined a la Turque on excellent venison furnished by Mr. Aitken Jr." McLeod's journal entry is followed by a notation, "25th, Jany 37. Just heard that Mr. Aitken has been shot dead by an Indian; John H. Fonda, "Early Reminiscences of Wisconsin," in *Collections of the State Historical Society of Wisconsin*, vol. 5 (Madison, 1868), p. 27, offers a brief account of the murder and trial of Alfred's assassin; and see Return Ira Holcomb (et al.), *Minnesota in Three Centuries*, 4 vols. (Mankato, 1908), vol. 2, chap. 10, pp. 125-130, for an account of the murder and subsequent trial. Recent general histories of Minnesota do not discuss the Alfred Aitkin murder case in spite of its serious ramifications.

45. Schoolcraft, *Thirty Years*, p. 554.

46. Edmund F. Ely, Journal No. 9, Saturday, January 7th, 1837, NEMHC.

47. Letter from Boutwell to Crooks, January 19th, 1837. AFC Papers; Schoolcraft, *Thirty Years*, p. 554.

48. Holcomb (et al.), *Minnesota in Three Centuries*, vol. 2, p. 127, contains a description by eyewitness William L. Quinn of the murderer lashed to a sled and quotes from a letter by Aitkin to Henry Sibley written in January of 1837.

49. Indian Agent Taliaferro's letter to Governor Henry Dodge, March 19th, 1837, National Archives, U.S. Office of Indian Affairs, Wisconsin Superintendency Records, 1836-1848. Letters Received.

50. Holcomb (et al.), *Minnesota in Three Centuries*, vol. 2, p. 129.

51. Letter from Governor Dodge to Commissioner Crawford, Superintendent of Indian Affairs, February 8th, 1839, in John Porter Bloom (ed.), *Territorial Papers*, vol. 27, p. 1186; see also, Letter from Lucius Lyon to Commissioner Crawford, July 16th, 1839, and Chippewa Half-breeds to Daniel P. Bushnell, July 24th, 1839, in Bloom (ed.), *Territorial Papers*, vol. 28, pp. 12-13, and 16-18.

52. Letter from George Bonga to William T. Boutwell, June 7th, 1838. Henry Hastings Sibley Papers, Minnesota Historical Society.

53. Letter from Thomas Pendleton Burnett to William A. Aitkin, May 28th, 1838. Henry Hastings Sibley Papers, Minnesota Historical Society.

54.   Delia Cook's remarks concerning the funeral of Alfred Aitkin on February 25th, 1837, are found in John Nelson Davidson, *In Unnamed Wisconsin: Studies in the History of the Region Between Lake Michigan and the Mississippi* (Milwaukee, 1895), p. 160, n. 1.

55.   See Spates' entry for Tuesday, October 5th, 1841, p. 10, in the Diary of Samuel Spates, Minnesota Historical Society.

56.   Florantha Thompson Sproat, "La Pointe Letters," *Wisconsin Magazine of History*, vol. 16, no. 2 (December, 1932), p. 206.

57.   See Mary Clara Post, "From Lake Superior," unpublished typescript, 1854, in the collections of the Northeast Minnesota Historical Center.

58.   For the text of the Chippewa Treaty signed in 1837, see Charles J. Kappler (ed.), *Indian Treaties: 1778-1883* (1911; reprint ed., New York, 1973), p. 492, Article 4.

59.   Letter from Lyman M. Warren to William Aitkin, September 8th, 1838. Henry Hastings Sibley Papers, Minnesota Historical Society.

60.   William A. Aitkin to Ramsay Crooks, October 1st, 1838. AFC Papers.

61.   Ramsey Crooks to William A. Aitkin, August 29th, 1837. Henry Hastings Sibley Papers, Minnesota Historical Society

62.   Charles Borup to William Davenport, January 22nd, 1839. AFC Papers.

63.   Lucy Lewis to James R. Wright, May 29th, 1844. William Lewis Papers, Minnesota Historical Society.

64.   Charles H. Oakes to Ramsay Crooks, January 2nd, 1840. AFC Papers.

65.   Charles Borup to Ramsay Crooks, November, 16th, 1840. AFC Papers.

66.   See letters from James McKay to William Brewster, July 4th and 17th, 1841. AFC Papers.

67   William A. Aitkin to Henry Sibley, July 6th, 1841. Henry Hastings Sibley Papers, Minnesota Historical Society.

68.   Kappler (ed.), *Indian Treaties*, pp. 545 and 567-569. Aitkin received nine hundred thirty-five dollars and sixty-seven cents in traders claims under provision of the Treaty with the Chippewa, 1842. The Treaty with the Chippewa of the Mississippi and Lake Superior concluded in 1847, did not contain a provision for the payment of any trader's claims.

69.   Lavender, *Fist in the Wilderness*, pp. 418-419; Rhoda R. Gilman "Last Days of the Upper Mississippi Fur Trade," *Minnesota History*, vol. 42, no. 4 (Winter, 1970), pp. 122-140.

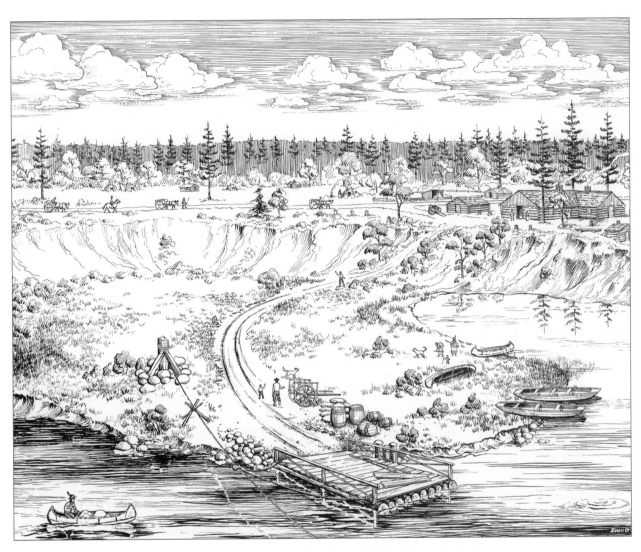

An artist's impression of "Aitkinsville" by Evan A. Hart.
Author's collection

His establishment, at present, consists of a large comfortable dwelling, several storehouses, and barns, stables, &c.; he raises corn and potatoes in fields near the house, and has a good stock of cattle. The soil about the lake and rivers is rich, but, with the exception of a small portion about the house, is subject to inundation during the early spring freshets, when Sandy Lake overflows with the Mississippi, and the great flood covers the country for many miles around.

Lt. James Allen's description of Aitkin's post at Sandy Lake, July 3, 1832.

Summer on the St. Louis River. During the 1840s and 1850s, the river was
the scene of excursions by tourists intent on seeing the wilderness.
Photo by Allen Anway

Part IV ⚙ The Changing Frontier

Chapter 10 ✂ Chronicles of a Changing Country

The year 1850 was a watershed in the story of the Northwest Trail. For two centuries prior to that date, the major commercial enterprise associated with the trail was the fur trade. After 1850, the emphasis changed to the timber and mining industries. With the growth of these new enterprises, the historic old Northwest Trail inspired what might be called a "new" Northwest Trail comprised of railroads and highways that in many cases paralleled the earlier water and land route.

Changes came slowly–almost imperceptibly–on the frontier, but they inevitably came. The changes involved a new economy, new forms of transportation, and the new policies of the government. All of these changes whether political, economic, or social were noted in some fashion in the writings of those who traveled along the ancient route. Many of these travelers were ordinary people or tourists who wished to satisfy their curiosity about the West. Others were officials or missionaries who ventured into the wilderness to work with the local people. All contributed significantly to the story of the trail.

Travelers' Tales

One might say there is nothing novel about the literature which described the Northwest Trail, yet explorers such as Pike, McKenney, Schoolcraft, Beltrami, and Nicollet wrote popular books based on their individual experiences with the historic route. One motivation for writing, aside from the obvious need to earn a modest profit, was a desire on the part of these explorer-authors to acquaint a prospective audience with their experiences, the nature of the country they passed through, and the people they met.

Many of the early explorer-authors had one thing in common: they were part of an expedition whose main purpose was scientific in nature and not exclusively intended for the gathering of material for a book. Most early expeditions discharged a specific function, such as tracing a river to its source or mapping the countryside. The ranks of these early writers were subsequently joined by individuals who made excursions through the country and wrote about their adventures. Their experiences can be found in diaries, magazine articles, and guide books.

One example of a traveler who left an informative record of his experiences was a Canadian named Martin McLeod. McLeod confided his colorful experiences in a diary as he traveled along the Northwest Trail. He was part of "The

Army of the Liberator of the Indian Nations," or who, for want of a better description, can be called "Filibusters" after the nineteenth century mercenaries who sought to expropriate portions of Mexico or territory belonging to Central American republics through military means.[1]

In addition to McLeod, who held a commission as "Major," the group consisted of the leader "General" James Dickson, a Polish officer Captain Ignatius Parys, five lieutenants, and seven soldiers all bound for the Red River of the North where they hoped to recruit an army of *metis* (mixed-bloods) and descend on northern Mexican settlements. Although Dickson and Parys had served in the Texas Army, their enterprise was doomed from the start. The expedition left Buffalo, New York, on October 1st, 1836, with sixty enthusiastic members but rapidly dwindled to less than twenty by the time it departed Sault Sainte Marie.[2]

As the "army" traveled along the Northwest Trail and ascended the Mississippi, it encountered more and more ice in the rivers and lakes and finally had to abandon its canoes at Ball Club Lake and travel on foot over the frozen waterways. The expedition ultimately disintegrated in the face of howling blizzards on the open plains near the Red River. McLeod's friend, Captain Parys, died from the effects of frostbite; and another expedition member, a Mr. Hayes, simply vanished in a blinding snowstorm and was never seen again. In the end, McLeod's descriptions of the conditions and the country he traveled through, account for far more than any dreams of glory in some far-off backwater province of Mexico. A few excerpts from McLeod's journal capture his impressions of the Northwest Trail:

> November 5th, 1836. Got to the Savannah Portage which we found so damnable that we had to wade in water up to our hips for nearly 3 miles and had to carry our trunks etc. to boot. 8th November. Started in west Savannah river. Came to a small lake [Little Savanna Lake] which we found frozen and had to break our way through. Made 2 portages 60 and 450 yards and encamped. Wednesday, 9th November, 1836. General Dickson and Capt. Parys left encampment to proceed to Sandy Lake on foot. About 11 o'clock started in Canoes and found great difficulty in getting through water so shallow.[3]

It is relatively easy to picture the difficulties involved in crossing the Savanna Portage from the entries in the journal. Evidently McLeod's day ended better than it began because he mentions:

> 2 P.M. entered Sandy Lake which is surrounded with lovely scenery, and is itself one of the most delightful lakes I have ever seen. On our arrival at the Am F. Co, trading house situated on the Mississippi near the upper end of the lake found our friends had arrived before us both those in the second Canoe and the Pedestrians. Met a highland welcome from Mr. [Allan] Morrison the person in charge of the Sandy Lake establishment.[4]

McLeod was not the only traveler to experience extreme difficulties negotiating the trails and waterways of Minnesota. In some cases couples braved the wilderness together to start a new life at a remote outpost. A good example of this sense of commitment can be seen in the reminiscences of Mr. and Mrs. George E. Nettleton from Ashtabula, Ohio, who traveled over the Northwest Trail and later recorded their adventures.

The Nettletons arrived in the Northwest in 1852 and joined George's brother William, who was a government farmer assigned to assist the Ojibway living at Gull Lake. George Nettleton was employed as a clerk in Clement Beaulieu's store in the village of Crow Wing. Mrs. Nettleton later recounted her experiences for an early twentieth century history of the region. On one occasion, during the fall of 1852, she and others in her party en route to Fond du Lac were forced to flee the onrushing flames of a forest fire as they crossed the Savanna Portage. The surrounding countryside had suffered from prolonged drought, and the tinder dry vegetation provided ample fuel for a serious conflagration.

In another incident, Mrs. Nettleton related how her husband was seriously injured when a disgruntled Indian threw a knife at him and hit him in the face. Mr. Nettleton was forced to travel all the way from Crow Wing to Fond du Lac to have his wound sutured. Nettleton reached the village of Fond du Lac where Susan Carlton, the wife of government blacksmith Reuben B. Carlton, started to perform the stitching required for Nettleton's facial wound. Unfortunately, the process so unnerved her that Mr. Carlton had to finish the job. Such were the trials and tribulations of people living in the sparsely settled country west of Lake Superior. The Nettletons persevered and later were associated with the pioneer settlement that became the modern city of Duluth, Minnesota.[5]

George Nettleton and his wife were typical of the pioneers who traveled the Northwest Trail in the 1850s.
Flower, *The Eye of the North-west*

Other individual experiences provide further colorful vignettes of life on the frontier in the 1850s. One notable story concerned a lone newspaper reporter's trip along the Northwest Trail and was later featured in an article in the *Superior Chronicle* for Tuesday, December 11th, 1855. The reporter, known only as "G," represented the *Missouri Republican* and was traveling to St. Paul by canoe after having toured the Great Lakes and the pioneer settlement at Superior, Wisconsin.[6]

His feature article began in considerable detail at Mackinac Island and continued until he arrived at the infant settlement of St. Anthony (Minneapolis). Along the way he remarked about the Grand Portage of the St. Louis or of cruising along the sinuous rivers which marked his passage from east to west. Part of his narrative, however, described both the villages found at Fond du Lac and at Sandy Lake. In the case of Fond du Lac, which he called "Nagogiwanang" (*Nagadgiwan*), he characterized it as follows:

It is beautifully situated on an elevated plateau, almost entirely sur-rounded by hills, which shut it in from the cold winds of winter. A per-pendicular rock on the edge of the plateau commands a fine view of the surrounding country. Beneath you lay the village with its dome-shaped wigwams, from whose tops the blue smoke curled most gracefully, whilst the glassy stream wound through its center and lost itself among the hills beyond. In the north, the pine-covered heights of the Grand Portage loomed up in the distance, and all around, the country spread out in hills covered with groves, and valleys verdant with the tall grass of the prairie.[7]

Of Sandy Lake village, he had this to say:

There is a small village on the west shore of the lake, which flourished under the euphonious title of "Gomaitonghigogima" [*Ga-mitawangaga-mag* or Sandy Lake], and which, with the neighboring wigwams, num-ber about two hundred and fifty Chippewas. The men were mostly absent at Crow Wing, receiving their annuities; and the women were among the small streams around about gathering wild rice.[8]

These short, vivid versions are typical of the brief recollections of early travelers along the Northwest Trail.

Some personal accounts, such as those mentioned here, became part of the priceless collection of pioneering experiences. Along with these first person accounts were the products of professional writers who visited the area and con-tributed their more lengthy observations of the country and people through pub-lished works. Spurred on by curiosity, possibly kindled from reading the works of explorer-authors, such as Henry Schoolcraft, they sought to experience firsthand the wilderness scenes so aptly described in the travel literature of the time. Perhaps unknowingly, these authors turned adventurers, were also agents of change, because of what they in turn wrote about, and the exciting images they projected of the country they passed through.

In reviewing the sources of information about the period, travel literature dealing with the wilderness represents the largest single source of contemporary materials about the Northwest Trail. Some accounts such as Martin McLeod's, which contribute significant information, also allow the reader to capture the essence of the country while other books add little new information. In fact, not everyone who wrote about the West or the Northwest Trail actually visited it, and some who did write about the region tended to color their stories to enhance their own deeds.

A number of versions fall into the category of travel literature. Among these are works which mentioned certain features of the Northwest Trail by authors such as Joseph Le Conte, Charles Lanman, Increase A. Lapham, E. Sandford Seymour, Laurence Oliphant, Christopher Columbus Andrews, and a Prussian officer, Count Ferdinand von Zeppelin.[9]

Charles Lanman, a landscape painter and friend of Henry Schoolcraft, wrote about his trip in the summer of 1846. His book, *A Summer in the Wilderness: Embracing a Canoe Voyage up the Mississippi and Around Lake Superior*, was published in 1847. Only two episodes from his book link Lanman in any way with the story of the Northwest Trail. The first incident occurred when Lanman became lost along the overland trail from Sandy Lake to the Savanna Portage and had to spend the night in a tree. The second incident concerned a side trip he took while crossing the Grand Portage of the St. Louis. His objective was to see the highest falls on the St. Louis River, which he claimed to have "discovered."[10]

Engraving of Charles Lanham, landscape painter, author, and friend of Henry Schoolcraft who claimed to have "discovered" the Dalles of the St. Louis in 1846. *J.V. Brower, The Mississippi River and Its Source*

William Warren in his *History of the Ojibway* castigated authors of travel books in general who claimed the discoveries of others as their own. He singled out artist and author George Catlin as well as Charles Lanman in particular:

> It is thus that a man who travels for the purpose of writing a book to sell, and who, being a man of letters, is able to trumpet forth his own fame, often plucks the laurels due to more modest and unlettered adventurers.[11]

Regarding the "discovery" of the falls of the St. Louis River, Warren pointed out that veteran traders such as Aitkin, Morrison, and Sayer were familiar with the features of the river long before Charles Lanman happened to pass by.

Increase A. Lapham and E. Sandford Seymour included some useful details in their books about the country west of Lake Superior; and Christopher Columbus Andrews may have been trying to live up to his famous namesake when he published a guide book in 1856 entitled *Minnesota and Dacotah*. Andrews listed the contemporary books that inspired him, but from the narrative one gets the impression he did not venture too far afield.[12]

In 1863, the Prussian Count, Ferdinand von Zeppelin; two Russian companions; and a crew of voyageurs completed a trip along the Northwest Trail. Zeppelin briefly described his impressions of it:

> There is the strange way of traveling by canoe, and when the highest ridge of land is reached, of carrying it across over your head. There is the rocky island [Fortress Island] in the midst of a rushing stream, as described by [James Fenimore] Cooper in his novels, and the stillness of a lake [Sandy Lake] on whose shore the Indian erects his fleeting wigwam.[13]

It may have been an interesting summer excursion, but Zeppelin left little besides a short narrative and a sketch map to tell of his experiences on the Northwest Trail. His real fame was not as a travel author but as a future aeronautical pioneer and designer of rigid airships.

In contrast to the brief mention afforded the Northwest Trail in the previous books and articles, two works stand out in the travel literature of the period which include significant observations of the Northwest Trail. The first is the story of a wilderness vacation by a young medical student, Joseph Le Conte, the second account was written by Laurence Oliphant, a career government official from Canada. These works were published by travelers who really used the Northwest Trail and later wrote accounts of their respective experiences. The first of these adventures by Joseph Le Conte, was not actually published until many years after the event. Nonetheless, that part of his work concerning the route provides the reader with a fresh perspective.

Summer Excursions in the Wilderness

Joseph Le Conte was a twenty-one year old college student from Georgia. He had graduated from the University of Georgia in 1841 and was attending medical school in New York, when apparently the thought occurred to him to take some time off from his studies and tour the rapidly changing American West. In the summer of 1844, Joseph and his cousin John L. Le Conte decided to take a trip to Minnesota by way of the Great Lakes.[14]

The Le Contes' journey employed nearly all forms of watercraft and began at Buffalo, New York, a favorite jumping-off place for travelers bound for the Northwest by way of the Great Lakes. The Le Contes traveled through the Great Lakes by steamboat to Mackinac Island and from there to Sault Sainte Marie. They changed vessels at the upper end of Saint Mary's Rapids and continued by schooner to La Pointe on Madeline Island.

Once at La Pointe, Joseph and his cousin hired a twenty-four foot "North Canoe" and voyageurs to man it. Joseph's first lesson in canoe travel came at the hands of his guide, a Mister "Robindeau." The guide abruptly informed the young men that moccasins were the only suitable footwear for a fragile birch-bark canoe, not heavy leather boots.

When all was ready, the party left La Pointe and followed the south shore of Lake Superior past sandy beaches and imposing sandstone cliffs. The voyageurs threaded their way through the Apostle Islands, and coasted as far as the Bois Brûlé (Burnt Wood) River. At that point, the Le Contes decided to cross to the lake's north side which they could faintly see in the distance.

Although the lake was calm, the voyageurs were apprehensive, because Superior changes its temperament quickly. A sudden squall could capsize the canoe, and the occupants would quickly succumb to hypothermia in the icy water. In spite of their misgivings, the voyageurs "struck out vigorously" and crossed the lake in four hours.

After following the irregular northern shoreline, the Le Contes and their men soon reached the site of the present city of Duluth and the imposing sandbar formed by the St. Louis River, known as Minnesota Point. A short "carry" (portage) over what the Ojibway referred to as the *Onigamins*, or "Little Portage," near the present location of the Duluth ship canal, brought them from the intensely cold waters of Lake Superior to the warm water of Superior Bay. Here, Joseph Le Conte, who was an excellent swimmer, could not resist the temptation to swim in the comfortable waters of the bay.

As Joseph proceeded up the St. Louis River, he remarked about the beauty of the area, "I can never forget the glory of that afternoon voyage up the river. The afternoon was warm, the air still and languorous, the river wide, smooth as a mirror, and very tortuous."[15]

The party stopped briefly at the Fond du Lac post of the American Fur Company where Joseph and his cousin met the clerk Clement Beaulieu. The next morning, the travelers moved upstream and began the laborious crossing of the Grand Portage of the St. Louis. Joseph was amazed at the loads borne by the voyageurs:

> ...I know of no beast of burden of equal size that could compare at all with these men in amount of work accomplished. They would take two hundred pounds on their backs and trot off with apparent ease, and during twelve hours, one-half the time they were thus loaded.[16]

Joseph and his cousin found the trail rough-going in spite of not having to carry heavy burdens. They stayed at the foot of the portage while the voyageurs carried the baggage and canoes across the height of land, "About three P.M. we started and walked to camp in good time, although the walking over stony ground in moccasins was at first trying to our feet."[17]

The greatest challenge to the men, both on the portage and along the river, was the seemingly endless horde of insects that swarmed around them. Travelers normally wore gloves and veils of mosquito netting. According to Joseph, the insects reached their "acme" by the time the party arrived at the East Savanna River. Earth was placed in the bottom of the canoe and a smokey fire kindled to ward off the bloodthirsty pests, but such measures proved only mildly effective, "The paddlers in front, and therefore unprotected by the smoke, were so covered with mosquitos that you could not tell the color of their hats or clothing. It was all a uniform gray."[18]

In spite of adversity compounded by insects, the voyageurs maintained a steady pace over the portages and up the rapids, singing boat songs as they went. Joseph enjoyed "their rude but rhythmic and inspiring music." Voyageur cuisine, however, was not to his liking. The standard meal consisted of "Chunks of mess pork and balls of the kneaded dough called boudin [bannock?] boiled together in the same kettle. No stomach but that of a voyageur could digest it."[19]

Finally Joseph's party reached Sandy Lake. There he found only two Americans. The two men, an Indian agent, and a Methodist missionary were "...the first except Boilieau [Beaulieu], we have seen since leaving La Pointe ten days ago." Joseph, his cousin, and the voyageurs stayed at Sandy Lake several days to rest and enjoy a change of diet. During that time, he frequently amused himself by taking daily swims in, as he termed it, "the deliciously pleasant water of the lake."

After a short respite, the travelers left Sandy Lake and turned south on the rapid current of the Mississippi River for the long trip home. After leaving Sandy Lake, they did not see another American until they arrived at Fort Snelling. The scenery along the route between Sandy Lake and the Falls of St. Anthony was characterized by Joseph Le Conte as consisting of "...only the dull monotony of boundless plains thickly sprinkled with little lakes."

Although the details of Joseph Le Conte's trip are as vivid today as when he made his summer excursion along the Northwest Trail, the account itself was not written until forty years later as part of a presentation he gave to the Geological Society of America. Further details of the trip were subsequently published in an autobiography printed in 1903. It was not until 1951 that Joseph's story was introduced to a wider audience through an article that appeared in *Minnesota History*. The passage of time has certainly not dimmed this colorful tale.[20]

Ten years after Joseph Le Conte's trip, English traveler Laurence Oliphant embarked on a tour of the same country by the same route. Following the completion of his tour, he wrote a very detailed version of his travels; and, judging from his descriptions, one can easily appreciate what it was like to visit the region west of Lake Superior when only the most primitive of accommodations or of conveyance was available.

Laurence Oliphant was an admirable candidate for a trip through the wilds of North America. His extensive travel experience abroad and his position as Civil Secretary and Superintendent-general of Indian Affairs in Canada undoubtedly provided him with a very realistic impression of what to expect when traveling in a rustic setting. Oliphant was certainly no stranger to travel literature when he began his trip in the summer of 1854. From his narrative, it is apparent he was well-read and had already published a travel book entitled *The Russian Shores of the Black Sea.*

He later published an account of his tour through Lake Superior and over the Northwest Trail in a series of six articles called "Notes on Canada and the North-West States of America" in *Blackwood's Magazine* from April to September of 1855. The serial articles were followed by a book, *Minnesota and the Far West,* also published in 1855.[21]

Oliphant's writing style is typical of the period with lengthy sentence structure, which differs from Joseph Le Conte's more spontaneous prose; but his descriptions are nonetheless quite evocative and his work is both informative and entertaining.

Oliphant's tour of the West began in Canada and followed the Great Lakes to their farthest end at the fledgling community of Superior, Wisconsin. He arrived there on the steamer *Manhattan* and set about preparing for his trip inland. Oliphant was accompanied over the Northwest Trail by three companions, but he barely mentions them in his narrative. Apparently they were all seeking the same experience. While in Superior, Oliphant succeeded in retaining the services of two experienced voyagers, Baptiste Cadot and Jean Le Fêve, and a canoe. From his account of the country, it is evident his voyageur guides were well-acquainted with the route west and freely shared their knowledge with him.

During the process of procuring supplies and preparing the canoe for the voyage ahead, Oliphant attracted the attention of various local "experts" who offered advice about a host of subjects in exchange for a customary libation, "Conflicting advice was tendered in every direction by people who knew nothing whatever of the matter, but who all expected a drink for their trouble...[22]

Some of Oliphant's most intriguing revelations occurred in frontier Superior and involved topics such as the unsolicited advice he received, the "hotel" where he lodged, and the efforts of a typical frontier real-estate promoter to sell him some lots consisting of completely impenetrable wild land in a future development. How long in the future was not specified by the agent.

Ignoring the barrage of wisdom showered on him, Oliphant finally succeeded in completing the necessary arrangements for the voyage. In summing up his experiences in Superior, Oliphant observed that the conversation of the backwoodsmen was punctuated with "a singular variety and quantity of oaths" and all but incomprehensible. He concluded that, "... familiar intercourse with the denizens of the West is neither profitable nor attractive."[23]

Oliphant left the rough frontier settlement and its equally crude inhabitants behind and set off upstream toward the village of Fond du Lac and the Grand Portage of the St. Louis River. The voyage up the broad river was slow work beneath a broiling August sun. It took seven hours to canoe a distance of twenty-one miles from the mouth of the river to the village. After a brief stop at Fond du Lac, the weary travelers pushed on.

Taking a shortcut to the foot of the portage, Oliphant was impressed by the beauty of the countryside. As he rested along the trail high above the river, he could look back at a pristine setting with the village of Fond du Lac nestled in the center of the valley below:

> The view from our resting-place was striking. Below us the river wound between islands, and on the opposite shore the Indian village dotted the cleared country; behind it a high range clothed with forest rose abruptly....[24]

After much toil, Oliphant's party finally reached the head of the Grand Portage. There they found the river swollen from a recent rainstorm. With great difficulty the voyageurs and their passengers managed to reach Fortress Island and Knife Portage:

> At last, after having forced our canoe, by dint of immense yelling and punting, up rapids that would have given a salmon pleasant exercise, we reached a rocky island [Fortress Island] about eighty feet high, dividing the stream into torrents that were quite impracticable. We therefore

were compelled to make a portage of three miles, called the 'Knife portage,' because the surface of the ground is covered with masses of slate, which cut through moccasins.[25]

As he traveled upstream, Oliphant noticed little evidence of human habitation and a lack of game with which to augment his provisions:

> The principal drawback to traveling in this part of America is the almost utter absence of all game; so that not only is sport out of the question, but there is an actual difficulty in procuring means of subsistence....[26]

In spite of difficulties encountered on the trip, Oliphant remained confident in the ability of his voyageurs. Whether it involved navigating a treacherous rapid, carrying enormous loads, cooking meals "with inadequate materials," or making a cozy camp, the voyageurs it seemed were never lacking resources.

Leaving the St. Louis River behind them, the travelers turned southwest and proceeded up the East Savanna River. Here the nature of the waterway changed from a rapid rock-strewn river to a winding stream flowing slowly between low banks. Overhead, a dense canopy of vegetation almost completely shut out the sunlight:

> It was just such a jungle as would have been considered good tiger-cover in India; and yet here not even the chirp of a bird broke the perfect stillness, which is one of the most striking peculiarities of American forests.[27]

Oliphant finally reached the source of the East Savanna River in a great swamp. It was with some difficulty that the voyageurs forced a passage because the main channel was choked with a lush growth of wild rice. His guides had never seen the rice so abundant.

At the east end of the Savanna Portage the men labored through deep mud. After passing the first *posés*, they camped for the night on a small knoll scarcely above the level of the swamp. Unknowingly, the weary travelers had chosen a campsite covered with a luxuriant growth of poison ivy. When they awoke they were covered with the unmistakable rash. Oliphant noted his companion, a Mr. Bury, was particularly afflicted:

> His face and head were so much swollen that his eyes were scarcely visible, and his hands and arms were double their natural size...although neither Petre nor myself were so much disfigured, our fingers looked much like Bologna sausages.[28]

The next day the men began the final crossing of the Savanna Portage. Oliphant mentioned the existence of two portage paths: one path was used by the voyageurs with the canoe and a second path for the passengers who carried their own luggage. The second path led to Little Savanna Lake, where from a promontory Oliphant's party saw their canoes being towed through a lush growth of aquatic plants down the shallow Little or West Savanna River:

> At our feet lay the Savanna Lake... We could just discern in the distance our Indians towing the canoe.... Meanwhile we dived into the woods again, sometimes to come out upon grass country, sometimes to wander through a forest of red pine, where no underwood impedes one's progress, or spoils the effect of those straight lofty columns which shoot upwards to a height of forty or fifty feet, and then, spreading out their evergreen capitals, completely roof in one of nature's grandest temples.[29]

Nature's "spotlight" is focused on the old Savanna Portage near Little Savanna Lake. Here the trail passes tall virgin pine and little brush grows on the forest floor. Photo by Larry Luukkonen

Oliphant's account of the crossing of the Savanna Portage provides some new insights on the exact nature of the route and the problems encountered by travelers during the crossing.

Laurence Oliphant finally reached Sandy Lake after walking most of the way on the banks of the West Savanna River. He and his traveling companions arrived at the lake late in the day. While crossing the lake, they were fortunate to encounter a fisherman from whom they purchased a quantity of fresh fish to augment some "wood pigeons" shot earlier on the portage.

The party camped at the Methodist mission where Oliphant obtained valuable information from Reverend Samuel Spates about conditions on the Mississippi River and his route home. He remarked that later during the night they were annoyed by thunder showers and mosquitos, such that "we courted sleep under considerable difficulties."

The next morning, after receiving some letters from the missionary to be mailed in St. Paul, Oliphant's party departed Sandy Lake. As the travelers left the

Sandy Lake River and turned south on the Mississippi, one of the voyageurs remarked about the deserted trading post at the junction of the rivers. The post, originally built by William Aitkin, was a reminder to all of the former importance of the fur trade, and as Oliphant noted, of "the change which the country was gradually undergoing..."

Thus ended the second account of a summer excursion on the Northwest Trail. The stories of Joseph Le Conte and Laurence Oliphant are significant, not only for the information they contain about the route between the waters, but also for the various experiences of each man. These stories contain wonderful descriptions of the country for those interested in tracing the Northwest Trail.

Ten years separated the journey of Joseph Le Conte from that of Laurence Oliphant, yet within that short span of time many changes occurred. For example, the sparse population Le Conte noted on his journey along the south shore of Lake Superior and on the trek over the Northwest Trail contrasted markedly with the scenes of bustling activity in the fledgling frontier town of Superior, Wisconsin as described by Oliphant.

One must also consider that Oliphant's account was written after Minnesota had become a territory and his trip took place on the eve of the signing of an important Indian land cession. It was no accident that persons flocked to the rough frontier town of Superior, Wisconsin. The focus of many of the newcomers lay beyond the crude haphazard collection of buildings facing the St. Louis River and far to the west in the heart of what was then commonly referred to as "Indian Country." Oliphant saw the raw wilderness west of Lake Superior on the eve of a major change before townsite promoters and real-estate agents lured prospective settlers into what up until that time had been virtual wilderness.

By 1854, people no longer confined their reasons for traveling over the Northwest Trail to the fur trade or for government business. In addition to these time-honored pursuits, prospective settlers, miners, and lumbermen were attracted to the area. More importantly, a new generation of tourists wanted to see the far west, and they could afford to hire experienced voyageurs and canoes to take them on an excursion into the wilderness.

It is strangely symbolic that both travel accounts of the Northwest Trail by Le Conte and Oliphant have as a common bond the voyageurs and guides who accompanied them. These colorful boatsmen represented a lingering vestige of the large-scale fur trade in the Northwest. The men who transported Le Conte and Oliphant were part of the last generation that could still proudly list its occupation as "voyageur" in the government census. With the passage of another decade that title disappeared forever from the roster of residents' names thus signaling yet another change.[30]

While tourists and travelers recounted their collective experiences along the Northwest Trail, another significant group left an important record of their presence in the region. In addition to travelers' accounts, the records of the early missionaries who operated along the Northwest Trail from the 1830s up until the 1850s also offer a fascinating glimpse of the country and the people.

The First Missionaries

"...thus I have been brought through the greatest difficulties in my long journey without harm, or scarcely fatigue that was worth mentioning–my path has been made smooth..."[31]

So wrote Reverend Edmund Franklin Ely, a young missionary for the American Board of Commissioners for Foreign Missions, on the eve of his arrival at the American Fur Company's Sandy Lake post. This remote station became his new home and the site of his first mission in the wilderness.

Reverend Ely was one of the first permanent missionaries to reside west of Lake Superior in what is now the state of Minnesota. Missionaries such as Allouez and Hennepin, visited the Great Lakes during the French regime; but neither of these men actually entered the country by way of the Northwest Trail or stayed for any appreciable length of time to work with the indigenous people.

With the many responsibilities of his mission at Chequamegon Bay and his work in mapping the coast of Lake Superior, Father Allouez was too occupied to engage in further lengthy exploration or additional missionary work in the interior of Minnesota. On the other hand, Father Hennepin was sent as part of a small exploring party by La Salle simply to find the source of the Mississippi. In the process, Hennepin was detained by the Dakota, who probably did not know what to do with him or his companions.

The writings of both men include many valuable contributions to the general geographical knowledge of the country. Father Allouez produced a remarkable map of Lake Superior. In Hennepin's case, his observations of the people he met and the country he passed through were included in his book *Description de la Louisiane* (Description of Louisiana), which perhaps earned him more attention than he deserved. While a great deal of missionary activity was undertaken on the Great Lakes during the French regime in North America, it did not spread west along the Northwest Trail. The closest early French mission was located at La Pointe.

Missionary activity west of Lake Superior truly began in earnest after the War of 1812. In 1823, a Presbyterian missionary, Reverend William M. Ferry, and his wife opened a boarding school on Mackinac Island. The school served the children of traders including those living on the far western end of Lake Superior in the old Fond du Lac Department. In addition to his school, Reverend Ferry was also pastor of a small church which included members of the American Fur Company in the congregation. One member in particular, Robert Stuart, resident manager of the company, looked very favorably on Ferry's missionary efforts.[32]

Apparently both company and independent traders alike approved the idea of the mission school. As mentioned earlier, William Aitkin, like many other traders, sent his three eldest children to Mackinac Island. Surviving letters include the cost of room, board, and other matters related to keeping his children at the school.

In the 1830s, the American Board of Commissioners for Foreign Missions, which included representatives from the Congregational and Presbyterian churches, responded to growing interest in missionary activity in the Lake Superior region. One of its first measures was to commission Reverend Sherman Hall to establish a mission at La Pointe in 1831. It was a post he retained until 1853, when he moved to the Crow Wing Indian Agency.[33]

Reverend Hall labored to teach his charges, mostly the children of clerks and traders, the basics of reading and writing. Hall also counted among his pupils a number of children of local Indian families. He soon found out that to be an effective teacher or missionary it was essential to communicate with these children in their own language. Reverend Hall's approach, like that of other early missionaries sent out by the American Board, was to educate prospective converts before receiving them into the church. In that respect, Hall differed from the earlier French missionaries who believed in receiving individuals into the church and then instructing them in the basic tenets of the faith. It was the new emphasis on education that set the nineteenth century missionary efforts apart from earlier endeavors.

In 1832 William Aitkin invited the American Board to send a missionary to his post at Sandy Lake to instruct the children of his clerks and voyageurs. A young catechist by the name of Frederick Ayer responded to the request. Frederick Ayer, the son of a Presbyterian minister, had studied for the ministry. In 1829 he began teaching as a volunteer missionary at Reverend Ferry's school, and in 1831 he moved to La Pointe and served for a year with Sherman Hall.[34]

Ayer's school at Sandy Lake was situated at a remote crossroad. It consisted of one room in Aitkin's house and was equipped with only the most spartan facilities. Nonetheless, the mission school was the first of its kind in Minnesota. Ayer faced similar problems to those encountered at La Pointe. Like Hall, he quickly realized that it was very beneficial for his Ojibway students to be able to receive instruction in their own language. During his year at Sandy Lake, Ayer completed a spelling book he had started while at La Pointe; and in the spring of 1833 he left for Utica, New York, to have his book published. His wife, Elizabeth T. Ayer, later recounted that William Aitkin contributed eighty dollars toward the cost of printing the book. Later that same year Ayer placed himself under the care of the American Board and opened a mission at Yellow Lake, in what is now Burnett County, Wisconsin.[35]

In the fall of 1833, two new missionaries arrived at Fond du Lac from La Pointe. Reverend William Thurston Boutwell, who had accompanied Henry Schoolcraft on his expedition to the source of the Mississippi in the summer of 1832, and a young Presbyterian clergyman, Reverend Edmund Ely, were bound for their new mission stations. Boutwell proceeded to Leech Lake while Ely continued the school Ayer had started at Sandy Lake.[36]

Although Ely was not the only missionary to visit the settlements at Sandy Lake and Fond du Lac, he kept the most complete record of any missionary ever stationed there. Ely's daily experiences were faithfully entered in his diary during the years he was at Sandy Lake (1833-1834) and at Fond du Lac (1834-1839). His diary provides various insights as to the activities of his mission, his relationships with the people he encountered, and much introspection.[37]

Reverend Edmund Franklin Ely, c.1856.
Northeast Minnesota Historical Center, S3045 b2f10

Katherine (Goulais) Bissell Ely, c. 1860.
Northeast Minnesota Historical Center, S3045 b2f10

Like Frederick Ayer before him, Reverend Ely took up quarters in Aitkin's house overlooking the confluence of the Mississippi and Sandy Lake rivers. He began teaching the children of the fur company employees and local Sandy Lake band members, but apparently attendance was rather sparse. On September 29th, 1833, he wrote:

> My Temple is my Chamber. My Congregation–from 6 to 10 Children–occasionally two or three women. They have assembled– three times today–about one hour each–to sing–also spent some time in teaching the "Lord"s Prayer" in Ojibue, & spent some time in prayer with them.[38]

Several days later he described his contact with two of Aitkin's men who desired instruction. John Russell visited Ely one evening and asked if he would help him learn to read. Russell claimed, "he had not touched a book in eight years." Ely went on to say:

> Another man, Mr. Jas. McCormick–expressed a determination to leave the country & return where he could Enjoy Gospel privileges–requested me a day or two since to furnish him a Hymn Book. He was originally from Watertown (I think)–near Boston Mass–a Soldier in the U.S. Army–& discharged at Mackinaw. Is a Carpenter–Cooper by trade. It is good to hear even such faint longings for instruction....[39]

Interspersed between Ely's accounts of his teaching duties are frequent refer- ences to his lonely existence at the isolated fur post near Sandy Lake, "...feel that I require some Genial spirit whose sympathies would unite with mine. Such feelings are most delightful to me–but in a few minutes they are unendurable–they want vent."[40]

One can only wonder at the motivation of Ely and others after reading their comments. Many missionaries gave up comfortable lives to labor in the wilderness. The words of an old Baptist hymn "The Missionary's Farewell," by Reverend Samuel Francis Smith, suggest their sacrifices:

> Yes. My native land, I love thee;
> All thy scenes, I love them well,
> Friends, connections, happy country,
> Can I bid you all farewell?
> Can I leave you,
> Far in heathen lands to dwell?[41]

Smith's hymn may not be familiar, but the lyrics seem to capture the feeling in passages from Ely's diary, which tell of the daily trials of a man alone in the wilderness.

Ely wrote about different situations he encountered in his daily routine at Sandy Lake, especially one of the most troubling circumstances facing any missionary—illness. Ely described an incident where he was stricken with an unknown malady and how he treated it:

> ...was taken with a shaking unattended with Chills. Every nerve was in Motion. My teeth chattered with the agitation. I took a little Peppermint–gradually became more composed in nerve–it was unattended with the least pain. Sank into a gentle slumber attended with perspiration–felt rather debilitated this morning–but have attended to my School &c. as usual.[42]

The "Peppermint" Ely referred to was a highly alcoholic concoction with peppermint oil designed to soothe the stomach.

In spite of illness, Ely continued teaching and began work on an "Ojibue Vocabulary" with the assistance of William Aitkin. Occasionally instructional materials were sent from La Pointe or other eastern cities to supplement his meager stock of teaching tools. Ely commented on one item he received, "Our copy of Dr. James, edition of the Ojibue Testament, complete was forwarded from Le Pointe. We have long [been] wishing this."[43]

Unfortunately, Ely's efforts to conduct a school for the children were hampered by the need of families to hunt game, fish, or gather wild rice and maple sugar. All of these seasonal activities lured his charges from the classroom. In addition to the many interruptions, Ely faced countless bad influences from traders and trappers who visited the post. He recorded one shocking incident:

> I today, for the first time, heard an Indian use profanity. He was endeavoring to repair a trap in the Vice, but not succeeding, he gave vent to his

vexation in an imprecation of the most horrid kind—in English—that some ungodly man had doubtless learned him. There is nothing in the Indian language capable of Expressing oaths as used in Eng. & French. They sometimes Call each other "Mojianim"—a bad dog—this, is the extent of their profanity....[44]

In the spring of 1834, Ely left Sandy Lake after a short visit with Reverend Boutwell at Leech Lake. Ely then accompanied William Aitkin to Fond du Lac. There, the fur company clerk Pierre Cotté built a mission for him. On August 30th, 1835, Ely married Catherine Bissell, a missionary worker who was part Ojibway, in a ceremony officiated by Reverend Boutwell. Ely remained at Fond du Lac from 1834 until 1839, when the American Board decided to concentrate all missionary effort at a new station on Pokegema Lake near the modern town of Pine City, Minnesota. Ely served at the Pokegama mission from 1839 until 1842. In the meantime, the abandoned stations at Sandy Lake and Fond du Lac were eventually occupied by missionaries sent out by the Methodist Episcopal Church.

Reverend William Thurston Boutwell
Minnesota Historical Society

In 1840, a number of Methodist missionaries traveled up the Mississippi River with the intention of operating the mission stations formerly staffed by the Congregationalists and Presbyterians. The Methodists had tried to establish schools at Elk River and later at Rabbit Lake, but these were unsuccessful because of the proximity of hostile Dakota.

The initial influence behind the involvement of the Methodist missionaries in what appeared to be a very promising mission field came from Reverend Alfred Brunson, who had read the accounts of Henry Schoolcraft and Lieutenant James Allen describing the land and people found along the Mississippi River. Brunson encouraged others in the denomination to accept the challenge and commit not only missionaries but financial resources to the Minnesota mission stations. One of the new missionaries, Reverend Samuel Spates, was assigned to serve at Sandy Lake. It was a position he held from 1840 until the fall of 1855.[45]

Samuel Spates, originally from Kentucky, traveled to Sandy Lake with an assistant, Reverend John Johnson (En-me-gah-bowh) formerly of the Rice Lake, Ontario, Band of Ojibway. Other missionaries in the party included Johnson's cousin Reverend George Copway (Kah-ge-ya-gah-bowh), Reverend H. J. Brace, and the Superintendent of the Indian Missions District, Reverend Benjamin T. Kavanaugh. All were bound for Fond du Lac, but Kavanaugh paused at Sandy Lake long enough to assess prospects for the mission station there. From a description given later by Reverend Alfred Brunson, the Methodist mission apparently occupied the old abandoned North West Company trading post. [46]

Three Methodist missions were established in Minnesota in 1840: the first was at Sandy Lake under Brace and Spates; the second mission was at Whitefish Lake under Reverend John Johnson; and a third at Fond du Lac under Reverend and Mrs. George Copway.

The Methodist Mission at Sandy Lake as pictured in Oliphant's book, *Minnesota and the Far West.* Note what appears to be a stockade in the center of the picture.

Like the Congregationalists and Presbyterians, the Methodist missions were located far apart and were dependent on the support provided by different established churches. Many of the Methodist congregations in the West were very poor, and sponsoring missionary work took money and willing workers. Various church officials regularly toured Sandy Lake, Fond du Lac, and other missions to check on their progress and reported to the churches sponsoring those missions. Still, the lack of local resources on the part of many frontier congregations can be seen in the frequent changes of sponsors.

Reverend John H. Pitezel was one who served in a supervisory position and visited the missions at Fond du Lac and Sandy Lake for some time beginning in 1849. Pitezel later published an account of his work in a book entitled *Lights and Shades of Missionary Life.* The book included detailed information about conditions in the region. Undoubtedly, works like Pitezel's in turn inspired people to enter the missionary field.[47]

Samuel Spates was evidently a highly motivated missionary judging by the various hardships he and his family endured during their long tenure in missionary work. For example, in his diary for Tuesday, September 22nd, 1841, Spates recorded the privations he suffered while returning to Sandy Lake by way of Lake Superior. The weather was so rough it caused him to "cast up my accounts" from seasickness. Added to the discomfort of the voyage, the Mackinaw boat he was riding in sank somewhere along the south shore of Lake Superior. Soaked to the skin and numb with cold, Spates nonetheless retrieved his belongings and camped by the lake. "But we are now on shore and have a fire kindled, a tent pitched, and are comfortable...."[48]

Spates, like Ely, was employed at Sandy Lake to instruct the local Indian children and those of the resident traders and voyageurs. Also, he was to oversee the spiritual well-being of the adult population. In one instance in October of 1841, Spates even got into a protracted discussion with William Aitkin over religious matters, "Mr. Ait—came in, a little while ago to see me and to talk about religion... I took the "sword of the Spirit," which is the word of god, and faught him for about an hour...."[49]

Spates tried to explain some trying situations that he encountered, such as the case of a domestic dispute between American Fur Company employee Stephen "Bounga" (Bonga) and his "wife:"

Friday 22 [October, 1841] I have had a na[s]ty case this day. Stephen drove his Squaw off last night, about midnight, and I knew nothing about it until this morning. So I gave him a good sitting down about it, after which he asked me to speak to his wife, as he called her. So I did, and made him and her promise to get married. I also cauchened them not to sleep together until they were married, and farther saied, "if you do, you will commit a <u>dultrey</u>." Now in view of this case, Are we Missionaries clear? we have let this man and woman remain at our house, for some days, and sleep together as man & wife, and yet, they are in trouth, no more man & wife, then I and Queen Victory [Victoria] are.[50]

Spates' Ojibway assistant, John Johnson, summed up the conditions at Sandy Lake mission after six years of effort in a letter to the Indian agent at La Pointe dated June 9th, 1846:

The present prospect of this mission is cheering of doing good in spiritual matters, though I have many difficulties to contend with; but I feel for these, my red brethren, that I cannot let them go without making a fair trial.[51]

Relations between individual missionaries and persons employed by the trading companies or local residents were sometimes anything but cordial. Ely had difficulties with the American Fur Company's resident clerk at Fond du Lac, Pierre Cotté. Spates lost his temper and called a Sandy Lake Indian "a dog," which insult earned him the undying enmity of the offended party. The most scandalous incident, however, occurred at Fond du Lac in 1848, when a trader attacked Mrs. Johnson. The unnamed trader's motive was not clear, but Reverend Johnson and James Tanner caught him and held him while Johnson's wife administered a sound flogging. For that episode, Reverend Johnson was expelled from the Methodist Church. Following Johnson's departure, the school at Fond du Lac was continued under the direction of Reverend J. W. Holt and his wife.[52]

Reverend John Johnson
(En-me-gah-bowh) and
Mrs. John Johnson
A Pioneer History of Becker County

Other forms of hostility were a bit more subtle. Some local residents simply refused to cooperate with the missionaries. Most importantly, Spates lamented his lack of ability to communicate with the Indian people without an interpreter:

> I asked a man to day, if he would interpret for me tomorrow to preach
> to the Indians, and said he could not, and, yet it is his mother tonge. If
> he spooke the trough, is it possible for me ever to preach in their lan-
> guage?[53]

The work of the missionaries became progressively easier as they became fluent in the language of the Ojibway. Over time, the amount of religious material translated into Ojibway increased. Some of the missionaries mentioned thus far contributed to the growing store of linguistic knowledge with works such as Ayer's spelling book and Hall's translation of the New Testament with the assistance of Henry Blatchford, described as "a Chippewa half-breed."

The work of men in the mission fields of the Northwest is well-known, but from the start there were also women mission workers. In addition, many of the wives of the ordained male clergy accompanied their husbands into the wilderness and shared their modest rewards and privations. A few of the women, such as Florantha Thompson Sproat and Lucy Lewis, left personal accounts of their experiences at the far-flung mission stations.

Lewis' accounts can be found in letters which describe the country and the inhabitants. In one letter, Lucy mentioned her precautions to insure a dry crossing of the notorious Savanna Portage. She earnestly believed high top India rubber boots were the answer, and circumstances almost reinforced her opinion. Unfortunately, near the end of her journey across the portage, she managed to step into a puddle that was deeper than anticipated, and the foul swamp water rose over the top of her boots. She had to endure wet muddy feet for the remainder of the crossing. It was a minor incident perhaps, but an uncomfortable experience nonetheless.[54]

This and other accounts are of particular interest as they expose the colorful human side of missionary work. Florantha Sproat noted the events of a traveling camp while en route to visit the mission at Fond du Lac in April of 1842:

The next morning–Thursday–I arose before any of our company and cleaned some ducks (Dr. B. [Borup] got from an Indian the day before) and prepared a fricassee for our breakfast. We ate it with keen appetites. After it, as we thought we should arrive at Fondulac in a few hours, we dressed ourselves for an introduction to our missionary brothers and sisters at that place, making our toilets in the wildwood. Dr. B. and his band took off coats and vests and prepared for shaving. Husband had brought a little glass which he hung on a bush and with a long sober face prepared to remove his beard. At the same time Dr. B. scrubbing himself near by, Mrs. Borup washing and combing her children, Miss [Abigail] Spooner washing & combing, and changing her frock, at the same time every bush hanging with different articles of apparel, the birds singing delightfully above our heads, careless of confusion beneath. I looked on and a wish arose as I have often had before, that you could see us just as we were.[55]

After her stay at the mission Mrs. Sproat, along with her party and the resident missionaries, paddled a short distance up the St. Louis River by canoe to view the rapids. Once at Shingle Rock, the group had a picnic which Mrs. Sproat described as including a menu of "cold beef, bread, ginger-bread and beer." After the party, the visiting missionaries prepared to leave Fond du Lac and return to La Pointe.[56]

Another well-known missionary was Hester Crooks, the mixed-blood daughter of the president of the American Fur Company, Ramsay Crooks. Hester Crooks entered the mission field while still quite young and worked at Yellow Lake before arriving at Fond du Lac. After serving there for a time, she met and later wed Reverend William Boutwell. On September 10th, 1834, they were married in the first Christian wedding ceremony performed at Fond du Lac. The next day they departed on their "honeymoon," which consisted of a long tiring trip over the Northwest Trail retracing Boutwell's steps to his Indian mission housed in a birch-bark lodge at Leech Lake. He commented on the perseverance of his new wife while crossing the Savanna Portage, "My dear Hester, like a true heart followed through mud and water half leg deep, encumbered with a few small cooking utensils."[57]

In June of the following year, Hester, now great with child, left Leech Lake and returned with her husband over the same difficult route on their way to the mission house at La Pointe on Madeline Island. Two weeks after the birth of their child, the couple once again started back to Leech Lake. Their second child, although born at the Leech Lake mission, was brought to La Pointe for baptism shortly after it was born. These sometimes harrowing trips by missionaries and converts alike from the interior to La Pointe for purposes of receiving baptism or saying marriage vows became increasingly common as the influence of the missions expanded.

Samuel Spates' wife and children shared his long tenure at the Sandy Lake mission. They also endured hostility from the local population, which clearly intended to drive Spates away. Spates' presence apparently represented something foreign or threatening to the local Indian community, and they grew increasingly hostile to him. Spates claimed that someone attempted to poison his little boy, but the plot was foiled. Unable to endure threats against his family, Spates left his mission station precipitously in October of 1855, never to return to the shores of Sandy Lake.[58]

Even if they were not completely successful with propagating the faith, the missionaries in the field recorded conditions on the frontier, provided local residents with basic instruction, and studied the Ojibway language. Among the significant contributions to this process were those by three Roman Catholic missionaries from Carniola, a part of the Austrian Empire.

Bishop Frederic Baraga holding a copy of his *A Dictionary of the Otchipwe Language.*
Photo by Mathew Brady Studio, Library of Congress

Father Frederic Baraga, the first of three Slovenian missionaries to the Great Lakes region, was sponsored by the Austrian Leopoldine Society. He began work at La Pointe in 1835. Although assigned to La Pointe, Baraga visited Fond du Lac in the fall of 1835 and again in the spring of 1836. He was heartened to find the resident clerk of the American Fur Company at Fond du Lac, Pierre Cotté, assiduously performing the work of a lay minister. Baraga also met several times with Reverend Ely.[59]

During the years of his ministry, Father Baraga compiled material, which he eventually incorporated into a dictionary of the Ojibway language. His lasting contribution was the eventual publication of *A Dictionary of the Otchipwe Language* in 1853. Although Baraga's work appeared too late to be of assistance to the first missionaries, nonetheless it still served as a valuable foundation for the later study of the Ojibway language.

Shortly after Baraga reached La Pointe in 1835, a second Slovenian priest, Father Francis Xavier Pierz (Slovenian Pirec), arrived in the Great Lakes region to assist in missionary work. Pierz originally intended to proceed to La Pointe and assist Baraga, but he was assigned instead to L'Arbre Croche (Harbor Springs, Michigan). Eventually his missionary duties extended along the northern shore of Lake Superior from Sault Sainte Marie west to Grand Portage. He did not venture as far as the Northwest Trail at Fond du Lac, as that area was Baraga's responsibility. Instead, Father Pierz was assigned to the Crow Wing area after Minnesota became a territory in 1849.[60]

Father Francis Xavier Pierz served the Ojibway living at Sandy Lake
Rezek. *Diocese of Sault Sainte Marie and Marquette*

Baraga was superseded at La Pointe by a third Slovenian priest, Father Otto Skolla. Skolla visited Fond du Lac but the situation had changed there. Pierre Cotté had been transferred to the Grand Portage fishing station in 1836; and without his leadership among the local people, the observance of religion apparently needed encouragement. Furthermore, the Indian school which had been in operation for many years at Fond du Lac was discontinued in May of 1850.

Unfortunately, other pressing matters at La Pointe kept Father Skolla from regularly visiting the area at the eastern end of the Northwest Trail. One day in 1853, while holding services at Fond du Lac, Skolla was surprised by a visit from Father Pierz, who informed him that Fond du Lac and Sandy Lake were included in an area newly assigned to Pierz. Meanwhile, another assignment awaited Father Skolla.

After eight years of mission work at La Pointe, Father Skolla was selected to work with the Menominee on the Keshena Reservation in Wisconsin.[61] As for Father Baraga, he received appointment as Bishop and visited Fond du Lac in 1856 and again in 1858. Both times he stayed with a devout resident trader, Francis Roussain. Father Pierz was the last of the early missionaries to travel the Northwest Trail.

It is said that while at his new Crow Wing mission, Father Pierz received an invitation from Fond du Lac Chief Naganub. Pierz's resulting visit to the head of Lake Superior was the first of his many trips across country to the far northern end of his frontier parish. It took nine days of difficult travel for Father Pierz to reach Fond du Lac from Crow Wing on the Mississippi. At times, he shared the difficulties experienced by the local people such as when the region suffered from a famine. His final visit to the area was in 1867. A number of years passed before regular missionaries once again visited the residents along the Northwest Trail.

To a growing number of government officials, the labors of the missionaries were appreciated, but the effort spent to educate the Ojibway children was deemed a waste of time, money, and talent. In 1846 James P. Hayes, Indian Sub-Agent at La Pointe, recommended that the government concentrate all of the Indians west of the Mississippi to expedite the distribution of government services and that the mission schools be replaced with manual training boarding schools. Hayes' statements were merely a reflection of the long-standing feeling on the part of some who not only saw too little gain compared to the investment in instruction, but also felt the proximity of the Indians to settled areas made them easy prey for whiskey sellers. Hayes' sentiments were echoed by Territorial Governor Alexander Ramsey who issued an order in 1852 closing the remaining schools. In 1853, Ramsey's successor, Willis A. Gorman, expressed similar sentiments.[62]

All of the missionaries who passed over the Northwest Trail experienced some degree of hardship. Like the Congregationalists, Methodists, or Presbyterians, the three Roman Catholic Slovenian missionaries were too few for the immense territory they were expected to cover. After the era of Baraga, Pierz, and Skolla, the mission fields gradually became smaller and more manageable. Still one can only wonder how any of the missionaries, regardless of denomination, were effective in meeting the spiritual needs of the local population given the enormous distances they had to cross and the few resources available to them.

The seasonal activities of the bands along the Northwest Trail often prevented some children from regularly attending school. In spite of irregular attendance, a rudimentary education for the Ojibway children was provided by the men and women in missionary service. Of all the many labors performed by the early missionaries, perhaps their most significant achievements were recording their impressions of the country and the people and converting the Ojibway language from an unwritten into a written form. By creating a written language, the missionaries helped preserve the language and provide a key to understanding Ojibway culture.

Missionary work that continued after the 1850s followed a different emphasis. Education shifted from reading and writing to the manual-labor schools advocated by many government officials. In addition, to prevent the students from interrupting their course of study, the concept of the boarding school was introduced. The change of direction in education was but the first of many changes for the Ojibway living along the Northwest Trail.

Chapter 10 - Chronicles of a Changing Country
Notes

1. "The Diary of Martin McLeod," ed. by Grace Lee Nute, *Minnesota History Bulletin*, vol. 4, nos. 7-8 (August-November, 1922), pp. 351-439.

2. General Dickson's private army was the second force to march west from Lake Superior to the Red River settlements. The first was a one hundred man contingent of former Swiss mercenaries recruited by Lord Selkirk in 1816 from the recently discharged Regiment de Meuron.

3, Ibid., p. 384.

4. Ibid.

5. The Nettletons' experiences can be found in Dwight E. Woodbridge and John S. Pardee (eds.), *History of Duluth and St. Louis County, Past and Present*, 2 vols. (Chicago, 1910), vol. 1, pp. 203-207.

6. "A Voyage From Lake Superior to St., Paul in a Bark Canoe," typescript copy of the *Superior Chronicle*, vol. 1, nos. 25 and 26 (Tuesday, December 11th, 1855).

7. Ibid.

8. Ibid.

9. Some of the works listed here not only contain travel information but also a great deal of information designed to promote settlement in the region. Much useful information about various travel accounts can be found in Margaret Irene Snyder, "Travel Literature of the Minnesota Frontier: 1804-1858," (Master's Thesis, University of the City of Toledo, 1932), and the bibliography in Philip P. Mason (ed.), *Schoolcraft's Expedition to Lake Itasca: The Discovery of the Source of the Mississippi* (East Lansing, 1993), pp. 370-373.

10. Charles Lanman, *A Summer in the Wilderness; A Canoe Voyage up the Mississippi and Around Lake Superior* (New York, 1847), pp. 117-118, and 122.

11. William Whipple Warren, *History of the Ojibway People* (1885; reprint ed., St. Paul, 1984), pp. 114-115.

12. I. [Increase] A. Lapham, *Wisconsin; Its Geography and Topography, History, Geology, and Mineralogy* (Milwaukee, 1846); E. S. [Sanford] Seymour, *Sketches of Minnesota, The New England of the West* (New York, 1850); and C. [Christopher] C. [Columbus] Andrews, *Minnesota and Dacotah: in Letters Descriptive of a Tour Through the North-West* (Washington, D.C., 1857).

13. Rhoda R. Gilman, "Zeppelin in Minnesota: The Count's Own Story," *Minnesota History*, vol. 40, no. 6 (Summer, 1967), p. 275.

14. June Drenning Holmquist (ed.), "Frontier Vacation: Joseph Le Conte's Geological Excursion," *Minnesota History*, vol. 32, no. 2 (June, 1951), pp. 81-99.

15. Ibid., p. 91.

16. Ibid., p. 92. The endurance displayed by the voyageurs stood in stark contrast to that of Joseph and his cousin.

17. Ibid.

18. Ibid.

19. Ibid., p. 94. Le Conte probably meant "bannock," a Scottish fry bread or scone. "Boudin" was a type of sausage made with buffalo intestines and does not match the description in the text.

20. Ibid., p. 95.

21. Laurence Oliphant had an interesting and productive career according to the information on the title page of his book, *Minnesota and the Far West* (Edinburgh, 1855). Oliphant's comments about the people and country are quoted several times in the text.

22. Ibid., p. 165.

23. Ibid., p.160.

24. Ibid., p. 170.

25. Ibid., p. 173.

26. Ibid., p. 177. Oliphant was able to barter some bear meat from a woman above Knife Falls.

27. Ibid., p. 181.

28. Ibid., p. 185.

29.   Ibid., p. 188.

30.,   The occupational title "voyageur" appears in only a few entries in the 1860 census of Minnesota. For example, see United States Census, 1860, Schedule 1. Free Inhabitants in Crow Wing Village, State of Minnesota, June 4th, 1860, p. 4.

31.   Edmund F. Ely Journal No. 2, Wednesday, September 18th, 1833. The original documents are in the Northeast Minnesota Historical Center, Duluth, Minnesota (hereafter referred to as NEMHC). Typescript copies of the diaries are in the collections of the Minnesota Historical Society.

32.   The degree to which Stuart sought to impose morality on the everyday operation of the fur company is described in David Lavender, *The Fist in the Wilderness* (1964, reprint ed., Albuquerque, 1979), p. 480, n. 14.

33.   Grace Lee Nute, "The Letters of Sherman Hall, Missionary to the Chippewa Indians," *Minnesota History*, vol. 7, no. 1 (March, 1926), pp. 62-65. The activities of the early missionaries along the south shore of Lake Superior are summarized in Hamilton Nelson Ross, *La Pointe: Village Outpost* (St. Paul, 1960), pp. 73-107.

34.   Elizabeth T. Ayer, "Frederick Ayer: Teacher and Missionary to the Ojibway Indians 1829-1850," in *Minnesota Historical Society Collections*, vol. 6 (1894), pp. 429-43. Ayer's work is also mentioned by a contemporary, Reverend Stephen R. Riggs, in "Protestant Missions in the Northwest," also in *Minnesota Historical Collections*, vol. 6 (1894), pp. 119-123.

35.   Ayer, "Frederick Ayer," p. 429. William Aitkin's charity to Reverend Ayer is mentioned by Elizabeth Ayer. Ironically, Frederick Ayer's first assignment away from La Pointe was Aitkin's trading post near Sandy Lake. Nineteen years later, his first case as Judge of Probate Court for Benton County, Minnesota, was the settlement of the estate of William A. Aitkin.

36.   For a history of Ely's work at Sandy Lake and Fond du Lac see Roy Hoover, "To Stand Alone in the Wilderness," in *Minnesota History*, vol. 49, no. 7 (Fall, 1985), pp. 265-274. The trip to Sandy Lake was described by Reverend William Thurston Boutwell in a letter to David Greene dated, Sandy Lake, September 21st, 1833. See Boutwell to Green in, *American Board of Commissioners for Foreign Missions*, MSS., vol. 74, no. 84, from a copy in the collections of the Minnesota Historical Society.

37.   A study of the reaction of the Ojibway to the missionary activity of Reverend Ely can be found in Elaine Johnson, "A Pair of Scales: A Drama of Early Minnesota," (essay submitted for the Funk Prize in History, Macalester College, 1935).

38.   Edmund F. Ely, Journal No. 2, Sunday, September 29th, 1833, NEMHC.

39.   Ibid., Journal No. 2, Tuesday, October 1st, 1833, NEMHC.

40.   Ibid., Journal No. 2, Sunday, October 13th, 1833, NEMHC.

41.   Reverend Smith was also the author of "America" or "My Country 'Tis of Thee." Although written in 1832, the song did not become popular until the time of the American Civil War.

42.   Edmund F. Ely, Journal No. 2, Friday, November 15th, 1833, NEMHC.

43.   Ibid., Journal No. 3, Saturday, March 1st, 1834, NEMHC.

44.   Ibid., Journal No. 3, Thursday, February 27th, 1834, NEMHC. Although Ely complained about the use of profanity by fur company employees, his diary entry mentions the lack of profanity in the Ojibway language.

45.   Anna V. Olson, "The Work of the Methodist Missionaries Among the Chippewa Indians of Minnesota," college paper (1927), in the collections of the Minnesota Historical Society; Margaret Lowe, "Methodist Missions in Minnesota 1837-1845" (Honors Thesis, Hamline University, May, 1930).

46.   Alfred Brunson, *A Western Pioneer*, 2 vols. (New York, 1872), pp. 201-202.

47.   John H. Pitezel, *Lights and Shades of Missionary Life* (Cincinnati, 1861).

48.   Samuel Spates, "Diary of Samuel Spates, Methodist Missionary to the Chippewa Indians, September 21st-October 31st, 1841," typescript, 1926, Minnesota Historical Society. See entry dated Tuesday, September 22nd, 1841.

49.   Ibid., "Diary," Wednesday, October 13th, 1841.

50.   Ibid., "Diary," Friday, October 22nd, 1841.

51.   Letter from John Johnson to James P. Hayes, Indian Sub-Agent, Indian Department, Sandy

Lake, June 8th, 1846, quoted in Leroy Jackson, "Enmegahbowh-A Chippewa Missionary," in *North Dakota State Historical Society Collections*, vol. 2 (1908), p. 479.

52.   The James Tanner mentioned here was the son of the famous Indian captive John Tanner who served as United States Interpreter at Sault Sainte Marie, Michigan and was later wrongly accused of the murder of Henry Schoolcraft's brother, Dr. James Schoolcraft. John Tanner disappeared in 1846, before he could clear his name. James Tanner reportedly died a violent death in Winnipeg, Manitoba, during the Reil Rebellion.

53.   Spates "Diary," Friday, October 22nd, 1841.

54.   Letter from Mrs. William (Lucy) Lewis to her brother James R. Wright, dated Leech Lake, May 29th, 1844, in the William Lewis Papers, 1843-1848, Minnesota Historical Society.

55.   Florantha Thompson Sproat, "La Pointe Letters," *Wisconsin Magazine of History*, vol. 16, no. 2 (September, 1932), p. 205.

56.   Ibid., p. 207.

57.   Edward D. Neill, "Memoir of William T. Boutwell, The First Christian Minister Resident Among the Indians of Minnesota," in *Macalester College Contributions*, 2nd series-no. 1(1890-1892), p. 28.

58.   Several reasons for the failure of Spates mission at Sandy Lake are given by Reverend Pitezel. See Pitezel, *Lights and Shades*, p. 298.

59.   Anna Marry Keenan, "Pierre Cotté," in *Acta et Dicta*, vol. 6, no. 1 (October, 1933), pp. 86-96. For information on Father Baraga, Father Skolla, and Father Pierz, see Antoine Ivan Rezek, *History of the Diocese of Sault Sainte Marie and Marquette* (Houghton, Michigan,1906).

60.   The community of Pierz, Minnesota, as well as a township, are named for Father Pierz.

61.   Rezek, *Diocese of Sault Sainte Marie*, p. 369.

62.   Newton H. Winchell, The *Aborigines of Minnesota* (St. Paul, 1911), pp. 642-643 and 651-652.

A page from Bishop Frederic Baraga's *A Dictionary of the Otchipwe Language.*

Brown's Point - Sandy Lake

Garden Area & Graves

Blacksmith Shop

Village

Aerial photograph of Brown's Point, Sandy Lake showing the location of the
Ojibway village, government blacksmith, gardens, and burial ground.
U.S. Department of Agriculture photo, 1939

Chapter 11 ✄ An All Too Brief and Tragic History

As the fur trade developed, it brought about changes in the the lives of the Ojibway including those living at Fond du Lac and Sandy Lake. Historically, these two Ojibway bands at either end of the Northwest Trail had been in the forefront of the fur trade west of Lake Superior. That favorable position, however, did not last. The increasing need to obtain furs for trade goods had to be balanced with the necessity of providing subsistence for the trapper's own family, and sufficient subsistence was difficult to find.

In addition to changes in the fur trade, changes in government policy influenced the future of the local Ojibway bands. The first change involved treaty provisions which required the government to furnish teachers and artisans to assist the Ojibway in learning the "arts of civilization," plus the payment of an annual annuity consisting of trade goods and cash. The second change concerned the establishment of the Sandy Lake Indian Agency in 1850, and the third was the attempt to consolidate the indigenous population through a series of treaties from 1837 to 1867. The writings of travelers, government officials, and missionaries chronicle the impact of these changing conditions in trade and policy on the Ojibway living at either end of the Northwest Trail.

The "Indian Trade"

By the 1830s, the fortunes of the Ojibway at Fond du Lac and Sandy Lake were effectively tied to the fur trade through their growing dependence on trade goods and their obligations to the resident traders. During the same period, the term "Indian Trade" was increasingly used to define the commercial relationship between the individual hunter and trader. The use of the term suggests a changing role for the hunter. Over time, the changes which took place in the fur trade had a profound impact on the Ojibway hunter.

Originally, the Ojibway operated with a subsistence economy. Any surplus generated from seasonal activities or home manufacture were used for trade. Once the tribe became involved with the European fur trade, it increasingly turned to barter with other western tribes to obtain the furs needed to purchase trade goods. The Ojibway functioned as middlemen. In fact, they became the vanguard of the fur trade on the Great Lakes, but in the words of the famous Indian captive John Tanner, "Wherever the Indian went, the traders were sure to follow as the wolves and buzzards follow the buffalo." Like the Ottawa and Huron, who held the same position before them, the Ojibway became indebted to the traders who followed them inland.[1]

To maintain their position as middlemen, the Ojibway hunters had to spend an increasing amount of time either harvesting or bartering for furs at the expense of domestic pursuits such as fishing, hunting, and gathering. Increased hunting for furs also meant the individual band members had to move about more as the population of fur bearing animals was exhausted. The steady westward movement of the Ojibway, however, was not only caused by the quest for fur but also by the need to obtain necessary subsistence chiefly in the form of big game which abounded along the edge of the western prairie.[2]

Unfortunately, the supply of beaver and other furs varied from area to area and from season to season. If an individual's hunt for beaver was poor, the trapper could and often did substitute other types of furs. The traders used a book entry system to keep track of an individual hunter's accounts. The prime beaver pelt was the standard of value against which trade goods or other types of furs and hides were measured.[3]

An indication of the shift from a barter to a cash economy came in 1820, when the North West Company introduced the beaver token to be used with the credit system. What effect the introduction of the beaver token may have had on the cash-starved Minnesota frontier over the long term is problematical because the North West Company's activities were confined largely to the northern border region. Although the North West Company merged with the Hudson's Bay Company in 1821, both the Hudson's Bay and American Fur companies used the beaver token and other forms of fiat money in their daily transactions. Also, fiat money issued by local banks circulated to a limited extent at frontier trading posts along the Northwest Trail. For example, a five *sou* copper token dated 1837 and issued by the Bank of Lower Canada was found on the site of William Aitkin's trading post.[4]

When Ramsay Crooks became president of the American Fur Company in 1834, the company enjoyed a dominant trade position in the former Fond du Lac Department. After he assumed leadership, Crooks sought to increase the profitability of the company not only by diversifying its operations to include the shipping business, banking, copper mining and commercial fishing, but also by controlling expenses. In particular, he sought to eliminate the time-honored credit system. He finally succeeded in this last endeavor.

In a letter dated March 13th, 1839, Crook's agent at La Pointe, Dr. Charles Borup, reported the credit system was finally eliminated.[5] Instead of the hunter receiving his supplies or "outfit" in advance of the year's hunt, Crooks substituted the cash-and-carry system familiar in most retail establishments of the era. Under the new system, "cash" in the form of beaver or other furs was tendered by the purchaser for the types of goods received. In addition, the old custom of gift giving by the trader before any trading occurred ended. Under the new system, a poor harvest of furs meant no trade. In contrast, under the old credit system, accounts could be carried on the company's books to tide over hunters who experienced a poor season. Although Crooks favored cash over credit, some of the old practices were retained. For example, prices for trade items tended to remain fixed in terms of a specific number of beaver pelts in spite of supply and demand.

Under the old credit system, the hunter was in an advantageous position to barter or negotiate with the trader. Abuses in the credit system by both parties were frequent. Hunters who "took out credits" on their anticipated winter's hunt sometimes cheated their trader by not paying for the full value of their outfit in furs. Knowing that he could be and often was shortchanged, the trader usually allowed a huge markup on the trade goods he offered in anticipation of only receiving partial payment in fur for those goods. Under the new system, the hunter could either accept the trader's price or go elsewhere.[6]

The prices of trade goods were stated in terms of beaver pelts.
Dover, *Animals*

Meanwhile, as the American Fur Company gained more of a monopoly in the region, it pressured delinquent hunters to either pay their balances or forfeit future trade with the company. Conversely, where small independent traders were present, they tended to undermine the position of the large company because the small trader offered credit to the Ojibway hunters. If the independent traders continued to undercut the large company by using credit for any length of time, it usually led to a price war. Morrison, Aitkin, and other American Fur Company traders often resorted to underselling whenever a rival trader appeared in the region to eliminate the threat of competition.[7]

There was another side to the trade that was not readily apparent to the trader. The individual Ojibway hunter was used to taking only what he needed when it came to nature's bounty. He and his family lived a very modest lifestyle that was closely in tune with nature. Their wants were simple and few; and, as can be seen by comparing invoices of trade goods over the years, their needs did not change much, if at all.[8] Changes which took place in the fur trade, however, affected everyone from an individual hunter to a large company like American Fur. Faced with a national depression following the Panic of 1837, increasing debt, and competition, the American Fur Company was forced to suspend payments in 1842. After paying off its indebtedness, the company sold off its remaining assets and ceased operation in 1847.[9]

On the surface, the fur trade seemed to continue as it always had; even after the dissolution of the American Fur Company. The trade along the Northwest Trail, however, was increasingly characterized by small traders, storekeepers, and individual trappers. Also, newly arrived settlers on the fringe of Indian territory saw the fur harvest as a means of supplementing their meager income. Contrary to the oft-repeated story that the fur trade ended with the introduction of the silk hat, the fur trade actually expanded. By the end of the nineteenth century more furs were being exported from the United States than at the beginning of the century. The fur trade never ended, instead it was transformed. Trapping, however, was no longer exclusively dominated by the Indian hunter.[10]

In addition to increasing competition for fur, the Ojibway also had to contend with periods when the seasonal hunt was simply unproductive. When the hunt for furs failed, the impact was felt throughout the band. An example of such a failure was witnessed by traders such as William Aitkin and Charles Oakes in 1842. The local hunters experienced not only a poor fur harvest but also a lack of big game to sustain themselves and their families.

Faced with a total failure of their hunt during the winter of 1841-1842, the Sandy Lake Ojibway, needing subsistence, sent hunting parties to the contested lands near the Crow Wing River, where they hoped to find relief from both hunger and a lack of furs. Instead, they faced potential conflict with the Dakota, who resented their incursions. In a letter to Ramsay Crooks dated February 18th, 1842, Oakes described the failure of the hunt for small furs and the desperate plight of the residents of Sandy Lake. He wrote, "I never saw a more wretched set of beings."[11]

The pressure to gather furs and his growing appetite for trade goods meant the individual hunter had less time to forage for his own food. In order to retain the hunters' loyalty, individual traders often resorted to offering them provisions so they could spend even more of their time trapping. During its existence, the American Fur Company increasingly hired hunters and fishermen to provide subsistence for the people employed during the winter hunt. Following the demise of the large company, the small traders were unable to provide the same amount of subsistence.[12]

Even if they received rations to tide them over the winter, there was no guarantee the amount could support the hunter, let alone his entire family. John Tanner related an account of his experience with the problem of subsistence while working for the American Fur Company trader Pierre Cotté at Fond du Lac and Rainy Lake. The individual ration provided each man in Tanner's party amounted to eighteen quarts of wild rice. Unable to supplement the rice with any fresh game, the men were eventually forced to eat their sled dogs. Having exhausted that source of food, they scavenged an abandoned Indian camp and feasted on the remains of a dead dog and some scraps of leather. In spite of adversity, Tanner was able to survive the winter and returned to Fond du Lac with a respectable pack of furs. Much to Tanner's chagrin, Cotté deducted ten dollars from his balance for the cost of the company sled dog that he had eaten.[13]

Experienced traders like William Aitkin could see the increasing problems confronting the continued viability of the fur trade. The growing competition for a dwindling supply of fur near Sandy Lake and a lack of sufficient game to sustain the Sandy Lake Ojibway undoubtedly convinced Aitkin to move south, first to Crow Wing, then to a site near the mouth of the Swan River located below Little Falls, Minnesota.

There was some relief for the Ojibway's plight. Beginning with the treaty negotiated at the confluence of the Mississippi and St. Peter's (Minnesota) rivers in 1837, the Ojibway received an annuity which was paid to them in both trade goods and cash in return for ceding certain lands. Bales and boxes of goods were distributed to individual families, and the cash payment in the form of specie (gold and silver coins) was shipped in closely guarded sealed kegs. Since the annuity was paid in part with cash, the Ojibway not only had a source of money with which to purchase provisions but also a remedy for any debts incurred by the Indian hunters. Traders' claims were allowed and, if approved, any outstanding debt was paid out of funds earmarked for the tribe.

Interestingly enough, there is evidence the Ojibway readily allowed traders' claims by those who had advanced them credit in the past. Similarly, those who were parsimonious, particularly in providing emergency food supplies to help tide hunters' families over in time of scarcity, could expect little sympathy from the tribe which had to approve those claims in advance.[14]

The introduction of the cash-and-carry system by the American Fur Company, the need to provide necessary subsistence for their families, and the uncertainty of the supply of large game were all factors which reduced the Ojibway to an increasing state of dependence on their traders. To counteract the Ojibways' growing dependency, an effort was made to help them become more self-sufficient. In response, the government offered the services of trained artisans to teach them useful skills. The treaty of 1837 contained a provision for the services of farmers, blacksmiths, and carpenters. Beginning in the 1840s artisans were stationed at Fond du Lac and Sandy Lake.

Tales of Farmers, Smiths, and Carpenters

Early travelers and missionaries described their experiences along the Northwest Trail in extensive written accounts. By contrast, the government farmers, blacksmiths, and carpenters who followed them left comparatively few records. The introduction of trained artisans to assist the local Indians represented an attempt by the government to change the hunter-gatherer into a self-sufficient farmer. Although the success of the effort varied, the government farmers, blacksmiths, and carpenters nonetheless attempted to introduce new skills at places like Fond du Lac and Sandy Lake.

The first problem addressed by the government employees was subsistence. The ability of the area to support selected crops was frequently noted by visitors to the region. The frontier trading posts situated at Fond du Lac and Sandy Lake were especially noteworthy for their rudimentary farming operations. In fact, whether one speaks of trading posts or contemporary military posts, all were intended to be as self-sufficient in food supply as possible. What could not be transported into the interior was either raised in the vicinity of these posts by the occupants or purchased from local tribes. Individuals had long sold maple sugar, fish, big game, and wild rice to soldiers and traders. It was but a short step from raising one's own commodities to selling the surplus to someone else, and the local people were encouraged to raise crops for eventual resale. For example, the residents at Red Lake were known for their production of corn, much of which was traded to villages closer to Lake Superior.

The existence of trading post gardens was proof that crops suitable for the climate could be grown in the region. In 1806, Zebulon Pike mentioned the existence of post gardens at Sandy Lake that annually produced four hundred bushels of potatoes. William Aitkin's post gardens were also productive according to Reverend William Boutwell, who viewed them in 1832:

> He [Aitkin] raised 600 or 700 bushels of potatoes last year. He has from 12 to 15 acres under improvement, cultivates barley, peas, and potatoes to a considerable extent, but no corn. Still I am persuaded it would grow here. His potatoes look exceedingly well. His barley has been overflowed by the Savannah [Sandy Lake River] and mostly destroyed.[15]

Aitkin's fields, first opened in the 1820s, were known to be exceedingly fertile, possibly because they were periodically inundated by the overflow of the Mississippi River. Flooding was an unexpected factor shared with other gardens established on Sandy Lake by local residents. As a testament to the continued productivity of the soil, Aitkin's fields were still being farmed in the twentieth century. An aerial photograph taken in 1940 shows the fields plowed and apparently planted to a crop.

Given the success of agriculture at local trading posts, the establishment of productive government farms for the Ojibway at places like Fond du Lac and Sandy Lake seemed assured. Following the Treaty of 1837, succeeding agreements with the Ojibway contained provisions for employing qualified artisans. For example, Article 2 of the treaty concluded in 1837 provided for the employment of farmers and blacksmiths at locations, "...as shall be designated by the Superintendent of Indian Affairs...."

Early records describe some of the persons employed by the government. In 1843, Julius T. Clark was appointed government farmer and John P. Bardwell blacksmith for the Sandy Lake Indians. The Superintendent of Indian Affairs also appointed a government carpenter, Mr. Benjamin F. Smith. Mr. Smith was to "itinerate" (rotate) between Fond du Lac and Sandy Lake.[16]

It is interesting to note that Julius Clark wrote a letter in February of 1844 to James D. Doty, then Governor of Wisconsin Territory (which included Sandy Lake), complaining of illicit liquor traffic at the mouth of the Crow Wing River. Very shortly thereafter, the Indian Sub-Agent in charge at La Pointe, Mr. James P. Hayes, suspended Clark:

> Mr. Clark is not a practical farmer and does not endeavor to perform the duties of his station. The Indians receive no instruction or assistance from him and say with truth the money might as well be thrown into the Lake.[17]

Hayes recommended the governor appoint Mr. John Stannard to fill Clark's position. Julius Clark later admitted he took the job at Sandy Lake for the experience of living on the frontier, but one cannot help noticing the interesting coincidence between his reporting the traffic in liquor and his subsequent dismissal. For his part, Clark is perhaps best remembered not as a farmer but as the author of an account of the Ojibway Chief Hole-in-the-Day.[18]

Farmers, however, were not the only skilled workers to be employed on behalf of the government to benefit the local Ojibway. Blacksmiths were probably the first skilled artisans to be represented in the wilderness.

During the French regime in Canada, blacksmiths were needed to repair equipment at isolated posts. Due to a scarcity of gunsmiths in the French colony, the local blacksmiths were also called upon to repair firearms of both French traders and local Indian tribes. In fact, the French authorities sent blacksmiths out amongst the tribes not only to repair tools and weapons, but also to gather information. The smithies served as goodwill ambassadors and in turn provided the colonial authorities with intelligence about the tribes—especially their sentiments toward rival English or Dutch traders.[19]

Tools and ironware found by Evan A. Hart on the site of the government blacksmith shop at Sandy Lake. Author's Collection

The policy of providing blacksmiths did not continue after the British conquest of Canada. Instead, blacksmith services were provided for the most part by traders. In more remote areas, various tribes quickly learned to repair their own tools in so far as possible, especially when it came to firearms. Caches of spare parts at village sites found throughout the country date back to the first introduction of firearms and indicate that people attempted to repair weapons on a surprisingly large scale.

The United States recognized the need to provide blacksmith services, particularly at remote locations. One repeatedly finds the provision for farmers, blacksmiths and carpenters in the various treaties concluded between Indian tribes and the government.[20]

Carpenter's skills were useful on the frontier. The policy of providing government carpenters to teach the Ojibway how to build dwellings, barns, and useful household articles resulted in the production of untold numbers of boards, squared timbers, shingles, doors, frames, fence rails, and even coffins. Wood products of various kinds were widely used on the frontier when available.

Government carpenters, like the farmers and blacksmiths, were appointed to serve the various Indian tribes. These government positions, unlike those maintained by the fur companies, were temporary and often went unfilled. Early official correspondence indicates the difficulty of obtaining or retaining qualified people for any of these three occupations. Also, the remote location often prevented men from reaching their assigned stations.

In February of 1845, Indian Sub-Agent Hayes writing from La Pointe, noted that John W. Hunter, the government farmer at Fond du Lac, had resigned his post and that Paul Beaulieu was appointed farmer in his place. He also indicated that Mr. Smith Mooers was appointed government farmer at Sandy Lake, but owing to difficulties experienced by Mr. Mooers in getting to his post, Hayes hired Mr. Clement Beaulieu to plow and plant for the Sandy Lake Band.[21]

Tombstone marking the final resting place for Clement Beaulieu's two daughters who perished from an unknown ailment at Sandy Lake. Photo by Larry Luukkonen

Getting to one's assigned post often presented almost insurmountable problems. Once there, living conditions at the isolated frontier stations were often harsh as indicated by an incident experienced by Clement Beaulieu. While performing his duties at Sandy Lake, Beaulieu's youngest daughters Margaret Elizabeth and Julia Sophia were stricken with an unknown ailment. Unable to secure medical assistance at the remote Sandy Lake station, both children eventually succumbed to the disease. Their remains were taken by Beaulieu from Sandy Lake to Father Frederic Baraga's mission at La Pointe for burial in the church cemetery.

Difficult living conditions undoubtedly plagued government blacksmith John P. Bardwell who resigned his post at Sandy Lake in 1845. Indian Sub-Agent Hayes recommended Mr. Erasmus D. Fowler for the post, but it is doubtful if Fowler ever served at Sandy Lake. Instead, a roster of men employed by the government listed William F. Vantassel and Peter Chouinard as blacksmiths assigned to Sandy Lake.[22]

In the spring of 1846, Wisconsin Territorial Governor, Henry Dodge, recommended Reuben B. Carlton, a native of Onondaga County, New York, for the post of blacksmith at Sandy Lake. Other than Dodge's correspondence, there is no further mention of Carlton serving at Sandy Lake. Instead, records indicate he worked as a government blacksmith at Fond du Lac beginning in August of 1845 for an annual salary of six hundred dollars. Carlton and his wife Susan lived in a small two-room house in Fond du Lac and for a time were reportedly the only Americans residing in the area.[23]

At first, Carlton's presence at Fond du Lac was not mentioned by early travelers, but his name and that of William Aitkin appeared as witnesses to a treaty concluded at Fond du Lac on August 2nd, 1847. Aitkin and Carlton knew each other, and both men eventually had counties and towns named after them. In fact, both Aitkin and Carlton counties were created on the same day, May 23rd, 1857. Carlton remained at Fond du Lac all his life and was very involved in promoting businesses and settlement in the region up until shortly before his death in 1863.[24]

Meanwhile, the ranks of the farmers, smiths, and carpenters continued to change as new men were hired to fill vacant positions. Paul Beaulieu, who had been appointed farmer at Fond du Lac, was transferred to Sandy Lake. Known for his ability as an interpreter, Beaulieu served both as government farmer and interpreter. He was present at the "Treaties with the Chippewa," concluded in 1854 and in 1855. These treaties relinquished claim to a large section of northeastern Minnesota, including the Northwest Trail.

In September of 1847, Paul Beaulieu reported his activities at Sandy Lake, which is remarkable for its scope considering the conditions he had to work under and the difficulty of the type of work he had to perform. Apparently the local people were motivated by Beaulieu's example:

> ...it is really encouraging to see that they mean to help themselves, they have took right hold of their work, and have Cleared for themselves about twelve Acres of land, which I ploughed. With the twenty-three I had last year, makes thirty five acres of land under cultivation for the indians at present.

Beaulieu went on to say,

> The indians have planted this year 290 Bushels of potatoes, & twelve bushels of peas that I sowed for them, and I hope that by the 15th of October they will see safe in store, potatoes & Peas, pumkins &c to live on with the help of the game they kill through the winter. I should request of you to buy 8 Bushels of corn for the indians to plant this spring, if it is practicable the corn from Red Lake would better suit the Climate. I have finished my barn & would finish my house if I had lumber. I have also made about 22 tons of hay, made fence about 1 week, & in fact made all in my power to make to benefit the indians.[25]

As government policy towards the Ojibway changed, the location of the farmers, blacksmiths, and carpenters shifted. In 1850, it was decided to close the La Pointe Indian Sub-Agency and move it to Sandy Lake. It was expected the Ojibway living in Michigan and Wisconsin would relocate to an area reserved for them in the northern part of Minnesota Territory, which would be closer for obtaining government services.

The result of the agency move concentrated government services at Sandy Lake. Minnesota Territorial Governor, Alexander Ramsey, noted the new situation in his annual report for 1850, which also credited the Sandy Lake Indians with the services of a farmer and a blacksmith. The employee roster for the newly established Sandy Lake Sub-Agency lists the persons employed and their salaries.

As of December, 1850, the records show two blacksmiths with an annual salary of six hundred dollars, two assistant blacksmiths at a salary of two hundred and forty dollars, and a farmer (Benjamin Gates) at a salary of six hundred dollars. The status of these workers was reflected in their wages. In comparison, the newly appointed Indian Sub-Agent, John Watrous, received an annual salary of seven hundred and fifty dollars.[26]

The establishment of the Sandy Lake Sub-Agency proved to be only a temporary move. The initial plan created a single large Indian reservation at Leech Lake, provided the Pillager Band which lived there agreed to the proposal. After protracted discussion, however, the Pillagers refused to accept the proposed reservation so Sandy Lake was chosen as an alternative. The Sandy Lake Sub-Agency lasted two years. In 1852 the agency was moved to Gull Lake near the present town of Brainerd, Minnesota. It was believed the Indians could be better supplied at Gull Lake both from a recently established government farm and by boat from St. Paul.[27]

Today, one is sometimes reminded of the former presence of the farmers, smiths, and carpenters. Occasionally local residents find a rusted tool or scrap of metal at the site of the farmers' fields or the blacksmiths' shop. In 1957, Evan A. Hart, an amateur archaeologist and later Historic Sites Supervisor for the Minnesota Historical Society, published an article detailing the location of the government blacksmith's shop at Sandy Lake. Mr. Hart and his family excavated the site. The building measured roughly fourteen by fourteen feet and contained numerous fur trade era relics and blacksmith tools. The location of the site on Brown's Point on Sandy Lake was only a short distance from the supposed site of the North West Company's trading post uncovered in 1926 by Hart's father, Professor Irving Hart.[28]

It is very likely that the building occupied by the government blacksmith was formerly one of several built in the vicinity by the American Fur Company in 1838. One clue as to the location of the agency buildings is provided in an estimate of expense written on December 10, 1850. An expenditure of six hundred and fifty dollars was incurred for an "office 18 by 20 ft. addition on dwelling house 16 by 20 ft. and repairing dwelling and two out-houses." The additions matched previous structures.[29]

Territorial Governor Alexander Ramsey offered another clue which suggested the the agency was either close to the government farm or one and the same, "...the slight improvements, which with great economy have been made during the past summer at Sandy Lake, could be turned to account as the residence of an Indian farmer...."[30]

Further evidence as to the approximate location can be found in a statement by Indian Agent Watrous in September of 1852:

> The past season has been very unfavorable for business, in the vicinity of Sandy Lake and Fond du Lac, on account of heavy rains. The farms at these two stations have been over-flowed; the water at Sandy Lake came quite into my house and stood three feet in depth on the floor, and continued at this height for nearly three weeks.[31]

A similar flood to the one Watrous mentioned occurred at Sandy Lake in 1950, when the water inundated the site of the former American Fur Company post and Indian agency to the same depth of approximately three feet.

In addition to the brief hints regarding the site of the agency buildings, the site of a large Indian village at the tip of the point and the existence of patches of cleared ground to the south of the blacksmith building all point to the location of the agency. Interestingly enough, local accounts refer to the area occupied by the farm fields as "Indian Gardens," a name possibly derived from the farming activities performed there in the 1840s and 1850s.

Other than a name, however, nothing tangible remains to tell the story of the farmers, smiths, and carpenters. The sight of oxen breaking ground, the ring of the blacksmith's hammer, or the rasping sound of the carpenter's pit saw are neither seen nor heard. The farmers, smiths, and carpenters came for the purpose of turning hunter-gatherers into self-sufficient farmers and artisans. Some of the government employees left their mark in the form of cleared fields long since abandoned, others are memorialized in local place-names, while still others left only the scattered rusted tools of their respective trades to remind one of their presence and that they too once traveled along the Northwest Trail.

The Sandy Lake Sub-Agency

Of the many historic sites that once existed along the Northwest Trail, one that has been conspicuously overlooked by authors and historians is the Sandy Lake Indian Sub-Agency. Virtually nothing has been written describing its location, and very little about the circumstances associated with its creation in 1850. This omission is remarkable, since the agency at Sandy Lake was also the proposed location of the first Ojibway reservation for Minnesota and the scene of a tragic epidemic.[32]

Perhaps the lack of information can be explained because the agency was never intended to be a permanent station, In fact, were it not for an epidemic that occurred there in the fall of 1850, few would know or care about its existence. Originally classified as a sub-agency and later an agency, the Sandy Lake Sub-

Agency replaced a similar facility located at La Pointe on Madeline Island. The agency transfer from La Pointe to Sandy Lake was part of a plan to relocate the remaining Ojibway bands residing in Michigan and Wisconsin.

The policy of Indian removal in western United States had its roots deep in the history of North America extending at least as far back as the French and Indian War (1755-1763). In fact, that conflict began over the enormous tract of land lying northwest of the Ohio River, subsequently known as the Northwest Territory. Both France and Great Britain, claimed the area. The inhabitants who dwelt there sought to retain their land in the face of a much larger conflict and sided with the European power which best represented their interests. Later, during the American Revolutionary War (1775-1783) and the War of 1812 (1812-1815), the same region was once again the scene of fierce conflict, as the local tribes sought to push back the advancing American settlers. When viewed in the context of the prolonged struggle for control of the Northwest Territory, it is understandable how the policy of Indian removal by the United States came to fruition following the War of 1812.

Mindful of the long struggle with various tribes over the Northwest Territory, Secretary of War John C. Calhoun is credited with developing the Indian removal policy in 1823, which was later announced by President Monroe in 1825 and widely applied by President Andrew Jackson. The passage of removal legislation in 1830 was met with resistance in the Old Northwest in the form of the Black Hawk War (1832) and in the southeast by the outbreak of the Second Seminole War (1835-1842). Most tribes, however, relocated reluctantly.

Proponents of removal stated it was meant to ensure peace between settlers and nearby tribes by moving the Indians to a specially reserved tract of land sufficiently far enough from settled areas to keep disreputable elements and whiskey traders from corrupting the Indians—a cause embraced by most missionary groups. It was reasoned that if the Indians were gathered in villages and separated from outside influence, they could be successfully educated and ultimately assimilated into the general population.[33]

By 1848, pressure for removal of the Michigan and Wisconsin Ojibway was building in some quarters, particularly since Wisconsin was about to achieve statehood. Interest in timber stands and mineral lands along the south shore of Lake Superior also aroused interest in favor of removal from those who sought to benefit from their acquisition.

In 1849, Alexander Ramsey, the newly appointed Territorial Governor of Minnesota, envisioned the establishment of a large Indian reserve at either Leech Lake or Ottertail Lake. Ramsey, a Pennsylvania Whig politician, was also the de facto Superintendent of Indian Affairs for the new Minnesota Territory. To test his idea, Ramsey and a group of officials traveled to the sites to see for themselves where a reserve could successfully be established. They settled on Sandy Lake as the logical place for the first reservation in the territory until the Pillager band at Leech Lake could be won over to the idea of absorbing the population of Ojibway residing near Lake Superior.

Evidence suggests Ramsey envisioned a large resettlement of Ojibway at

Sandy Lake; but the Indian Agent at La Pointe, John Livermore, appraised him of the difficulty the local band had at times in obtaining sufficient subsistence. The addition of more people to the area would only exacerbate an already bad situation. Also, the lack of cooperation by the Pillagers had to be considered as well as the required protocol of the Wisconsin and Michigan bands receiving an invitation from the Sandy Lake (host) Band prior to moving.[34]

Meanwhile, the removal order was issued. Although President Zachary Taylor signed the order, outright removal of the Great Lakes bands to Sandy Lake did not take effect immediately. Instead, preliminary steps were taken to notify the Indians that the La Pointe Sub-Agency would close and all annuity payments and other matters stipulated under previous treaties would henceforth occur at Sandy Lake. The negative reaction by Indian and non-Indian groups such as missionaries, traders, settlers, and lumbermen, who relied on the Ojibway for various services and labor, was not anticipated. In spite of protest, however, the first steps were begun in the creation of the new sub-agency followed by the scheduling of the annual annuity payment for the fall of 1850.[35]

The new Indian Sub-Agent, thirty-one year old John S. Watrous, had little beside his political party affiliation to recommend him for the job. In 1848, the Whig Party emerged victorious in the national elections and, in keeping with the tradition of the spoils system, party bureaucrats reviewed all federally appointed positions and replaced Democrats with Whig loyalists, such as Watrous.[36]

Watrous, a native of Ohio, and his twenty-one year old wife Martha set off for the new Sandy Lake Sub-Agency west of Lake Superior after he learned of his appointment. Upon his arrival at Sandy Lake, Watrous found a small community existed near the future agency compound. In addition to a few resident government employees, fur traders such as Crittenden & Lynde, David Fuller, and Julius Austrian operated trading establishments at one time or another on or near Sandy Lake. Veteran trader William Aitkin also maintained commercial ties to the area judging from trade invoices of the time.

Engraving of Reverend
John H. Pitezel

Pitezel, *Lights and Shades of
Missionary Life*

Other neighbors on the lake included Reverend Samuel Spates and his family at the Methodist Episcopal Church mission. The mission was located at the old North West Company post site on the southwest side of the lake. It was the missionaries, Spates and his supervisor Reverend John Pitezel, who later recounted events that took place at the agency in the fall of 1850. The center of the small community at Sandy Lake was the Ojibway village located at the end of Brown's Point. In 1850, the site was not as totally surrounded by water as it is today. The village was situated on the tip of a gradual bend in the shoreline. The Sandy Lake village became the focal point for a chain of events beginning with the announcement in September of 1850, that the annual payment of the annuities promised in previously concluded treaties would be distributed at the new sub-agency.[37]

Documents of the time reveal the annual payment was the intended means for bringing about the eventual removal to Minnesota Territory of those bands of Ojibway still residing on or near Lake Superior. Money and goods promised under terms of the treaties were paid in person at the agency, and each recipient was expected to sign for his share. It was believed by officials like Ramsey and Watrous that the Indians would see the wisdom of permanently relocating to Minnesota rather than continue to reside in their old locations.[38]

Ramsey wanted the payment to be completed in June, but apparently preparations had not included securing the permission of the host band. The payment was finally scheduled late in the year; and on September 23rd, 1850, Agent Watrous dispatched word to the Ojibway to assemble at Sandy Lake by October 25th. In a report written in December of 1850, Watrous underestimated the attendance since he believed, no Grand Portage, L'Anse, Lac Vieux Desert, or Wisconsin Ojibway could cover the hundreds of miles without experiencing difficulties crossing Lake Superior. The "high and contrary winds" effectively prohibited travel.[39]

The plan for the payment proceeded slowly. Food supplies, including subsistence rations for the anticipated multitude, were stored at Sandy Lake. Government invoices from the period indicate five hundred dollars worth of tobacco (worth ten to twelve cents a pound), fifteen hundred dollars worth of corn, a thousand dollars worth of flour, and fifteen hundred dollars of "mess pork" (salt pork) was on hand. The money portion of the payment, however, had not yet arrived.

On October 6th, Watrous left Sandy Lake for St. Louis to personally receive the shipment of treaty money destined for Sandy Lake. He arrived at St. Louis, Missouri, on October 21st, but no money awaited him. Instead, he was informed that Congress had not appropriated the necessary funds.

Watrous left St. Louis without the promised specie on October 26th aboard the steamer *Dr. Franklin*. Delayed by low water and accidents, the steamer did not reach St. Paul until November 13th. From there Watrous was forced to travel overland by wagon to Crow Wing, and then by canoe up the Mississippi River. As he worked his way upstream, Watrous eventually found the river frozen and had to abandon his canoe and walk the remaining distance to Sandy Lake. He arrived there on November 24th, almost a month after the scheduled treaty payment was supposed to begin. Meanwhile, conditions at Sandy Lake began to deteriorate for those Ojibway who attended the payment.[40]

The Ojibway, anticipating a short stay at the payment place, traveled lightly. Since it was customary to expect the host to provide meals and lodging, most arrived with few provisions or adequate means of shelter. Watrous later noted in his report that the Ojibway expected to be subsisted by the government. Wisconsin Territorial Governor Henry Dodge, who was familiar with the arrangements for the treaty of 1837, strongly recommended that agents responsible for payment gatherings lay in ample stores of food.[41]

The Sandy Lake Ojibway were of little help in arranging the food supply since their previous year's rice crop had been damaged by high water. In addition, many surrounding tribesmen, facing mass starvation, descended on the Methodist mission at Sandy Lake, and hoped to get some meager supplies to help them survive the winter. Unfortunately, the situation had not improved by the fall of 1850.[42]

To compound matters, the weather during October and November turned unexpectedly harsh. Those who attended the payment were forced to seek shelter within the crowded wigwams and cabins of local residents. The arrangements furnished a fruitful breeding ground for disease. Two weeks before Watrous returned, an epidemic of what was described as measles and dysentery broke out. Some observers thought the affliction was Asian Cholera, since an outbreak of that disease had occurred at Sault Sainte Marie in 1849. Regardless of the disease present at Sandy Lake, starvation, malnutrition, and epidemics were all too common on the frontier, and the conditions present at Sandy Lake proved ideal for the onset of an epidemic.[43]

Seeing a potential problem, Watrous authorized the release of additional food stored in the government warehouse. Prior to his return, the Ojibway had been reduced to a daily ration of one pound of flour and a half pound of salt pork. Watrous arranged to issue additional supplies from the government storehouse only to find that some of the flour was damaged by river water which had flooded part of the storehouse floor.[44]

To supplement existing stocks of food, Watrous purchased six thousand dollars worth of additional provisions from nearby traders. Flour was available at twenty dollars per sixty pound barrel, but mess pork was in short supply. Watrous bought pemican instead, since it was cheaper than pork and much more nutritious.

The issuance of additional provisions did not appear to have any effect on those who were ill. As the people waited for the payment to conclude, many more sickened and died. How many local residents and visitors actually perished from disease is not known, but estimates range from one hundred fifty to as high as four hundred. The plowed fields around the village were turned into a graveyard. As the days wore on, the ground froze, and the residents resorted to digging shallow graves inside their wigwams to take advantage of the soft earth and then moved the structures to new sites after the burials were completed.[45]

Few eyewitness accounts of the disaster which struck the Ojibway at Sandy Lake have survived. Some who wrote about the calamity, such as Reverend John Pitezel, arrived after the epidemic had run its course. Pitezel noted evidence of a disaster as he approached the village:

> All over the cleared land graves were to be seen in every direction, for miles distant, from Sandy Lake; they were to be found in the woods. some, it is not known how many, were interred by their friends on their way home.

Pitezel continued his graphic description of events:

On my way to Sandy Lake I saw a number of those recent graves, and, in some places, there were remaining racks constructed for the support of the sick. The evidence of a terrible calamity every-where met the eye.[46]

Before leaving Sandy Lake, tribal leaders held a council and requested ammunition for hunting in order to supplement their rations. Watrous and Captain J. B. Todd of the 6th U.S. Infantry asked trader Clement Beaulieu to provide powder and shot sufficient for the Indians. Beaulieu was apprehensive of ever being paid, but eventually complied with the request and furnished six hundred and twenty-six dollars worth of gunpowder and shot for distribution.[47]

Finally, on December 3rd, 1850, the Ojibway left Sandy Lake for their distant homes. Leaving a number of their sick to be tended at Sandy Lake, the remainder departed quickly over land, as the rivers were frozen. Canoes that had been left at the mouth of the East Savanna River were totally useless. As the homeward bound Ojibway moved through the snow-covered landscape with their burdens, many continued to drop out of the line of march. Reverend Pitezel remarked:

...there were instances in which the sick were unable to accompany their relatives, and were left alone to perish in the wilderness. One man, it is said, importuned his wife to remain with him and not suffer him to die alone. She replied that if she should remain she must die too, and thus left him.[48]

The retreat from Sandy Lake was not a forced march in the sense of people being driven at the point of a bayonet, but something far more insidious. A persistent killer stalked the Ojibway, and their desire to escape its suffocating grasp drove them, as in times past, to flee to their respective homes. To what extent the disease followed them home is problematical since no further record has been found to show the spread of an epidemic resulting from the incident at Sandy Lake or what happened there following the payment. Pitezel mentioned an outbreak of scarlet fever occurred shortly after the payment which undoubtedly resulted in more casualties.[49]

There has been some discussion as to exactly what caused the outbreak, and several reasons have been given including the timing of the payment late in the year. It seems reasonable to conclude, however, that any large gathering in that era which included crowded or unsanitary conditions brought with it the real prospect of an outbreak of some highly communicable disease. In fact, a treaty negotiation at Prairie du Chien in 1825 was marred by a similar outbreak of disease which killed a number of those attending. At the time, conditions such as overcrowding, lack of knowledge as to how diseases are transmitted, and an absence of basic hygiene contributed to numerous outbreaks of disease in both isolated areas and overcrowded cities throughout the country.

Various claims as to the cause for the disease, including tainted food, have been advanced. It is significant that most of the types of rations that were available at Sandy Lake would have required preparation. For example, it is difficult to conceive that the existence of damaged flour alone would have caused illness since its condition was clearly noticeable and certainly it was not eaten raw. Likewise, the heavily salted pork would have been thoroughly soaked in water to remove the excess salt for palatability. One would think that in the process of preparing the flour or meat any spoiled product would have been detected.[50]

Regardless of the specific cause of the epidemic, the tragedy that occurred in 1850 convinced the Ojibway residing on or near Lake Superior not to return to Sandy Lake. In spite of the disaster that occurred and the widespread reluctance of the Ojibway to attend payments there in the future, plans were approved by the government in the spring of 1851 to relocate the Lake Superior Ojibway. This time supply depots were established at La Pointe, Fond du Lac, and at Sandy Lake. Mindful of the lack of provisions the Ojibway brought to the previous payment gathering, large quantities of foodstuffs were assembled by the government.

Sandy Lake monument commemorating those who perished from the epidemic during the annual payment in 1850.
Photo by Larry Luukkonen

Simultaneously, the Sandy Lake Sub-Agency was upgraded to the status of a full agency known as the "Chippewa Agency," and John Watrous received a promotion in spite of a badly botched job. For their part, the Michigan and Wisconsin Ojibway wanted nothing further to do with Sandy Lake, even if it meant forfeiting their annuities. Undoubtedly the adverse publicity garnered from events at Sandy Lake in the fall of 1850 influenced subsequent decisions.[51]

In the summer of 1852, President Millard Fillmore rescinded the removal order directed against certain tribes in Michigan and Wisconsin. At the same time the Chippewa Agency was relocated near the village of Crow Wing. Ultimately it took an epidemic that no one could possibly have foreseen to counteract the removal order. The concept of concentrating the Indian population on a large reservation, however, did not die as a result of the tragedy at Sandy Lake.[52]

If the Indian Department in the nineteenth century increasingly suffered from neglect and incompetence, it was certainly not unique among government agencies then. A leading cause was the rampant political patronage system practiced by all parties during the era. The popular notion that "to the victor belong the spoils" contributed its own peculiar woes by insuring that party hacks would be regularly appointed to government positions regardless of qualifications or experience.

As for John Watrous, his career as an Indian Agent ended with a Democratic victory in the election of 1852. He was swept out of office by the broom of political patronage just as quickly as he had been brought in. Watrous settled near the head of Lake Superior, and reportedly platted the townsite of "Clifton." It was not long before he once again turned to a political career. Although known as a staunch Whig, he suffered a miraculous transformation and became a Democrat. Watrous, elected as a representative to the first state legislature, with state senator and pioneer blacksmith Reuben B. Carlton, represented St. Louis County and the scattered settlements along Lake Superior. Watrous was later appointed as Receiver at the United States Land Office established at Buchanan (modern Knife River, Minnesota) and served in that capacity until January of 1860. He later moved to California and died there in 1897.[53]

Unfortunately the story of the Sandy Lake Sub-Agency and the tragedy that befell many Ojibway in the fall of 1850 has faded with the passage of time. The location of the agency itself, like the shallow graves along the Northwest Trail, has been forgotten.

Three Decades of Transition (1837-1867)

Efforts to relocate the Ojibway still living in parts of Michigan and Wisconsin between 1850 and 1851 were unsuccessful largely due to the timing and the epidemic that struck those who attended the first payment. There is much more to the story, however, than the abortive efforts to establish a reservation at Sandy Lake. While removal of some Indian populations from Michigan and Wisconsin were abandoned, the process of consolidating the Indian population remaining within Minnesota Territory, including those permanently residing along the Northwest Trail, continued unabated.

The period from 1837 to 1867 saw the fruition of a policy which grew out of the early efforts at Indian removal. The policy can be summarized by four words: relocate, congregate, educate and assimilate. Its gradual implementation is reflected in the provisions of a series of treaties involving land cessions. Government officials reasoned once the Ojibway were gathered into permanent villages, government services could be provided more efficiently. As for the children, they could be educated through manual labor boarding schools run by the government or religious groups. The goal of the policy was to educate and eventually assimilate the tribal population. A review of the series of treaties with the Ojibway from 1837 to 1867 shows a clear picture of what gradually transpired.

The first Chippewa or Ojibway land cession in Minnesota was accomplished by a treaty concluded at the mouth of the St. Peter's River in 1837. In return for relinquishing any claim they had to certain lands, the Ojibway were assured they could continue to use the land for domestic pursuits such as hunting and fishing, much as they had always done in the past. In addition, people affected by the treaty received an annuity of both specie and goods. Furthermore, a provision in the treaty allowed for the employment of farmers, blacksmiths, and carpenters, as noted previously. Teachers were provided largely by missionary societies.[54]

The government employees were to teach the Ojibway useful trades and perform work for them. There was no land set aside for reservations for the Ojibway in the treaty of 1837, but the provision for various services, mentioned in the text of the treaty, carried with it the notion of consolidation. The services were not easily moved from place to place although some of the farmers, blacksmiths and carpenters were expected to rotate among various established villages. The teachers, however, were most effective if the population was sedentary. In practice, the traditional seasonal activities repeatedly interrupted the children's education. Ten years after the conclusion of the first treaty at the St. Peter's River, two additional land cessions were concluded.

The Chippewa Treaty of Fond du Lac, concluded on August 2nd, 1847, provided for the second Ojibway land cession. The treaty included both the Chippewa of the Mississippi and of Lake Superior. The area in question was bounded by the Mississippi, Crow Wing, and Long Prairie rivers and the Chippewa-Sioux boundary as far as the Watab River. In return for their agreement, the Lake Superior bands received seventeen thousand dollars in specie. The Mississippi bands likewise received seventeen thousand dollars in specie plus an annual payment of one thousand dollars for forty-six years.[55]

The third land cession was represented by the Chippewa Treaty of Leech Lake, concluded on August 21st, 1847. This treaty between the government and the Pillager band of Ojibway resulted in the cession of certain lands in exchange for an annual supply of trade goods for the next five years. In addition, at the first payment the government was to furnish as a present, two hundred warranted beaver traps and seventy-five Northwest guns (trade muskets specially manufactured for the Indian hunters).[56]

The 1847 treaties came at almost the same time and were meant to address questions with the boundary separating Indian lands from those formerly ceded by the treaty concluded in 1837. The treaties not only brought the frontier line closer to the southern edge of the Northwest Trail but also effectively removed areas formerly part of the contested ground where Ojibway from Sandy Lake were accustomed to hunt buffalo.

In 1853, Superintendent of Indian Affairs for Minnesota Territory, D. B. Herriman, recommended a treaty be concluded with the Ojibway for the timber and mineral lands lying east of the Mississippi River. Accordingly, in the following year the fourth land cession of the Ojibway occurred in the Chippewa Treaty at La Pointe, which was ratified on September 30th, 1854.[57]

The 1854 treaty is significant since it was the first to establish specific reservations, including one for the Fond du Lac Band. The reservation's metes and bounds description, however, did not include the band's village at the foot of the

Grand Portage of the St. Louis. Instead, the point of beginning for the reservation was located several miles up the St. Louis River at the Paw-paw-sco-me-me-tig islands. The boundary ran west from the island, then north along a line that eventually intersected the St. Louis River, then down that stream to the point of beginning.[58]

Upon the completion of a survey of the reservation boundary, it was found that the description used to delineate the area of the reservation did not match the area intended. Worst of all, a village at Perch Lake was actually several miles due south of the proposed boundary line. An adjustment was proposed and approved by President Buchanan to extend the southern boundary to include the village.[59]

What had once been the main village of the Fond du Lac Band had to be abandoned since it was outside the boundary of the new reservation, and the residents relocated upstream. Fields and gardens that had formerly been used by the village residents were subsequently opened to purchase by settlers who could file a claim on the property once the treaty was ratified.

A fifth land cession in 1855, known as the Chippewa Treaty of Washington, included a reservation for the Sandy Lake Band. The boundary of the Sandy Lake Reservation included the land surrounding the lake and for some distance south. The reservation included not only Sandy Lake and its resources but also Great Wild Rice Lake located southeast with its rich rice beds, fishery, and birch groves. Although the Sandy Lake residents did not have to relocate like their neighbors at Fond du Lac, the size of their reservation was vastly smaller than that of Fond du Lac. The Gull Lake, Rabbit Lake, Pokegama Lake, and Rice Lake reservations were likewise much smaller than Fond du Lac.[60]

It is not clear from simply reading the text of the various treaties how the exact sizes of the respective reservations were determined. It appears that the Fond du Lac Reservation may have been larger due to the fact that the area was covered in many places by swamps and pine groves, which were regarded as being less productive both in terms of agriculture and in the amount of game, fish, wild rice, and maple sugar compared to lands farther west. The opinion that the region near Lake Superior was essentially a sterile country had been repeated by numerous travelers and may have influenced the decision concerning the amount of land to include in the reservation.[61]

The respective populations of the various bands were also a factor that may have been considered. It is clear, however, that the size of the individual reservations did not correspond to the historic significance or primacy of the Fond du Lac and Sandy Lake villages, which formed the heart of each reservation created by the terms of the treaties of 1854 and 1855.

The treaties of 1854 and 1855 were the first to attempt to address the problem posed by the introduction of liquor. Article 7 of the 1854 Treaty not only prohibited liquor on the reservations created by the treaty but also stated none could be sold to Indians on the lands ceded by the treaty. This provision was substantially repeated in the Treaty of 1855. In spite of the best intentions of those who drew up the treaty to remove liquor from the newly created Indian reservations, the whiskey peddlers avoided the prohibition by simply giving liquor to the Indians as an inducement to trade rather than selling it.[62]

Although both the people of Fond du Lac and Sandy Lake were included within the new reservations, Minnesota Territorial officials were already committed to a policy of further concentrating the Indian population on a large reservation in the northern part of the state instead of maintaining the numerous smaller reservations. Less than a decade after the reservations were created, most of the smaller reservations, including the Sandy Lake Reservation and nearby Rice Lake (included as part of Sandy Lake Reservation) were abolished by provisions of the seventh land cession, known as the Chippewa Treaty at Washington, May 7th, 1864. At Sandy Lake, only a single section of land was reserved for Chief Misqua-dace under the provisions of the treaty.[63]

Following the abolition of the Sandy Lake Reservation by the Treaty of 1864, the Ojibway population there tended to migrate toward Lake Pokegama, White Oak Point on the Mississippi, and Leech Lake, but, contrary to popular accounts, not everyone left the Sandy Lake area. There were simply not that many settlers in the area to exert significant pressure on the local Indian population to move. Also, there is ample evidence that those Ojibway who remained provided a valuable source of labor.

In 1855, the territory around Sandy Lake was opened for commercial log-

Sandy Lake Ojibway in canoe c. 1910. In spite of the treaty of 1864, which abolished their reservation, the Sandy Lake Ojibway have maintained a constant presence in the area. McGregor Public Library

ging. For the next several decades, local residents of Sandy Lake were recruited to work on the log drives or supplied area logging camps with fresh game on a regular basis. Furthermore, the beginning of construction of a transcontinental railroad west from Northern Pacific Junction (Carlton, Minnesota) in 1870 provided additional employment. In the 1890s, construction of the Sandy Lake Dam by the United States Army Corps of Engineers employed many Sandy Lake Ojibway. After the turn of the twentieth century, the same structure was upgraded and again required the labor of local Ojibway.[64]

The Fond du Lac Reservation remained intact following the 1864 Treaty, but an act of Congress in May of 1872 sought to have the reservation lands appraised and sold. This act failed when it was discovered the residents of the reservation had not approved the measure, but the idea of selling off "surplus" reservation land lingered. The passage of the General Allotment Act of 1887 was closely followed by the Chippewa Agreement of 1889, which included the tenth land cession. The last treaty included language ceding all title and interest in the Fond du Lac Reservation and all the rights in such parts of the Red Lake Reservation as were not needed for allotment to the United States.[65]

The creation of the allotment system broke up the traditional tribal organization. Instead, the new legislation encouraged individuals to become assimilated by acquiring an enumerated tract of public domain offered by the government and developing a self-sustaining homestead. To prevent abuse of the allotment system, the piece of land that was selected could not be sold and remained in the family. The allotment system and the goal of assimilation of the Indian into the general population remained in effect until 1934.

Charlie Grasshopper resting on what some refer to as "Indian Portage," c. 1910. Charlie held an eighty acre allottment north of Sandy Lake, in what is now Savanna Portage State Park, where he maintained a sugar camp.
McGregor Public Library

The policy of gathering the native population on reservations, educating them, and then assimilating them by making them self-sufficient yeoman farmers was undertaken ostensibly for the well-being of the Indians. Unfortunately, the policy also had negative effects not imagined by its various proponents. Not the least of these consequences was the gradual loss of the history and the language, which are the very roots of the cultural identity of any population. Policy makers took no interest in the history of the inhabitants of Fond du Lac and Sandy Lake. For example, the abolition of the Sandy Lake Reservation, after a very brief existence, was done without any recognition of the historical importance of that location to the Ojibway. The village of Fond du Lac suffered a similar fate in 1854. Sadly, the story of the people and the villages which once anchored each end of the historic Northwest Trail, has gone largely unnoticed.

In spite of events, the respective populations of the earliest footholds of the Ojibway in Minnesota remained as determined as any other people to retain their identity and dignity. From the beginning, when their villages were the spearhead of Ojibway expansion in the Northwest, neither band has ever given up in the face of adversity. Today there are many reminders of the presence of the Ojibway. Hopefully, they will continue to be remembered for their important contributions to our collective history.

Chapter 11 - An All Too Brief and Tragic History

Notes

1. Edwin James (ed.), *A Narrative of the Captivity and Adventures of John Tanner (U. S. Interpreter at the Saut de Sainte Marie) During Thirty years Residence Among the Indians* (1830; reprint ed., Minneapolis, 1956), p. xxiv.

2. The conflict between harvesting furs for trade and providing adequate subsistence for a trapper's family is a major theme of Harold Hickerson: "Ethnohistory of Mississippi Bands and Pillager and Winnibigoshish Bands of Chippewa," in *Chippewa Indians II* (New York, 1974), and "Ethnohistory of the Chippewa of Lake Superior," in *Chippewa Indians III* (New York, 1974). See also, Harold Hickerson, *The Chippewa and Their neighbors: A Study in Ethnohistory* (1970; reprint ed., Prospect Heights, Illinois, 1988).

3. The prime beaver pelt, known in the trade as a "plus" or "plue," is mentioned frequently as the standard of value. For a schedule of relative values of other furs compared to beaver (as of 1839) see Lucius Lyon to Commissioner of Indian Affairs T. Hartley Crawford, December 16th, 1839, in John Porter Bloom (ed.), *The Territorial Papers of the United States: The Territory of Wisconsin, 1839-1848*, vols. 27-28 (Washington, D.C., 1975), vol. 28, pp. 91-98 (hereafter cited as Bloom, *Territorial Papers*, vol. 28). For a summary of the fur trade see Carolyn Gilman, *Where Two Worlds Meet: The Great Lakes Fur Trade* (St. Paul, 1982).

4. Beaver notes and tokens were the first signs of a shift from a barter economy to a cash economy. These articles are described by Grace Lee Nute in "Beaver Money," *Minnesota History*, vol. 9, no. 3 (September, 1928), pp. 287-288. Similar tokens and paper notes were still in circulation in the early twentieth century. A photograph showing specimens of both can be found in Philip H. Godsell, *Arctic Trader: An Account of Twenty Years With The Hudson's Bay Company* (New York, 1934), photograph facing page 32; Gilman, *Two Worlds Meet*, p. 55; and in Charles E. Hanson, "Trade Notes and Tokens," *Museum of the Fur Trade Quarterly* (Spring, 1968), pp. 1-5.

5. Charles Borup to Ramsey Crooks, March 13th, 1839. American Fur Company Papers, New York Historical Society. Microfilm copies in the collections of the Minnesota Historical Society, (hereafter cited as AFC Papers).

6. Allan Morrison, "History of the Fur Trade in the Northwest" unpublished manuscript, n.d., Minnesota Historical Society collections, pp. 16-17.

7. The treatment meted out to competitors is reflected in the very title of David Lavender's work. See *The Fist in the Wilderness* (1964; reprint ed., Albuquerque, 1979), p. 418.

8. Arthur Woodward, *The Denominators of the Fur Trade: An Anthology of Writings on the Material Culture of the Fur Trade* (Pasadena, 1970), p. 116. In fact, some of the articles noted by Woodward were still being offered for sale during the author's travels in the Arctic in the 1990s.

9. The events which culminated in the end of the American Fur Company are summarized in Lavender, *Fist in the Wilderness*, pp. 418-419.

10. James L. Clayton, "The Growth and Economic Significance of the American Fur Trade, 1790-1890," in *Minnesota History*, vol. 40, no. 4 (Winter, 1966), pp. 210-220.

11. Charles H. Oakes to Ramsay Crooks, February 18th, 1842, AFC Papers.

12. Hickerson, *Chippewa Indians II*, p. 271.

13. James (ed.), *Narrative of Captivity*, pp. 262-263.

14. Hickerson, *Chippewa Indians II*, p. 271.

15. Philip P. Mason (ed.), *Schoolcraft's Expedition to Lake Itasca* (East Lansing, 1993), p. 323.

16. Bardwell's nomination as blacksmith is found in a letter from Robert Stuart to Commissioner Crawford, dated June 2nd, 1843, in Bloom, *Territorial Papers*, vol. 28, p. 552. (see also n. 15 for information on the nomination of Clark and Smith).

17. Ibid., pp. 72 and 648-650, for James P. Hays' letter to Commissioner Crawford, August 16th, 1844, wherein he explains the firing of Clark; and letter from Wisconsin Territorial Governor, James Duane Doty to Crawford dated February 23rd, 1844, discussing Clark's report on the use of liquor in the fur trade.

18. Julius T. Clark, "Reminiscences of Hole-in-the-Day," *Collections of the State Historical Society of Wisconsin*, vol. 5 (1869), pp. 378-386.

19. For an informative account of frontier gunsmithing see T. M. Hamilton, *Firearms on the*

Frontier: Guns at Fort Michilimackinac 1715-1781, Reports in Mackinac History and Archaeology, no. 5 (Williamston, Michigan, 1976).

20. For the text of various treaties containing the provision for farmers, blacksmiths, and carpenters see Charles J. Kappler (ed.), *Indian Treaties, 1778-1883* (1911; reprint ed., New York, 1973).

21. Government appointments are mentioned in a letter from Wisconsin Territorial Governor Tallmadge to Commissioner Crawford, February 10th, 1845, in Bloom, *Territorial Papers*, vol. 28, pp. 792-793.

22. "Statement of all persons employed within the Sandy Lake Sub-Agency in the quarter ending December 31st, 1850," in National Archives Record Group 75. Records of the Bureau of Indian Affairs. National Archives Microcopy 234, Letters Received by the Office of Indian Affairs, no. 102, (hereafter cited as NAM. 234 Letters Received OIA).

23. See letter from Wisconsin Territorial Governor Henry Dodge to Commissioner of Indian Affairs, Medill, in Bloom, *Territorial Papers*, vol. 28, p. 944, n. 25.

24. For a summary of Reuben Carlton's career see Larry Luukkonen, *Reuben B. Carlton: Frontier Blacksmith and Visionary* (Cloquet, Minnesota, 2005).

25. Paul Beaulieu's report is in Bloom, *Territorial Papers*, vol. 28, p. 1107.

26. See n. 22 above.

27. The re-establishment of the Chippewa Agency to "a favorable site" on Crow Wing River near Gull Lake is discussed in Newton H. Winchell, *The Aborigines of Minnesota* (St. Paul, 1911), p. 650.

28. Evan A. Hart, "A Frontier Smithy in Wisconsin Territory," *Wisconsin Magazine of History*, vol. 40, no. 4 (Summer, 1957), pp. 261-269.

29. See "Estimate for Removal of Sub-Agency Existing Temporary Buildings..." in NAM 234, Letters Received OIA, no. 120.

30. Alexander Ramsey's report can be found in *Senate Executive Document No. 1* (31st Congress, 2nd Session) serial 587, p. 94. Report of the Commissioner of Indian Affairs; No. 13, Minnesota Superintendency, St. Paul, October 21st, 1850, p. 185. An abbreviated version is available in Winchell, *Aborigines*, pp. 644-648.

31. Ibid., p. 650.

32. Outside of official reports and correspondence, few contemporary accounts exist concerning the Sandy Lake Sub-Agency. More recent accounts refer chiefly to the writings of Reverend John H. Pitezel for details. See especially John H. Pitezel, *Lights and Shades of Missionary Life: Containing Travels, Sketches, Incidents, and Missionary Reports* (Cincinnati, 1861). Unfortunately, Pitezel served as an itinerant mission supervisor and was not a resident at Sandy Lake except for brief visits. The resident missionaries, such as Samuel Spate, left very fragmentary records. A brief but useful summary of events at Sandy Lake for the period 1850 to 1853, is found in John Nelson Davidson, *In Unnamed Wisconsin: Studies in the History of the Region Between Lake Michigan and the Mississippi* (Milwaukee, 1895), pp. 168-169. Winchell, *Aborigines*, p. 649. The idea of a large reservation for the Ojibway was discussed by Ramsey in 1849, prior to the creation of the Sandy Lake Sub-Agency and in his report on the treaty with the Red Lake and Pembina Ojibway concluded in 1851.

33. Ibid., pp. 641-643 and 649. The idea of concentrating the Ojibway on a single large reservation antedates the appointment of Ramsey as Territorial Governor of Minnesota. In 1842 the Indian Agent at La Pointe, Daniel P. Bushnell, recommended the relocation of all the Ojibway east of the Mississippi. His initial recommendation was followed by similar sentiments from Indian Agent James P. Hayes in 1846 and again in 1848.

34. See Alexander Ramsey to John S. Livermore, March 2nd, 1850; and Livermore to Ramsey, March 26th, 1850, in NAM 234, Letters Received OIA. Alexander Ramsey's comments regarding the Pillagers can be found in his annual report for 1850.

35 Several petitions were circulated against Indian removal to Sandy Lake including one from Reverend J. B. Treat, representing the American Board of Commissioners for Foreign Missions, dated January 21st, 1851; and one from the Wisconsin Assembly dated February 7th, 1851. Copies of both can be found in NAM 234, Letters Received OIA.

36. See Elisha Whittlesey to Commissioner of Indian Affairs Luke Lea, November 16th, 1850, in

NAM 234, Letters Received OIA, for John Watrous' appointment as Indian Sub-Agent to the new post at Sandy Lake. Details of Watrous' career can be found in J. R. Carey, "History of Duluth and of St. Louis County to the Year 1870, *Collections of the Minnesota Historical Society*, vol. 9 (1898), p. 250; and Dwight E. Woodbridge and John S. Pardee, *History of Duluth and St. Louis County, Past and Present*, 2 vols. (Chicago, 1910).

37.   The location of the Methodist mission on the site of the old North West Company post is discussed in chap. 7 above.

38.   For further discussion of the reasons for the removal project consult, Edmund Jefferson Danziger, Jr., *The Chippewas of Lake Superior* (Norman, 1978); Edmund Jefferson Danziger, Jr., "They Would Not Be Moved: The Chippewa Treaty of 1854," in *Minnesota History*, vol. 43, no. 1 (Spring, 1973), pp. 175-185; and James A. Clifton, "Wisconsin Death March: Explaining the Extremes in Old Northwest Indian Removal," a reprint from *Transactions of the Wisconsin Academy of Sciences, Arts and Letters*, vol. 75 (1987), pp. 1-39.

39.   Ramsey and Watrous apparently believed the Ojibway would stay at Sandy Lake rather than risk the rigors of the return trip home. See Watrous' report to Ramsey dated Sandy Lake, December 10th, 1850, in NAM 234, Letters Received OIA.

40.   Ibid.

41.   The importance of timely distribution of provisions and tobacco was mentioned in a letter from Wisconsin Territorial Governor Henry Dodge to Commissioner of Indian Affairs Harris, dated July 6th, 1838, in Bloom, (ed.), *Territorial Papers*, vol. 27, *The Territory of Wisconsin, Executive Journal, 1836-1848*, p. 1030.

42.   Ramsey, although aware of the failure of the Ojibway's rice crop for two previous years and the general scarcity of game near Sandy Lake, nonetheless persisted with his plan to relocate all Ojibway east of the Mississippi to Sandy Lake (see n. 30 above for a reference to his annual report for 1850).

43.   No one is certain exactly what diseases were present at the payment in 1850. The best information indicates there were three epidemics in succession: dysentery, measles, and scarlet fever. The last disease occurred after the payment concluded.

44.   The man who was supposed to be overseeing the removal effort, Sandy Lake trader Charles H. Oakes, resigned his position on January 10th, 1850. See Oakes to Watrous, January 10th, 1850, in NAM 234, Letters Received OIA.

45.   Pitezel, *Lights and Shades*, p. 300; see also "Extract from a Letter of Reverend Sherman Hall, dated La Pointe, Lake Superior, December 30th, 1850," in NAM 234, Letter Received OIA. Pitezel believed about two hundred Ojibway perished as a result of the delayed payment. Hall estimated the casualties at about one hundred. He claimed at least seventy or eighty were buried at Sandy Lake.

46.   Pitezel, *Lights and Shades*, p. 301.

47.   NAM 234, Letters Received OIA, includes an invoice from C.H. Beaulieu dated St. Paul, April 6th, 1851, for one hundred and fifty pounds of gunpowder and two hundred and fifty pounds of shot.

48.   Pitezel, *Lights and Shades*, p. 300.

49.   Helen Hornbeck Tanner (ed.), *Atlas of Great Lakes Indian History* (Norman, 1986), cites several epidemics which occurred at Sandy Lake, but does not mention any incident in 1850.

50.   The only documented complaint regarding the rations distributed during the 1850 payment concerned some spoiled flour.

51.   See Davidson, *Unnamed Wisconsin*, pp. 168-169, for the reaction to the payment at Sandy Lake. Note especially Reverend E. P. Wheeler's remarks concerning the existence of an "Indian Ring" and his accusation of rampant corruption.

52.   Hickerson, *Chippewa Indians II*, pp. 250-251, cites various reasons for the failure of the removal plan at Sandy Lake.

53.   John R. Carey, "History of Duluth, and of St. Louis County to the year 1870," *Collections of the Minnesota Historical Society*, vol. 9 (1898), p. 250, provides details of Watrous' later career in Minnesota.

54.   Kappler (ed.), *Indian Treaties*, pp. 491-493. Article IV describes the services provided by the

government. See Winchell, *Aborigines of Minnesota*, part 8, chap. 2, pp. 636-702, for an historical sketch of the Ojibway from 1837 to 1889.

55.   Kappler (ed.), *Indian Treaties*, pp. 567-569.

56.   Ibid., pp. 569-570.

57.   Ibid., pp. 648-652.

58.   Chrysostum Verwyst, "A Short Account of the Fond du Lac Mission," *Acta et Dicta*, vol. 4, no. 2 (July, 1914), p. 236, mentions a mission at "Papashkominitigong" which means a "treeless island in a river." See chap. 2, n. 21 above, regarding *Paw-paw-sco-me-me-tig* or Posey Island. The Fond du Lac mission was located on a bluff overlooking Paw-paw-sco-me-me-tig island.

59.   Winchell, *Aborigines of Minnesota*, p. 681.

60.   Kappler (ed.), *Indian Treaties,* pp. 685-690. For a map showing the various reservations see Charles C. Royce, *Indian Land Cessions in the United States*, in Eighteenth Annual Report of the U.S. Bureau of American Ethnology to the Secretary of the Smithsonian Institution 1896-1897 by J. [John] W. [Wesley] Powell, 2 vols. (Washington D.C., 1899), vol. 2, Map MN 2, plate CXLI. See also Winchell, *Aborigines of Minnesota*, p. 616, for a copy of the map by Royce showing the reservations set aside for the various bands in Minnesota.

61.   Hickerson, *Chippewa Indians III*, pp. 129-144, noted large sections along both sides of the St. Louis River in the northwestern corner of the Fond du Lac Reservation consisted of swamp lands.

62   Kappler (ed.), *Indian Treaties*, p. 650.

63.   Ibid., pp. 862-865; see also Royce, *Indian Land Cessions*, pp. 830-831.

64.   The Ojibway of Sandy Lake, like their counterparts at the Fond du Lac Reservation, found employment in harvesting timber and driving logs on area rivers.

65.   See Royce, *Indian Land Cessions*, vol. 2, p. 856; and Winchell, *Aborigines of Minnesota*, pp. 678-679, regarding the sale of surplus land and timber harvesting. For reservation boundaries see Kappler (ed.), *Indian Treaties*, p. 648; Royce, *Indian Land Cessions*. Lingering concern over the boundary issue was noted in Winchell, *Aborigines of Minnesota*, p. 681.

A Sandy Lake Ojibway man and canoe filled with wild rice.
McGregor Public Library

A group of Sandy Lake Ojibway are pictured outside
their birch-bark wigwam around 1910.
McGregor Public Library

Scene on the St. Louis River looking south. At the left, loads of logs wait to be dumped into the river for sorting and storage before being turned into useful products by the mills in Cloquet. In the background is the Posey Island railroad bridge, and on the far right the clearings and buildings of the Fond du Lac Reservation settlement dating from 1854. Carlton County Historical Society

Chapter 12 ✂ Old Routes and New Ways

"Just as the acquisition of 1854 was a miners' proposition,
so that of 1855 was a lumbermen's."[1]

Such was the observation of the Ojibway land cessions of 1854 and
1855 by the noted historian William Watts Folwell. Judging by what
transpired following their ratification, the treaties also affected not only
the people living along the Northwest Trail but also the future of the
trail itself. With the opening of the land to settlement, and a large influx
of population, more and better means of transportation were required.
The Northwest Trail played an important role in the determination of
the future routes of roads and railroads.

Merchants, Miners, and Lumbermen

The news of first one then another Ojibway land cession in 1854 and 1855
was greeted with enthusiasm on the frontier. Townsites appeared almost
overnight all along the Northwest Trail. For example, the town of "Palmburg" was
platted in 1856 by Benjamin C. Borden at the western end of the trail on the site
of William Aitkin's Sandy Lake trading post. The town existed only on paper and
was typical of the type of development that accompanied the opening of frontier
land to settlement.

Midway along the trail, a three hundred and twenty acre site named
"Cloquette" was founded at the confluence of the Cloquet and St. Louis rivers.
Articles of incorporation were filed in St. Louis County for the town of Cloquette,
but no further evidence in the form of a plat map or other suitable documentation has been discovered which provides additional information about this particular community.[2] The town existed only on paper and should not be confused
with the later plat (1883) of the village of Cloquet farther downstream. Cloquette
may have been a paper town, but its very creation is a testament to the spirit of
the time.

The area of greatest development was on the eastern end of the trail with
fourteen townsites being platted and recorded in 1856. The new towns with
names such as Oneota, Fremont, Portland, Endion, and Belleville sprouted along
the cutover hillside overlooking the St. Louis River and Superior Bay. A short distance out on Minnesota Point was another new village named Duluth. These new
townsites joined the established villages of Fond du Lac, at the head of navigation
on the St. Louis River, and Superior City, near the mouth of the St. Louis River.
People from all walks of life invested in these and other fledgling communities
which appeared to offer the promise of wealth. Reverend Ely, who had left the
mission field in 1849 and later moved to St. Paul, returned to the head of Lake
Superior in 1855 and settled in the new town of Oneota, where he invested in
town lots and a sawmill.[3]

Persons who were already residing in the country or along the fringes of settlement, such as government surveyor turned fur trader, George Riley Stuntz, welcomed the new settlers and merchants who flocked to the area. Most of the new arrivals came in anticipation of the development of mineral wealth thought to be located in northeast Minnesota. Under the guise of fishing excursions, some adventuresome folk even scouted potential mine locations along the northern shore of Lake Superior.[4]

The enthusiasm which initially accompanied news of the opening of vast areas in northern Minnesota to settlement quickly vanished with the onset of a financial crisis known as the Panic of 1857. Faced with a sudden financial disaster in the country, panic spread rapidly throughout the West. During the weeks and months that followed the first news of a business crisis, there were few accounts of anyone traveling over the Northwest Trail. Living conditions in the infant settlements at the head of Lake Superior were so bad that over seventy-five percent of the population left the area. Those few who remained either hoped for some relief from the harsh economic conditions or simply did not have sufficient money to buy passage out of the wilderness on the few ships that still called at Superior, Wisconsin. Pioneer settler John A. Bardon wrote:

No money, no work, no lumbering, no market, no railroads. Superior and Duluth were entirely isolated–two hundred miles by land from St. Paul and Minneapolis and five hundred miles by boat to Detroit.[5]

The economic slump caused by the Panic of 1857 continued into succeeding years and was followed by the outbreak of the American Civil War in the spring of 1861. One of the original settlers on the site of what is now the city of Duluth, Minnesota, Mr. Robert Jefferson, determined to leave the city and enlist in the First Minnesota Volunteer Infantry Regiment mustering at Fort Snelling. Jefferson, who had the distinction of having built the first frame dwelling in Duluth, could not afford the thirty-five dollar fare to ride the stage coach over the recently constructed Military Road connecting Superior with St. Paul and the Mississippi River. Instead, Jefferson with his wife and infant child left by canoe on a journey over the Northwest Trail to Sandy Lake, then down the Mississippi River to Fort Snelling. He was later killed in the war.[6]

Although the depression following the financial panic of 1857 and the outbreak of the Civil War seriously curtailed interest in traveling to the new settlements at the head of Lake Superior, there was apparently a continual interest in the mineral resources of Northeastern Minnesota dating back to the French regime in Canada. Reports of natural copper deposits along the shore of Lake Superior led many to search for further evidence of minerals, not only by the lake, but also in the hinterland.[7]

Neither the French nor British governments followed up on reports of known copper deposits as noted in Chapter 8. By the early 1800s word of the existence of copper outcroppings was sufficiently well-known. Officials of the newly independent United States were keenly aware of the potential existence of deposits of copper. Beginning with the treaty signed at the Grand Council at Fond du Lac in 1826, the government sought to acquire title to and mine any copper deposits located in the Northwest Territory.[8]

Geological surveys of Lake Superior began in 1820 with Governor Cass' Northwestern Expedition. Additional surveys such as performed by Doctor Joseph Norwood in 1847-1848, not only mapped the country but sought to uncover any evidence of important mineral deposits. A further series of geological surveys leading up to an extensive geological report in the 1890s conclusively documented the existence of mineral resources long-suspected to lie beneath the surface.

In 1865, reports of gold outcroppings on Lake Vermillion were enough to create a gold rush to that remote location. At first the Northwest Trail furnished the quickest route by water to the gold fields. Prospectors in search of El Dorado followed the St. Louis River north from Fond du Lac, past the mouth of the Cloquet and Whiteface rivers, to the height of land, then by portage to Pike River, which flowed into Lake Vermilion.[9] In 1866, a substantial road was finally built from Duluth to Lake Vermillion to accommodate the heavy influx of prospectors, but by the time it was completed rumors of any wealth to be found evaporated. Very little gold was ever found, but the existence of iron deposits were frequently noted.

The gold seekers were not the only people aware of the iron. Surveyors trying to map the countryside complained about the iron deposits which caused what they described as "a great deal of local attraction" in their compasses. Awareness of the existence of iron deposits gradually led to systematic searches to see if commercial quantities of the metal existed in the remote interior of Minnesota. The fate of one early resident along the Northwest Trail also lends an element of mystery to the first search for minerals.

North Albert Posey, commonly known as N.A. Posey or Joe Posey, was a little-known figure who, according to some accounts, became embroiled in a tragic situation involved with the search for iron. Posey, like Reuben Carlton, was a government blacksmith for the Ojibway. He not only served both the Fond du Lac and Bois Forte bands, but also operated a trading post out of one end of his cedar log house. Local accounts indicate Posey supposedly knew of the location of rich iron ore outcroppings.[10]

In 1863, Posey brought some samples of iron ore obtained from local Indian people living near Lake Vermilion to George Riley Stuntz, a central figure in the early exploration for minerals in northern Minnesota. Posey was later given credit by Stuntz and other mining pioneers for being the first man to find iron deposits at the future sites of the Lee and Breitung mines on the Vermilion range. As so often happens, Posey derived nothing but tragedy from his reported discoveries.

Joe Posey and two of his children died under very mysterious circumstances in January of 1882 when their house burned. From the available evidence gathered by a coroner's inquest, it appeared he and two children were murdered by a party or parties unknown. Accounts of the incident vary. Some claimed the motive was robbery while others believed Posey knew of more sources of iron ore and was murdered for not revealing those sources and his house set on fire to hide the crime.[11]

Today, the only reminder of Posey's sad fate is an overgrown island (Paw-paw-sco-me-me-tig) in the St. Louis River renamed for him. Posey Island, long a local landmark, was the reported site of gardens planted by the Ojibway who occupied a new village overlooking the river at that point. More recently, the island was the site of the Posey Island railroad bridge built to haul the timber harvested from the rich pineries along the St. Louis and its tributaries to the new sawmills at Cloquet. The island was also the point of beginning for the legal description of the Fond du Lac Reservation created in 1854 out of lands ceded to the United States by treaty in September of that year.[12]

In 1875, a search team headed by geologist Albert H. Chester was sent by iron mining developer Charlemagne Tower to investigate the location first known to Posey. The team arrived by railroad at what was then called Northern Pacific Junction (Carlton, Minnesota), the scene of the beginning of the Northern Pacific Railroad construction in 1870. From there, the men walked over the system of trails and portages to the head of Knife Portage, where they met two local guides with two large birch-bark canoes. Proceeding upstream, the party passed Posey's log house, which was the last sign of civilization they saw for the rest of their trip. Subsequent iron prospectors fanned out over the country and left evidence of their search in the form of a scattering of test pits, including some, which can still be seen today along the St. Louis River.[13]

With the discovery of valuable iron deposits, mine owners sought a faster and more direct means of reaching the mine sites. Even the Vermilion Trail, built to bring gold prospectors to the lake of that name, was soon supplanted by railroads capable of hauling large tonnage. The railroads were either built inland from the shore of Lake Superior, or wound their way up the St. Louis River valley to the mouth of the Cloquet River and then extended directly north.[14]

The Northwest Trail largely ceased to be a factor in further exploration or development of the iron mining industry once reliable rail transportation was extended to the mining district. The development of railroads to serve the iron mines, however, did not yet signal the end of the useful life of the Northwest Trail. As if to underscore the point, loggers arrived hard on the heels of the iron prospectors. From the 1850s through the 1920s, the timber industry utilized the Northwest Trail's water and land routes intensively and in some cases improved them.

When word of rich stands of virgin white pine was reported by surveyors and prospectors as far north as the headwaters of the St. Louis and Mississippi rivers, enterprising lumbermen lost no time in investigating this information. The first development for handling timber cut along the St. Louis was begun in 1872, with the creation of the Knife Falls Boom Company, founded by James Smith Jr., a director of the Saint Paul & Duluth Railroad.[15] Two years later lumbermen from Duluth improved the river with the hope of capturing some of the wealth represented in the vast pineries of northern Minnesota.[16]

Photograph of pioneer timber cruiser Dan Cameron who first estimated timber in the St. Louis River watershed in the 1870s. Carlton County Historical Society

In July of 1877, a group of timber cruisers canoed up the St. Louis River for the first time to survey the reported forest resources of the watershed. They were instructed to concentrate their efforts in townships 51 through 55, of range 17, located north of the Cloquet River. Among their number was a timber cruiser named Dan Cameron, who left written notes about his various experiences. Cameron and his comrades traveled by rail from Chippewa Falls, Wisconsin, to Komoko immediately west of Northern Pacific Junction, where the St. Paul & Duluth tracks met the Northern Pacific Railroad. From there the men traveled overland on a trail which led to Posey Island. Cameron recalled Joe Posey maintained a trading post and residence there and mentioned the reservation settlement comprised of houses and wigwams stretching along a bluff overlooking Posey Island and the St. Louis River.

Traveling up the St. Louis River in two birch-bark canoes manned by local voyageurs, the men experienced how difficult and uncertain river travel could be when they encountered the channel choked with logs at the Grand Rapids of the St. Louis. They had to drag their canoes carefully upstream from there. The timber cruisers also encountered difficult conditions on the Cloquet River. They established a camp that first season and spent the winter cruising the assigned territory. They returned for several seasons thereafter to survey additional territory for logging operations.[17]

Bateaux, like those shown here, were used in the fur trade and later by loggers along the Mississippi and St. Louis rivers to transport men and supplies. Carlton County Historical Society

These first beginnings date the origin of the city of Cloquet, which became for a brief period in history, a center for the logging and processing of timber harvested from the St. Louis River watershed. In 1879, a railroad spur, which later became part of a major transcontinental railroad route, was first extended from Northern Pacific Junction to Knife Falls. In that same year the first of five sawmills was built at the future site of Cloquet. For a time the ancient travel route up the St. Louis River was important to the newly established logging operations, since the bulky logs could easily be moved to the mills by water in the spring.[18]

Logging railroads were used to transport timber out of the forests.
Carlton County Historical Society

From the 1870s to the 1920s, the annual spring log drive downstream resulted in the St. Louis being choked with saw logs so thick in places that a man could walk dry shod from one side of the river to the other. However, a new method of handling logs was needed since timber cruisers' reports showed vast areas of prime timber were located too far from suitable logging streams. To access those stands of timber, the logging companies increasingly turned to the railroad. Tracks could be laid to any spot, and increasingly more and more logging was done by railroad compared to the traditional river drive.[19]

This photograph of the St. Louis River choked with logs is typical of logging streams throughout northern Minnesota from the 1850s to the 1920s. The entire surface of the river is covered in logs to such an extent that a man could walk across the river dry shod. Carlton County Historical Society

The story of the rapid development of logging on the St. Louis River watershed after 1872 was only one part of the race to tap the pine forests of northern Minnesota. Actually large-scale logging began twenty years earlier when lumbermen first thrust their operations up the Mississippi River past the Northwest Trail to the very headwaters of the river itself. The story of logging and the timber industry in the region west of Lake Superior began long before the treaties of 1854 and 1855, opening the land to commercial development were even ratified.

Interest in the timber resources along the Mississippi River dates from the first sawmill built to furnish timber for the construction of Fort Snelling. From that event, the ever expanding logging operations in Minnesota followed the rivers flowing from the north; and by the early 1850s, lumbermen already knew of the rich pine forests along the Northwest Trail. The arrival of the lumbermen, however, was gradual; and the transition from fur trade to logging often involved the same individuals.

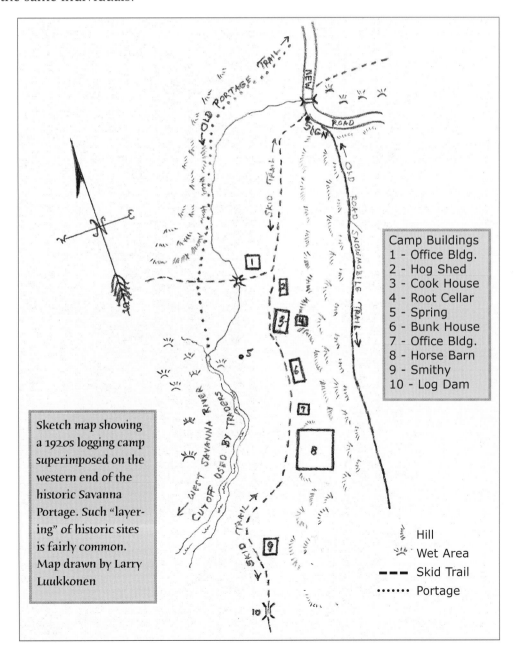

Camp Buildings
1 - Office Bldg.
2 - Hog Shed
3 - Cook House
4 - Root Cellar
5 - Spring
6 - Bunk House
7 - Office Bldg.
8 - Horse Barn
9 - Smithy
10 - Log Dam

Sketch map showing a 1920s logging camp superimposed on the western end of the historic Savanna Portage. Such "layering" of historic sites is fairly common. Map drawn by Larry Luukkonen

Hill
Wet Area
Skid Trail
Portage

The Last Trading Post

There are few surviving sites of former times when the economy of northern Minnesota was based not on mining or timber resources, but on fur. There is, however, a place where physical reminders of the transition of these economies can still be seen. Early timber operations occurred near the site of the last trading post on the Northwest Trail and involved some of the owners of that site. In fact, two buildings from that period are still standing at the junction of the Mississippi and the Sandy Lake rivers in mute testimony to the historical events that transpired there beginning in the 1850s. Largely overlooked today, the story of the last trading post and of the people associated with it is an interesting chapter in the history of the Northwest Trail.

The last trading post on the Northwest Trail c. 1910. The same building was photographed by the author in 1994.
Photos from Author's Collection

Of all the many fur trade sites formerly located along the Northwest Trail, only one remains nearly intact. Referred to by some as the "Old House," the site comprises two standing structures and the foundations of what were apparently a storage building elevated on wooden piers, and the remains of a barn. Although in disrepair, the trading post buildings still stand on the southern slope of a hill overlooking the junction of the Sandy Lake and Mississippi rivers.

The main building is a two-story structure of vertical squared log construction, which is presently covered with narrow clapboard siding. A single story one-room addition is located at the rear, or north side, which evidently served as a trading room and later as a general store. Early photographs also show a lean-to on the southwest side of the building. The addition was probably a storage area and does not exist today.

East of the main building is a small one-room hewn log structure with large windows flanking either side of the entrance. It appears no heat was provided in the building; however, a wooden vent located on the ridge of the roof provides ventilation. The exact purpose of the little log building is not known but it fits the description of a typical trading post.

Few written descriptions of the old buildings survive. In fact, it is possible descriptions of existing buildings at the site have been confused with those of William Aitkin's trading post, which adjoins it. Written descriptions of Aitkin's post boasted many structures including a two-story dwelling, storage buildings, shops, a barn, and other outbuildings. No records, however, have been uncovered to verify that the two buildings which exist today were ever part of Aitkin's original trading post.

The location of Aitkin's two-story dwelling can be reasonably fixed on the narrow peninsula separating the Sandy Lake River from the Mississippi. An eyewitness account by Reverend William Boutwell in 1832 placed Aitkin's house fifty to eighty feet from each river. Boutwell gives further interesting details about the establishment:

> Aitkin has a large establishment here, a two-story dwelling house, from 40 to 48 feet by 30, I should judge: a store house still larger, besides a small house for his men. One or two other small out houses, besides stables for 30 head of cattle, 3 or 4 horses and 15 swine.

Boutwell provided the measurements and location of Aitkin's house:

> Mr. A's post is located on a point of land where the Savannah [Sandy Lake River] unites with the Mississippi. It faces the former on the east, and the latter on the west elevated 15 or 20 feet above either, and perhaps 3 to 5 rods from each.[20]

Several other accounts refer to a trading post at the junction of the two rivers. Doctor Joseph Norwood remarked about passing, "...the old Trading House of Mr. Aitkin..." when he visited the region during a geological survey in the summer of 1848. Six years later the English traveler Laurence Oliphant remarked about Aitkin's former post at the confluence of the rivers, "We passed a deserted trading post and village, where Le Fêve told us he had formerly lived." The similarity between the two-story buildings suggests that it was entirely possible the Old House included materials from Aitkin's former dwelling. Such "recycling" was common on the frontier. Still, the relative positions of the Old House and that of William Aitkin do not agree.[21]

Oliphant's reference to the deserted trading post was the last mention of the site for several years. Two years after Oliphant's visit, the plat for the town site of Palmburg, previously mentioned, encompassed both the former area occupied by William Aitkin's trading establishment and the site of the Old House. The area of the village of Palmburg included all the land east of Aitkin's post as far as the future site of the government dam. The map of the town showed several existing buildings, including one on the site of the Old House.[22]

Interestingly enough, when the official government survey of the area was undertaken in 1870, records do not mention any buildings in either the survey notes or on the survey map. The record shows only that the land was part of Government Lot 2, in Section 25, Township 50 North, Range 24 West of the 4th Principal Meridian. Subsequent records of the property show that it was part of a lavish land grant given under a Congressional enactment on July 2nd, 1854, known as: "An Act to Aid the Construction of the Railroad and Telegraph Line, from Lake Superior to Puget Sound on the Pacific Coast, by the Northern Route."[23]

The next mention of the existence of the Old House came in the summer of 1872. While on a trip down the Mississippi River in his canoe named the "Dolly Varden," Julius Chambers, a Fellow of the Royal Geographical Society and member of the National Geographic Society, stayed there overnight. In 1910, Chambers published an account of his adventure in a book entitled *The Mississippi River and its Wonderful Valley*. In his narrative, Chambers mentions the Old House:

> We slept that night at the mouth of the Sandy Lake River, upon the floor of Mr. Libby's historic trading post. "Libby's" has been known for three generations as the point of portage for the "Big Sea Water"...[24]

What is most intriguing about Chamber's statement is the time frame associated with the trading post buildings and his reference to "Libby's." Chambers implies the post was active for three generations and that it was owned by the Libby family. Actually the story of the Libbys and their relations, the Wakefields, is inextricably tied to the history of the Old House. Both families were from Maine, but the Libby family was occupied with the logging business, not with the operation of a trading post. Furthermore, there is no record they ever operated a trading post for three generations at the junction of the rivers.

The first member of either family mentioned in connection with the area was Joseph Libby. Born January 12th, 1805, in Gouldsborough, Maine, Joseph Libby moved to Cherryfield, Maine, in 1830. From there he moved to Minnesota Territory in 1850 and located in the village of St. Anthony, later part of modern Minneapolis, Minnesota.

Biographical sketches of Joseph Libby indicate he engaged in the lumber business on the Rum River and in 1851 cut and rafted logs down the Mississippi that were used to build the second sawmill in the village of St. Anthony. In 1855, he reportedly built the first flatboat above St. Anthony Falls and traveled upstream all the way to Pokegama Falls, the site of the modern town of Grand Rapids, Minnesota.

Joseph Libby and his wife Priscilla, also from Maine, had nine children. Of these, his fourth child, Mark Wilson Libby, and his ninth, Joseph Eugene Libby, were later associated with him in various logging operations on the upper reaches of the Mississippi River. Both sons later resided in the Sandy Lake area where they married local Ojibway women. Although Joseph Libby and his son Mark operated in the Sandy Lake area, there is no specific reference about either of them constructing a trading post at the junction of the Mississippi and Sandy Lake rivers. That distinction was left to a near relation.[25]

The connection between the Libby and Wakefield families mentioned earlier came through Joseph Libby's third child, Edward G. Libby, who married Martha E. Wakefield, also of Cherryfield, Maine. Martha had two brothers, William Lord and Joseph W. Wakefield, both of whom moved to Minnesota. It was Joseph W. Wakefield whose name first appeared prominently in connection with the Old House in the 1860s.

Joseph Wakefield's biography states he learned the millwright's trade from his father, Louis Wakefield. He was also credited with supposedly inventing a roller process of flour milling, which unfortunately was stolen from him. Joseph Wakefield arrived in St. Anthony in 1856 and after briefly engaging in flour milling, became interested in the timber business. He and his brother, William Wakefield, traveled to northern Minnesota about the same time that Joseph and Mark Libby ventured into the area. Joseph Wakefield continued in the logging business for four years. In 1860 he decided to enter what was then described as the "Indian Trade." It was a pursuit he followed from 1860 until interrupted by what was referred to as the "Sioux Outbreak" in the summer of 1862.[26]

Mr. and Mrs. Joseph W. Wakefield. Wakefield and his brother William had extensive business dealings in the region extending from Sandy Lake to Superior, Wisconsin; Grand Rapids, Minnesota; and the White Earth Reservation.
Compendium of Northern Minnesota History and Biography

While Joseph Wakefield was busy trading at the Sandy Lake River, his brother, William, continued in the timber business. With the onset of the American Civil War in the spring of 1861, William was among the first to respond to the call for volunteers. On May 23rd, 1861, William Wakefield enlisted in the First Minnesota Volunteer Infantry then organizing at Fort Snelling. It was during his service in the First Minnesota that William Wakefield met a future business partner in the person of Edwin Barry Lowell. Lowell, also from Maine, enlisted on the same day and both he and William Wakefield were assigned to Company E of the First Minnesota Regiment.[27]

William Wakefield and Edwin Lowell saw action together in various campaigns. Both men were present at Gettysburg on July 2nd, 1863, and participated in the gallant but suicidal charge of the regiment's two hundred and sixty-two men against an advancing Confederate column led by General Wilcox. The next day, the forty-seven men who survived the onslaught of the Confederate host faced still another charge led by General George E. Pickett, at the head of fifteen thousand veteran troops. That any man of the First Minnesota Regiment lived to fight another day was a miracle.

Wakefield was discharged for disability on January 4th, 1864. It is interesting to note in passing that he was elected by the men of the regiment to the vacant position of second lieutenant. The vote, however, was disregarded and the regiment's commander appointed another man who received twenty-one fewer votes than Wakefield. As for Edwin Lowell, he continued in service for several more months and was finally discharged on May 3rd, 1864, having been wounded at the battle of Bristow.[28]

Meanwhile, back in Minnesota, Joseph Wakefield faced a war of his own. He had successfully pursued his trade at Sandy Lake until the summer of 1862. On August 17th of that year, discontent with the terms of the land cessions and mismanagement on the part of the Indian Department, culminated in an outbreak of violence marking the beginning of the "Sioux Uprising."

War raged throughout the Minnesota River Valley and for a time threatened to spill over into Ojibway country. In fact, hostilities expressed by some Ojibway led by Chief Hole-In-The-Day, convinced traders like Joseph Wakefield to abandon his trading post at Sandy Lake and seek shelter at Fort Ripley. In his biography, Wakefield mentioned that he was supposedly chased on foot by Indians for the last three miles to the fort and barely escaped capture.[29]

All along the Northwest Trail the possibility of a general Indian uprising was greeted with alarm. The citizens of Superior, Wisconsin, appealed for assistance and a small contingent of troops was actually sent to that frontier community to quell fears and provide a show of force on the northern flank. In St. Louis County, the county board authorized "Colonel" Reuben B. Carlton, the local government blacksmith, "...to employ, if to him it shall appear necessary or advisable, a suitable person to keep watch over...the Indians near us...." Carlton employed an unidentified French-Canadian as a spy for thirty dollars.[30]

The threatened hostilities with the Ojibway never materialized, and Joseph Wakefield resumed his trading activities. He was active not only at Sandy Lake but throughout the territory and assisted the government with various Ojibway bands during the remainder of the Sioux Uprising. In a letter dated July 22nd, 1906, Joseph Wakefield described his work for the government, including preparing land and transporting materials for the new Indian reservation established at White Earth in 1868. Joseph Wakefield and Edwin Lowell were also active in commercial affairs in the Crow Wing area.[31]

Apparently the Wakefield brothers were aware of developments concerning the disposition of the land where their trading post was located. Records show Joseph Wakefield and Edwin Lowell, operating as Wakefield & Lowell, purchased from the trustees of the Northern Pacific Railroad the land where the Old House stood. The handwritten deed described the sale of Government Lot 2 to "Wakefield & Lowell" on December 14th, 1874, for the sum of seventy-five dollars and sixty-five cents.[32]

After the purchase of the site of their trading post, the business activity of the brothers and their partner Edwin Lowell increased. Regular steam navigation of the Mississippi River between the city of Aitkin and Pokegama Falls began in 1870 with the voyage of the steamer *Pokegama*. Edwin Lowell took a special interest in the development of river commerce. With the advent of steam navigation, the Old House became a regular scheduled stop, refueling point, and a frequent destination for persons traveling on the Mississippi or along the Northwest Trail.[33]

For ten years, from 1874 until 1884, the Old House was a hub of commercial activity for the Wakefield brothers and Edwin Lowell. In addition to serving the needs of the logging camps in the area, new settlers, arriving on the completed Northern Pacific Railroad, required necessary supplies to sustain themselves until their homesteads were sufficiently developed. The prospects for transportation and general merchandising looked very bright indeed. At one time the Wakefield's operated twelve stores throughout the region. Joseph Wakefield moved to the city of Aitkin and for a time operated a general merchandising business. In 1884, Joseph left the general merchandise business and concentrated instead on the growing logging business, but not before selling his interest in the Old House.[34]

On April 4th, 1884, Joseph and Sophia Wakefield transferred the property to Edwin Lowell, who held it until 1902. Interestingly, while Lowell owned the property, his friend William Wakefield continued to live in the building and operate a trading post. This arrangement continued for almost twenty years.

In the 1890s, work started on the construction of the Sandy Lake Dam, and William Wakefield's store provided many of the supplies for the crews engaged in the construction. Wakefield operated a highly successful general store, and the steamboat business brought a steady flow of travelers. Several guest rooms were created on the second floor of the Old House for passengers.

During the construction of the dam, Wakefield not only sold supplies but also rented his draft horses. The government paid for the use of the animals and their care including buying feed. Of course William Wakefield was happy to provide horse feed along with other supplies for a reasonable fee. Being the only storekeeper in the immediate area certainly had its advantages.[35]

On June 29th, 1891, a United States Post Office was established at Sandy Lake to serve the new settlement of "Libby" growing up around the site of the newly completed dam. William Wakefield was the first postmaster. The post office continued in operation until October 30, 1953. Although the post office has long since ceased to exist, a road sign denoting the town of Libby is still present alongside State Highway 65.[36]

In 1902, Annie Lowell received title to the Old House, but William Wakefield continued to live there as before. The following year, however, William became ill and left Sandy Lake for the last time. He traveled to Minneapolis to stay with his sister, Mrs. Edward Libby. On Friday, June 12th, 1903, Joseph Wakefield received a telephone call at his Aitkin residence informing him of the death of his brother from stomach cancer. The news of William Wakefield's passing appeared in the local newspaper on June 16th. Though a lengthy obituary described his life and times, it did not mention the Old House.[37] After William Wakefield's death, Annie Lowell sold the property to Al Torrey, who continued to operate the general store. Torrey was short and was accordingly nicknamed "Shorty" by the local residents. "Shorty's store" was a favorite neighborhood gathering place.

Under Torrey's management the Old House continued as a trading post and country general store. While he stocked all of the necessities usually associated with a general mercantile store, Torrey continued to trade a little on the side. Stories of furs bartered for provisions, and bags of wild rice piled to the ceiling suggested a brisk trade with the local Ojibway.

By the 1920s, while business at the store began to increase with the influx of summer tourists, Al Torrey's health began to decline. In November of 1925, Shorty's Store ceased operation, and the property was sold to the I. K. Knights Company of Minneapolis in August of 1926. A newspaper story stated that Knights hoped to develop the area around the Old House as a park or historic site. Instead, the property was sold to a private party and has remained a private residence.[38]

Ironically, it was in that same summer of 1926 that Professor Irving H. Hart endeavored to uncover what he believed to be the North West Company post on Sandy Lake. Unfortunately, no attention was paid to the old trading post at the confluence of the Sandy Lake and Mississippi rivers.[39] So the cycle of history came full circle in 1926 with the closing and sale of the last trading post. Throughout its history, the Old House at the crossroads has served as a dwelling, hotel, post office, trading post, and later a general store. Indeed, some of the old fixtures from former times still repose within its walls. In spite of its place in the history of the region, the building has been allowed to slowly deteriorate. For now it still basks in the sunlight on the banks of the Mississippi, a fading monument to all those who passed over the Northwest Trail.

Pioneer Roads and Iron Rails

As long as waterways were the primary means of travel and commerce, the Northwest Trail from Lake Superior to the Mississippi River remained an important artery of trade and travel in northern Minnesota. The ancient network of rivers, portages, and winter trails provided the first major connection between the watersheds. Part of the story of travel, however, involved changing modes of transportation and their collective effect on the use of that network. Some historical accounts of travel in early Minnesota state that the traditional water routes were simply abandoned in favor of pioneer roads and railroads. A careful reading of the sources suggests a different sequence of events occurred.[40]

Beginning in the 1850s the pattern, or flow of trade goods and the shipment of furs changed. Trade goods were increasingly purchased and brought into the country not from the Great Lakes, but from St. Paul, which had become a fur buying center in the northwestern states following the demise of the American Fur Company. Trade goods were sent upstream to Sandy Lake, then east over the Savanna Portage to the confluence of the East Savanna, Floodwood, and St. Louis rivers.[41] From that point, the goods were then sent north up the St. Louis, across a portage to the Pike River and on to Lake Vermilion, where the traditional seasonal fur trade continued as it always had along the border lakes.

Neither the advent of roads nor railroads meant the immediate end of the waterways as major transportation arteries. Two early roads have been commonly cited as alternatives to the Northwest Trail, but neither achieved its objective.

The first of these roads, officially known as the Point Douglas-St. Louis River Military Road, was one of four road building projects of its kind undertaken in Minnesota Territory. Begun in 1852 and opened to traffic in 1856, it was designed to link the Mississippi River at Point Douglas with the St. Louis River and Lake Superior.[42]

Called "government roads" or "military roads," because they were built with federal funds and the help of the United States Army engineers, such roads were actually a means for opening the frontier to settlement. Every state and territory competed for funds to construct military roads. Many were built, but few ever saw any appreciable military traffic. The money Congress appropriated for their construction, however, meant jobs for local contractors and a welcome infusion of cash to the local economy wherever the roads were built.[43]

The Point Douglas-St. Louis River Military Road has been commonly referred to by some local authors as simply "The Military Road." Perhaps this familiarity is because it was the longest and most costly of the four roads constructed in Minnesota during the 1850s. Whatever it was called, its proponents claimed it would facilitate trade between St. Paul and neighboring communities with the ports on the Great Lakes. This economic argument became especially significant after 1855, when a ship canal was completed at Sault Sainte Marie.

As far as the Point Douglas-St. Louis River Military Road being a competing trade route with the Northwest Trail is concerned, the road began at the confluence of the Mississippi and St. Croix rivers and ran in a northerly direction roughly parallel with the St. Croix. At no point did the road ever truly follow the path of the Northwest Trail. Furthermore, except for a branch road to St. Paul, the Military Road ran through country bereft of any significant settlement.[44]

Photograph of a stage stop at Twin Lakes on the Military Road.
Carlton County Historical Society

The road passed through Pine County and continued into southern Carlton County. At a stage stop located at Twin Lakes, a few miles south of the present city of Carlton, Minnesota, the road turned east and followed a course terminating at a point opposite the mouth of the St. Louis River in Superior, Wisconsin.

LABORERS WANTED
Two hundred laborers are wanted on the north-western division of the Point Douglas and St. Louis Military road, by Mr. O. [Orrin] W. Rice, the contractor. Twenty-six dollars per month, and board, will be given.
Superior Chronicle, Tuesday, October 5th, 1855

The route chosen for the Military Road is significant in that all later means of transportation including railroads such as the Lake Superior & Mississippi, the state trunk highway system, and the more recent interstate highway system, followed a similar route.

While construction was underway on the Military Road, another road was being built to connect the settlement at Crow Wing with Lake Superior by intersecting the Military Road. Known as the "Crow Wing-Lake Superior Road," or the "Mille Lacs Road," the road differed from the Military Road only in that it was a territorial road built with funds appropriated by the Minnesota Territorial Legislature.[45]

The Crow Wing-Lake Superior Road began at the trading settlement of Crow Wing on the river of that name about nine miles south of the present city of Brainerd, Minnesota. The road extended eastward to the north shore of Mille Lacs near the present town of Garrison. From there it followed close by the shore of the lake taking advantage of the high gravel banks along the shoreline.

The road ran through the townships of Hazelton, Wealthwood, and Malmo in Aitkin county. After entering Malmo Township, the road turned northeast skirting the west side of Twenty Lake and rounded the northwest side of Sugar Lake before heading northeasterly through Lee Township. Midway through Lee Township, on the southwest corner of Section 22, the road headed due east intersecting present State Highway 65. From there, it continued roughly parallel with State Highway 27 into Carlton County.

Once in Carlton County, the road passed around the south end of Coffee Lake and headed in a northeasterly direction, eventually intersecting with the Point Douglas-St. Louis River Military Road, northeast of the present city of Moose Lake, Minnesota.[46]

Both the Point Douglas-St. Louis River Military Road and the Crow Wing-Lake Superior Road were hardly today's modern highways. In fact, neither road was ever completely finished. Both roads required constant maintenance as noted in a newspaper article in the *Superior Chronicle* for Saturday, July 23rd, 1859:

> The most important part of this work, however, is repairing the Military Road from here [Superior] to the Mille Lacs Road, for by fixing up that portion, we will be met by the people of Snake River, thus giving us a good road to St. Paul, at the same time we are progressing toward Crow Wing. Neither the road to St. Paul, or the Crow Wing will, or can be available, until we repair the Military Road from here to the Mille Lacs Road...[47]

Part of the problem with the roads lay in their construction. Building early frontier roads mainly involved clearing a right-of-way by sawing off trees and brush at ground level. Roots and stumps were grubbed out by hand, and the surface of the road filled and graded by horse-drawn equipment usually built locally out of hewn timber. What little fill existed was provided by excavating material from shallow ditches on both sides of the right-of-way and depositing it in the middle or where most needed. The cross section of a typical road had a highly convex shape designed to shed water. Lack of regular maintenance caused deterioration in the shape of the road; and the traffic rapidly wore deep ruts in the soft material, which delayed travel over some stretches of the road after a heavy rain.

Many stories exist about travel on these early roads—or what passed for roads. John T. Trowbridge described his experience traveling the Military Road:

> August 14th, —Weather cold and drizzling. Roads this day worse than ever, though worse had seemed impossible. Every little while a wagon sticks in the mud. Now a wiffletree breaks, now a king-bolt; now a baggage wagon upsets, or a horse is down; and now we must wait for a gulf of mud to be bridged with logs and brush. At every accident the whole train comes to a halt. We get through only by keeping together and helping each other. The shouts of the drivers, the calls for help, the running forwards, the hurrying back, the beckoning signals, the prying up of mired wheels, the replacing of broken bolts, make ever a picturesque and animated scene.

At the end of the journey Trowbridge remarked,

> We have made this grand portage laboriously (in wagons for the most part), and we have been three days and more about it. The railroad com-

pleted, it will be made comfortably in a few hours. This terrible mud-canal navigation through the wilderness will soon be obsolete...[48]

Regular stagecoach service on the Military Road began before the road was ever completed. William Nettleton reportedly established a stage line connecting Superior with St. Paul in 1854-1855; but the Minnesota Stage Company, headquartered in St. Paul, quickly absorbed the new business. Although stagecoach service was well-advertised, actual travel conditions were primitive. Fares were high and often a passenger literally had to fight for a decent place to sit. George Barnum, who was employed by the Lake Superior & Mississippi Railroad, related his experiences during the spring of 1868. Barnum had paid seventy-five dollars for a seat on the St. Paul to Superior coach only to find that he had to ride in an ordinary freight wagon filled with boxes. After arguing with the driver to no avail, Barnum mounted the wagon and began tossing the boxes out on the ground. This act infuriated the driver:

> Exasperated at the way things were going, I started to toss the boxes from the wagon when he dared me to do just this thing, and turned suddenly to find him rushing at me with an ugly black snake whip in his hand. Dodging the whip, I ran to a woodpile nearby, singled out a four-foot birch stick, and laid into him, but not until I received several severe cuts with the lash. The stick did the business and ended the fight. I forced him to mount the wagon and toss the boxes to the ground.[49]

Obstreperous teamsters were not the only difficulty experienced by travelers on the Military Road. Poor accommodations, high prices, delays, mosquitoes, mud, rude passengers, and a host of other annoyances confronted the early traveler. Faced with such conditions, it was little wonder that many residents and travelers alike chose to continue traveling by canoe on the traditional water routes.

While work progressed with road building in early Minnesota, a new method of transportation was slowly gaining ground. As early as the 1840s, the idea of building a railroad to connect the Great Lakes with the Mississippi River was presented in the writings of travelers such as Charles Lanman and Christopher Columbus Andrews. Their thoughts were echoed by Alexander Ramsey. Ramsey's comments regarding the proposed railroad may have been based on a tour to the headwaters and Sandy Lake in 1849. In 1850, writer Sanford Seymour described a similar plan in his book *Sketches of Minnesota the New England of the West*:

> If the Mississippi should be found practicable for steamboat navigation as far as Sandy Lake, it will probably be connected, in the course of time, with the head of the lake, by a railroad running along the valley of the St. Louis and Savannah Rivers....[50]

Most of the early schemes for building a railroad between the watersheds were predicated on the idea that railroads, like portages, were designed to connect waterways and not necessarily intended to operate as independent transportation systems. It took a very long time for the concept of an independent railroad system to be accepted by policy makers. To most people, the railroad was merely the successor to the portage. In fact, prior to the construction of the Northern Pacific Railroad, there is evidence in the form of sketch maps and surveys showing a proposed portage railroad extending from the main Northern Pacific right-of-way to the Prairie River east of Sandy Lake.[51]

In 1857, the territorial legislature chartered two railroads with the intention of connecting the Great Lakes with the Mississippi rivers at different points. The Lake Superior & Crow Wing Railroad was to extend due west from Duluth to the village of Crow Wing. A second railroad, the Nebraska & Lake Superior, was supposed to connect Lake Superior with the Mississippi further south. Only the Nebraska & Lake Superior fulfilled the goals set forth in its charter. Renamed the Lake Superior & Mississippi Railroad, the company succeeded in completing a line from St. Paul to Duluth. Nonetheless, this new railroad was initially designed to connect two major waterways and only later became part of a larger independent transportation system.[52]

Once completed, the Lake Superior & Mississippi Railroad effectively drove the stagecoach and freight lines that operated over the Military Road out of business. The freight companies quickly discovered they could not compete with the railroad in speed, quantity of goods carried, or accommodations. Interestingly, the first few miles of the Lake Superior & Mississippi Railroad followed part of the Northwest Trail through the valley of the St. Louis River before turning south toward St. Paul and away from the portage along the bank of the river.

In addition to the great interest in road and railroad building, other schemes were advanced to supersede the old Northwest Trail by connecting the watersheds with a canal cut between the St. Louis River and Sandy Lake. In 1850, the noted geologist Doctor Joseph Norwood witnessed the arrival of the screw steamer *Manhattan* at the village of Fond du Lac and later included the event in a footnote in the official geological report published in 1852. Norwood commented, "This brings the steam navigation on Lake Superior within thirty-five miles of the Mississippi at the mouth of Sandy Lake River...."[53]

In 1857, the same legislature that chartered the two railroads just mentioned also chartered the Lake Superior and Mississippi Ship Canal Company. The enterprise, capitalized at five million dollars, was an enormous undertaking for the time; but the possibility of such a venture was certainly not new. Reuben B. Carlton, the government blacksmith at Fond du Lac, envisioned such a project and, in fact, was associated with a number of companies seeking to link the head of navigation on Lake Superior with St. Paul and the Mississippi River.[54]

Of course the construction of a canal depended on the navigability of the Mississippi River as far as Sandy Lake. Speculation on whether or not steamboats could complete the trip from the rapids at Little Falls to Sandy Lake was eliminated in the summer of 1858, when Anson Northrup's stern wheel steamer *North*

Star not only successfully cruised the Mississippi from above Little Falls to Pokegama Falls, but also took a side trip into Sandy Lake and up the Prairie River for several miles before encountering a fish weir.[55]

Although the spectacular voyage of the *North Star* showed it was possible to navigate the Mississippi, the problem of fluctuating seasonal water levels remained. Further work on any form of transportation was effectively put aside with the outbreak of the American Civil War in April of 1861. It was not until several years after the conclusion of the war that the government turned its attention to improving navigation on the Mississippi.

In the 1880s, attention was focused on the construction of a thirty-seven mile long ship canal connecting the St. Louis and Mississippi rivers. The project, as envisioned in an 1880 publication sponsored by the Duluth Chamber of Commerce, went far beyond merely connecting the two river systems. Instead, what was confidently put forward was a system of canals linking the Great Lakes and Mississippi waterways with the Red River of the North and ultimately Hudson Bay![56]

The navigation lock and control house at the Sandy Lake dam.
photo by Larry Luukkonen

The results of a Mississippi River survey by the United States Army Corps of Engineers showed the need for building a series of dams on the headwaters in order to regulate the continual flow of the Mississippi. In 1891, uncertain whether or not a canal would ever be built to connect Lake Superior with the Mississippi, lumbermen in Aitkin, Minnesota, petitioned the federal government to at least provide a navigation lock in the new dam scheduled to be built at the outlet of Sandy Lake.[57] The result of the petition was the addition of a wood and stone crib control structure complete with what was referred to as a "bear trap lock," capable of lifting boats from the Mississippi into Sandy Lake.

In 1907, the idea of a barge canal connecting Lake Superior to the Mississippi once again briefly surfaced. The Aitkin newspaper proclaimed "From Lake Superior to the Sea by Mississippi Waterway." The journalistic euphoria was short-lived, however, as the water required to operate a canal and lock system sufficient to raise barges from Lake Superior into the Mississippi would seriously reduce the amount of water available in area streams to allow log drives. Although several individuals proposed to build a canal above Cloquet on the St. Louis River, any attempt to divert water from the river met with stiff opposition from timber interests who saw their extensive transportation and lumber processing operation at the Cloquet mills adversely effected. Today, the only reminder of the canal scheme first envisioned in 1850 are faded newspaper accounts and the remains of the navigation lock at the Sandy Lake Dam.[58]

Of all the modes of transportation built in northern Minnesota, the railroads were the most influential in hastening settlement along the Northwest Trail. The unique strength of the railroad lay in its ability to extend anywhere within the region and provide transportation. The Northern Pacific Railroad was not a portage railroad but an independent system. The railroad, however, closely followed the general direction of the Northwest Trail and quickly assumed primary responsibility for moving freight and passengers from the Great Lakes to western destinations—stretching ultimately to the Pacific Ocean.[59]

Once work began on the Northern Pacific Railroad, construction proceeded so swiftly that the rails quickly reached the Mississippi at the future site of the city of Aitkin, and, by the end of the year, had crossed the river on a massive wooden trestle at the site of Brainerd, nine miles north of the old trading center of Crow Wing. Bypassed by the railroad, the fur trading center of Crow Wing soon faded into oblivion as businesses and settlements were drawn north to the new bustling town of Brainerd.

In 1878, a second railroad founded by Duluth businessmen and known as the Duluth & Winnipeg began laying track northwest up the valley of the St. Louis River from Knife Falls (Cloquet). The new railroad also paralleled the route of the Northwest Trail as far as Floodwood, Minnesota. From there, it continued across country until it intersected the Mississippi River at Grand Rapids. Once again the railroad continued alongside the former trade route to Cass Lake, due west leaving the old water route to meander toward Red Lake and the Red River of the North. In time, this railroad became part of the Great Northern Railroad system, which also provided transcontinental service. Both the Northern Pacific and Great Northern operated as a system, and any interconnection with waterways merely enhanced their commercial position instead of limiting it.[60]

Although the railroads quickly replaced the Northwest Trail as a means of moving cargo and large numbers of people, the fine harbor provided by the St. Louis estuary expanded as a transportation center to meet the growing need for shipping facilities. New cargoes of iron ore, wheat, coal, timber, and manufactured products passed through the port, which eventually developed from an insignificant frontier port of call into a world class shipping center. At the same time, the old water route continued to serve the timber industry.

From the 1870s to the 1920s, the St. Louis River and its tributaries such as the Cloquet, Whiteface, East Savanna, Floodwood, and East Swan were the scene of annual log drives. The river was used for commercial log driving and log storage from Knife Falls to the head of the major affluents of that important stream.

The same commercial change from freight hauling to log driving also occurred on the western end of the Northwest Trail. The Mississippi River was the setting for major log drives from 1855 until 1920. In addition, both the West Savanna and the Prairie rivers were the scene of large-scale timber harvesting and log drives. In fact, the West Savanna boasted four logging dams constructed to insure a plentiful supply of water to wash the winter's harvest of timber downstream to Sandy Lake and on into the Mississippi River.[61]

Even the East Savanna River with its notorious swamp and serpentine course was changed to improve its flow so that adjoining land would be more accessible and tillable. Shortly after the turn of the twentieth century, huge floating steam dredges were brought into the area and work was begun to straighten the main channel of the East Savanna and drain the surrounding countryside. The reclamation project was officially known as Judicial Ditch Number 3; however, to most people the "channelized" stream is all that remains of the East Savanna River.

Professor Irving H. Hart, who had devoted much time to the study of the history of the area, commented on the extensive drainage projects associated with the East Savanna River while retracing the Savanna Portage in 1926 and 1927. Less than two decades after the steam dredges had finished their work, Hart believed the project was a dismal failure. Aside from altering the vegetation in the immediate vicinity of the river, no appreciable change ever took place to turn the area into productive homesteads.[62]

In addition to the use of the rivers for commercial log drives, there was an interest in developing the potential water power of the St. Louis River. Shortly after the turn of the twentieth century a series of dams were built to harness the considerable horsepower of the river. The end result was the construction of reservoirs and hydroelectric stations that used the same water five times to generate electricity. The most ambitious part of the whole power project was the construction of a large dam and reservoir at Thomson, Minnesota, and the diversion of the main water supply of the St. Louis River around the Dalles.

To accomplish this task, a canal was constructed extending several miles to the east of the Thomson Reservoir to a height of land overlooking the river valley. There, the water from the canal was sent down a steep hill through three huge wooden pipes to a generating station located on the bank of the river. During its construction, the series of dams and reservoirs on the St. Louis River represented the largest hydroelectric generating facility west of Niagara Falls. Today, the production of electricity represents a major commercial use of the St. Louis River, second only to shipping from the twin ports of Duluth and Superior.[63]

Thus from the 1850s onward, the Northwest Trail provided the inspiration for an unprecedented era of innovation. The notion that the use of the rivers and

FALLS OF THE GREAT NORTHERN WATER POWER PLANT AT THOMSON, MINN.

An early view of the Thomson reservoir dam that was constructed
on the St. Louis River. Carlton County Historical Society

trails that comprised the historic route somehow ceased operation almost on cue
with the coming of the railroads fails to recognize the steady evolution which has
taken place along the route. The Northwest Trail was in reality as much an idea
as it was a trade route. New railroads and highways, not to mention new ways of
using the old route, developed after 1850. The concept of a canoe route to the
Northwest took on a whole new meaning as a network of improved transportation was either superimposed upon or paralleled the Northwest Trail.[64]

Finally, one interesting indication of the process of change can be seen in the
way early communities such as Fond du Lac, Cloquet, Duluth, and Superior were
first platted. Initially, their main streets and important buildings faced the St.
Louis River waterfront; but as new transportation developed, these same communities increasingly turned their attention from the rivers and the Northwest
Trail to face first the railroad and later the highways that formed the new main
street. As we enter a new century, the emphasis along the Northwest Trail has
once again shifted—this time to recreation. Perhaps this recent change is a real-
ization of our former attachment to waterways. Communities are once again facing the river in anticipation of the recreational potential the waterways afford.

Today, instead of each end of the trail being anchored by Ojibway villages,
two state parks sit astride the route. The Jay Cooke and Savanna Portage state
parks not only preserve portions of the Northwest Trail but also afford visitors
the opportunity to enjoy the scenic beauty of the area.

And so the story of the Northwest Trail, like the rivers and portages along its
path, has taken many twists and turns from 1850 to the present. It is still possible
to follow parts of the old route either by canoe or on foot. Those who have hiked
the portages or paddled the historic waters separating the Great Lakes from the
Mississippi River know the feeling of discovery engendered by such a trip. One
soon realizes that he or she is but the latest traveler along an historic route
between the waters—a route that still beckons the adventurous.

Notes to Chapter 12
Old Routes and New Ways

1.   William Watts Folwell, *A History Of Minnesota*, 4 vols. (1921; reprint ed., St. Paul, 1956), vol. I, pp. 306-307.

2.   "Articles of Agreement for Cloquette filed with the St. Louis County Register of Deeds at 10.00 AM, July 20th, 1857, by Charles A. Post, John D. Howard, William A. Farr, and Patrick O'Brien," Cloquet File, Carlton County Historical Society, Cloquet, Minnesota.

3.   John R. Carey, "History of Duluth, and of St. Louis County, to the Year 1870," in *Collections of the Minnesota Historical Society*, vol. 9 (1898), pp. 246-247, 262, and 267. For additional information of Ely's career, see "The First Missionaries" in chap. 10 above.

4.   Walter Van Brunt, *Duluth and St. Louis County Minnesota: Their Story and People*, 3 vols. (Chicago, 1921), vol. 1, p. 86.

5.   John A. Bardon, "Miracle Mud," unpublished manuscript, n.d., John A. Bardon Papers, Minnesota Historical Society.

6.   Carey, *History of Duluth*, pp. 257-259.

7.   Folwell, *History of Minnesota*, vol. 1, pp. 40-42.

8.   Charles J. Kappler (ed.), *Indian Treaties: 1778-1883* (1911; reprint ed., New York, 1973), pp. 268-271. See Article 3, p. 269, for the provision regarding mineral exploration and mining.

9.   David A. Walker, "Lake Vermilion Gold Rush," *Minnesota History*, vol. 44, no. 2 (Summer, 1974), pp. 42-54; Newton H. Winchell, "Historical Sketch of Explorations and Surveys in Minnesota," in *The Geology of Minnesota 1872-1882, The Geological and Natural History Survey of Minnesota*, vol. 1 of the Final Report (Minneapolis, 1884), vol. 1, p. 110.

10.   Van Brunt, *Duluth*, vol. 1, p. 345. Van Brunt's account of the exploration of George Riley Stuntz for iron near Lake Vermilion in 1865, credits N.[North] A. [Albert] Posey, a government blacksmith serving the Bois Forte and Fond du Lac reservations, with being the first outsider to report the existence of iron in 1863; see also Betty Dahl, "The Posey Family," in Thomas D. Peacock (ed.), *A Forever Story: The People and Community of the Fond du Lac Reservation* (Cloquet, Minnesota, 1998), pp. 203-205. North Albert Posey, or N. A. Posey, was also known as Joe or Joseph Posey after his father.

11.   Dahl, "Posey Family," pp. 203-205; "The Cloquet Calamity, Joseph Posey and his Two Daughters Burned to Death at Knife Falls—Suspicion of Foul Play," in *Duluth Tribune*, January 13th, 1882. The apparent murder-arson of Posey and his children took place on January 9th, 1882. The story appeared in the newspaper four days later. Official information about the deaths of Posey, and his two daughters Mary and Lenora, appear in Book 1, *Register of Deaths*, p. 10, nos. 16, 17, and 18 in the Carlton County Recorder's Office, Carlton, Minnesota.

12.   Kappler (ed.), *Indian Treaties*, p. 648.

13.   Van Brunt, *Duluth*, vol. 1, p. 352, includes a description of the canoe route used by the Chester Expedition of 1875; see also Walker, "Lake Vermilion," p. 48 for a map showing both the St. Louis River route and the Vermilion Trail.

14.   See Marvin G. Lamppa, *Minnesota's Iron Country: Rich Ore, Rich Lives* (Duluth, 2004), for a comprehensive history of the development of Minnesota's iron mining industry.

15.   See Francis M. Carroll, *Crossroads in Time: A History of Carlton County Minnesota* (Cloquet, Minnesota, 1987), pp. 129-154, for a thorough summary of logging operations along the St. Louis River and its tributaries.

16.   Dan Cameron, "notes," n.d. in Dan Cameron Papers, Carlton County Historical Society, Cloquet, Minnesota. Cameron's handwritten manuscript is accompanied by a typescript prepared by his daughter Grace Cameron dated March 9th, 1926.

17.   Ibid.

18.   Carroll, *Crossroads*, pp. 139-144.

19.   Frank A. King, *Minnesota Logging Railroads* (San Marino, 1981), pp. 87-101; C. J. Ryan, "Reign of the Logging Railroads," *Early Loggers in Minnesota*, 4 vols. (Duluth, 1973-1986), vol. 1, pp. 32-38.

20.   See Paul Masson (ed.), *Schoolcraft's Expedition to Lake Itasca* (East Lansing, 1993), p. 323, for Boutwell's description of William A. Aitkin's trading post.

21.   Laurence Oliphant, *Minnesota and the Far West* (London, 1855), p. 205.

22.   Reference to the town of Palmburg can be found on the "Historico-Geographical Map" in Elliott Coues, *The Expeditions of Zebulon Montgomery Pike*, 2 vols. (1895; reprint ed., Minneapolis, 1965). A copy of the plat map of Palmburg by Benjamin C. Borden is in the Alfred J. Hill Papers, Minnesota Historical Society.

23.   Warranty Deed, Northern Pacific Railroad to Wakefield and Lowell, no. 432. *Deed Record A*, Aitkin County Recorder's Office, Aitkin, Minnesota.

24.   Julius Chambers, *The Mississippi River And Its Wonderful Valley* (New York, 1910), p. 169.

25.   Charles Thornton Libby, *The Libby Family in America* (Portland, Maine, 1882), pp. 472-473.

26.   *Compendium of History and Biography of Northern Minnesota*, s.v. "Joseph Wakefield," (Chicago, 1902), pp. 266-269.

27.   John Quinn Imholte, *The First Volunteers: History of the First Minnesota Volunteer Regiment, 1861-1865* (Minneapolis, 1963), pp. 76, 155, and 157.

28.   Ibid., p. 155.

29.   Wakefield, *Compendium*, p. 269.

30.   "Early History of Superior," n.d. Superior Public Library, Superior, Wisconsin.

31.   For Joseph Wakefield's work with the government, see letter from Wakefield to Wilcox, dated Aitkin, Minnesota, July 22nd, 1906, in Alvin H. Wilcox, *A Pioneer History of Becker County* (St. Paul, 1907), pp. 240-241.

32.   See n. 23 above.

33.   "Passenger Rate Schedule, Season of 1909." Copy in author's collection. Passage from Aitkin to Sandy Lake was one dollar.

34.   See n. 26 above.

35.   Lori McDonald, "History of the Army Corps of Engineer's Sandy Lake Dam Runs Deep," *Aitkin Independent Age* (October 6th, 1999), p. 3.

36   Alan H. Patera and John Gallagher, *The Post Offices of Minnesota* (Burtonsville, Minnesota, 1978), pp. 34 and 242.

37.   *The Aitkin Age*, Tuesday, June 16th, 1903.

38.   "Site of Fort Benton at Sandy Lake Bought by Mill Citian May Be Park," *The Duluth Herald*, Monday, August 28th, 1926. The "Fort Benton" referred to in the news article was a name give by Indian Agent Lawrence Taliaferro to William Alexander Aitkin's trading post established at the junction of the Mississippi and Sandy Lake rivers in 1822. See also chap. 9, n. 22 above.

39.   Professor Irving H. Hart, "The Site of the Northwest Company Post on Sandy Lake," *Minnesota History*, vol. 7, no. 4 (December, 1926), pp. 311-325. Hart's study of the old North West Company post appeared the very year the last trading post in the area was sold by the I. K. Knights Company of Minneapolis. Curiously, Hart never mentioned the last trading post.

40.   Interview with Herbert William Larson, Saturday, December, 4th, 1982, regarding the western terminus of the portage and a logging camp site (c. 1927-1928) superimposed on the trail.

41.   Crittenden & Lynde and Francis Roussain represent two of the small firms trading along the Northwest Trail in the 1850s. For a list of traders operating in the vicinity of the village of Fond du Lac see Ellworth T. Carlstedt, "A History of the Fond du Lac Trading Posts With Some Mention of the Fond du Lac Department," unpublished manuscript, University of Minnesota, December 9th, 1933, chapter 10. Typescript copy in the collections of the Carlton County Historical Society, Cloquet, Minnesota.

42.   Grover Singley, *Tracing Minnesota's Old Government Roads*, Minnesota Historic Sites Pamphlet no. 10 (St. Paul, 1974). See the maps on pages 16, 18, 20 and 21 showing sections of the Point Douglas to St. Louis River Military Road; Arthur J. Larsen, *The Development of the Minnesota Road System* (St. Paul, 1966), pp. 44-47; and John R. Carey, "History of Duluth and of St. Louis County to the Year 1870," *Minnesota Historical Collections*, vol. 9 (1898), pp. 245-246.

43.   Singley, *Old Government Roads*, pp. 1-5.

44.   Ibid., see maps 16 and 18, showing the route of the Point Douglass-Lake Superior Military Road along the St. Croix River.

45.   Interestingly enough, Superior business interests vigorously supported the construction of the Crow Wing Territorial Road because it intersected the Red River Trail. It was widely believed by Superior merchants that they could interdict trade from the Hudson's Bay Company otherwise destined for St. Paul. Plans went so far as to include the erection of a warehouse in Superior for the use of the company.

46.   The route of the Crow Wing-Lake Superior Road is shown in A. T. Andreas, *Illustrated Historical Atlas of the State of Minnesota* (Chicago, 1874); see "Map of Todd, Morrison, Crow Wing, and Aitkin Counties;" see also J. William Trygg, *Composite Maps*, sheets 13 and 14.

47.   *Superior Chronicle*, Saturday, July 23rd, 1859.

48.   John T. Trowbridge, "Through the Woods to Lake Superior," *The Atlantic Monthly*, vol. 25 (April, 1870), pp. 419-423.

49.   "Interview with George Barnum," *Duluth Herald*, April 10th, 1933.

50.   E. Sanford Seymour, *Sketches of Minnesota, The New England of the West* (New York, 1850), pp. 231-232.

51.   Sketch maps of Sandy Lake area, Alfred J. Hill Papers, Minnesota Historical Society.

52.   The quality of the service and accommodations provided for passengers, not to mention the condition of the newly built road, were all subjects of numerous comments from travelers who followed the Military Road and other early trails. See nn. 48 and 49 above.

53.   For Dr. Joseph Norwood's comments, see David Dale Owen, *Report of a Geological Survey of Wisconsin, Iowa, and Minnesota; and Incidentally of A Portion of Nebraska Territory* (Philadelphia, 1852), p. 270.

54.   The Lake Superior Ship Canal Company is mentioned in Dwight E. Woodbridge and John S. Pardee (eds.), *History of Duluth and St. Louis County*, 2 vols. (Chicago, 1910), pp. 76-77.

55.   Details concerning the *North Star* (later renamed the *Anson Northrup*) can be found in the *St. Paul Daily Times*, September 24th, 1856, p. 2, cols. 1 and 3; Captain Russell Blakeley, "Opening of the Red River of the North to Commerce and Civilization," in *Collections of the Minnesota Historical Society*, vol. 8 (1898), pp. 44-66.

56.   See *Duluth Tribune*, January 14th, 1881, for article regarding canal project put forth in 1880 by the Duluth Chamber of Commerce.

57.   *Aitkin Age*, May 9th, 1891, "Resolution of the Aitkin Board of Trade." The city of Aitkin's proactive stand concerning the building of a canal connecting the Mississippi and St. Louis rivers may have stemmed from the belief the periodic flooding experienced by that community could be prevented by diverting the runoff from the Prairie River into the St. Louis. In an article in the *Aitkin Age*, dated January 19th, 1904, Captain Viebahn of the steamer *Irene* believed the Prairie River and other tributaries contributed to the flooding.

58.   The *Aitkin Age*, July 30th, 1907, reported the canal project was being reviewed favorably. The estimated cost would be nine million dollars for a ninety-four mile long canal.
For the impact the proposed canal project would have had on towns along the St. Louis such as Cloquet, see Carroll, *Crossroads*, pp. 208-209. The canal project, which had various names including: The Minnesota Canal & Power Company (1893), and the Highland Canal & Power Company (1902), intended to divert the St. Louis River to Duluth for barge traffic and the production of hydroelectricity.

59.   See John C. Luecke, *The Northern Pacific in Minnesota* (St. Paul, 2005), pp. 2-3. The concept of the Northern Pacific Railroad evolved beyond the stage of a portage railroad designed to merely link the major watersheds in Minnesota.

60.   See Carroll, *Crossroads*, pp. 101-124, for a thorough summary of the impact the construction of the Northern Pacific Railroad had on the area.

61.   *Aitkin Age*, May 23rd, 1896, reported over eighty-nine million board feet of timber arrived at Sandy Lake. This splendid harvest was during the height of commercial logging in the region. The last major log drive on the Mississippi was in 1920, and included one million one hundred thousand board feet of timber. The last drive on the St. Louis was in 1924. After that date, logs were shipped to the mills at Cloquet by rail, sorted and then stored in the St. Louis River above Cloquet in an elaborate system of booms which separated each company's logs.

62.   Irving H. Hart, "The Old Savanna Portage," in *Minnesota History*, vol. 8, no. 2 (June, 1927),

p. 136. Regarding the attempt to reclaim wetlands for agriculture, Hart observed, "The land is still hopeless swamp, and so far as anyone can now see will always remain so."

63.   For the development of hydroelectricity on the St. Louis River see Bill Beck, *Northern Lights: An Illustrated History of Minnesota Power* (Duluth, 1986). Several stories surround the spelling used for the reservoir dam and nearby town of Thomson. According to Warren Upham, *Minnesota Geographic Names* (1921; reprint ed., St. Paul, 1969), p. 76, the name "Thomson," was allegedly meant to honor the famous North West Company Geographer David Thompson who made a survey of the St. Louis River in 1825, but the spelling actually used was the same as that of the Scottish poet, James Thomson. Another version of the tale maintains the spelling was the same as that of J. Edgar Thomson, President of the Pennsylvania Railroad and partner in the construction of the Northern Pacific Railroad.

64.   John Fritzen, "Portages and Old Trails In And Adjacent To Jay Cooke State Park," unpublished manuscript, c. 1935, Carlton County Historical Society, Cloquet, Minnesota, pp. 27-28. According to Fritzen, the Fond du Lac to Cloquet Wagon Road was superimposed on a major portion of the Grand Portage of the St. Louis (see also chap. 2, n. 11 above).

Photograph of a steam dredge used to straighten the Mississippi and Savanna rivers, and for land reclamation c. 1910. Note the size of the machine and the number of men standing on the boom. Photo by J.W. Sarff from the Author's Collection

Epilogue

A reader's literary journey along the Northwest Trail may end with the thought: Are there any more tales to tell about this historic pathway? The answer is an unqualified yes. My own interest in the topic dates from the 1950s and in some areas I have only scratched the surface. Fascination with the subject has kept me coming back to explore not only new source material but also selected portions of the route itself.

For instance, my first encounter with the Savanna Portage was in 1959 when I explored the western end of the trail. There was a great deal of discussion at the time about creating a new state park to preserve the historic Savanna Portage, and I was understandably curious about the reasons why the portage was chosen for such a distinction. I have subsequently explored and photographed other sections of the Northwest Trail. Sometimes the exploration amounted to little more than taking a group of students down a stream like the West Savanna River for a fun filled day trip by canoe. Other times, the exploration was more intense.

In 1983, several companions and I set out to explore the East Savanna River. What began as a leisurely one day excursion by canoe turned into an overnight trip when we encountered a series of almost insurmountable obstructions in the river. Although there were some anxious moments on the East Savanna, we completed the trip without incident. That experience pales in comparison to more serious challenges I have faced including an incident where I was marooned on a deserted island in Hudson Bay. My Inuit guide was more concerned with hunting whales than in helping me search for the site of a 1719 shipwreck.

Part of the pleasure of exploration or travel in connection with scholarly research is the added perspective it provides. Actually seeing an historic site helps me understand and therefore communicate my own enthusiasm for the story to others. In the case of the Northwest Trail, the experience is doubly rewarding because parts of the story have not been told before.

Until now, there was no single volume that covered the story of the Northwest Trail and the travelers who ventured into the unknown country west of Lake Superior. Perhaps this lack of coverage was due to the preoccupation most writers have had with other regions of Minnesota. A few local histories tell part of the story of the Northwest Trail, but their scope is confined within narrow boundaries. None cover the entire route or know it by name.

In contrast to the limited coverage in published accounts, there are many valuable documents that provide further information about the Northwest Trail. Each chapter in the book lists sources which contain additional leads. I have patiently followed these leads while exploring the route. If I learned anything in the process it was that nothing can be accomplished quickly. The Northwest Trail did not give up its secrets easily. A weekend stroll along its twisting course can only tempt the reader to further examine the story.

In addition to information gleaned from researching and exploration, some valuable lessons were learned in the process of writing this narrative. The lessons include the importance of listening, observing, and critically assessing available oral history. These three elements were particularly helpful during several interviews I had with the son of an early pioneer. The interviews concerned both the route of the overland trail from West Savanna River to Northeast Bay on Sandy Lake, and the western end of the Savanna Portage. I am grateful for the privilege of hearing the stories and actually walking the routes. Unfortunately, it was an experience that cannot be repeated.

While writing the story of the Northwest Trail, I have tried to avoid the many pitfalls that have snared other authors. For example, some writers have either accepted information without critical analysis or have failed to follow significant leads. Others have displayed an occasional desire to jump to unwarranted conclusions over the location of a trading post or portage. In each case, the zeal to find an historic site has far outweighed the available information concerning the true location. In other instances, authors have ignored information in contemporary records. In the worst case, one author did not even bother to visit the site he wrote about. My interest in comparing written descriptions with actual historic sites has helped avoid perpetuating that serious mistake.

After reading this book, some may wish to explore both the written sources and the actual route. I am confident they will see that far from abandoning the old Northwest Trail, people have adapted portions of it to new uses. My research has shown that the water and land route evolved—sometimes in different directions, but it certainly did not vanish. For those interested in tracing the Northwest Trail, this book is but the first step on a long and interesting journey.

A view of the landing in front of the American Fur Company post site at Fond du Lac. The pilings were part of a later dock erected to serve steamboat passengers. A plaque describing the fur post is located in a grove to the right of the landing.
Photo by Larry Luukkonen, 1994.

Winter on the St. Louis River.
Photo by Allen Anway

Appendices

Appendix A: A chronological listing of the references to Sandy Lake trading posts

1. A possible French trading post or "wintering" cabin, c. 1752-1754, conceivably used by the Chevalier de la Vérendrye.

2. A trader's cabin built by Meniclié de Morachon c. 1791, as described by Jean Baptiste Perrault. Perrault probably meant 1792, since he was off one year in his Narrative.

3. The old North West Company trading post built by John Sayer & Company, 1794-1795.

4. A possible XY Company post based on a map and statements concerning the location of voyageurs supposedly employed by the company in 1805.

5. William Alexander Aitkin's establishment near the confluence of the Mississippi and Sandy Lake rivers was built and used by him from 1822 until 1842. It also served as the American Fur Company's second post in the Sandy Lake area from 1830-1838.

6. Le Vieux Fort (the old fort), was marked on a sketch map of Sandy Lake drawn by Joseph N. Nicollet in 1837 during a visit to the lake in company with William A. Aitkin. This site may also represent an XY Company post or an early trading post used by Perrault, who indicated a post location nearby marked with a zero apostrophe on a sketch map of Sandy Lake and vicinity.

7. American Fur Company Post Number 3 1838-1847, on the northwest corner of Sandy Lake midway on Brown's Point. This site was later used as the Sandy Lake Indian Agency and evidence exists of the location of the government black-smith and government farm for the Sandy Lake Ojibway as provided for in the treaty of 1837 and subsequent treaties.

8. Crittenden & Lynde trading post 1851-1855. Crittenden & Lynde most likely either used the buildings on Brown's Point or Aitkin's old post as the scene of their operations, since there is no reference to a separate post constructed by them. They maintained trading facilities not only at Sandy Lake, but also at Leech, Vermillion, Otter Tail, Cass, Winnipeg, Pokegama, and Red lakes, and at Fond du Lac.

9. Wakefield & Lowell trading post and later general store c. 1855-1926.

Appendix B: "The Ojibway Maid"
by Jane Johnston Schoolcraft

(lyrics)

That stream, along whose bosom bright,
With joy I've seen your bark appear;
You cross no longer, with delight,
Nor I, with joy, your greeting hear.

And can such cause, alone, draw tears
From eyes, that always smiled before?
Of parting–can it be the fear;
Of parting now–to meet no more?

But heavily though now you sigh;
And tho' your griefs be now sincere,
To find our dreaded parting nigh,
And bid farewell to pleasures dear–

When o're the waters, wide and deep,
Far–thine Ojibway Maid shall be,
New loves will make you please to weep,
Nor e're again, remember me!

A version of this music is included in Thomas L. McKenney, *Sketches of a Tour to the Lakes*, published in Baltimore, in 1827, pp. 187-189.

> **"THE O-JIB-WAY MAID."**
>
> *Original of the O-jib-way Maid.*
>
> Aun dush ween do win ane
> Gitchy Mocomaun aince
> Caw auzhaw woh da modē
>   We yea, yea haw ha! &c.
>
> Wah yaw burn maud e
> Ojibway quainee un e
> We maw jaw need e
>   We yea, yea haw ha! &c.
>
> Omowe maun e
> We nemoshain yun
> We maw jaw need e
>   We yea, yea haw ha! &c.
>
> Caw ween gush shā ween
> Kin wainyh e we yea
> O guh maw e maw seen
>   We yea, yea haw ha! &c.
>
> Me gosh shā ween e yea
> Ke bish quaw bum maud e
> Tehe won ain e maud e
>   We yea, yea haw ha! &c.

The lyrics for the Ojibway Maid in the original Ojibway language.
From McKenny

THE O-JIB-WAY MAID.

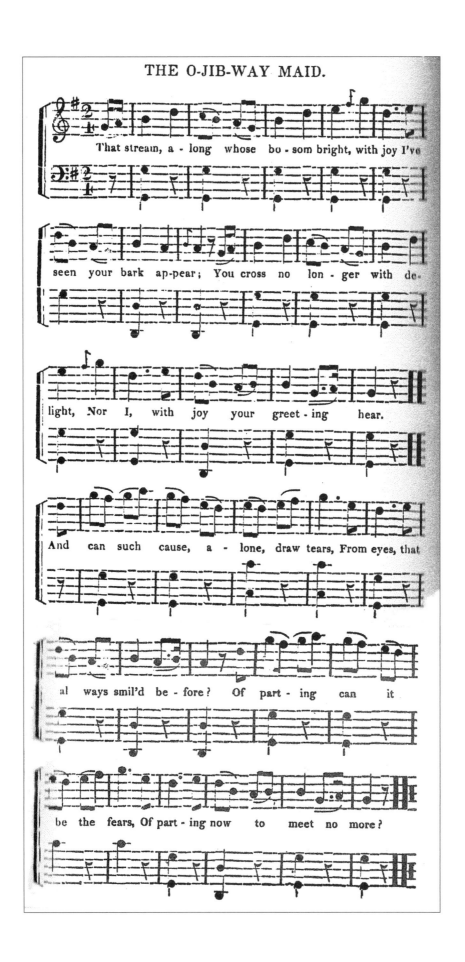

That stream, a - long whose bo - som bright, with joy I've

seen your bark ap-pear; You cross no lon - ger with de-

light, Nor I, with joy your greet - ing hear.

And can such cause, a - lone, draw tears, From eyes, that

al - ways smil'd be - fore? Of part - ing can it

be the fears, Of part - ing now to meet no more?

Appendix C: William Aitkin's Family

First wife:
    Madeline or Bay-ji-quod-o-qua (Pa-zhuk-wad-o-qua)

Children:
    Alfred, born 1816
    John, born 1818
    Nancy (aka Anna), born 1819 or 1820
    Matilda, born 1825
    Roger, born 1827
    Elizabeth, born 1830
    Anne, born 1840

Second wife:
    Julia Quatice or O-be-be-won-o-quay

Children:
    Julia, born 1837
    Selim (Salem), born 1839
    Robert, born 1842
    Monema (Jemima), born 1839
    Childa (Othilda? aka Nah-zheek), born 1846
    Isabella (Belle), born 1848
    Edgar, born 1850

Selected Bibliography*

Adney, Edwin Tappen and Charles I. Chapelle. *The Bark Canoes and Skin Boats of North America*. (Bulletin 230) Washington, D.C., 1964.

"With the American Fur Company in the Michilimackinac Dependencies, 1818-1822." *The Moorsfield Antiquarian* (May,1938), vol. 2, no. 1, pp. 5-24.

Bell, Charles Napier. "The Earliest Fur Traders on the Upper Red River and Red Lake, Minnesota (1783-1810."*The Historical and Scientific Society of Manitoba*. Transaction no. 1, n.s. (November 24th, 1926), pp. 1-16.

Blair, Emma Helen. ed. and trans. *The Indian Tribes of the Upper Mississippi Valley and Region of the Great Lakes, as described by Nicholas Perrot...Bacqueville de la Potherie...Morrell Marston... and Thomas Forsyth...* 2 vols. Cleveland, 1911-1912.

Bray, Martha Coleman. ed. André Fertey. trans. *The Journals of Joseph N. Nicollet: A Scientist on the Mississippi Headwaters With Notes on Indian Life*. St. Paul, 1970.

Brebner, John Bartlett. *The Explorers of North America, 1492-1806*. 1933. Reprint. Cleveland, 1968.

Brunson, Alfred. *A Western Pioneer*. 2 vols. New York, 1872.

Burpee, Lawrence J. ed. *Journal and Letters of Pierre Gaultier de Varennes de la Vérendrye and his Sons*. Toronto, 1927.

Butterfield, Consul Wilshire. *Brulé's Discoveries and Explorations*. Cleveland, 1898.

Campbell, Marjorie Wilkins. *The North West Company*. Vancouver, 1983.

Carlstedt, Ellworth T. "A History of Fond du Lac Trading Posts With Some Mention of the Fond du lac Department." University of Minnesota. December 9th, 1933.

Carroll, Francis M. *Crossroads in Time: A History of Carlton County, Minnesota*. Cloquet, Minnesota,1987.

Coleman, Sister Bernard. *Where the Water Stops: Fond du Lac Reservation*. Duluth, 1967.

Cormir, Louis-Phillipe. ed. *Jean-Baptiste Perrault: marchand voyageur parti de montre al le 28e de mai, 1783*. Montreal, 1978.

Coues, Elliott. *The Expeditions of Zebulon Montgomery Pike*. 3 vols. in 2. 1895. Reprint Minneapolis, 1965.

_____ *New Light on the Early History of the Greater Northwest. The Manuscript Journals of Alexander Henry, fur trader of the Northwest Company, and David Thompson, official Geographer and Explorer of the Same Company, 1799-1814. Explorations and Adventure among the Indians on the Red, Saskatchewan, Missouri and Columbia Rivers*. 3 vols. 1897. Reprint. New York, 1965.

Curot, Michel. "A Wisconsin Fur Trader's Journal, 1803-1804." *Collections of the State Historical Society of Wisconsin*, vol. 20 (Madison, 1911), pp. 396-471.

Danziger, Edmund Jefferson, Jr. *The Chippewas of Lake Superior*. Norman, 1979.

Duckworth, Harry W. "The Last Coureurs de Bois." *The Beaver*, outfit 314, no. 2 (Spring, 1984), pp. 4-12.

Fritzen, John. *The History of Fond du Lac and Jay Cooke State Park*. Duluth, 1978.

Gilman, Carolyn. *Where Two Worlds Meet: The Great Lakes Fur Trade*. St. Paul, 1982.

Gilman, Rhoda R. "Last Days of the Upper Mississippi Fur Trade." *Minnesota History*, vol. 42, no. 4 (Winter, 1970), pp. 122-140.

Glover, Richard. ed. *David Thompson's Narrative*, 1784-1812. Toronto, 1962.

Greer, Clifford. *Twelve Poses West*. McGregor, Minnesota, 1967.

* Each of the works listed here is linked to a person, place or event concerning the Northwest Trail.

Hart, Evan A. "A Frontier Smithy in Wisconsin Territory." *Wisconsin Magazine of History*, vol. 40, no. 4 (Summer, 1957), pp. 261-269.

Hart, Irving H. "The Old Savanna Portage." *Minnesota History*, vol. 8, no. 2 (June, 1927), pp. 117-139.

_____. "The Site of the Northwest Company Post on Sandy Lake." *Minnesota History*, vol. 7, no. 4 (December, 1926), pp. 311-325.

Hartley, Alan H. "The Expansion of Chippewa and French Place-Names into the Lake Superior Region in the Seventeenth Century." *Names*, vol. 28 (March, 1980), pp. 43-68.

Hay, John. "Journal in the N.W. by S. Side of L. Superior," in "Extracts from Capt. McKay's Journal—and Others." *Publications of the State Historical Society of Wisconsin, Proceedings of the Society at its Sixty-third Meeting, October, 21st, 1915* (Madison, 1916), pp. 200-210.

Heidenreich, Conrad E. "Mapping the Great Lakes, The period of Exploration, 1603-1700." *Cartographica*, vol. 17, no. 2 (Autumn, 1980), pp. 32-64.

Henry, Alexander. *Travels & Adventures in Canada and the Indian Territories Between the Years 1760 and 1776.* ed. by James Bain. 1809. Reprint. Boston, 1901.

Hickerson, Harold. "Ethnohistory of the Mississippi Bands and Pillager and Winnibigoshish Bands of Chippewa." *Chippewa Indians II*. New York, 1974.

_____. "Ethnohistory of the Chippewa of Lake Superior." *Chippewa Indians III*. New York, 1974.

Holmquist, June Drenning, ed. "Frontier Vacation: Joseph LeConte's Early Geological Excursion." *Minnesota History*, vol. 32, no. 2 (June, 1951), pp. 81-99.

Jackman, Sydney W. and John F. Freeman eds., assisted by Donald S. Ricard and James L. Carter. *American Voyageur: The Journal of David Bates Douglass.* Marquette, 1969.

Jackson, Donald. ed. *The Journals of Zebulon Montgomery Pike.* 2 vols. Norman, 1966.

James, Edwin. ed. *A Narrative of the Captivity and Adventures of John Tanner (U. S. Interpreter at the Saut de Sainte Marie) During Thirty years Residence Among the Indians.* 1830, Reprint, Minneapolis, 1956.

Keaton, Anna Mary. "Pierre Cotte." *Acta et Dicta*, vol. 6, no. 1 (October, 1933), pp. 86-96.

Kellogg, Louise Phelps. *Early Narratives of the Northwest, 1634-1679.* New York, 1917.

_____. *The French Régime in Wisconsin and the Northwest.* Madison, 1925.

Knuth, Helen E. "Economic and Historical Background of Northeastern Minnesota Lands. Chippewa Indians of Lake Superior." *Chippewa Indians III*. New York, 1974.

Lanman, Charles. *A Canoe Voyage up the Mississippi River and Around Lake Superior.* New York. 1847. Reprint, Grand Rapids, Michigan, 1978.

Lass, William E. *Minnesota's Boundary With Canada: Its Evolution Since 1783.* St. Paul, 1980.

Lavender, David. *The Fist in the Wilderness.* 1964. Reprint. Albuquerque, 1979.

Luukkonen, Larry. *Cloquet: The Story Behind The Name.* Cloquet, Minnesota, 2000.

Lydecker, Ryck and Lawrence J. Sommer. eds. *Duluth, Sketches of the Past: A Bicentennial Collection.* Duluth, 1976.

MacKenzie, Sir Alexander. *Voyages From Montreal on the River St. Lawrence Through the Continent of North America to the Frozen and Pacific Oceans in the Years 1789 and 1793.* Master Works of Canadian Authors Series. 1801. Reprint. Toronto, 1927.

McLeod, Martin. "The Diary of Martin McLeod." ed. by Grace Lee Nute. *Minnesota History*, vol. 4, nos. 7-8 (August-November), 1922.

McNeice, Gladys. *The Ermatinger Family of Sault Ste. Marie.* Sault Sainte Marie, Ontario, 1984.

Monk, George Henry. "A Description of Northern Minnesota by a Fur trader in 1807." ed. by Grace Lee Nute. *Minnesota History*, vol. 5, no. 1 (1923-1924), pp. 28-39.

Nute, Grace Lee. *The Voyageur.* 1931. Reprint. St. Paul, 1955.

_____. "Posts in the Minnesota Fur Trading Area." *Minnesota History*, vol. 11, no. 4 (September,1928), pp. 353-385.

_____."Marin versus La Vérendrye." *Minnesota History*, vol. 32, no. 4 (December, 1951), pp. 226-238.

_____. *Caesars of the Wilderness*. New York, 1943.

Norwood, Joseph. in David Dale Owen. *Report of a Geological Survey of Wisconsin, Iowa, Minnesota; and Incidentally of a Portion of Nebraska*. Philadelphia, 1852.

Oliphant, Laurence. *Minnesota and the Far West*. Edinburg, 1855.

Perrault, Jean Baptiste. "Narrative of the Travels and Adventures of a Merchant Voyageur...May, 1783 (to 1820)." ed. by John Sharpless Fox. *Historical Collections and Researches Made by the Michigan Pioneer and Historical Society*, vol. 37 (1909-1910), pp. 508-619.

Pitezel, John. *Lights and Shades of Missionary Life*. Cincinnati, 1861.

Sackett, Richard R. "An Unidentified Trading Post on the Portage La Savanna." *The Minnesota Archaeologist*, vol. 7, no. 4 (October, 1941), pp. 75-77.

Sproat, Florantha Thompson. "La Pointe Letters." *Wisconsin Magazine of History.* vol. 16, no. 1(September, 1932), pp. 85-95 ,and, vol. 16, no. 2 (December, 1932), pp. 199-210.

Tanner, Helen Hornbeck. ed. *Atlas of Great Lakes Indian History*. Norman, 1987

Upham, Warren. Minnesota *Geographic Names: Their Origin and Historic Significance.* 1921. Reprint. St. Paul, 1969.

Warren, William Whipple. *History of the Ojibway People*. 1885. Reprint, St. Paul, 1984.

Williams, Mentor L. ed. *Schoolcraft's Narrative Journal of Travels*. East Lansing. 1992.

Winchell, Newton H. *The Aborigines of Minnesota*. St. Paul. 1911.

Index

A view of the Sandy Lake River looking northeast.
photo by Larry Luukkonen

About the Author

photo by Kathryn Nordstrom

Larry Luukkonen was born and raised in Cloquet, Minnesota. He has lived a good part of his life near the sites he describes in this book. He attended the University of Minnesota where he received his Bachelor of Science, Master of Arts, and was admitted to candidacy for the Ph.D., all in history. He taught history at the University of Minnesota, Bemidji State University, and in the Minnesota Community College System. He has written several scholarly works including *Terms of the Trade: Some Words and Expressions Used in the Fur Trade* (1999) and *Cloquet: The Story Behind the Name* (2000). In 2004, he was commissioned by the Carlton County Historical Society to work on a centennial history of Cloquet. The result of this project was *A Hometown Album: Cloquet's Centennial Story* (2004) which he co-authored with Marlene Wisuri, director of the Carlton County Historical Society. In 2005, Larry completed *Reuben B. Carlton: Frontier Blacksmith and Visionary*, a biography of the county's namesake. He has written over sixty feature articles in magazines and newspapers, all dealing with various aspects of Minnesota's early history. He is a frequent guest lecturer and has appeared on public radio and television. He has also served as a consultant for museums and video productions concerning northern Minnesota.